Security as Practice

CW01022213

This important text offers a full and detailed account of how to use discourse analysis to study foreign policy. It provides a poststructuralist theory of the relationship between identity and foreign policy and an in-depth discussion of the methodology of discourse analysis.

Part I offers a detailed discussion of the concept of identity, the intertextual relationship between official foreign policy discourse and oppositional and media discourses and of the importance of genres for authors' ability to establish themselves as having authority and knowledge. Lene Hansen devotes particular attention to methodology and provides explicit directions for how to build discourse analytical research designs.

Part II applies discourse analytical theory and methodology in a detailed analysis of the Western debate on the Bosnian war. This analysis includes a historical genealogy of the Western construction of the Balkans as well as readings of the official British and American policies, the debate in the House of Commons and the US Senate, Western media representations, academic debates, and travel writing and autobiography.

Providing an introduction to discourse analysis and critical perspectives on international relations, this book will be essential reading for students and scholars of international relations, discourse analysis and research methodology.

Lene Hansen is an Associate Professor in the Department of Political Science at the University of Copenhagen, Denmark.

The New International Relations

Edited by Barry Buzan, *London School of Economics* and Richard Little, *University of Bristol*

The field of International Relations has changed dramatically in recent years. This new series will cover the major issues that have emerged and reflect the latest academic thinking in this particular dynamic area.

Security as Practice

Discourse analysis and the Bosnian war

Lene Hansen

LONDON AND NEW YORK

First published 2006
by Routledge
2 Park Square, Milton Park,
Abingdon, Oxon, OX14 4RN

Simultaneously published in the USA and Canada
by Routledge
270 Madison Avenue, New York, NY 10016

Routledge is an imprint of the Taylor & Francis Group

© 2006 Lene Hansen

Typeset in Garamond by Keyword Group Ltd

All rights reserved. No part of this book may be reprinted or reproduced or
utilized in any form or by any electronic, mechanical, or other means,
now known or hereafter invented, including photocopying and recording,
or in any information storage or retrieval system, without permission
in writing from the publishers.

British Library Cataloguing in Publication Data
A catalogue record for this book is available from the British Library

Library of Congress Cataloging in Publication Data

Hansen, Lene.
Security as practice : discourse analysis and the Bosnian war / Lene Hansen.
    p. cm. — (The new international relations)
Includes bibliographical references and index.
ISBN 0-415-32653-2 (hardback : alk. paper)—ISBN 0-415-33575-2
(pbk. : alk. paper) 1. Language and international relations. 2. Discourse analysis.
3. Bosnia and Hercegovina—History—Partition, 1995. I. Title. II. Series.
JZ1253.5.H36 2006
327.1'01—dc22   2005018281

ISBN10: 0-415-32653-2 (hbk)
ISBN10: 0-415-33575-2 (pbk)
ISBN13: 9-78-0-415-32653-7 (hbk)
ISBN13: 9-78-0-415-33575-1 (pbk)

For Helle Venzo

Contents

List of Illustrations

Figures

Tables

Series Editor's Preface

This book should make even the skeptics about poststructuralist approaches to International Relations sit up and take notice. In a clear and accessible form, Lene Hansen offers the first full and detailed account of how to use discourse analysis to study foreign policymaking. This is an invaluable and long overdue contribution that will give critics a better idea of what they are trying to attack, and give enthusiasts concise practical guidance about how to get on with it. Critics will, I think, find their task made more challenging. Enthusiasts will find their task made easier (which is not to say easy). Although it contains a sophisticated analysis of the Bosnian war in its own right, the book is set up as a useable text that should fill many an awkward gap in methodology courses.

Hansen confronts the rationalist critique that discourse analysis fails to expose causal relations by showing how representations of identity and foreign policy are co-constitutive and cannot be staged in cause–effect terms. She gives a concrete sense of what discourses are and how they can be approached and analyzed systematically as the key components of the social and political world. The book shows in detail how discourses frame and give meaning to facts, and how different takes on given facts go to compose competing political positions. It gives a firm sense of how discourses grow and change, and how selective memory causes older discourses to be either forgotten or remembered at opportune times. For the uninitiated, it makes clear what otherwise daunting terms such as *intertextuality* actually mean (and why they are not, in fact, particularly daunting). Hansen offers clear explanations of how to choose texts for a discourse analysis, addressing the difficult questions of how much is enough, and what types of sources count as relevant and why.

She then takes the reader through a meticulously researched sample case study on the Western discourses surrounding the Bosnian war using this to demonstrate the co-constitutive character of representations of identity and various foreign policy positions. This approach reveals how the politics of the Bosnian war were composed around competing discourses about genocide, ancient hatreds, human rights and Western responsibilities. It exposes the tensions within the EU and the US over Bosnia, and also the tensions between them, and shows how politicians and others incorporate events and changes in policy into their discourses. Using this method, Hansen is able to offer a whole range of deep and incisive insights into the various literatures and political positions surrounding the Bosnian crisis. She is coolly even-handed in her judgments, ruthlessly exposing both the intended and unintended 'spin' that different discourses impart to the awful events of the Bosnian war. Hansen successfully shows how competing discourses destabilize each other, and how the dynamics of self versus other pervades, indeed constitutes, much of the process of foreign policymaking.

This is a landmark book that should set a standard for a long time to come. It is a very welcome addition to 'The New IR' series.

Barry Buzan
LSE

East, by Pedro Lujan (oil paint and gold leaf, 85 × 137.5cm).
Copyright Pedro Lujan, 1995. Reproduced with his kind permission.

Preface

This book is about the importance of identity for foreign policy, and it tries to do three things: to develop a discourse analytical theory of identity and foreign policy, to present a methodology for how to apply it, and to provide an extensive analysis of the Western response to the Bosnian war.

I will argue that poststructuralist discourse analysis, built on Foucault, Derrida, Kristeva, and Laclau and Mouffe, can be used to theorize the constitutive relationship between representations of identity and foreign policies as suggested by heads of states, governments, oppositional politicians, the media, and academics. Foreign policies need an account, or a story, of the problems and issues they are trying to address: there can be no intervention without a description of the locale in which intervention takes place or of the peoples involved in the conflict. There can be no understanding of development policies without a description of who the underdeveloped are, where they differ from the developed West, and how they can transform their identity. Foreign policies are legitimized as necessary, as in the national interest, or in the defense of human rights, through reference to identities, yet identities are simultaneously constituted and reproduced through formulations of foreign policy. Policies require identities, but identities do not exist as objective accounts of what people and places 'really are,' but as continuously restated, negotiated, and reshaped subjects and objects. To theorize foreign policy as discourse is to argue that identity and policy are constituted through a process of narrative adjustment, that they stand, in social science terminology, in a constitutive, rather than causal, relationship.

Identity, politics, discourse—these key words indicate that this book is based on multiple literatures and that it seeks to speak to several audiences. The focus on foreign policy discourse locates the book within the discipline of International Relations (IR), where it takes sides with so-called poststructuralist approaches. Foreign policy is, however, merely one form of politics, and the argument about the constitutive importance of identities is relevant for policy debates more broadly. Debates on immigration and multiculturalism in Europe and North America, to take a prominent example, concern not only how many people can be allowed into the European Union countries or the United States, but the very identity of 'Europe' and 'America' and hence what is constituted as 'foreign.' To debate the marital and adoptive rights of homosexuals is to invoke constructions of the deviant and the normal, of the identity of the 'proper family' as opposed to the non-nuclear subversive one, and of the boundary between the public and the private. Identity, in short, is not only at work in the constitution of inter-state relations, but in any significant political decision—and the constitution of what is different or foreign is not confined to Foreign Policy as conventionally understood.

Official foreign policies as declared by heads of states and their foreign ministers have distinct formal authority and hence have traditionally been the main subject of foreign policy analysis. The discourse analytical perspective developed in this book argues that this focus might be retained but that official foreign policies should be situated within a wider discursive terrain. Official declarations present themselves as unobjectionable definitions of the issues at hand, and the chosen policy as the logical and necessary response thereto. But in doing so, they need to speak to a wider political field. There might be competing discourses advocated by oppositional politicians or the media, and consensus is often achieved through the mobilization of identities with a powerful conceptual history. To speak, for instance, of the irrationality and fanaticism of the Islamic world is to invoke a Western Orientalist discourse with long historical traits, and to describe the wars of the former Yugoslavia as 'Balkan' is to draw discursive strength from a conception of Balkan identity which goes back to the 1920s.

That official foreign policy is always speaking to and from contemporary as well as historical discourses indicates the convergence between the discourse analysis developed here and writings on identity and discourse from a series of other fields, most prominently comparative literature, conceptual history, media studies, and cultural studies. These convergences are further strengthened by this book's analytical attention to the way in which discursive agents constitute themselves as having authoritative knowledge about the policy problems they face. This book shows that politicians legitimate their stances through references not only to 'serious' academic analysis and 'objective' reports but also to personal experiences and such non-scientific forms of text as travel writing. Adopting the concept of intertextuality, the use of multiple genres in foreign policy debates is theorized with particular attention to how subjective and narrative forms of knowledge are part and parcel of how seemingly rational and objective Western foreign policymakers argue.

This book's contribution to the debates on identity and foreign policy within the discipline of IR could not have been made had it not been for Derrida's deconstruction, Kristeva's intertextuality, Foucault's account of power and knowledge, Laclau and Mouffe's view of discourse and hegemony, the work on travel writing by Marie Louise Pratt, Eakin's rendition of the genre of autobiography, as well as the canon of poststructuralist IR, including Richard Ashley, Rob Walker, James Der Derian, Michael Shapiro, David Campbell, Cynthia Weber, Iver B. Neumann, and Ole Wæver. And, while the most explicit conversational partner in the first chapter of the book is an imaginary IR theorist, it has been the intention to speak to those working on questions of identity and discourse within the social sciences and the humanities as well. To that audience, a preliminary note of clarification might be in order: the term 'poststructuralist discourse analysis' is used in this book in accordance with conventional IR terminology to capture a theoretical approach that draws on Foucault, Derrida, Kristeva, and so on, but other fields might follow different conventions. It should be noted though that while I refer to my theoretical framework as poststructuralist discourse analysis, it is not the case that poststructuralism and discourse analysis are completely identical. Poststructuralism includes, for instance, a body of works that take a psychoanalytical and Lacanian route not incorporated here, and discourse analysis as a general field of research covers as diverse approaches as content analysis, ethnomethodology, functional pragmatics, Critical Discourse Analysis as developed most prominently by Norman Fairclough and Ruth Wodak, as well as the work by Laclau and Mouffe. The discourse analytical approach taken in this book is located in the tradition of Foucault, Derrida, and Kristeva, and hence is closer to Laclau and Mouffe than to Fairclough, but there are also significant points of convergence between the discourse analysis developed in the pages ahead and Critical Discourse Analysis, in particular in the latter's concern with media representations.

Those well versed in poststructuralist theory might wonder how Derrida and Foucault can be fitted into one theoretical framework, or where the exact difference runs between poststructuralist and critical discourse analysis, but I should lay my cards on the table and say that the goal of this book is to speak to the subject matter—how to theorize the constitution of identity within foreign policy discourse—and that intra-theoretical debates and differences have been downplayed accordingly. While obviously debatable, it was a choice influenced by my desire to couple the theory of discourse analysis with a thorough concern with methodology and to address both the methodology of reading, the development of research designs, and the choices involved in making textual selections.

The foregrounding of methodology runs up against one of the few axioms shared within the discipline of IR, namely that poststructuralism and methodology don't mix. From Stephen Walt's realist warnings against the seductive sirens of poststructuralism to Katzenstein, Krasner, and Keohane's programmatic statement that poststructuralism denies the use of evidence, there has been rationalist consensus that poststructuralism is defined by its incapacity for epistemological and methodological rigor. That leading constructivist of the thinner persuasion have concurred in constituting 'postmodernism' as a theoretical and methodological detour only adds to the branding of poststructuralism as anti-method. Yet, pointing the accusatory finger at neo-epistemologists and constructivists alone would be too easy as a search through the canon of poststructuralist IR reveals that explicit concern with methodology has not been given prominence of place. This methodological vow of silence gives the impression of poststructuralists emerging from years of Foucaultian-Derridarian-Nietzschean-Kristevian studies that obliterate the need for discussions of the methodology of reading or accounts of how source material might be selected.[i]

To be fair, there were good reasons why poststructuralists focused on abstract theory and deconstructivst readings of the discipline and history of IR when poststructuralism was first developed: to challenge the privilege accorded to realism and liberalism, particularly in their neo-neo incarnations, required an exposure of ontological and epistemological foundations, and methodology could never be the medium through which this was done. But, as a long-term branding strategy, leaving methodology to rationalists and constructivists alike has been a problematic move. Or, to put it constructively, it's time for poststructuralism to take methodology back.

A poststructuralist methodological turn has two advantages: it speaks to poststructuralism's critics by explicating the rigorous work that does indeed underpin much of poststructuralist analysis. No reading of, say, Foucault's *The Order of Things*, or James Der Derian's *On Diplomacy*, could dispute that these are works built on an enormous wealth of material analyzed through a sophisticated optic. Yet to foreground poststructuralist methodological questions is not only a defensive maneuver, but a move which facilitates research within poststructuralism itself. What is methodology? That is itself a contested issue, with Derrida arguing that methodology is intimately tied to Western rationalism and positivist truth claims, and deconstruction henceforth must be a non-method. But while this might be a defensible philosophical position, it is also one which reiterates a dichotomous choice between rationalism and methodology on the one hand, and poststructuralist methodological emptiness on the other. Rather, I would argue, it is more productive to see methodology as a way of communicating choices and strategies that all writing, deconstructivist and poststructuralist included, must make. Rationalists cannot claim to be the sole keepers of the methodological grail, but neither can Derridarian notions of deconstruction conjure a space free of strategies, inclusions, and exclusions. This is not to say that methodology could ever take the place of theory, nor that it could be a platform from which all IR theorists could arbitrate their ontological and epistemological differences, but that to put methodology in these broader terms creates a space for making and debating poststructuralist analyses, for better understanding how analyses might compete or complement each other, and for a stronger theoretical account of the use of identity in foreign policy.

---

i A series of more recent books has been devoted to presentations of the methodology of discourse analysis (Titscher *et al.* 2000; Wetherell *et al.* 2001; Wodak and Meyer 2001). Yet, as valuable as these overviews are, they are not explicitly focused on policy discourses, nor do they formulate principles for how to build research projects and select bodies of data. A series of Scandinavian books has pointed to the need for a methodology of discourse analysis, but these books too have not offered an integration of theory and methodology or explicit methodological guidelines of the kind suggested here (Hjort 1997; Dyrberg *et al.* 2000; Jørgensen and Phillips 1999; Neumann 2001).

The theoretical framework and methodological guidelines developed in the first part of this book are illustrated by short examples. The second part turns to a thorough analysis of the Western response to the Bosnian war, which broke out in 1992 and lasted for more than three and a half years. This study is, on the one hand, a case study in that it illustrates the application of the theory, but it is also a 'case plus' in that it wants to offer a thorough analysis of the Western debate on Bosnia. The 'case plus study' thus has a triple purpose: it shows how the often complex theoretical and methodological arguments of the first five chapters can be applied to a particular situation and material; it points to fruitful new research agendas in need of further research, as summed up in the Conclusion, and it offers an extensive analysis of the Western debate on Bosnia. The analysis covers the policies adopted by the United States and Western Europe, the media representations of leading British and American newspapers, travel writing, memoir, and IR debates between neorealists, feminists, and poststructuralists. The analysis points to the importance of history, not as an explanation of the conflict itself, but as a discursive construction of temporal identity, and it speaks to broader debates on Western post-Cold War security as well as conceptual, literary, and cultural studies of 'the Balkans' and 'the West,' most crucially Maria Todorova's *Imagining the Balkans* and Vesna Goldsworthy's *Inventing Ruritania*.

To speak to the politics of identity is to acknowledge the link between the construction of the Other and 'our' understanding of Self. The Other has often come in the form of the East, from the Huns, the Russians, the Orientals, the Turks, the terrorists, the Chinese, to, in this book, the Balkans. That this, and any, Other is mirrored in but not fully identical with the Self is beautifully captured by Pedro Lujan's painting 'East,' which appears on the cover of the paperback edition of the book. May it be a political and aesthetic overture for the pages ahead.

Acknowledgements

Writing a book can be one of those experiences that truly convinces you of the importance of family, friends, and colleagues, and I have been fortunate over the past years of book-making to find myself within an incredibly supportive set of professional and social networks. As a research assistant and graduate student I benefited enormously from the environment at the Copenhagen Peace Research Institute (COPRI), where Barry Buzan and Ole Wæver formed the nucleus of the group on European Security, 'EUR', later known as The Copenhagen School. The monthly meetings of the EUR group provided a candid and supportive setting for presenting work in progress—and sometimes distress—and Barry and Ole were great examples of how to combine academic discipline with creativity and open-mindedness. Numerous participants joined the group over the years, and the following deserve particular mention for their comments on a series of 2002–3 chapter drafts: Christopher Browning, Stefano Guzzini, Ulla Holm, Pertti Joenniemi, Anna Leander, Noel Parker, Vibeke Schou Pedersen, and Jaap de Wilde. I am grateful to all of them for their critical engagement and suggestions as well as for their patience with yet another version of the Balkan discourse.

Working under the supervision of Alexander Wendt at Yale University in 1996 provided another formative graduate student experience. Having agreed with me that my previous drafts were rubbish, Alex taught me the need for rigor, reason, and textual care, particularly when working with complex philosophical and methodological questions. Although our understandings of discourse and poststructuralism differed and differ, Alex was always extremely supportive and generous with his time, and I have learned more from him than is perhaps immediately apparent from the pages ahead.

Time is perhaps the most precious commodity of academic life, and I am grateful to all of those who contributed some of theirs over the years. Particular thanks go out to Tom Biersteker, James Der Derian, Yale Ferguson, Jef Huysmans, Lis Højgaard, Gearóid Ó Tuathail, Michael Pugh, Iver B. Neumann, Michael Shapiro, Anders Wivel, the audiences at presentations at the University of Southern California, Brown University, and the ISA in Montreal in February and March 2004, and to the International Relations group in the Department of Political Science at the University of Copenhagen.

A more impersonal but equally heartfelt appreciation goes to my Copenhagen masters thesis students and the participants in my courses on discourse analysis and international relations who convinced me of the need for a book which took theoretical discussions of discourse analysis and poststructuralism into the realm of concrete methodological choices. A smaller group of graduate students provided particularly valuable substantial and pedagogical suggestions at a one-day workshop on the full manuscript in October 2004, many of which have been incorporated into the text.

By early 2004, I had compiled a series of drafts, but needed to start from page 1 and write my way onwards. A research sabbatical allowed me to focus fully on the book, and a research grant from the Danish Social Science Research Council took me to New York City, where Ted Magder, the Chair of the Department of Culture and Communication at New York University, was an incredibly generous host. I am deeply indebted to Ted, Helen Nissenbaum, and Judi Stevens for making my stay at NYU possible, productive, and enjoyable. As the editors of the *New International Relations* series, Barry Buzan and Richard Little have encouraged the project from the start. Barry offered extensive and detailed comments on the full final draft, as did Michael C. Williams, whose comradeship over the years has made an enormous professional and personal difference. At Routledge, I had excellent support from my editor Heidi Bagtazo, as well as from Grace McInnes and Harriet Brinton. Last but not least, I am thankful for a departmental research grant that allowed me to hire Kristoffer Astrup as my research assistant. I have no doubt that without Kristoffer's commitment, reliability, and independence, this book would have been longer in the making and the process much more arduous.

Over the past years, I have been fortunate to have supremely supportive friends and family. My parents set up the ultimate writer's retreat for me on the island of Langeland in Summer 2003, where I spent six weeks pondering how to bring structure to it all. In New York City, John Phillip Santos provided unwavering support for bringing in travel writing, memoir, and other non-academic genres, and his thoughts on the politics of identity have made a deep impact on the chapters ahead. Another eminent Mexican-Texan-American New Yorker, Pedro Lujan, kindly allowed me to use his painting, 'East', for the cover of the paperback edition—many thanks to him, and to Leah Gitter too, for their hospitality during my time in the city. In Copenhagen, Markus von Hedemann provided more loving support during the final revisions than I could possibly imagine, and my brother Peter, my sister Anne, and my friends, Stine Krøyer, Thomas Opstrup, Karen Lund Petersen, Helle Johansen, Lisa Richey, and Anja Besser Schmuhl provided food, wine, and patience as I kept promising that it would be just one more month, or week, before the book was done. The book is dedicated to my oldest friend, Helle Venzo, for her generous and indefatigable encouragement and insights over the years. Neither life nor book would have been the same without her.

Smaller parts of chapters 6, 8, and 9 have been adapted from: Hansen, L., 'Past as Preface: Civilizational Politics and the "Third" Balkan War,' *Journal of Peace Research*, vol. 37, no. 3, 2000, pp. 345–62 (© International Peace Research Institute (Oslo) PRIO, 2000), reproduced by permission of Sage Publications Ltd; and Hansen, L., 'Gender, Nation, Rape: Bosnia and the Construction of Security', *International Feminist Journal of Politics*, vol. 3, no. 1, 2001, pp. 55–75, journal website at www.tandf.co.uk, reprinted by permission of Taylor and Francis. I thank the editors and journals for the permission to include this material in the book.

Lene Hansen

1 Introduction

The relationship between identity and foreign policy is at the center of poststructuralism's research agenda: foreign policies rely upon representations of identity, but it is also through the formulation of foreign policy that identities are produced and reproduced. Understanding foreign policy as a discursive practice, poststructuralism argues that foreign policy discourses articulate and intertwine material factors and ideas to such an extent that the two cannot be separated from one another. It also argues that policy discourses are inherently social because policymakers address political opposition as well as the wider public sphere in the attempt to institutionalize their understanding of the identities and policy options at stake.

This approach to identity sets poststructuralism apart from liberal and constructivist studies of ideas as a variable in foreign policy analysis by arguing that identity is not something that states, or other collectivities, have independently of the discursive practices mobilized in presenting and implementing foreign policy (Goldstein and Keohane 1993; Laffey and Weldes 1997; Katzenstein 1996). It is, as a consequence, impossible to define identity as a variable that is causally separate from foreign policy or to measure its explanatory value in competition with non-discursive material factors. Critics of poststructuralism and discourse analysis have often portrayed this absence of causal epistemology as the road to theoretical, methodological, and political anarchy, but this book will show that poststructuralist discourse analysis can indeed create a theoretically vibrant and rigorous research agenda that speaks to pertinent political issues. It is a research agenda which engages classical questions of foreign policy—how do states generate responses to the problems they face and how do politicians rally support for their calls for action?—as well as bridges to the importance of media and political opposition for how political debates unfold.

Without theory there is nothing but description, and without methodology there is no transformation of theory into analysis. Poststructuralism has traditionally not engaged in explicit methodological discussions and hence there is a need to address the methodological challenges that arise from a poststructuralist theoretical perspective. Many International Relations (IR) poststructuralists have drawn on Derrida, who declared methodology is intimately tied to positivist forms of science and his own deconstruction is a non-method, and on literary, philosophical, and sociological traditions that place less emphasis on questions of validity and reliability than do IR and political science. But if the link between methodology and positivist epistemology is loosened, and the former seen as the procedures and choices by which theory becomes analysis, then a poststructuralist methodology is not only possible, but also desirable. Many of the methodological questions that poststructuralist discourse analysis confronts are those that face all academic work: what should be the focus of analysis?, how should a research design be built around it?, and how is a body of material and data selected that facilitates a qualitatively and quantitatively reliable answer? Poststructuralism's focus on discourses as articulated in written and spoken text calls in addition for particular attention to the methodology of reading (how are identities identified within foreign policy texts and how should the relationship between opposing discourses be studied?) and the methodology of textual selection (which forums and types of text should be chosen and how many should be included?).

The goals of this chapter are to situate poststructuralist discourse analysis within the field of IR and to discuss rationalist demands for 'real world research questions' and causal epistemology in more detail. The first section links poststructuralism's concern with identity to the history of IR and traces the development of rationalist, constructivist, and poststructuralist approaches. The second section argues that poststructuralism can speak directly to 'real world' foreign policy questions from its conceptualization of identity as discursive, political, relational, and social. The third section continues the discussion of real world relevance by theorizing official foreign policy discourse as challenged or reproduced by the media, oppositional politicians, commentators, and popular culture. The chapter returns in the fourth section to the demand for causal theorizing that was issued by the most comprehensive political science introduction to qualitative causal research design, *Designing Social Inquiry: Scientific Inference in Qualitative Research* by King, Keohane and Verba (1994). It is argued that poststructuralism cannot be formulated as a causal theory because the relationship between identity and policy is co-constitutive or performative. The methodological demands which ensue are addressed in the fifth section, which also presents the methodological status of the case to be explored in the second part of the book, the Western debate on the Bosnian war. The chapter closes with a brief presentation of the structure of the book and the content of each chapter.

Poststructuralism and the field of IR

The question of identity has been at the center of disciplinary debate for the past 15 years, perhaps even since the inception of the field of IR. Is the abstract essence of IR not best seen as a continuous political and normative debate over the identity—the ontology—of the state, the difference between domestic politics and international relations, and the scope for transforming the latter? These questions, albeit not exactly phrased in these terms, were at the fore- front of classical IR texts by E. H. Carr, Reinhold Niebuhr, Norman Angell, Hans Morgenthau, John Herz, Arnold Wolfers, and Kenneth Waltz, yet buried under the epistemological cloak of the growing behavioralism and positivism of American social science in the 1950s and 1960s.

By the end of the 1970s Waltz's *Theory of International Politics* (1979) had canonized positivist and causal epistemology and combined it with an abstract, transhistorical structuralism. But as *Theory of International Politics* became the key text for the following decade, it provided the starting point for a burgeoning uncovering of the philosophical and political roots of IR as a discipline and a political practice. Richard Ashley praised the classical realism of John Herz and coined the term 'neo-realism,' which was faulted for its denigration of history and its celebration of structural determinism (Ashley 1981, 1984, 1987); Robert Walker traced the ontological and political importance of state sovereignty for the discipline of IR (Walker 1987, 1993); Friedrich Kratochwil, Nicholas Onuf and John Ruggie pointed to the impor- tance of norms, regimes and legal reasoning (Kratochwil 1989; Onuf 1989; Ruggie 1992; Kratochwil and Ruggie 1986); Alexander Wendt brought the structure–agency debate into IR while arguing that Waltz's structuralism was paradoxically dependent upon a particular construction of the individual state (Wendt 1987); James Der Derian showed that diplomacy was not simply a convention for managing interstate relations but a cultural practice through which the foreign and the strange were mediated (Der Derian 1987); and Michael J. Shapiro held that foreign policies took place not in abstract dis- embodied neorealist space, but through the mobilization of particular cul- tural, racial, and political identities (Shapiro 1988).

After Robert Keohane's famous 1988 presidential address, this group was given a name—'reflectivists'—as well as legitimacy; 'reflectivism,' argued Keohane, offered important insights into the importance of institutions for international politics, insights not adequately acknowledged by realist and neoliberal approaches, which he subsumed under the juxtaposing label of 'rationalism' (Keohane 1988). Yet, it was crucial that reflectivism adopted an epistemology, and ensuing methodologies, which would provide it with the capacity to engage rationalism (Keohane 1988: 389–93; Katzenstein, Keohane and Krasner 1998: 677; Walt 1991). Keohane conceded that reflectivists were right in pointing to the importance of identity, culture, norms, regimes, and ideas, but argued that they needed to formulate causal hypotheses and subject them to more rigorous testing to assess their applicability.[1] The con- struction of this rationalist–reflectivist research agenda privileged a particular form of research modeled on the natural sciences and microeconomics over forms of knowledge that drew upon philosophical, historical, and humanistic traditions of understanding.

The rather amorphous group of reflectivists quickly began to splinter along constructivist and poststructuralist lines, and by the mid-1990s the constructivists had further subdivided into 'conventional' or 'thin' constructivists on the one hand and 'critical' or 'thick' constructivists on the other (Katzenstein 1996; Adler 1997; Price and Reus-Smit 1998; Wendt 1999; Zehfuss 2001). But the influence of Keohane's programmatic distinction cannot be overestimated: it had successfully privileged epistemology over ontology as the area where the importance of non-material factors should be assessed, and epistemological differences continued to be key to the construction of separate positions within the fracturing reflectivist camp. As Alexander Wendt exclaimed in his much anticipated *Social Theory of International Politics*, 'when it comes to the epistemology of social inquiry I am a strong believer in science—a pluralistic science to be sure, in which there is a significant role for "Understanding," but science just the same. I am a "positivist"' (Wendt 1999: 39).

But where constructivists had been willing—or perhaps even seen a strategic advantage—to embrace a disciplinary label, over the years very little work had declared itself to be postmodernist or poststructuralist. When it did, it usually opted for the latter category, arguing that 'poststructuralism' pointed to the theoretical roots in poststructuralist (not anti-structuralist) linguistics, philosophy, social theory, and literary theory (more specifically to writers like Nietzsche, Kristeva, Foucault, and Derrida), whereas 'postmodernism' referred to a particular historical order (Hansen 1997; Wæver 2002). This absence of self-declaration implied that attempts to present poststructuralism as a coherent approach were carried out largely by its critics (for exceptions see Der Derian and Shapiro 1989; Ashley and Walker 1990; George 1994). Rationalists chastised 'postmodernism' for seeking to seduce the field (Walt 1991), for being 'self-referential and disengaged from the world,' and for denying the 'use of evidence to adjudicate between truth claims' (Katzenstein, Keohane and Krasner 1998: 678). Yet, in spite of these shortcomings, in their *International Organization* fiftieth anniversary survey of the field Katzenstein, Keohane and Krasner warned that 'it is easy to underestimate the direct importance and indirect influence of this intellectual current. Postmodernism has found many adherents both in the broader international studies field in the United States and in Europe where major journals and book series are dedicated to publishing the results of this work' (Katzenstein, Keohane and Krasner 1998: 678). By the mid-1990s, constructivists began to chime in to set themselves aside from 'some exotic (presumably Parisian) social theory' (Jepperson *et al.* 1996: 34; see also Adler 1997; Wendt 1999; Wæver 1998; Price and Reus-Smit 1998).[2] Even Richard Price and Christian Reus-Smit, who state their ambition to be an open exploration of the terrain between constructivism and 'postmodernism,' fault the latter for, among other shortcomings, neglecting 'conceptual elaboration and sustained empirical analysis,' not explaining or predicting the end of the Cold War, and not bringing causality to the study of why one discursive formation prevails over another (Price and Reus-Smit 1998: 264–5, 279).[3] Constructivism was, not surprisingly, claimed to rectify these shortcomings by combining the best of the old 1980s poststructuralism with an epistemological rapprochement to rationalism (Price and Reus-Smit 1998: 283–4).

The application of labels to schools of thought and academic approaches is important for how disciplinary debates are conducted (Wæver 1998). Labels function as codes to the reader and as meeting points for theory-building and research programs, and the absence of a clearly delineated programmatic post-structuralism made it harder for a non poststructuralist audience to assess the validity of these charges (for a few responses see Walker 1993: 81–6; Der Derian 1992: 8–11; Campbell 1998b: 207–27). Indeed, as will be apparent from this book, most of what has been said about poststructuralism is misleading at best.[4] Or, to put matters more constructively: it is indeed both possible and valuable to build a theory of identity and foreign policy which draws upon the writings of poststructuralist theorists, inside and outside of IR, but which differs significantly from the image conjured up by rationalists and conventional constructivists. Poststructuralism has strengths and weaknesses, as do all theoretical approaches—no theory can pursue all relevant research questions simultaneously—but it can be drawn upon to show not only that identities matter for foreign policy, but also how they can be studied systematically through the adoption of a theory of discourse. In doing so it pursues a particular set of research questions, centered on *the constitutive significance of representations of identity for formulating and debating foreign policies,* and it argues that *adopting a non-causal epistemology does not imply an abandonment of theoretically rigorous frameworks, empirical analyses of 'real world relevance,' or systematic assessments of data and methodology.*

Representations as 'real world' research questions

How does one decide the scope of one's research project? In their authoritative study *Designing Social Inquiry*, King, Keohane, and Verba (1994) argue that there are essentially no rules from which to determine whether to study ethnic conflict or educational policy, NATO or the EU, poverty or war. The only criterion that one can meaningfully establish is that it *'should pose a question that is "important" in the real world.'* That is, it 'should be consequential for political, social, or economic life, for understanding something that significantly affects many people's lives, or for understanding and predicting events that might be harmful or beneficial' (King *et al.* 1994: 15, italics and quotation marks in original). This of course points to a very broad array of research projects, in fact it is hard to imagine anyone studying international politics who would not claim to be in compliance with this 'real world programmatic.' When poststructuralism is chastised for being removed from the study of the real world, what is at stake is thus a more specific contestation of what it means to study significant events and effects: that poststructuralism's preoccupation with philosophy and texts takes it away from concerns with 'real foreign policy' as it is practically conceived and implemented.

But even with a narrow definition of 'real world relevance,' poststructuralist analysis has a research program that speaks directly to the conduct of foreign policy. This research program is based on the assumption that policies are dependent upon representations of the threat, country, security problem, or crisis they seek to address. Foreign policies need to ascribe meaning to the situation and to construct the objects within it, and in doing so they articulate and draw upon specific identities of other states, regions, peoples, and institutions as well as on the identity of a national, regional, or institutional Self. To take an example, the Bosnian war was frequently represented by the Clinton administration as a 'Balkan war.' It followed from this representation that the war was seen as fought by a barbaric, violent people with a 'Balkan identity' who had hated each other for at least 500 years. This in turn made the war an intractable 'problem from hell,' as US Secretary of State Warren Christopher called it, which the West did not have the means to solve (Friedman 1993). Western intervention was, as a consequence, a dangerous undertaking which should be avoided unless there were clear implications for Western security.

The poststructuralist assumption that foreign policies draw upon representations of identity is linked to a conceptualization of identity as discursive, political, relational, and social. To say that identity is *discursive* and *political* is to argue that representations of identity place foreign policy issues within a particular interpretative optic, one with consequences for which foreign policy can be formulated as an adequate response. To theorize identity as constructed through discourse, and for policy to be dependent thereon, is to argue that there are no objective identities located in some extra-discursive realm, hence identity cannot be used as a variable against which behavior and non-discursive factors can be measured. This implies a conceptualization of identity existing only insofar as it is continuously rearticulated and uncontested by competing discourses (Anderson 1983). The emphasis on the political in poststructuralism's concept of identity sets it aside from a conceptualization of identity as 'culture,' as in anthropological studies of marriage rituals, or aesthetic analyses of cultural artifacts such as architecture, music, and literature.[5] Nor can a conflict be explained by 'a people's culture.' Poststructuralism's *relational* conception of identity implies that identity is always given through reference to something it is not. To speak of the 'American,' 'European,' 'barbaric' or 'underdeveloped' is to constitute another identity or set of identities as non-American, non-European, civilized or developed. To conceptualize identity as *social* is to understand it as established through a set of collectively articulated codes, not as a private property of the individual or a psychological condition—not that individuals do not understand themselves as having identities, instead individual identity is constituted within and through a collective terrain.

The conceptualization of identity as discursive, political, relational, and social implies that foreign policy discourse always articulates a *Self* and a series of *Others*. Security discourses have traditionally constituted a national Self facing one or more threatening Others, whose identities were radically different from the one of the Self. But identities are not necessarily constructed through juxtaposition to a radically different and threatening Other

(Campbell 1992). Constructions of identity can take on different degrees of 'Otherness,' ranging from fundamental difference between Self and Other to constructions of less than radical difference, and the Other can be constituted through geographical representations as well as political representations such as 'civilizations,' 'nations,' 'tribes,' 'terrorists,' 'women,' 'civilians,' or 'humanity.' Geographical and political constructions of identity are usually articulated with a particular temporal identity through themes of repetition, progress, transformation, backwardness, or development. Temporal representations locate a contemporary foreign policy question within a historical discourse, but they are, from a poststructuralist perspective, precisely *discourses*: framings of meaning and lenses of interpretation, rather than objective, historical truths.

The scope of foreign policy analysis: situating official discourse

If representations of identity are always employed in the legitimization of foreign policy, where do representations come from and how do official representations relate to those argued by oppositional political parties and groups, the media, and public intellectuals? Poststructuralist discourse analysis argues that foreign policy decision-makers are situated within a larger political and public sphere, and that their representations as a consequence draw upon and are formed by the representations articulated by a larger number of individuals, institutions, and media outlets. Top politicians rarely have detailed knowledge about the issues put before them and therefore rely upon their advisors, media coverage, and, in some cases, background literature to establish a representational framing of the policy (to be) adopted. In 'speaking back' their representation of a foreign policy issue, politicians are in turn influencing what count as proper representations within a particular foreign policy issue. This is not to say that there is necessarily a complete congruence between official foreign policy discourse and the representations argued from other sources: politicians do not always (or even rarely) reproduce media and expert representations slavishly, nor does official discourse determine which representations can be argued by other sources and agents, at least not in democratic societies. It would, however, be extremely unlikely—and politically unsavvy—for politicians to articulate foreign policy without any concern for the representations found within the wider public sphere as they attempt to present their policies as legitimate to their constituencies.

Understanding official foreign policy discourse as situated within a wider discursive field opens up a theoretical and empirical research agenda that examines how foreign policy representations and representations articulated by oppositional political forces, the media, academe, and popular culture reinforce or contest each other (Hansen and Wæver 2002; Holm 1993, 1997; Shapiro 1988, 1997; Der Derian 1992; Hansen 1996; Neumann 1996a). Some foreign policy questions are less contested than others, leading to less diversity in terms of the representations argued. One might therefore be prone to focus the analysis on official policy and discourse as not much new will be uncovered when including a larger set of actors and media.[6] But, such a hegemonic situation might also be seen as worthy of an extensive study of nongovernmental sources in as much as this generates important knowledge of the way in which governmental representations are dispersed and reproduced.[7] To study foreign policy by examining patterns of reproduction and contestation across official discourse, political oppositional parties, and media discourses, as well as more popular forms of writing, also points to the importance of genre. Official foreign policymakers seek to constitute themselves as having authority to speak about a foreign policy issue: their formal authority is derived from their institutional location, but authority is also built on *knowing* about a particular issue. Knowledge, therefore, becomes important for establishing authority, and this in turn creates a new analytical optic for discourse analysis of foreign policy, as different genres—policy speech, journalistic reportage, and academic analysis, for instance—establish particular forms of knowledge as acceptable. How texts construct acceptable knowledge becomes an empirical question in need of analysis; it is not a matter of deciding upon a proper social science epistemology as in the rationalist–constructivist–poststructuralist debate. That different genres of foreign policy writing adopt different forms of knowledge becomes particularly salient when foreign policy discourses are seen as intertextually linked. An intertextual understanding of foreign policy argues that texts build their arguments and authority through references to other texts: by making direct quotes or by adopting key concepts and catchphrases.[8] In making links to older texts, new texts rely upon the status of the older, but this process of reading and linking also produces new meaning: references never reproduce the originals in a manner which is fully identical, but weave them into the present context and argument.

Foreign policymakers reference media reports and academic analysis to support their discourse, but they also, more surprisingly, point to texts not normally considered scientific or explicitly political. The Western debate on Bosnia showed that a diverse set of texts and genres had an influence on not only the broader debate but also the central foreign policy decision-makers. Clinton backed down from the Vance–Owen Peace Plan and a policy of 'lift and strike'—shorthand for lifting the arms embargo imposed upon the Bosnian Muslims and bombing Bosnian Serb positions—after having read the travel book *Balkan Ghosts* by Robert D. Kaplan (Kaplan 1993a; Drew 1994). Kaplan's primary source was another travelogue, Rebecca West's *Black Lamb and Grey Falcon*, written on the verge of World War II, which was said to have instilled a pro-Serbian attitude into two generations of readers, policymakers, and diplomats (Holbrooke 1998: 22; Simms 2001: 179). These might at first seem to be unique instances, but a further analysis in chapter 4 shows that not only travel writing, but memoir as well have played an important role in developing the Western view of international politics from the age of exploration to contemporary foreign policy debate. Memoir and travel writing can be described as 'literary non-fiction' in that they invoke factual academic forms of knowledge, in particular in making historiographic claims, while also relying upon subjective forms of knowledge and literary techniques and themes.[9]

Epistemological challenges

Deciding the scope and research questions is at the core of building a research agenda, but the delineation of which questions can and should be asked is intertwined with questions of epistemology. King, Keohane, and Verba demand that research projects, in addition to being concerned with 'the real world,' should *make a specific contribution to an identifiable scholarly literature by increasing our collective ability to construct verified scientific explanations of some aspect of the world*' thus privileging causal epistemological research projects over those which use, and require, other forms of knowledge (King *et al.* 1994: 15, italics in original).

The debate over what constitutes the proper conception of causal epistemology and how rigidly and fully IR research programs should comply with it is extensive and inconclusive. Rationalism, as comprehensively stated by King, Keohane, and Verba, argues that social science theories should generate falsifiable hypotheses about the relationship between dependent and independent variables. This allows some room for 'description' as inspiration and data for theory-building, but description 'loses most of its interest unless linked to some causal relationship' (King *et al.* 1994: 34). Determining the causal mechanisms between variables in situations of 'multiple causality,' where 'the same outcome can be caused by combinations of different independent variables,' can be difficult, however this should not lead to the abandonment of causality but to a definition of 'the counterfactual conditions making up each causal effect very precisely' (King *et al.* 1994: 87, 89). There is no scope, in short, within the rationalist epistemological position for research projects that cannot be conceptualized in causal epistemological terms.

Constructivists have argued in response that the separation between description and causal theory is misleading: constitutive theories of foreign policy might not make causal claims, but their theorization of the constitutive relationship between structures and agents or identity and foreign policy make them theories rather than mere descriptions (Wendt 1999: 87). Furthermore, from a sociology of knowledge perspective it is doubtful whether 'pure description' ever exists as what is described, and how it is described depends on a selection of particular aspects of a phenomenon. One should also distinguish between description as the gathering of 'raw' or disjunctive data, such as levels of armament, and descriptive theories concerned with relationships between sets of phenomena. Yet, while conventional constructivists allow more scope for non-causal theory as part of a research agenda incorporating multiple epistemological ambitions (Katzenstein 1996), they still mobilize causal concepts of testing to assess theoretical validity. In Wendt's words, constitutive theories 'imply hypotheses about the world that can and should be tested' (Wendt 1999: 87). Price and Reus-Smit argue that constructivism should 'answer the hard and good question inevitably asked by traditional scholars—"show me your discourse matters and how much",' and that some measure of causality and variability is necessary to assess the importance of discourses and identity (Price and Reus-Smit 1998: 279, 282; Wendt 1999: 55–6; Wight 1999; Campbell 1999).[10]

King, Keohane, and Verba stress that building good causal research design is often a complex task—social life is much more multifaceted, and its patterns of influence more interwoven, than the experiments in the controlled laboratory of the hard sciences allow—but it should be noted that their concept of causality is itself narrowly and rigorously defined.[11] It is, however, not uncommon to encounter vaguer conceptions of 'causality' as pointing to the 'impact' or 'influence' of identities and discourses on policies and state action, conceptions which draw upon the everyday use of the word '(be)cause.' Yet it is problematic to move from the rigid conception of King, Keohane, and Verba and to the vaguer everyday use as this would make the concept of causality so broad as to be virtually meaningless: there would be virtually nothing which would not be considered a causal relationship as humans—and institutions run by humans—almost universally describe their actions as driven by causes. That is, agents employ 'discursive causality' in explaining their actions, but these are, from an epistemological perspective, single observations, not causally related classes of phenomena.

This is not to say that there is one undisputed conception of causality that should be honed by everyone at all times, or that there are no important conceptual questions to be pursued in the space between the rationalist conception and everyday use. The conception of causality has a history of its own, and the Humeian one of King, Keohane, and Verba is not the only one which can be uncovered (Kurki, forthcoming). That said, this conception has become the ideal of social science research, and it stands as the model around which constructivist and poststructuralist scholarship have had to cast themselves.

In contrast to conventional constructivism's embrace of causal epistemology, for poststructuralists what constitutes 'proper knowledge' is not a theory's ability to uncover causal truths as knowledge is historically and politically situated. Causal epistemology is therefore a particular discourse of knowledge, which cannot sustain its privilege outside of its own historical and political location (Foucault 1970, 1974). Engaging rationalism's and constructivism's faulting of poststructuralism for its unwillingness to engage in causal theorizing, this book argues that representations of identity and policy are linked through discourse, but that they do not stand in a causal relationship with one another as representations of identity are simultaneously the precondition for and (re)produced through articulations of policy. Contrary to rationalism's and constructivism's linkage of causal epistemology to theoretical and methodological rigor, and the absence thereof with intellectual insularity, the first part of the book formulates a general theoretical framework for the study of the processes through which identities and policies are constitutively or performatively linked while simultaneously insisting that applications of this framework need to be historically and contextually grounded.

Methodology and the status of the 'case plus study'

The first part of this book presents a comprehensive poststructuralist discourse analytical framework and develops a methodology for reading as well as a methodology for developing research designs and selecting texts. These chapters make continuous use of examples and illustrations. The second part of the book turns to a detailed study of the Western debate on the Bosnian war. This study provides an in-depth application of the theoretical framework and methodological principles from the first half of the book. This analysis is a case study in that it shows the application of the theory and methodology from the first part of the book, but it is not a test as the basic propositions of post-structuralist discourse analysis are constitutive rather than causal. It is also more than a case study, if 'case study' is taken to mean the application of theory to a particular phenomenon without ensuing theoretical elaboration. Rather, the study will be used as a medium for continued theoretical and method-ological discussions, summed up in chapter 10 by a series of suggestions for a future research agenda.

The Western debate on Bosnia was chosen because it illustrates the width and depth of the theoretical framework and hence the widest empirical scope of the theory: it had competing representations as well as competing policies; constructions of the Other as radical as well as non-radical; a transformation of representations and policy over time; the articulation of historically preg-nant concepts as part of the construction of identity; political dissent as well as hegemony; the influence of the media and literary non-fiction on foreign policy discourse; and it was a foreign policy issue which was constructed as so politically important that it mobilized responses from Western powers and institutions. The Western debate on Bosnia is not, in turn, a representative case, in the sense that not all foreign policy debates would follow a similar pattern. Whether there would be consensus rather than contestation, radical difference rather than varying degrees of difference, continuity over time rather than change, and less explicit influence by the media and literary non-fiction are empirical questions, but ones that the theory allows to be posed.[12] One might ask why one large study rather than a series of smaller ones was chosen, and the answer is that while poststructuralist discourse analysis can be applied to a wide variety of topics, it is a form of analysis which requires extensive knowledge of the case in question and which can therefore only be undertaken in a small number of cases.

The content of this book

This book is divided into two parts, Part I: 'The theory and methodology of discourse analysis' and Part II: 'A discourse analysis of the Western debate on the Bosnian war.' Part I opens with chapter 2, 'Discourse analysis, identity, and foreign policy,' which presents the linguistic ontology and discursive epistemology of poststructuralist discourse analysis. The chapter argues that policy and identity are performatively linked and that one cannot therefore theorize their relationship in causal terms. The concern should instead be with the combinations of identity and policy delineated within a foreign policy debate and on the ability of these combinations to incorporate discursively constituted 'facts' and 'events.'

Chapter 3, 'Beyond the Other: analyzing the complexity of identity,' is devoted to a more detailed discussion of the concept of identity. Drawing on works by David Campbell and William Connolly, it is argued that identity is relational, discursive, political, and social, and that the national Self constitutes 'the Other' through degrees of difference, ranging from the radically different to the familiar. This constitution of Self and Other can be theorized as taking place through two simultaneous logics—a logic of differentiation and a logic of linking—as well as through the articulation of identity in spatial, temporal, and ethical terms. Foreign policy debates evolve around a wealth of texts, and the last part of the chapter argues that these can be seen as structured by a smaller number of basic discourses, which articulate radically different relationships between Self and Other.

Chapter 4, 'Intertextualizing foreign policy: genres, authority, and knowledge,' continues the discussion of how to map discourses and their relationship and introduces the concept of intertextuality to capture the way in which texts draw upon other texts to establish legitimacy and authority for their constructions of identity and foreign policy. Discourse analysis can be applied to a multiplicity of foreign policy actors and arenas, and the chapter develops three intertextual research models with different research agendas and analytical objectives. One model focuses on official foreign policy discourse, the second on the wider discourse as articulated by political opposition, the media, and corporate organizations, and the third model incorporates popular culture and marginal political discourses. Taking an intertextual approach to official discourse implies that references to other texts are documented and analyzed, which in turn brings in texts from a variety of genres, including journalism, academe, travel writing, and autobiography. All texts and genres represent the author as knowledgeable, but what constitutes knowledge differs between policy speech, investigative journalism, and travel writing. Writings incorporating both the factual and the fictitious, particularly memoir and travel writing, have been noteworthy, yet undertheorized, importance to foreign policy debates and are therefore presented in more detail in the last part of the chapter.

The methodology of reading is given a prominent place in chapters 2 to 4, and chapter 5, 'Research designs: asking questions and choosing texts,' turns to the question of poststructuralist research design. The first part of the chapter develops a research design model that identifies a concrete study as produced through choices along four dimensions: intertextual model, number and types of Selves, temporal perspective, and number and kinds of events. The next methodological issue discussed concerns the selection of texts. The chapter first argues that one should select material from the time of study as well as historical material that traces the genealogy of important representations, and then argues that key texts with a prominent intertextual location as well as general material that allows for an identification of dominant discourses should be included. The last part of the chapter combines the choice of research design with the selection of texts in a presentation of the case study developed in the second part of the book, the Western debate on the Bosnian war.

Moving into Part II, chapter 6, 'The basic discourses in the Western debate over Bosnia,' identifies 'the Balkans' as one of two central representations within the Western debate and analyzes when and how it has been conceptualized. This historical genealogy identifies three discourses—a Romantic, a civilizational, and one of Balkanization—which articulate 'the Balkans' and 'the West' in very different terms. The Balkanization discourse is mobilized in the 1990s by one of the two basic discourses—'the Balkan discourse,' which constitutes the war in Bosnia as the product of ancient Balkan hatred and hence a conflict that the West could and should not solve. The opposing basic discourse, 'the Genocide discourse,' challenges this representation by arguing that the war was a genocide committed by Serbian military and political leaders and that the West had an ethical obligation to come to Bosnia's rescue.

Chapter 7, 'Humanitarian responsibility versus "lift and strike": tracing trans-Atlantic policy discourses,' draws upon the two basic discourses in an analysis of the official policy of the British and American governments and whether it was supported or challenged by parliamentary opposition and the media. The chapter identifies significant differences across the Atlantic: the British Conservative government modified the Balkan discourse by separating Bosnian leaders and innocent civilians and constructing a humanitarian responsibility toward the latter. This discourse was supported by the Labour Party and was furthermore remarkably resilient in the face of events in Bosnia. US policy, by contrast, was formulated by two Presidencies, and as Clinton came into office in early 1993 he articulated an unstable combination of the Balkan discourse and the Genocide discourse, settling eventually for the former. This discourse, although largely intact until mid-1995, was fiercely challenged in the US Senate, where an American Genocide discourse argued that the West had a responsibility toward the Bosnian government and that a policy of 'lift and strike' should be adopted.

Chapters 8 and 9 move from the level of policy discourse, and its chronological (re)production in the face of events in Bosnia and criticism at home, to more detailed intertextual studies of the links and key texts within the two basic discourses. Chapter 8, 'Writing the past, predicting the future: travelers, realism, and the politics of civilization,' is devoted to the intertextual web of the Balkan discourse established through two key texts: Robert D. Kaplan's

Balkan Ghosts, the travelogue which influenced Clinton's decision to abandon the Vance–Owen Peace Plan as well as 'lift and strike' in spring 1993; and Kaplan's primary source, Rebecca West's *Black Lamb and Grey Falcon*, a book from 1941, itself extensively quoted within the debate. Both Kaplan and West were commonly read as representative of the Balkan discourse, but the analysis shows that their works made prominent use of a Romantic discourse and that their policy implications were ambiguous. Locating these works inside the wider debate, two concepts stand out as intertextual points of reference: *civilizations* and *ancient hatred*. The concept of civilizations is traced through Samuel P. Huntington's article and book on 'the clash of civilizations' and through George F. Kennan's introduction to the 1993 re-publication of *Report of the International Commission To Inquire into the Causes and Conduct of the Balkan Wars* from 1914. The concept of ancient hatred leads from readings of readings of neorealism to a critical evaluation of writings by John Mearsheimer and Barry Posen. With the exception of Kennan, all of these authors articulate a modified version of the basic Balkan discourse and show that a variety of concrete policy proposals were linked to the identity of 'the Balkans.'

Chapter 9, 'The failure of the West? The evolution of the Genocide discourse and the ethics of inaction,' turns to the other basic discourse, the Genocide discourse, and its critique of Western policy. The first part of the chapter considers the key text within this discourse, Roy Gutman's reports, subsequently collected in *A Witness to Genocide*, which revealed the existence of camps in northern Bosnia in the summer of 1992. The second part of the chapter examines three variations on the Genocide discourses, a 'European responsibility for Genocide discourse,' a 'Balkanizing Serbia discourse,' and a 'gendering Genocide discourse,' in a discussion of discursive stability and the boundaries between the Genocide discourse and the Balkan discourse. A particularly noteworthy critique of the West is made by David Campbell in his *National Deconstruction*, a poststructuralist analysis of the Western debate that both supplements and challenges the analysis of *Security as Practice*. Reading *National Deconstruction* as a text within the debate, the third part of the chapter argues that Campbell is both critical of, yet leans toward, the Genocide discourse. The Genocide discourse's critical readings of the West are, finally, juxtaposed with the memoirs of the two most important mediators, David Owen and Richard Holbrooke.

The conclusion, chapter 10, summarizes the most important theoretical and analytical arguments, addresses the question of what constitutes good discourse analysis through a discussion of Campbell's *National Deconstruction*, and suggests a number of research questions for the future research agenda of poststructuralist discourse analysis.

Part I

The theory and methodology of discourse analysis

2 Discourse analysis, identity, and foreign policy

Theories of foreign policy are united by a concern with the way in which states understand and respond to the world around them. Beyond this broad focus there are, however, multiple perspectives on how questions should be asked and analysis developed, which is to say that theories rely upon a set of ontological assumptions and make a series of epistemological choices. Comprehending the deeper foundations of foreign policy theories and their research agendas and where and why they differ requires, therefore, a thorough consideration of questions of ontology and epistemology.

Poststructuralism's discursive ontology is, as laid out in the first section of this chapter, deeply intertwined with its understanding of language as constitutive for what is brought into being. Language is social and political, an inherently unstable system of signs that generate meaning through a simultaneous construction of identity and difference. The productive nature of language implies that policy discourse is seen as relying upon particular constructions of problems and subjectivities, but that it is also through discourse that these problems and subjectivities are constructed in the first place. Policy and identity are therefore conceptualized as ontologically interlinked. To help situate poststructuralism's ontology within current International Relations (IR) debates, it is pointed out that the concept of 'discourse' is not equivalent to 'ideas'; discourse incorporates material as well as ideational factors.

The poststructuralist view of language as relationally structured and ontologically productive is coupled to a discursive epistemology, which, as the second section 'Discursive epistemology and relational identity' explains, produces an analytical focus on the relational construction of identity. This in turn provides for a rather different conception of identity than the one adopted by the most influential conventional constructivist, Alexander Wendt, who claims the possibility of a pre-social intrinsic state identity. Having defined the concept of identity as relational and discursive, the third section 'The impossibility of causality' returns to the question of causality and argues that it is impossible to conceptualize the relationship between identity and foreign policy in terms of causal effects and that one cannot, as a consequence, formulate hypotheses about the (relative) explanatory power of discourse as opposed to material explanations. As the refusal of causal epistemology breaks with conventional rationalist assumptions, this section points out that poststructuralism produces analysis which can expand upon as well as question causal scholarship.

The relationship between foreign policy and identity is theorized in non-causal terms, but the absence of causality does not imply a lack of structure. The fourth section 'A theoretical model of combinability' argues that one should systematically examine how identity and policy are linked in a non-causal process of combinability, and it presents a theoretical model centered on the assumption that the goal of foreign policy discourse is to create a stable link between representations of identity and the proposed policy. Creating this link requires internal discursive stability between identity and policy and for the external constraints imposed on the discourse to be addressed. Situating combinability within a dynamic context further highlights the importance of the stability of combinations and their response to contestations, and the role of 'facts' in stabilizing or undermining established constructions of identity and policy.

The last section of the chapter, 'Challenges, changes, and facts,' turns to security, traditionally the field where non-discursive approaches have mustered their strongest defense of objective, non-discursive conceptualizations. Drawing upon the work of the Copenhagen School and David Campbell, it is argued that security can be seen as a historically formed discourse centered on the nation state and as a particularly radical form of identity construction with a distinct political force that invests political leaders with power as well as responsibility.

The ontology of linguistic construction

To poststructuralism, language is ontologically significant: it is only through the construction in language that 'things'—objects, subjects, states, living beings, and material structures—are given meaning and endowed with a particular identity. Language is not a transparent tool functioning as a medium for the registration of data as (implicitly) assumed by positivist, empiricist science, but a field of social and political practice, and hence there is no objective or 'true meaning' beyond the linguistic representation to which one can refer (Shapiro 1981: 218). To understand language as *social* is to see it not as a private property of the individual but as a series of collective codes and conventions that each individual needs to employ to make oneself comprehensible. The experience of coming to a foreign culture whose language one does not speak and where no locals speaks one's own illustrates the collective nature of language, as does the likely use of gestures and body language in the search for a common non-verbal language. Language's social character implies that individuals are socialized into connecting sounds with particular objects—one learns that the sound of 'chair' refers to an object on which a person can sit—and into a larger set of political discourses on, for example, 'national security,' 'democracy,' and 'the rule of law.'

To understand language as *political* is to see it as a site for the production and reproduction of particular subjectivities and identities while others are simultaneously excluded. For example, in nineteenth century Europe women were widely considered to have a political identity radically different from that of men (of a certain age and income). They were defined as motherly, nurturing, incapable of comprehending complex political and financial questions, and emotional—identities that made female political influence inappropriate if not outright dangerous (Pateman 1983; Elshtain 1981). This view was held to be an objective account of women's nature, not a particular construction of identity, and it was reproduced through linguistic practices which continuously reinstalled the male as the privileged political subject. It was also reinforced through political and economic practices which prevented women from obtaining political, economical, legal, and cultural rights. The political—and thereby also contestable and subjective—nature of these practices was only brought out as they came under attack from women's movements and women's rights advocates. Over time, the 'objective account of women's nature' went from being a widely accepted, or hegemonic, construction to being a politically contested one.

The collective and structured nature of language is emphasized in Foucault's suggestion that a discursive formation can be defined as 'a *system* of dispersion [whenever] between objects, types of statement, concepts, or thematic choices,' which form 'a *regularity* (an order, correlations, positions and functionings, transformations)' (Foucault 1974: 38; emphasis added). Language is, argues Derrida, a system of differential signs, and meaning is established not by the essence of a thing itself but through a series of juxtapositions, where one element is valued over its opposite (Derrida 1976, 1978). For example, the state's construction of 'its' national identity is only possible through a simultaneous delineation of something which is different or Other (Campbell 1992; Neumann 1996b); a 'terrorist' can only be identified through a differentiation from the legitimate 'freedom fighter' or 'state sanctioned soldier' (Der Derian 1992: 92–126), and the 'underdeveloped' world is not meaningful without a juxtaposition to a superior 'developed' world (Doty 1996).

To say that meaning is constructed through the discursive juxtaposition between a privileged sign on the one hand and a devalued one on the other leads to a conceptualization of identity in relational terms and as being constructed along two dimensions (Laclau and Mouffe 1985). It is constructed through a series of juxtaposed signs, to be a woman in nineteenth century discourse is to be different from—and inferior to—being a man, it is to be emotional rather than rational, to be motherly rather than intellectual, to be reliant rather than independent, and to be focused on the simple rather than the complex.

'Woman' is defined through a positive *process of linking* emotional, motherly, reliant and simple (Figure 2.1), but this female series of links is at the same time juxtaposed to the male series of links through a negative *process of differentiation*.[1] Although the two processes can be separated analytically, it is important to stress that they are both part and parcel of the process of identity construction and enacted simultaneously (Figure 2.2).

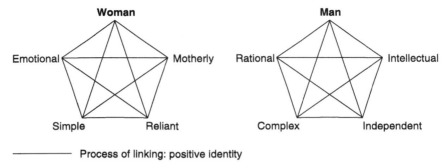

Figure 2.1 Process of linking.

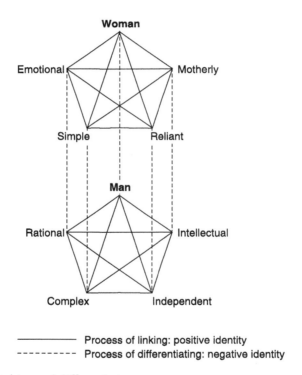

Figure 2.2 Linking and differentiation.

Language, and the construction of identity therein, is highly structured, but it is also simultaneously inherently unstable—poststructuralism is not only 'structure' but also 'post.' Discourses strive to fix meaning around a closed structure, but 'neither absolute fixity nor absolute non-fixity is possible' (Laclau and Mouffe 1985: 111). The ambiguous nature of language as both structured and unstable implies that discourses will try to construct themselves as stable, but that there will always be slips and instabilities, building up what Derridarian discourse analysis calls the 'undecidability' of any text (Torfing 1999: 95–6, 119). Seeing identity as built through processes of linking and differentiation shows the possibility for destabilization: the link between some of the 'positive signs' might become unstable; or a negatively valued term of one discourse might be constructed as positive within another discourse, making the clear attribution of inferior or superior value to signs more complicated. For example, the construction of 'women' in nineteenth century discourse is not solely negative. Women are constructed as an essential part of society and as performing crucial tasks. They are, in Derrida's terms, a supplement: secondary to the privileged male, but simultaneously necessary for societal completion and survival (Derrida 1976: 141–64; Elshtain 1987). The supplement is secondary to the privileged term or subject, but the latter would not be complete without the former. However, the positive value ascribed to 'women' is preconditioned upon women's acceptance of the subject position bestowed upon them. If 'women' were to be constructed, or construct themselves, as less motherly, less caring, and less publicly passive, their supplementary privilege would in all likelihood be suspended.

Language's structured yet inherently unstable nature brings to the fore the importance of political agency and the political production and reproduction of discourses and the identities constructed within them (Foucault 1977). Policy discourses construct—as do discourses in general—problems, objects, and subjects, but they are also simultaneously articulating *policies* to address them (Shapiro 1988). Policies are thus particular directions for action, whereas the construction of identity in discourse is seen more broadly as a political practice. The conceptualization of foreign policy as a discursive practice implies that policy and identity are seen as ontologically interlinked: it is only through the discursive enactment of foreign policy, or in Judith Butler's terms 'performances,' that identity comes into being, but this identity is at the same time constructed as the legitimization for the policy proposed (Butler 1990: 25; Campbell 1992: 8–9; Weber 1998). Identities are thus articulated as the reason why policies should be enacted, but they are also (re)produced through these very policy discourses: they are simultaneously (discursive) foundation and product.

Poststructuralism's ontological turn to discourse does not, it should be stressed, equal the adoption of an idealist position; as two prominent discourse analysts, Erneste Laclau and Chantal Mouffe, have stated, poststructuralists 'affirm the material character of every discursive structure. To argue the opposite is to accept the very classical dichotomy between an objective field constituted outside of any discursive intervention, and a discourse consisting of the pure expression of thought' (Laclau and Mouffe 1985: 108). The distinction between the material and the ideational is one of the cornerstones of Western philosophy of science, and it is therefore not surprising to find it central to recent debates between rationalists, conventional constructivists, and poststructuralists. The first two groups have converged on a research program which seeks to investigate the explanatory power of ideational factors on the one hand as opposed to material factors on the other. The ideational component is here expressed as ideas, ideals, norms, identity, or culture, but they are all separated from—and in some cases tested against—material sources of explanations (see for instance Moravcsik 1999a, 1999b; Wendt 1999; Katzenstein 1996). These approaches differ in their research designs and empirical conclusions, but they converge around an acceptance of the distinction between the ideational and the material and a reading of poststructuralism as privileging the former.[2]

Yet for poststructuralism neither ideas nor materiality have a meaningful presence separate from each other. A tank, for example, is not simply a material assemblage of metal and rubber but an object of warfare—or peacekeeping—whose material and social production is situated within an abstract discourse of national security ('states should be armed to defend themselves') as well as a specific, local one ('we have been threatened by Soviet forces in the past and we have no reason to believe they have changed their military doctrine and conception of themselves as an expansive power'). To adopt a discursive approach to foreign policy is therefore not, as is sometimes claimed, to hold that materiality does not matter or to say that the law of gravity is just an idea or that one would not feel the materiality of a punched fist (Wendt 1999: 55–6). The point is, rather, that Newtonian laws can be viewed as a mathematics and physics discourse, which offered a very different construction of the meaning of falling objects than had previously been articulated, and that this discourse was both situated within and helped reinforce the growth of a particular form of positivist, mathematical, and experiential knowledge that differentiated itself from earlier religious and philosophical discourses.

Emphasizing the material aspect of poststructuralism's conception of discourse, the point is not to disregard material facts but to study how these are produced and prioritized. Here it might be useful to distinguish between first-order factual questions and second-order factual questions, where first-order questions concern the constitution of the factual framework itself. For example, when analyzing the 'War on Drugs' of the George H. Bush administration, David Campbell asks why race is chosen as a meaningful category through which to document and represent drug use and why some drugs are considered 'dangerous' and 'criminal' while others are considered 'acceptable' or even encouraged. The selection of 'race' and 'dangerous drugs' as representational categories are dependent not on 'facts' themselves but on a wider set of societal discourses (Campbell 1992: 197–8).

It is a key goal of discourse analysis to show how these first-order facts are dependent upon a particular discursive framing of the issue in question and that this framing has political effects, in this case an aggressive set of policies aimed at urban blacks and Hispanics. That being said, once these 'facts' of 'race' and 'dangerous drugs' are stabilized, one might counter them at the level of their statistical accuracy and pose a second-order factual question: 'to what extent do alternative sets of data contradict or support the claims being made?' Here Campbell finds that 'Contrary to the competing narrative discussed above—which argue that levels of cocaine and crack consumption amongst suburban whites greatly exceeds those amongst urban blacks and Hispanics—it is the minorities in America who have become the target of "the war on drugs"' (Campbell 1992: 206). The strategy of discourse analysis is thus to 'incorporate' material and ideational factors rather than to privilege one over the other. The constitution of certain drugs as dangerous and others as acceptable, and particular ethnic groups as more susceptible to transgressive behavior, draws on ideational constructions, but these are both enacted through and reproduced by a set of material structures, for instance police tactics and systems of financial transactions. The analytical intent is not to measure the relative importance of ideas and materiality but to understand them as constructed through a discourse which gives materiality meaning by drawing upon a particular set of identity constructions.

Discursive epistemology and relational identity

The ontological conception of identity as both a precondition for and as constituted through foreign policy has epistemological consequences—and consequences for how research agendas are designed and methodological questions are formed and addressed. The adoption of a discursive epistemology implies that the poststructuralist analytical focus is on the discursive construction of identity as both constitutive of and a product of foreign policy. Consistent with the ontological emphasis on language, the practical epistemological focus is on how identities and policies are articulated.

Most discourse analysis has an epistemological and methodological focus on written or spoken language, but in principle language need not be verbal (Fairclough 2001: 122). For individuals, non-verbal language could be sign or body language, while for collectives such as states 'body language' could be the movement of troops or undertaking military exercises. One could also 'read' material objects, for instance war memorials, as texts that articulate a particular construction of national identity and the war in question (Edkins 2003). That said, it should be noted that political collectives, states in particular, are very verbal entities. States communicate widely, both domestically and internationally, leaving very little foreign policy action that is entirely non-verbal. This in turn is related to the social and political realm in which states are located: if a state moves its forces close to the border of its neighbor without any prior consultation a verbal as well as a non-verbal response is in all likelihood provoked and non-verbal foreign policy is brought into the realm of the verbal.

Turning more specifically to the epistemological conceptualization of identity in poststructuralism, identities need to be articulated in language to have political and analytical presence and they are thus dependent on political agency for their ontological and epistemological significance. States do not have identities operating underneath discursive articulations and as language is a referential system, identities will always be constructed through processes of differentiation and linking (Wæver 2002). This discursive and relational conception of identity sets poststructuralism aside from the most prominent conventional constructivist Alexander Wendt, who argues that identity need not be constructed as relational difference. First, because states have pre-social (corporate) as well as social identities and as the former is self-organizing 'there is no particular Other to which the Self is related' (Wendt 1999: 225); second, because one can distinguish between role identities and type identities, such as 'democracy,' which are intrinsic to the individual actor (Wendt 1999: 224–8; for critical discussions of Wendt's conceptualization of identity see Zehfuss 2001 and Rumelili 2004). At the ontological level, this conceptualization is at odds with poststructuralism's conception of identity as relationally constituted, but ontological questions cannot be solved at the level of empirical analysis: one cannot prove identity to be objectively relational or intrinsic as such a 'proof' is intertwined with which epistemology is chosen. The adoption of a discursive epistemology makes a pre-social, corporate and intrinsic identity an impossibility, and vice versa: if identity is assumed to be ontologically intrinsic, then it cannot be identified through a discursive epistemology but has to be attributed externally by the analyst.

To examine Wendt's conceptualization of identity in more detail, one might begin by looking at the assumption that identities could be pre-social. The strongest case for a pre-social collective identity appears to be an isolated community existing without knowledge of other human beings. But, one might argue, this group would still be composed of individuals and thus involve a construction of the individual in relation to the group, of what it means to be a member, and thereby what is implied in the collective identity of the group. Second, at the level of collective identity, the relational non-we might not necessarily be another human collectivity—it could be animals, for instance, or Easter Islands deities—and it might not be constructed around a spatial delineation but around a temporal construction of identity (Wæver 1996; Wendt 2003: 527–8).[3] Identity is in this case narrated through the mythological origins of the group, its development and survival, and its relationship to the spiritual and natural forces. Although this discourse employs different forms of representation than those of twenty-first century Western states, it can still be read in relational terms.

Moving from an isolated group to the social entity of the nation state and the possibility of intrinsic identity it would be impossible, to take Wendt's example of democratic identity, for a state to be 'democratic all by itself' in so far as this was a part of the discursive construction of state identity. 'Democracy' might be attributed to the state by an observing political scientist, but it would not be part of the state's own self-understanding and discourse.[4] One solution to this opposition between a Wendtian intrinsic and a poststructuralist relational conception of identity might be to underline that constructions of identity involve processes of linking. Thus the poststructuralist argument is not that there is no positive identity construction—what might appear as intrinsic—but that this is simultaneously constructed through a process of differentiation. 'Democracy,' to take Wendt's example of an intrinsic identity, is constructed as a privileged identity that other states could and should embrace. This articulates a relation of identity between 'all states' through an emphasis on their 'democratic potential' while situating this identity within a construction of spatial and temporal difference as not all states are yet sufficiently democratic.[5]

The impossibility of causality

To adopt a rigid definition of causality—as argued in chapter 1—is to demand that theories hypothesize about causal effects; for discourse analysis the challenge raised is to show 'how much discourse matters' for state action by proving first the relative explanatory power of discourse as opposed to material explanations, and second the causal effect of identity on foreign policy (Katzenstein 1996; Adler 1997; Price and Reus-Smit 1998). To begin with, the first challenge for poststructuralism is that there is, as laid out above, no extra- or non-discursive realm of explanations from which one might construct competing explanations. There is no 'extra-discursive' materiality that sets itself forward independently of its discursive representation—which, to reiterate, is not to say that the material has no importance, but rather that it is always discursively mediated.[6]

The view of materiality as discursively constituted implies that poststructuralism brings to the fore questions that are unexplored by rationalist scholarship. To take an example, Celeste Wallander's rationalist liberalist analysis argues that NATO's post-Cold War survival is due to its ability to address not only external threats but also a 'variety of security problems, including instability, uncertainty, and relations among allies' (Wallander 2000: 706). Yet, her analysis leaves unexplored how 'threats' or 'instabilities' become constituted as such in the first place—they are presumed to exist materially and objectively independently of NATO's own construction thereof. Poststructuralist analysis, however, shows how these 'threats' and 'instabilities' are not simply 'there' but appear through NATO's own discursive articulation of the alliance's (transformed) post-Cold War rationale. For example, the decision to consider the situation in Kosovo an 'instability' which warranted NATO's intervention—and legitimated the alliance's existence—required a particular construction of the parties to the conflict and the adoption of a discourse of humanitarian intervention (Hansen 1999; Williams and Neumann 2000; Huysmans 2002).[7] Poststructuralist analysis focuses on three issues: the way in which NATO's discursive construction of its 'new surroundings,' 'purposes,' and 'threats' is enacted, both by the institution itself and by key officials (like the ones interviewed by Wallander); how this produces and legitimizes

NATO's existence; and how this in turn might involve a reconstruction of NATO's institutional identity.

Having argued that there is no extra-discursive materiality against which a discursive analysis can be tested, the second challenging question is whether identity has a causal effect on policy. For a causal relationship to be hypothesized, a dependent and an independent variable need to be identified. This might at first seem possible inasmuch as political discourse is characterized by 'discursive causality'; that is, politicians will often present the adoption of a foreign policy as caused by a particular representation of identity. Yet adopting a rigid conception of causality, for discursive causality to be considered an actual causal effect, one needs to separate two variables and to observe each independently of the other. This, however, is precluded by poststructuralism's insistence on the ontological significance of discursive practice: identities are produced, and reproduced, through foreign policy discourse, and there is thus no identity existing prior to and independently of foreign policy. The analytical significance of poststructuralism's performative understanding of identity can be illustrated by contrasting it to Thomas Risse-Kappen's liberal constructivist analysis, which holds that NATO survived the disappearance of the Soviet Union because of a set of common democratic, liberal values. For poststructuralism, however, it is the alliance's own construction of its 'common liberal identity' from the early 1990s onwards which 'explains' NATO's continued existence[8] (Risse-Kappen 1996). The explanatory focus is thus shifted between constructivism and poststructuralism as the latter highlights the active discursive mobilization of NATO's 'old' identity in the attempt to reconstruct the legitimacy of the alliance's centrality to Western security.[9]

But if identities are produced through foreign policy discourse, perhaps policy might be said to cause identity? This might seem compelling at first insofar as there are no identities existing independently of human and political agency; if there were no reproduction of what it means to be 'American,' or 'German,' or 'Russian' these identities would disappear. Presuming that an archive existed, these identities might be mobilized in a revival of these identities, but it would be precisely that: a resurrection which would tell the national narratives anew. More generally, to say that policies caused identity would require that there was no feedback from the articulation of identities to policy. And, as was argued above, identities are simultaneously a product of and the justification for foreign policy. Foreign policy problems are furthermore not handled *de novo* as their solution is written into a discursive terrain that is already partially structured through previously articulated and institutionalized identities. These structuring discourses stretch from the general and abstract, from 'national identity,' 'national interest,' and 'strategic interests,' to particular ones like 'Danish identity,' 'civilization,' 'developed,' and 'European.' To argue policies that radically break with these constructions is not impossible, but it is a daunting task, in particular when political opposition can mobilize these historically (re)produced constructions[10] (Hansen and Wæver 2002).

Rationalists, poststructuralists, and constructivists build their analyses on different research packages: poststructuralists conceptualize identity and policy as ontologically inseparable and this inseparability is enacted through discourse, and they cannot therefore adopt an epistemology documenting the causal effects of identity on foreign policy. Rationalists and constructivists on the other hand see identity as one potential causal influence on foreign policy and as (partially) non-discursively constituted.

A prominent example of how this produces different research agendas is the thesis on the democratic peace: the claim that liberal, democratic states abstain from war against other liberal, democratic states. Rationalist explanation was at first located at the domestic level; it argued that checks and balances in conjunction with the reluctance of citizenry to bear the cost of war led democracies to less aggressive foreign policies. This explanation was expanded to account for the phenomenon of 'separate democratic peace'—that the peaceful nature of liberal foreign policy was not observable in dealings with non-liberal states—through the inclusion of international norms (MacMillan 2003). Bruce Russet argued that 'regimes apply the norms of conflict resolution they use domestically to international relations, and presume that others will do likewise' (MacMillan 2003: 237). This explanation introduced norms as an ideational component, but remained within a casual epistemology that traced the causal effects of particular regime types and their associated norms on foreign policy behavior. By introducing the premise that states base their behavior on the identification of other states' regime type, liberalist theory pointed to recognition as the process through which states come to see each other as democratic (Williams 2001: 527–31). But, Ido Oren argues, this process is not as unproblematic as the democratic peace theory assumes: not only is the construction of 'democracy' derived from a particular American political tradition, the 'normative and empirical content attached to "democracy" by American elites changed notably over the past two centuries' (Oren 1995: 151). It was only after 1917 that 'democracy' shed its connection with socialism and became 'America's chief self-portrayal' (Oren 1995: 152) and rather than being a trans-historical, trans-cultural, and objective description of a particular political form, 'democracy' is a historically and normatively constructed concept (Laclau and Mouffe 1985). Once established as a desirable form of government, the particular construction of 'American democracy' was one 'whereby objective dimensions on which America resembled its enemies were eliminated, whereas those on which America differed the most from its enemies became privileged' (Oren 1995: 153). Past patterns of foreign policy led to a particular construction of 'democracy,' argues Oren, patterns which the democratic peace theory is now, not surprisingly, able to explain. Understanding 'democracy' as a foreign policy discourse rather than as an independent variable calls, for instance, for a study of the way in which it has been articulated, from its adoption by President Clinton (Oren 1995: 147), over NATO's construction of its 'liberal obligation' to intervene in Kosovo in 1999, to American post-9/11 constructions of 'terrorists' as hating American freedom and liberal democracy. These political mobilizations of identity also point to democratic identity as relationally constituted against states or groups that are either becoming, non- or anti-democratic.

The adoption of a discursive epistemology does not lead poststructuralism to assume that states always follow the policy they publicly declare. It is, as numerous historical examples show, quite possible for politicians to proclaim a foreign policy which is not implemented or which functions as a foil for clandestine operations. The process of foreign policy making is not necessarily a public process, and discourse analysis is in principle applicable to analysis of deception and disinformation. Methodologically, analysis would draw upon classified documents and accounts of casual conversation or closed meetings; the problem is, however, that the empirical access to these kinds of documents is often limited (Weldes 1999).

For rationalists to have a non-causal relationship between variables would be an unacceptable condition to be solved through the deployment of counter-factual reasoning (King *et al.* 1994: 89). For poststructuralism, however, the theoretical—and ontological—core assumption is that representations and policy are mutually constitutive and discursively linked. Rationalists present causal epistemology as the unrivalled means through which knowledge can be generated; and many constructivists at least partially concur. Causal epistemology cannot, however, establish its privilege through reference to any objective truth as its own criterion for truth is enshrined within a historically situated discourse of knowledge, not in a trans-historical, trans-discursive universal objectivity. Poststructuralism's break with causality is thus not a flaw within its research design but an ontological and epistemological choice. Adopting a non-causal, discursive epistemology does not, however, imply that analysis should be conducted without any epistemological or methodological principles. Rather, what is opened up is a discursive research agenda focused on the construction of identity and policy and the way in which the two are linked within political discourses.

A theoretical model of combinability

The goal for foreign policymakers—as well as for other actors trying to influence foreign policy—is to present a foreign policy that appears legitimate and enforceable to its relevant audience. Thus, at the center of political activity is the construction of a link between policy and identity that makes the two appear consistent with each other. For example, speaking before the fall of Baghdad in early April 2003, President Bush constructed 'Iraq' as an identity split between two entities: the 'regime' of Saddam Hussein, the 'dictator,' and his 'thugs,' who had committed 'atrocities' on the one hand; and the 'oppressed Iraqi people' longing for the 'freedom' and 'liberty' provided by the American forces on the other. The Iraqi regime constituted 'a grave danger' to 'free nations,' it was 'evil' and composed of 'mass murderers' with 'weapons of mass destruction,' and it was an 'enemy' with the capacity to 'plot another September the eleventh.' This representation gave Bush's policy of military intervention a stable underpinning: the materiality of nuclear weapons in the hand of a 'mass murderer' discursively linked with terrorism attacking the 'free world' warranted 'defending our own security.' Yet, war was not only conducted in defense of *American* security but also to 'protect the world' as well as 'the Iraqi people,' and hence it was not only a matter of 'traditional' national security but also morally sanctioned as 'a great and a just cause' (Bush 2003).

An analytical separation of identity and policy facilitates analysis of how foreign policy discourse creates stability, but it is important to notice that this separation does not necessarily—or even frequently—mirror the concrete process through which politicians decide on foreign policy. Empirically, foreign policy decision-making usually does not separate the articulation of identity from the delineation of policy, but constructs identity and policy by mutually adjusting the two. Politicians rarely sit down and have an 'identity discussion' separate from a consideration of which policies can be pursued, nor are foreign policies decided without deliberations on identity. Even abstract foreign policy doctrines that involve conceptions of 'national interests,' 'military capabilities,' and 'security interests' are articulated inside discourses on 'national security' that draw upon constructions of national identity.

Theoretically, foreign policy discourse can be conceptualized as a simple model centered on creating a stable link between identity and policy. One might think of this model as a system of equilibrium; for instance, the human body has a salt–water balance which it has to maintain—if a person eats an excessive amount of salt, their body will retain water to reestablish the correct balance. Likewise in the case of foreign policy discourse: if there is an imbalance in the construction of the link between identity and policy there will be an attempt to make an adjustment to recreate stability through modification of either the construction of identity or the proposed policy. As argued above, it is impossible for discourses ever to reach absolute fixity and stability, thus on the one hand no policy–identity links or articulations of identity are ever completely stable. Yet as identities are constructed through an articulation of a larger number of signs in processes of differentiation and processes of linking, it is possible to analyze the *relative* ability of a discourse to present a construction of identity which is not (seen as) highly internally unstable. Discourses will be less stable if the articulation of identities is internally inconsistent; for example, if a discourse constructs 'Balkan identity' as barbaric and violent and 'European identity' as civilized and peaceful, while at the same time arguing that there is no boundary differentiating 'the Balkans' and 'Europe.'

Foreign policy, however, is not a closed system, like that of the body, but is formulated within a social and political space. This implies that the *internal stability* of a policy–identity construction cannot be determined in isolation from the broader social and political context within which it is situated.

Whether a discourse articulates a stable relationship between identity and policy is to be posed not only as a question of internal stability but also as a matter of whether the discourse is supported or criticized by other discourses. Put in more programmatic terms, politically contextualized discourse analysis combines the analysis of how texts seek to create stability with analysis of whether these constructions are being accepted or contested within the political and public domain.[11] For example, the extent to which Bush's construction of the identities of 'Saddam Hussein,' 'the Iraqi people,' 'the free world,' and 'America' is seen as supporting the war against Iraq is to be analyzed both at the level of the textual construction of identities and how they are linked with policy and at the level of the wider responses to Bush's policy and discourse. The contextualized and mutually adjusted character of the policy–identity constellation implies furthermore that their link is not a functionalist nor an essentialist one: stable links are constructed through and in response to discursive practices, practices which vary and depend on human agency, not on abstract functionalities.

The construction of the link between identity and policy is more specifically confronted by a set of *external constraints* that impact the deliberation of identity as well as policy. Beginning with the construction of identity, the fact that foreign policy questions are always articulated within a partially structured discursive field is, as argued above, both enabling and constraining for those constructing foreign policies. This is not to say that established identities cannot be contested, rather that such contestations need to engage with the dominant construction of identity already in place (Wæver 1995: 45). Moreover, as established discourses are mobilized anew, they reinforce and potentially modify the identity on which they are centered. For example, 'The Balkans' was powerfully employed within the Western debate of the 1990s as a representation of the war in Bosnia, and this representation drew upon a concept of 'the Balkans' which had been coined and developed from the late nineteenth century onwards (Todorova 1997; Goldsworthy 1998). Yet, through this deployment of 'the Balkans,' the ostensibly trans-historical concept was itself slightly modified.

Turning to the external constraints on policy, foreign policymakers usually face a series of limitations on which policy can be promoted, and thus which representations of identities can be articulated. Such constraints might be based on military capabilities, institutional pressures from bureaucracies and the armed forces, the media, or recent experiences of humiliation or defeat. These external constraints are not, however, objective material factors constituted outside of discourse but situated within, or products of, older and competing discourses.

The contextual constraints and creative aspects involved in foreign policymaking imply that discourse analysis has to proceed methodologically by investigating empirically the constructions of identity and the formulations of policy within a given debate. One cannot assume that a particular representation of identity will always lead to a particular policy; nor that a particular policy will always underpin a specific construction of identity. The importance of detailed empirical studies sensitive to the specificity and flexibility of the policy–identity linkage was underscored by the tendency within post-structuralist and critical constructivist studies of the Western debate on the Bosnian war to assume a quasi-causal link between representations and policy. These studies argued that a connection was made between a construction of the Bosnian war as a 'Balkan' phenomenon caused by ancient hatred and a policy of Western inaction and that a second connection was made between a representation of the war as 'genocide' which argued in support of a policy of Western intervention. While these two constellations of identity and policy were certainly present and important within the debate, they were not the only ones as the process of combinability between identity representations and policies was more complex and open-ended (Ó Tuathail 1996a; Crawford and Lipschutz 1997; Campbell 1996b; Fierke 1996). First, the uniformity of the two representations of 'Bosnian reality' was exaggerated; in fact one finds (as chapters 7 to 9 show) a number of variations of these two representations. Second, even among those who *did* construct their policies on the basis of a 'Balkan identity,' there was not a perfect correspondence between this representation and a policy of Western inaction. While policies and representations are related, they are related in ways that are more complicated than the more simple models assumed.

Challenges, changes, and facts

Situating the theoretical model of policy–identity combinability within a dynamic and political context, it is apparent that the policy–identity constellation is dependent on agency and that competing discourses might focus their attacks on different parts of the dominant model. The overall goal of oppositional foreign policy discourse is to bring forth a different policy, but in most cases this will involve attacking and rearticulating the construction of identity as well. A critical discourse might start by challenging the key representations of identity that underpin the policy in question. For example, John J. Mearsheimer and Stephen M. Walt challenged Bush's Iraq discourse by arguing that his construction of Saddam's identity 'as either irrational or prone to serious miscalculations' did not stand up to an examination of historical facts (Mearsheimer and Walt 2003: 52). Mearsheimer and Walt argued that this misconstruction of Saddam Hussein's identity made the Iraq war 'An Unnecessary War,' and that the policy that *should* have been pursued was one of 'deterrence and containment' (Mearsheimer and Walt 2003: 59). One might also find discourses that begin by questioning the policy side of the policy–identity constellation, for example as a policy is constructed as unenforceable or as ineffective. There were, for instance, voices within the American debate on Bosnia that argued that the USA did not have the resources to engage in the war and that action, if any, should be undertaken by Europeans. However, this discourse did not stay at the level of material constraints but brought with it an articulation of the identity of 'Bosnia' as a 'European responsibility,' as in its 'backyard,' of the war as 'civil' or 'ethnic,' and with no moral implications for the USA.

Discourses engage and contest each other by challenging policy, identity, and the logic through which they are linked, and in doing so they often provide different readings of facts and events—in particular as discourses develop over time. When analyzing how foreign policy debates unfold, it is methodologically useful to examine how facts are brought together to constitute events. The term 'key events' refers to those situations where 'important facts' manifest themselves on the political and/or the media agenda and influence the official policy–identity constellation or force the official discourse to engage with political opposition and media criticism. Mapping debates around key events offers a methodological technique for tracing the stability of official discourse as they can be used to construct a timeline which in turn can be employed when empirical material is selected.

The poststructuralist point is not, as argued above, that material facts do not exist, but rather that they are produced by and inserted into foreign policy discourses. For facts to become politically salient and influence the production and reproduction of foreign policy discourse there must be human and discursive agency; individuals, media, and institutions who collect, document and distribute them. For example, the deaths of thousands of Muslim men at the hands of Bosnian Serb forces at Srebrenica in 1995 was quickly documented by intelligence data and eyewitness accounts and accepted as facts, but (as is discussed further in chapter 7) there was no immediate agreement between British and American governments whether this constituted a 'massacre,' a 'genocide,' or was a 'part of warfare,' or on which policy should be employed in response (United Nations Security Council 1995; Secretary General of the UN 1999). While dependent upon agency and discourses for their production, facts do not carry with them automatic political responses; they need to be located inside a discourse and read to have a particular effect on policy and the representations of identity.

The goal of poststructuralism is therefore to study in an empirically rigorous and structured manner the ways in which facts are formed and how they impact on foreign policy debates. How are facts coupled with representations of identity and to particular policies? How do oppositional discourses present critical evidence in the attempt to destabilize official policy? How does governmental discourse respond? Studied in a dynamic perspective, as new facts are presented—whether by the media, governmental agencies, or non-governmental institutions—they present possibilities and challenges for official as well as oppositional discourse. Oppositional discourses might use new facts to destabilize the construction of identity or the proposed policy, thereby destabilizing the other part of the official policy–identity constellation as well.

Faced by critical discourses, governments can react on a sliding scale of decreasing responsiveness. First, a government might significantly change its policy–identity construction. Although a complete change is rather rare it is not impossible, as shown by the case of Srebrenica, which led to a change in official American policy from a passive advocacy of 'lift and strike' to an active policy culminating in the Dayton Accord and the deployment of 20,000 US ground troops. This policy change was accompanied by a revision of the representation of the war and the official policy–identity combination was thus changed in such a way that the oppositional discourse—which had argued in favor of a more active Bosnia policy—was largely, if not completely, accommodated.

Second, and very commonly, official discourse might acknowledge facts but explain them within the discursive framework already in place. For example, Bush confirmed the 'violence' aimed against 'coalition forces' in Iraq in April 2004, something which would appear to undermine his construction of 'a liberated Iraq' and grateful Iraqis. But Bush's discursive counter-strategy was to construct those who were attacking American forces as disconnected from 'the Iraqi people': as 'remnants of Saddam Hussein's regime,' 'Islamic militants,' and 'an illegal militia' supporting 'terrorist groups,' and the attacks on American forces as part of a global fight where 'enemies of the civilized world are testing the will of the civilized world' (Bush 2004a). Had Bush concurred with a representation of the events as 'a popular uprising' against the American forces, this would have seriously destabilized his construction of the American intervention as undertaken to free 'the Iraqi people' and would have raised a series of questions as to the conduct and purpose of the American forces in Iraq.

The third option, although difficult to execute in the event of massive media coverage and fierce criticism, is to seek to pass by the facts in silence. This strategy might be adopted when it is considered difficult to accommodate facts within the current discourse and a new policy impossible to design. The failure to find weapons of mass destruction in Iraq was thus a fact highlighted by parts of the American media, but the Bush administration responded by stating that the weapons might still be found and by silencing the issue through shifting the discursive emphasis onto a link between Hussein's Iraq as a 'haven for terrorism' and the goal of 'liberating the Iraqi people.'

Security as discourse

The discussion has proceeded so far as a consideration of how foreign policy discourse in general draws upon representations of identity, and this chapter concludes by turning to those particular foreign policies that are constructed in terms of security. Rationalist approaches, realist ones in particular, often claim that while ideational factors might have some importance for certain areas of foreign policy, when it comes to *security* the logic of material factors, military capabilities, and the defense against objective threats must take center stage (Walt 1991). As was argued above, for poststructuralism there is no extra-discursive realm from which material, objective facts assert themselves. For problems or facts to become questions of security, they need therefore to be successfully constructed as such within political discourse. This, obviously, is not to say that security is not of tremendous political importance, rather that one should understand its discursive and historic specificity. Underpinning the concept of 'national security' is a particular form of identity construction— one tied to the sovereign state and articulating a radical form of identity—and a distinct rhetorical and discursive force which bestows power as well as responsibility on those speaking within it (Campbell 1992; Wæver 1995).

The classical concept of security is either explicitly defined as national security or implicitly draws upon this connection with the state; not because the state is an immortal entity or because security is objectively provided by the state, but because 'the meaning of security is tied to historically specific forms of political community' (Walker 1990: 5). Because the specific community developed over the past 400 years is the sovereign state, national security has achieved a prerogative as *the* concept of security (Walker 1990: 7). This realist construction of state sovereignty promises a secure domestic life by taking violence out of inter-individual relations; as Hobbes argued, 'state security' is not just *one* precondition it is *the* precondition for 'individual security,' but to achieve security individuals have to give away their authority to define it (Campbell 1992: 63–4; Williams 1998).[12]

State sovereignty organizes authority, space, time, and identity by separating the domestic sphere on the one side from the international realm on the other. 'Inside' the state, progress, order, democracy, ethics, identity, and universal rights are promised; 'outside' is anarchy, power, difference, and repetition (Ashley 1987; Walker 1993). The national and the international are thus not simply two different political spheres but are constructed as each other's opposites, as each other's constitutive Other. This delineation of a radical difference between the national and the international has led 'security discourse' to construct identity in terms of a national Self in need of protection against a radically threatening Other (Campbell 1992). David Campbell writes that 'securing an ordered self and an ordered world—particularly when the field upon which this process operates is as extensive as a state—involves defining elements that stand in the way of order as forms of "otherness"' (Campbell 1992: 55). In this view, security is an ontological necessity for the state, not because the state has to be protected from external threats but because its identity depends on them. Threats and insecurities are not just potentially undermining of the state and things that could be eliminated, they constitute the state: the state only knows who and what it is through its juxtaposition against the radical, threatening Other. And, the protection of the state against an external Other is often intimately linked with the delineation of an internal Other, be that communism in 1950s America, immigration, or homosexuality (Campbell 1992: 71; Todorov 1992: 50).[13]

To construct something as a threat to security most often involves a mobilization of discursively important 'sub-security concepts,' such as 'strategic interests' and 'national interests' (Weldes 1999). The strength of the national security discourse is that while it draws upon the politically powerful identity of the national community it also simultaneously masks its specific, historical, and thus contestable nature by constructing security as an objective, dehistoricized demand. When something—or somebody—is constructed as a threat to 'national security' or as in 'our strategic interests' it takes on an objective character and a particular rhetorical and political urgency. To constitute something as a threat to security is, in Ole Wæver's terms, to *securitize* it, to present it as 'an existential threat to a designated object (traditionally, but not necessarily, the state, incorporating government, territory, and society)' (Buzan *et al.* 1998: 21). To construct it as *existential* implies that security discourse constructs a sense of heightened priority and drama, arguing that if a 'security problem' is not addressed it will have fatal consequences (Buzan *et al.* 1998: 25). Security problems thereby take on political saliency: not only will they be the subject of intense policy activity, they will also be favorably treated when resources are allocated.

Security discourse grants certain issues heightened priority, but it also bestows a particular legitimacy on those handling the policies in question. Security questions allow governments and political leaders to 'break free of procedures or rules he or she would otherwise be bound by,' for instance to suspend civil rights or political transparency, and to make policy decisions without consulting or informing parliaments (Buzan *et al.* 1998: 25). This is not to say that there are no limits to what a government might do when something is constructed as a security problem, but that what limits will remain in place is a question to be investigated empirically. Security discourses are thus characterized by a dual political dynamic: they invest those enacting security policies with the legitimate *power* to undertake decisive and otherwise exceptional actions, but they also construct those actors with a particular *responsibility* for doing so. These mobilizations of power and responsibility are intimately linked: the construction of something as so threatening as to warrant decisive action is followed by a responsibility for answering those threats. Once on the political agenda, politicians cannot turn their back on threats to national security without rearticulating the situation in such a manner that it is no longer one of security: in Wæver's terms, 'de-securitizing' it.

As security is seen as a political discourse that installs responsibility and legitimizes the exercise of power, it becomes apparent why some agents seek to draw upon the classical discourse of security and move it beyond the classical realist military security of the state. States have retained the modality of the classical security discourse but have employed it to areas outside of the traditional military focus, such as in the construction of 'drug consumption' and 'Japan's economic strength' as threats to national security within American post-Cold War security discourse (Campbell 1992). More radically, states, non-governmental groups, and academics have argued that the political urgency of security should be retained, but that the privilege of the sovereign nation state be questioned. Human rights violations, civil wars, hunger, AIDS, and poverty—questions that are included in the discourse of national security only if they pose a threat to the national Self—are articulated as 'international security problems' which the international community has a responsibility for countering (Booth 1991: 319; Krause and Williams 1996: 229–30). Conceptually, this has lead to the formulation of new security concepts that draw upon the traditional urgency, power, and responsibility of national security, yet indicates a distance by the use of terms such as 'common security' (Väyrynen 1989), 'human security' (Paris 2001: 89), 'world security' (Walker 1990), or 'comprehensive security' (OSCE 1996). These concepts have different institutional, political, and academic trajectories, but they all seek to rearticulate the unquestioned privilege of national security while maintaining its demands for action and responsibility. Some analysts and political activists have argued in favor of a conception of security in individual terms. However, in keeping with the understanding of discourses as *social*, it is important to point out that the crucial issue is not whether 'something' is an individual or a collective security problem but rather how certain threats are endowed with a collective signification while others are read 'only' as individual (Booth 1991). Even if one speaks security in the name of the individual, claiming the rights, threats, or concerns of the individual constitutes an engagement in the public and political field; 'individual security' is in this respect always collective and political. Rather than conceptualizing security along a collective–individual dichotomy, one should focus on how political practices individualize certain threats, thereby locating them outside of the public, political realm, while others become visible as collective concerns (Hansen 2001a).

3   Beyond the Other

Analyzing the complexity of identity

Identity is at the ontological and epistemological center of poststructuralist discourse analysis; it is, as discussed in chapter 2, produced through and constitutive of foreign policy, and it is relationally and discursively constituted. As particular constructions of identity underpin and legitimize policies, the broader political and ethical ambition is to show how these constructions impose particular constraints on which subjects can gain a legitimate if circumscribed presence and which foreign policies might in turn be meaningfully proscribed. It is therefore pertinent to develop an analytical perspective through which the empirical complexity of identity construction can be brought out and which more specifically allows not only for the construction of a national Self and a radically different and threatening Other, but also for degrees of difference and Otherness. As this chapter argues, even if constructions of radical Otherness constitute a crucial component of foreign and security policy, it is only parts of foreign policy that appropriate such radical measures, and even the radical Other is often situated within a more complicated set of identities.

This chapter continues the development of a theoretical framework for understanding the political construction of identity by suggesting four analytical steps through which the richness of identity construction can be systematically examined and a series of related methodological issues addressed. The first section argues that Campbell's theoretical conception of state identity as radical Other should be revised to allow the concept of identity to assume degrees of Otherness. The second section maintains that identity construction involves not a single Self–Other dichotomy but a series of related yet slightly different juxtapositions that can be theorized as constituting processes of linking and differentiation. Understanding identity as produced through processes of linking and differentiation provides a theoretical and methodological account of the way in which discourses seek to establish stability, and also how this stability can always be deconstructed. The third section suggests that the construction of identity in foreign policy discourse can be analyzed through a consideration of how identity is always spatially, temporally, and ethically situated. The manner in which boundaries are drawn, how subjects constituted by these boundaries are imbued with temporal identities, and to whom responsibility is applied are at the center of foreign policy discourses. Analyzing the way in which these three dimensions of identity construction are interlinked provides not only a richer account of how political subjectivities are constituted but also the possibility for analyzing differences between discourses and their changes over time. The fourth section builds upon the previous three in turning to a discussion of how discourses can be seen as organized within a field of debate. On the one hand, one might argue that every single text articulates a unique construction of identity and policy and thereby constitutes a separate discourse. But on the other hand, political debates are, as argued in chapter 1, held together by a concern with a set of shared issues, and one might therefore define a smaller number of basic discourses which structure debate.

Otherness, difference, and the construction of Selves

The classical discourse of national security constructs, it was argued above, a radical difference between the national community on the one hand and international anarchy on the other. The state, holds David Campbell, needs to articulate threats and radical Others to construct its identity, and hence there is a drive within the ontology of national identity for turning constructions of difference into Otherness. 'To constitute,' in William Connolly's words, 'a range of differences as intrinsically evil, irrational, abnormal, mad, sick, primitive, monstrous, dangerous, or anarchical—as other' (Connolly 1991: 65; Campbell 1992: 55; Neumann 1996b). Historically, political leaders have legitimized their security policies by constructing other countries, immigrants, homosexuals, and communists as Others who are threatening the security and social fabric of the national Self, thereby capitalizing on 'a fund of generalized resentment from those whose identity is jeopardized by the play of difference, contingency, and danger' (Connolly 1991: 209–10; Klein 1994). Going back to the Christian thinking of Saint Augustine, Connolly locates this pull toward constructing identity as radical Otherness in two problems of evil. The first problem, argues Connolly, comes from the human experience of the unfairness and suffering of life and the inescapability of death; a suffering which creates resentment and the desire that someone should be made responsible. A demand rises for agents and agency, for 'sites at which responsibility can be located.' The second problem of evil addresses this demand by situating responsibility in the Other 'by defining the other that exposes sore spots in one's identity as evil or irrational' (Connolly 1991: 8). Connolly describes the second problem of evil as structural, or ontological, inasmuch as it is built into the doctrine of agency, responsibility, and identity articulated from Augustine onwards (Connolly 1991: 8). For Augustine, the view of God as omnipotent and benevolent needed to be protected from 'heretics' such as the Manicheans, whose view of the world as a battle between the forces of good and evil (with the latter usually believed to be the stronger part) brought the proper Christian construction of God into question. The

Manicheans were constituted as Other, as a sect, and violently persecuted. Lifting the question of responsibility (and the tragedies of life, death, and resentment) out of a late-medieval Christian context, the need for protecting a flawless, omnipresent god might have disappeared, but the need for locating responsibility in the Other has been institutionalized at the individual as well as the collective or state level.

Both Campbell and Connolly leave open the possibility that identity need not be constructed through radical Otherness: Connolly by stating that it is a 'temptation rather than a necessity,' that even Augustinian discourse had elements which destabilized the construction of the Manicheans as Other, and that the identity of the Self can be constructed through a variety of non-selves comprising complementary identities, contending identities, negative identities, and non-identities (Connolly 1991: 8 and 64–5);[1] and Campbell by raising the possibility that foreign policy does not yield to 'the temptation of otherness' (Campbell 1992: 78). Yet in Campbell's *Writing Security*, the empirical focus on the construction of Otherness within elite and governmental discourses produces, not surprisingly, a study that demonstrates the importance of constructions of Otherness rather than more ambiguous articulations of identity. Thus, while *Writing Security* shows that constructions of Otherness are present in many instances of American foreign and security policy, it does not prove—nor does it seek to prove—that *all* foreign and security policies are always constructed through relations of radical Otherness.[2] Had this been the ambition, the study should have had a different research design, included oppositional discourses, and used instances of foreign policy that were less likely to fit into the processes of radical identity construction than the ones selected.

Moving beyond the instantiations of American foreign policy analyzed by Campbell, one finds numerous examples of foreign policies that draw upon more ambiguous or complex constructions of difference. 'Nordic identity,' for example, was constructed by Swedish, Danish, and Norwegian politicians during the Cold War as an identity transcending the nuclear rivalry of the antagonistically opposed superpowers and 'Nordic' policies of neutrality, disarmament, development aid, and peacekeeping as superior to the (dangerous) geopolitical and nuclear confrontation of the Soviet Union and the USA (Joenniemi 1990). The development of the Baltic Sea region from the end of the Cold War and throughout the 1990s as a cultural, political, and financial project also exemplifies an identity constructed as an attempt to integrate previously disjointed countries and people; an identity different from Western Europe and the Soviet Union but integrating elements from both (Wæver 1997; Browning 2002). Countries might also construct themselves as favorably positioned between geographical and cultural boundaries: Slovenian discourse of the 1990s, for example, articulated a rather sharp difference between 'Europe' and 'the Balkans,' yet while Slovenia was constructed as belonging to the former—and its 1991 independence evidence of its rightful 'return to Europe'—it was simultaneously constituted as being sufficiently familiar with the Balkans that it could function as a 'bridge' between the two (Hansen 1996).

Discourses of return to 'Europe' or 'the West' illustrate that the Self can be constructed through an identity that is articulated as both superior to the Self and as identical to it. The construction of a superior 'Europe' to be emulated was the dominant political discourse of the Central European countries after the breakdown of communism in 1989, but this discourse simultaneously pointed to numerous facts proving the 'Europeanness' of the country in question, thus making these countries identical with yet temporarily separated from Europe. Discourses that involve a construction of the Other as outright superior to the Self are less frequent but do exist. Iver B. Neumann's study of the history of the Russian idea of Europe shows how 'Westernizers' portrayed Europe as superior and Russia as inferior, and Russia's route to progress accordingly as copying Europe (Neumann 1996a: 13, 47, 167, 200). Taking a broader view of societal, literary, and academic discourses, the colonial Other has been constructed as exotic and different from the West yet mysteriously attractive (Said 1978). The female native who enjoys her uninhibited sexuality and offers it to the spellbound Western male is a figure of much colonial writing of the eighteenth and nineteenth centuries (Pratt 1992: 86–107), and Romanticism in the tradition of Byron constructed the Other as an object of admiration, vitality, and passion, which had been lost by the industrial, lifeless West (Goldsworthy 1998).

Broadening the scope beyond classical security discourse; threats, danger, and deterrence is not the only modality through which states meet the world, nor is the Other necessarily another state or even another bounded political subject. The EU, argues Ole Wæver, is constituted not against an external, geographical Other, but against a temporal Other: the fear of a return of its own violent past (Wæver 1996). While there might be an Other, it is thus one fundamentally intertwined with the construction of the European Self. Post-Cold War NATO (re)constructed itself as an alliance based on the defense of liberal values rather than as a deterrence against a territorial threat; and this identity holds out a universal promise—all states can and should become liberal democracies—while granting Western countries the privilege of defining the content of this universality (Hansen 1999; Williams and Neumann 2000). A parallel example is development discourse, which constructs a temporal distance between those who have developed and those who have not, but it is a distance that can be bridged, if not always eradicated, through the developing Other's adoption of Western policies and advice (Doty 1996). One should keep in mind, however, that the less-than-radical construction of the Other within development discourse is carried out by a privileged Western subject, who is constructing not only the identity of the Other but also the concrete policies it should be undertaking to comply with this proscribed identity (Todorov 1992; Doty 1996).

The articulation of less-than-radical Others within foreign policy discourse can also be shown by how the Other is situated within a web of identities rather than in a simple Self–Other duality. To return to the example of Bush's construction of the war in Iraq that is discussed in chapter 2, the discourse involved not only a construction of 'America' and 'Iraq,' but a splitting of the Iraqi subject into 'Saddam Hussein' and his regime on the one hand and 'the Iraqi people' on the other. This split reconstituted the war from being against the entire Iraqi state and society to being against a repressive regime, and while 'Saddam' was constructed as a radical Other, the relationship between the 'Iraqi people' and 'the USA' was more ambiguous (Weber 1995). On the one hand, the Iraqi people were imbued with a proto-democratic, liberal desire linking them to the identity of the USA, but on the other hand their captivity under Saddam Hussein implied that the manifestation of this desire could only be realized after 'liberation' had taken place. Theoretically, even if a radical Other—'Saddam'—is at the center of a security discourse, it is an Other constructed through and stabilized by a simultaneous articulation of a number of other identities of a less radical and more ambiguous character. Civil wars, and human rights violations more generally, confront the international community with situations where multiple Others are trying to gain political, military, and discursive support, forcing politicians to decide on the identity of a number of subjects. The theoretical point is not to measure the relative empirical prevalence of radical or non-radical forms of identity construction—if such a measure could be done at all—but to adopt an ontology of identity that is flexible as to the forms of identity construction that one might encounter in concrete foreign policies. To define *a priori* that radical forms of identity construction would be the only form of identity construction within foreign policy discourse would result in an unnecessary theoretical and empirical limitation and prevent an engagement with important parts of contemporary foreign policy. It would produce a static view of foreign policy discourse as incapable of change, indeed paradoxically as separated from political and discursive practices.

Linking and differentiation: the methodology of reading

Having made the case for a theory of identity whose ontological flexibility facilitates the empirical study of different degrees of radicalization, the next step is to develop an analytical framework and a methodology through which these identity constructions can be studied. Discourse analysis has, as laid out in chapter 2, a discursive epistemology, and its methodology is, as a consequence, located at the level of explicit articulations. As illustrated by the analysis of Bush's Iraq speech in chapter 2, it is the enunciation of signs such as 'evil,' 'dictator,' 'oppressed people,' and 'grave danger' that informs discourse analysis, not an extra-textual attribution of identity onto a case. Discourse analysis would not, for example, identify a construction of 'evil' within Bush's discourse without this being an explicit discursive articulation. Methodologically, one should therefore begin by identifying those terms that indicate a clear construction of the Other, such as 'evil,' 'dictator,' 'murderer,' and 'terrorist,' or of the Self, such as 'good,' 'civilized,' 'justified,' and 'attacked.' Identity construction is not, however, accomplished solely through the designation of one particular sign for the Other or the Self but rather through the location of this sign within a larger system. Chapter 2 argued that this could be theorized as a dual processes of linking and differentiation: that meaning and identity are constructed through a series of signs that are linked to each other to constitute relations of sameness as well as through a differentiation to another series of juxtaposed signs. For example, to construct 'the Balkans' as different from 'Europe' does not create much meaning unless this construction is situated within a discourse that links and differentiates these signs. One discursive possibility is to link 'the Balkans' to the violent, irrational, underdeveloped, barbarian, backward, tribal, primitive, and savage and differentiate it against a controlled, rational, developed, civilized, organized, national, orderly, and mature 'European' identity (Figure 3.1) (Todorova 1997).

Analytically, the construction of identity should therefore be situated inside a careful investigation of which signs are articulated by a particular discourse or text, how they are coupled to achieve discursive stability, where instabilities and slips between these constructions might occur, and how competing discourses construct the same sign to different effects. As an example of the latter, Todorov's analysis of the Spanish conquest of the Americas shows

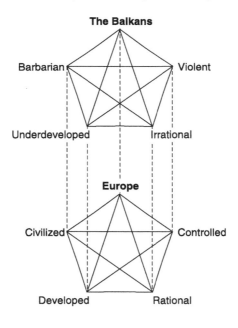

Figure 3.1 The linking and differentiation of 'the Balkans' and 'Europe.'

that there were two dominant discourses among the Spanish conquistadors, both of which constructed the Indians as 'savages' (Figure 3.2). On the one hand, the discourse articulated by Cortés coupled savagery to a further construction of the Indians as non-human, as incapable of change, and thus beyond Christian redemption. The priest Las Casas, on the other hand, situated the Indian 'savages' inside a construction of the Indians as humans, as heathens, but with the capacity for transformation and salvation (Todorov 1992: 165). Although both discourses constructed the Indians as 'savages,' they differed radically as to the ontological and temporal identity of this Other, and, accordingly as to which policy should and could be employed: Cortés' discourse legitimized the annihilation of the Indians, whereas Las Casas' discourse of Christian egalitarianism installed a Spanish responsibility for converting the Indians into Christendom. Thus, if analysis had focused only on the term 'savage' without analyzing how it was linked to other signs, it would have overlooked important differences in how the two discourses construct identity and policy.

The discourses of Cortés and Las Casas converged, however, on one important point: the Indian 'savage' was an Other who could and should be transformed, either by annihilation or through conversion to the Christian Self. Other discourses might differ even further by ascribing different values to the same sign, and thereby to the identity of the Other. Chapter 6 shows in more detail that 'passion' has been a key element in the Western construction of 'the Balkans' since the early nineteenth century. However, there is an important difference between its linking to violence, ancient hatred, barbarism, the primitive, irrational, treacherous, and Oriental within the 'Barbaric Balkanization discourse' that became dominant after World War I and its linking to the spontaneous, emotive, joyous, sensitive, poetic, convivial, mystic, and heroic within nineteenth century Romantic 'Byronic Balkan discourse.' While both

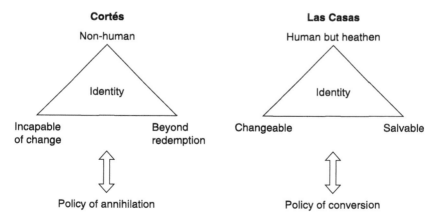

Figure 3.2 Competing constructions of Indian 'savages.'

discourses locate 'passion' as a central element in the construction of Balkan identity, it is valued very differently through its linkage to other signs.

Having argued that the methodological starting point for discourse analysis is the explicit articulation of identity within a web of signs, this should be qualified in three important respects. First, although identity is relationally constructed, and the Self therefore always articulated through a differentiation against an Other, one might not necessarily find that all texts construct this through a slavish juxtaposition of a Self and an Other. When Bush constructs Saddam Hussein as 'evil,' he does not explicitly say that he, himself, is 'not evil'; when the 'Iraqi people' are defined as 'oppressed,' he does not immediately declare that 'the American people are not oppressed.' Not only would such repetitive juxtapositions make speech unbearably cumbersome, but also the audience to whom he is speaking is supposed not to question the implicit American parts of the juxtapositions. Yet this implicit construction of the 'American' is not only assumed to resonate, it is reinforced by the articulation of Saddam Hussein's Iraq.

Second, as discourses are articulated through the course of a foreign policy debate, a particular discourse might become established to such an extent that texts no longer need to make as detailed constructions of identity as when 'the problem' first manifested itself on the political and media agendas. For example, when the wars in the former Yugoslavia broke out in the early 1990s, they were repeatedly constructed as 'Balkan,' and politicians and the media would elaborate the identity of 'the Balkans' through articulations of a longer series of signs. As war continued, and 'the Balkan' reference became established, it was no longer necessary to articulate as detailed a link of signs: 'The Balkans' was now familiar enough to readers that they would be able to 'fill in the signs' on their own.

Third, the methodological focus on explicit articulations raises the question of 'discursive disappearance': that identities articulated at one time might cease to be important. As an example, consider the importance of the monarchy–republic distinction for constructing European and American identities of the eighteenth and nineteenth centuries. Today, this representation has lost its saliency in terms of constructing Western states' international identity; there are still European monarchies, but 'monarchy' is no longer of political or representational significance for how countries differentiate themselves from one another.[3] Or, taking the opposite route, identities previously not articulated might become important, as with the articulation of a 'human species identity' in the face of an invasion by aliens, robots, or animals. This is a theme played out in popular culture, where humans have a remarkable capacity for allying rather than drawing aliens/robots/animals into a human balance of power system (Hansen 2001b).

The processes of linking and differentiation provide theoretical concepts and methodological tools for conducting empirical analysis and they allow for a structured and systematic analysis of: how discourses seek to construct stability, where they become unstable, how they can be deconstructed, and the processes through which they change. As the meaning of each sign is established through linking and differentiation, there is always a gap between them: they are linked to each other, but never fully the same. Instability might be explicitly articulated if the Other is constructed as radically different yet also as part of the Self, but discourses will usually seek to avoid such blatant contradictions, and tracing instability therefore usually involves more careful analysis of how links and juxtapositions come into conflict with each other. For example, as part of the construction of 'the Balkans' as radically different in Western discourse, an aggressive 'Balkan' masculinity was articulated. This, however, not only constituted 'the Balkans' as Other but also split the Balkan subject into two gendered parts: 'Balkan women' were victims of aggressive masculinity and therefore in need of Western protection. This gendering of the Balkans destabilized the construction of uniform radical Balkan identity as well as the abrogation of any Western responsibility for the course and casualties of the war. Adopting a dynamic perspective, one might also examine the way in which events put particular pressure on links within a discourse, for example Bush's construction of 'America' as a morally superior liberator of Iraq in the face of widespread prison abuse at Abu Ghraib prison. Bush's response to the pressure laid upon the link between 'America' and 'liberal human rights' was to construct violations as 'un-American,' a response that bred further political and discursive pressure for explaining the existence of the 'un-American' in the 'American' armed forces.

Understanding identity as constructed through processes of linking and differentiation also raises methodological questions concerning the reliability of discourse analysis: would different analysts come to the same result were they working with the same selection of texts? Is it possible to adjudicate between different readings and declare some discourse analyses as better than others? It is sometimes polemically argued by poststructuralism's critics that poststructuralism sees *any* reading as equally valid, that 'anything goes.' But this is misleading insofar as the methodology of discourse analysis insists on readings based on explicit discursive articulations of signs and identities and that one has to pay careful analytical attention to how signs are linked and juxtaposed, how they construct Selves and Others, and how they legitimize particular policies. Thus if analysis overlooks important signs, if it misinterprets the stability between linked and juxtaposed signs, if it exaggerates or downplays the degree of difference between Self and Other, or if it fails to identify the connection between identities and policy, then it makes a weaker reading. But to say that it is possible to establish methodological and theoretical criteria for good discourse analysis is not to say that there is one reading which will *exhaust* all others, or that texts cannot be subjected to multiple research questions and thereby to multiple and complimentary readings. Identity is constituted through the linking and differentiation of a series of signs, and one will usually focus on one in particular, for instance 'the Balkans' or 'Iraq,' and analyze how this privileged identity is constructed through the processes of linking and juxtaposition. Depending on the research question, another sign might be constituted as the privileged identity and its linkage to a web of signs analyzed. For example, if one is interested in the way in which 'civilization' was being employed in Western discourse after the end of the Cold War, one might read texts on the Bosnian war, many of which explicitly articulated the concept of civilization, and make this the privileged identity rather than the one of 'the Balkans.' Or, one might conduct a double reading, which traces the articulations and discursive linkages of these two identities (Hansen 2000b).[4] The multiple readability of texts produces another series of questions related to which research questions or discursive frameworks one might usefully select, and these questions are addressed in more detail in chapter 5.

Reading political identity: spatial, temporal, and ethical constructions

The first part of this chapter has already hinted at the importance of spatial, temporal, and ethical identities for the construction of identity and difference in foreign policy discourse and this should now be elaborated. At the grandest philosophical scale, space, time, and responsibility are the big concepts through which political communities—their boundaries, internal constitution, and relationship with the outside world—are thought and argued.[5] Even abstract discourses constitute subjects by situating them within particular boundaries, by investing them with possibilities for change or repetition, and by constructing ethical relations. Turning to foreign and security policies, national security discourse can be seen as a particular spatial, temporal, and ethical instantiation: the space of the national community is sharply differentiated from the anarchic international realm; within this national space progress can unfold while it is deferred on the outside; and responsibility is situated between governments and citizens while 'international responsibility' is absent, perhaps even dangerous (Walker 1993; Der Derian 1987). Methodologically, spatial, temporal, and ethical constructions are investigated through analysis of linking and differentiation, but one should not expect foreign policy discourse to explicitly use the concepts of space, time, and responsibility in formulations such as 'civilization is the proper spatial construction through which post-Cold War security should be understood,' or 'the temporality of the Balkans is one of recurring violence.' Spatiality, temporality, and ethicality are analytical lenses that bring out the important political substance of identity construction, not explicitly articulated signs.

Spatiality, temporality, and ethicality have equal theoretical and ontological status; there is not one dimension which is more fundamental than the others or which can be said to determine the other two. Particular texts might be more explicitly concerned with one of the three dimensions, for instance the importance of temporal identity for understanding regional conflicts or (under)development, but the overriding goal of foreign policy discourse is to articulate the three elements in such a manner that they draw upon and reinforce each other, in some cases to silence the possibility that 'international responsibility' could be applied. While discourses strive to create stable links in the articulation of spatiality, temporality, and ethicality, there is not just one constellation of the three dimensions of identity which is logically and empirically possible. To return to the constructions of the Indian 'savage,' both Cortés and Las Casas employed a spatial construction of identity that constituted the 'Indians' as 'savages,' yet they articulated radically different temporal identities in that Cortés constituted the 'Indians' as incapable of becoming Christian humans whereas Las Casas' construction was centered on exactly this temporal transformation. Or, as is laid out in chapter 6, the Western discursive constructions of 'the Balkans' have taken a spatial identity, 'the Balkans,' and constructed it within three different discourses: a Byronian Romanticism that constituted 'the Balkans' as different from the West, as an object of admiration that should not be transformed, but supported by the West in its struggles for independence; a civilizational Enlightenment discourse that constituted 'the Balkans' as different from the West but with the capacity for liberal political and economic transformation, a transformation for which the West had a moral responsibility as well as a financial and geopolitical interest; and, finally, a Balkanization discourse that constructed 'the Balkans' as radically different and threatening in its capacity to bring chaos and war to the West, as incapable of transformation, and to be isolated and deterred rather than supported.

Taking each of the three dimensions in turn, to understand identity as *spatially* constructed is to reiterate that identity is relationally constituted and always involves the construction of boundaries and thereby the delineation of space. In foreign policy discourse this delineation has historically centered on the nation state, abstractly through the privilege granted to national security discourse and concretely through the construction of the particular identities of other states, regions, and peoples. Spatial constructions of identity are immediately identifiable in the construction of other countries, 'Russia,' 'Israel,' 'Lebanon,' and so on, but representations of foreign policy will often involve a more complex set of spatial identities, drawing upon regional constructions, such as 'Africa,' 'Europe,' 'the Orient,' 'the Balkans,' and 'the Middle East' (Said 1978; Wolff 1994; Todorova 1997; Goldsworthy 1998). These territorially bounded identities are all imbued with political content, but spatial identity might also be articulated as abstract political space, boundaries, and subjectivities. One might find discourses which evolve around the construction of political subjects such as 'terrorists,' 'barbarians,' 'tribes,' 'heathens,' 'savages,' 'homosexuals,' 'women,' 'civilization,' 'the international community,' 'humanity,' and 'the people'; and identities are often constructed as a mixture of the territorially bounded and the abstract political. The identity of 'Latino' in American debates on immigration and assimilation articulates, for example, a geographical connection with Latin America, but it is also a political subject in its own right (Huntington 2004).

Understanding foreign policy discourse as constructed through a series of spatial identities casts light on the importance of universal discourse. What, it is sometimes argued, does a relational understanding of identity make of the construction of universal identities? Does not the articulation of 'international community,' 'universal human rights,' 'humanity,' and 'universal civilization' conflict with the assumption that identities are relationally and spatially constituted by suggesting an identity with no juxtaposing Other? The answer is that universal discourse does indeed articulate a boundless political subject, but this subject is on the other hand always discursively mobilized in relation to a set of particular identities. The construction of policies to be undertaken in 'defense of universal human rights' is made in response to *violations* of these rights, and hence particular political subjects who are not yet complying with the 'universal demand.' Universal discourse holds out the difference between universal principles and those who have adopted them, on the one hand, and those who have failed to, on the other, thereby constructing spatial as well as temporal identities.

Foreign policy discourse evolves, as shown by this discussion, not only around spatial constructions but also through articulations of *temporal identity*. Temporal themes such as development, transformation, continuity, change, repetition, or stasis are crucial for understanding and analyzing the construction of identity within foreign policy discourse, and one might distinguish between discourses of religious, civilizational, political, and other forms of *progress* on the one hand and discourses of *intransience* on the other.

Starting with the abstract discourse on state sovereignty and national security, the constitutive division between national and international space has been coupled to temporal identity by locating the possibility of progress—politically, financially, and culturally—inside the boundaries of the state, whereas international relations always revert to conflict and war, to a temporality of repetition (Walker 1993). Clearly, many political and philosophical discourses have challenged this simplified realist understanding of spatial and temporal identities, but these challenges also point to the continuing importance of understanding political spaces and subjects as constituted in time, and to the importance of different conceptions of time for what is considered politically feasible or morally necessitated. Turning to a broader set of foreign policy discourses, the construction of the Other as temporally progressing toward the (Western) Self is for instance a central component of development discourse as well as discourses on democratization and human rights. More specifically, one might ask first, how the temporality of the Other is constituted in relation to the temporality of the Self: if the Other is constructed with a temporal identity similar to the one of the Self, or if it is articulated as an object in a time different from the one of the Self (Fabian 1983). If the latter is the case, is it constituted as 'backward,' 'tribal,' 'savage,' 'barbarian,' or 'primitive'—in other words, as less temporally developed—or is it constituted as temporally superior to the Self and so as an object to be emulated in the search for progress and prosperity? If an Other is capable of transformation (Table 3.1), as with the heathen Indian 'savages' of Las Casas, it might transcend even radical Otherness to become like the Self, thus showing the difference between the current and the future identity of the Other. But other discourses, like the Western discourse on the violent, barbaric, and tribal Balkan Other, articulate the Other as unable to break with its backward identity. Thus in this case, the Other is doubly temporally displaced: it is constituted as backward *and* as permanently located within its violent and primitive backwardness.

It has been suggested, most explicitly by Ole Wæver, that identity construction need not involve the delineation of a spatial Other but can be based on the temporal construction of the Self. The EU, argues Wæver, is constructed not against an external Other but rather against the temporal Other of its own past (Buzan *et al.* 1990; Wæver 1996). Broadening the scope beyond contemporary EU Europe, the construction of national, regional, civilizational, and religious Selves are stories set in time, be that religious stories of wandering out from Old Testament Egyptian deserts, a national narrative of medieval tribal origins or New World immigration, or a universal discourse of civilizational progress. These are narratives of how struggles, defeats, and conquests distinguish and build the Self, usually to construct the contemporary Self as the product of a continuous process of refinement, but occasionally, as for instance in modern Greece, as a more ambiguous instantiation of a glorious past (Herzfeld 1987: 41–2). While temporal identity is clearly important for constructing foreign policy identities and discourse, one should not, however, take this to imply that temporality would be the *only* dimension of identity construction, and that identity therefore does not need to be spatially situated (Wendt 2003: 527). To take Wæver's study, the past is important for understanding the EU's discourse on European identity and integration, but it is not the only important construction of identity in play, nor is it disconnected from a spatial construction. The construction of the EU as

Table 3.1 Temporal identity

Capacity for change[a]	The Other	
	Superior	*Inferior*
Yes	Eastern Europe's construction of Europe in the 1980s	Western construction of 'developing countries'
No	'Despairing discourse,' impossible at the level of states	Western construction of 'the Balkans' after 1920

Note
[a] The capacity for change refers to a change in the inferior identity.

overcoming its violent past is simultaneous with a construction of (spatial) Others who have not and a series of 'neighbors' in Eastern Europe, the Mediterranean, the Middle East, and North Africa.

Turning to the construction of *ethical identity* one might at first consider this dimension difficult to conceptualize insofar as national security discourse locates responsibility within the national community, leaving no space for an international ethics (Walker 1993: 64). The goal of poststructuralist discourse analysis is not, however, to step outside of discourse to define how international ethics should be developed and applied, but rather to argue that foreign policy discourses always involve a construction of responsibility, even if only implicitly as applicable toward a national citizenry. For governments to legitimize their foreign policies as in the 'national interest' is to articulate a responsibility toward the national body politics, a responsibility which, as argued in chapter 2, invests political leaders with the power to make authoritative and far-ranging decisions. It is also an articulation of responsibility which effectively overrides any potential claim to an 'international responsibility.' The focus of discourse analysis on articulations of ethical identity implies, therefore, a concern with the discursive construction of ethics, morality, and responsibility; with the moral force of particular representations, for instance of wars as 'genocide' and interventions as 'humanitarian'; and with, in short, the Self's articulation of (non)responsibility toward the Other.

Moving beyond state sovereignty and realist security discourse, constructions of ethical identity and responsibility are not as uncommon as one might think. Las Casas' construction of a Christian obligation for christening the Indian 'savages,' nineteenth century Enlightenment philosophers' use of a universal conception of civilization to implicate Western countries in the global spread of science and reason, the humanitarian responsibility for combating hunger and natural disasters that is implied by the development discourse of the twentieth century, and the discursive rise of 'human rights' and 'human security' after the end of the Cold War all point to the explicit invocation of ethical identities in foreign policy discourse.

When foreign policy discourse articulates an explicit international responsibility, whether to stop 'genocide,' to combat 'humanitarian disaster,' or to prevent violations of 'human rights,' a powerful discursive move is undertaken in that the issue is moved out of the realm of the strategic and 'selfishly national' and re-located within the 'higher grounds' of the morally good. A similar dynamic is evident when non-governmental voices argue in favor of foreign policies based on ethical concerns, for instance that the West has a 'human responsibility' for coming to the aid of the defenseless, hungry, poor, and persecuted. All foreign policy discourses articulate constructions of ethical identity, yet some representations of identity, for instance of a war as constituting a 'genocide,' invoke a particular moral force, a call for action that in response constitutes the spatial and temporal identities of those involved as well as those called upon to intervene.

By combining the analytical concern with degrees of difference and Otherness and the three dimensions of identity construction, a theoretical double grip is produced: which Selves and Others are constituted in foreign policy discourse? How radical is the difference between them? And how is difference constituted through the articulation of spatial, temporal, and ethical identity? This double grip not only provides substantial knowledge of the identity construction taking place within foreign policy discourse, it also provides a lens through which discursive differences, similarities, and changes can be studied, thus ultimately furthering theoretical understanding of the links between identity and policy. Rather than simply identifying two constructions of identity as 'different,' how this difference is located in spatial, temporal and/or ethical constructions of identity can be traced. As discursive changes are studied, one can more systematically lay out whether this is a change in one of the dimensions or in all three, and analyze how change within one dimension builds up pressure on the others and how policy adjustments are being made.

From texts to basic discourses

This chapter has focused on developing an analytical framework for the study of the discursive construction of identity, yet what remains to be addressed is how one identifies 'a' discourse; more specifically, how one moves theoretically and methodologically from individual texts to discourses. Foreign policy discourses are, as laid out in chapter 2, analytical constructions—not empirical objects—through which the construction and linking of identity and policy can be studied. They are identified through the reading of texts, whether spoken or written. One might argue that each individual text constitutes identity through its own particular process of linking and differentiation, that no two texts are therefore ever completely identical and that there are as many discourses as there are texts. This view is certainly defensible from a strict deconstructivist perspective, which insists on the unique nature of every text, but adopting it as a theoretical and methodological principle for foreign policy discourse analysis would simultaneously downplay the social and structured nature of language and the location of foreign policy within a larger discursive and political field. Foreign policy debates are constituted through individual texts, but these texts converge around common themes, around certain constructions of identity and sets of policies considered viable, desirable or necessary; foreign policy debates are as a consequence bound together by a smaller number of discourses.

The view of foreign policy debate as constituted through a smaller number of discourses raises the question of *how* these particular discourses are identified. Since discourses are analytical constructions rather than empirically observable objects, it is necessary to theorize the choices and principles upon which the selection of a smaller set of structuring discourses is made. It is possible that an empirical case is dominated by just one discourse that has achieved hegemonic status, or that one chooses a focus on governmental discourse only. Often, however, it is pertinent to have a theoretical framework that allows for multiple discourses, either because the focus of study is a larger political and media debate; because contemporary discourse is analyzed in a historical and thereby comparative perspective or because one seeks to identify challenges to an otherwise hegemonic discourse. Those are situations where one would want to identify a smaller number of structuring *basic discourses* which: construct different Others with different degrees of radical difference; articulate radically diverging forms of spatial, temporal, and ethical identity; and construct competing links between identity and policy. Analytically, basic discourses point to the main points of contestation within a debate and facilitate a structured account of the relationship between discourses, their points of convergence and confrontations; how discourses develop over time in response to events, facts and criticism; and how discursive variations evolve.

Basic discourses are identified through readings of texts, but it should be stressed that 'basic discourses' is an analytical distinction of an ideal-type kind. This implies that while basic discourses should have some empirical prevalence, they are not necessarily the most frequently argued discourses, especially if a lengthy debate is examined, nor are they necessarily the ones argued by governments or international institutions. The analytical value of basic discourses is rather that they provide a lens through which a multitude of different representations and policies can be seen as systematically connected and that they identify the key points of structuring disagreement within a debate. The ideal-type character of basic discourses furthermore implies that they are often modified and variations constructed over time.

There is no fixed number of basic discourses that one should always identify within a debate, but it is useful to settle for a small number, usually two or three discourses. The goal is to identify discourses that articulate very different constructions of identity and policy and which thereby separate the political landscape between them. More concretely, the following points function as theoretical and methodological guidelines.

The first point is that, because basic discourses should indicate the main structural positions within a debate, it is pertinent that they are based on the reading of a larger number of texts, preferably from a wide variety of sources, media, and genres (chapter 5 discusses in more detail how a body of texts is selected). Having established basic discourses from a wider reading, one might subsequently (re)turn to a detailed study of the articulations of identity and policy within particular texts, media, or genres and situate them inside the context of the larger political debate. As no two texts are fully identical, the analysis of a set of texts will be more general than a reading of particular texts, but the discourse analysis principles should still be applied to identify the signs most frequently articulated, the relationship between Self and Other, the policy that is coupled thereto, and the articulations of spatial, temporal, and ethical identity. One should note that while a foreign policy discourse is identified as the construction of identity, policy, and the link between them, it is not necessarily the case that all texts explicitly articulate both identities and policy. Certain types of policy texts, legal documents and official communiqués for instance, are of a declaratory nature and do not elaborate on what constructions of identity are implicated. These texts are not separate from political discourse but are part of a larger textual and discursive corpus. As not all texts will explicitly articulate constructions of identity, not all texts will explicitly address policy—chapter 4 discusses how such texts become part of foreign policymaking and public debate as they are read and situated within a policy discussion.

The second methodological point is that basic discourses should be built on explicit articulations of key representations of identity, for example: 'the Balkans' and 'genocide' in the Western debate on Bosnia; 'civilization' in debates on the importance of religion and culture for post-Cold War conflicts; 'security' in studies of NATO's persistence and transformation; 'quagmire' and 'Vietnam' in the American debate on Iraq; or 'evil' in analysis of the importance of evangelical religion for George W. Bush's foreign policy. Key representations might be geographical identities, historical analogies, striking metaphors, or political concepts, yet it is impossible to construct an exhaustive list of potential representations because language itself develops.

Once the key representations have been selected one might turn to the third methodological point, which is to draw upon available conceptual histories of the representations chosen. Current representations might not repeat historical articulations slavishly, but they would have to relate themselves thereto. The importance of conceptual history is not only, however, to create a comparison with past discourses, but also, in Foucault's terms, to conduct a genealogical reading which traces the constitution of the present concept back in history to understand when and how it was formed as well as how it succeeded in marginalizing other representations (Foucault 1984).

Conceptual histories and genealogies are often written by historians, linguists, or historical sociologists and offer an empirical richness that can be subjected to a more structured reading that traces the processes of linking and differentiation and the articulation of the three dimensions of identity within the historical material. A structured reading of conceptual history provides, where applicable, important knowledge on how constructions of identity have been argued in the past and thus a good indication of where 'discursive fault lines' might be located in the present. As shown in chapter 6, the conceptual history of the Western construction of 'the Balkans' is structured around three very different discourses, and the analysis of the debate of the 1990s points out that one discourse was privileged by governmental, media, and literary voices.

The next points in the methodological guidelines draw explicitly on the theoretical framework laid out in chapters 2 and 3. The fourth point is that basic discourses should be composed in such a way that the Others and Selves they articulate differ both in how radical a relation of Otherness is constructed and in their spatial, temporal, and ethical constructions of identity; and potentially as to which Other(s) are articulated as the most significant. The fifth point is that, because basic discourses articulate very different Selves and Others and because identity and policy are interlinked, one will expect that basic discourses advocate rather different foreign policies. The sixth and final point is that, when viewed in a dynamic perspective, it is likely that at least one basic discourse will be argued relatively quickly as an issue manifests itself on the foreign policy agenda, while the other basic discourse(s) will be argued in response to and in criticism of this position.

4 Intertextualizing foreign policy
Genres, authority, and knowledge

Texts are simultaneously unique and united: each makes its own particular construction of identity, weaves a series of differentiations and juxtapositions, and couples them to a spatially, temporally, and ethically situated foreign policy. Yet, the inimitability of every individual text is always located within a shared textual space; all texts make references, explicitly or implicitly, to previous ones, and in doing so they both establish their own reading and become mediations on the meaning and status of others. The meaning of a text is thus never fully given by the text itself but is always a product of other readings and interpretations. This process, coined by Julia Kristeva with the concept of *intertextuality* (Kristeva 1980), is both theoretically and methodologically significant for discourse analysis of foreign policy. It highlights that texts are situated within and against other texts, that they draw upon them in constructing their identities and policies, that they appropriate as well as revise the past, and that they build authority by reading and citing that of others. It points analytically, politically, and empirically to seeing official foreign policy texts—statements, speeches, and interviews—not as entities standing separately from wider societal discourses but as entities located within a larger textual web; a web that both includes and goes beyond other policy texts, into journalism, academic writing, popular non-fiction, and, potentially, even fiction.

Understanding foreign policy texts as intertextually linked across a variety of media and genres calls for empirical analysis of how these links are made as well as for thoroughly theorizing the way in which texts build authority and their capacity to speak about a particular issue. As one examines different genres of text and the links between them, it becomes clear that textual authority is not generated or stabilized in an identical manner within prominent genres such as policy texts, journalistic reportage, historiography, quantitative analysis, or literary non-fiction (e.g., memoir and travel writing). All texts constitute themselves as knowledgeable, but their form of knowledge and the way in which it is linked to other modes of authority differ: political leaders construct their authority in part through their right and ability to exercise power; investigative journalism's authority comes from uncovering politically important facts; and literary non-fiction builds authority by mixing historiography and factual knowledge with experiential forms of knowledge, such as personal encounters and anecdotes.

Different genres employ different modalities of authority, and theorizing how they draw upon knowledge, power, and narrative techniques is important for understanding not only the internal workings of the genres themselves but also the process through which they are linked and politically mobilized. What happens when texts constructed within one modality of authority and knowledge are situated inside a policy text that employs different modalities? Perhaps most striking is when literary non-fiction, or even fiction, is intertextually linked to official foreign policy: such as when Clinton reads a travelogue that does not even broach the question of American foreign policy and changes his policy toward Bosnia, or when the best-selling apocalyptic evangelical *Left Behind* series' discourse of good and evil intertwines with the foreign policy discourse of the George W. Bush administration (Kirkpatrick 2004).

The first section of this chapter pursues these questions by presenting intertextuality as a concept through which the importance of textual influence and debate can be theorized, particularly within the field of foreign policy. The second section suggests three models for how texts and genres might be more systematically organized in relation to official foreign policy discourse. These models point to different research projects and emphasize different ways in which connections between official discourses and non-official material can be theorized, selected, and studied. The third section turns to a discussion of the importance of authority and the constructions and mobilizations of power, knowledge, and narrativity within the genres of policy texts, journalism, academe, and literary non-fiction. Literary non-fiction points most explicitly to the importance of subjective and narrative forms of knowledge, which is discussed in further detail in the fourth section.

Political intertextuality

All texts, including foreign policy texts, are situated within a wider web of writing: 'any text is,' argues Julia Kristeva in formulating her concept of *intertextuality*, 'constructed as a mosaic of quotations; any text is the absorption and transformation of another' (Kristeva 1980: 66). Kristeva's theory on the intertextual generation of meaning suggests in more concrete terms that no text is written without traces of previous texts, that a text is simultaneously drawing upon a textual past and constructing this past into a unique new text (Der Derian and Shapiro 1989). This process can be most clearly identified when texts make *explicit references* to older works, in particular when these are constructed as texts with a particular authority, or as classics that have to be assessed and criticized. One might consider Waltz's *Theory of International Politics*, a classic text within 1980s International Relations (IR) theory that other IR texts had to relate to. Moving to a higher level of abstraction, works such as Hobbes' *Leviathan* are classics within political theory and the continued subject of debate on the meaning and interpretation of sovereignty and state power. A more concrete example, which is discussed in chapter 8, is Robert D. Kaplan's *Balkan Ghosts*, which adopted Rebecca West's *Black Lamb and Grey Falcon* as the literary references through which Kaplan's Yugoslavian itinerary, encounters, and writing were constructed (West 1941; Kaplan 1993a). But intertextuality might also be more subtle, established through *secondary sources*. Brian Hall has noted, for instance, that West's *Black Lamb and Grey Falcon* was the most widely used source for journalists working on the Balkan wars of the 1990s, although their reporting did not necessarily quote her book (Hall 1996).

Intertextuality can also be employed through *conceptual intertextuality*, where the articulation of concepts such as 'the Balkans,' 'security,' and 'democracy' rely upon *implicit references* to a larger body of earlier texts on the same subject. Conceptual intertextuality might also come into play through programmatic *catchphrases*, such as Huntington's 'clash of civilization,' which became a common reference in Western politics and journalism even though Huntington might not always be explicitly quoted (Huntington 1993, 1996).[1] Table 4.1 summarizes the different forms of intertextuality.

As a text makes references to older texts it constructs legitimacy for its own reading, but it also simultaneously reconstructs and reproduces the classical status of the older ones. Rather than seeing new texts as depending on older, one should therefore see the two as interacting in an exchange where one text gains legitimacy from quoting and the other gains legitimacy from being quoted. This construction of an intertextual link produces mutual legitimacy and creates an exchange at the level of meaning. No quote or rendition of an original text is ever a complete reproduction of the original, and the meaning of original texts will therefore always be read and re-read through new texts. Even a direct quote is situated inside a new textual context, reconstructed by it, and meaning is therefore never seamlessly transmitted from one text to another.

This implies that the intertextual focus is not only on which texts are being quoted or which links are being made by other texts, but also on how texts are read and interpreted: how facts and knowledge are drawn from one text to

Table 4.1 Forms of intertextuality

Intertextuality	Intertextual linkages
Explicit	Quotes
	References
Implicit	Secondary sources
	Conceptual
	Catchphrases

another and located within a particular foreign policy discourse. At the abstract theoretical level, there is no original text that is not shaped by being re-read, but this process of textual appropriation comes out particularly strikingly in the case of historical texts. Historical texts are often read through the dominant categories of a contemporary debate, rather than the ones that might have been prevalent at the time of writing. Rebecca West, for example, in *Black Lamb and Grey Falcon* (from 1940–1) employed the term 'Slavic' extensively and with important political effects, but this term was not widely articulated in debates on Bosnia in the 1990s and hence not in contemporary readings of her book. Readings are performed through the central discourse of their present, thereby lifting parts with representational similarity out of older texts while ignoring or silencing others. The reading of older documents through the discourses of the present implies that texts might be located inside an entirely new foreign policy discourse. George F. Kennan, for instance, wrote an introduction to a 1993 re-publication of a report on the first two Balkan wars (which was originally published by the Carnegie Commission in 1914) situating the report inside a Balkanization discourse of eternal Balkan violence and Western non-intervention. The original report, however, was firmly embedded in an Enlightenment discourse of Balkan civilizational improvement and Western responsibility (see chapters 6 and 8).

This example points to historical texts whose foreign policy discourses are reconstructed by later readings. However, texts might also be textually appropriated as foreign policy texts even though they do not explicitly formulate policy. These texts are located by other texts inside a proper foreign policy discourse by adding or deducing policy. A prominent example of the political mobilization of a non-policy text, discussed in chapter 8, was Kaplan's *Balkan Ghosts*: it did not define a foreign policy, but its construction of Balkan identities is said to have led Clinton to abandon an American 'lift and strike' policy for Bosnia. Kaplan, in turn, later opined that this was not the policy course he thought should have been pursued.

The absence of an explicitly formulated foreign policy opens a text for incorporation into a policy discourse, but can one say that one construction of identity automatically necessitates a particular policy? In principle, no; as shown in the analyses in chapters 6 to 9, one might find empirically that multiple policies can be formulated around the same construction of identity. But while a text might not formulate or logically imply a particular policy, it is simultaneously empirically situated within a larger intertextual and discursive field that influences how identity constructions are being read. If a text articulates a particular construction of identity and this identity is routinely coupled to a specific policy by other texts, this will in all likelihood influence the reading of the policy implications of the text in question. The construction of identity within *Balkan Ghosts* was one that resonated with discourses that normally *did* couple this identity to a policy of Western non-intervention, and thus while perhaps not the intention of the author, it reinforced a discourse that advocated this policy. And, once the story of the book's impact on Clinton's foreign policy gained hold, it took on a textual importance of its own; the text's notoriety stabilized its status and legitimized construction of both Bosnia as 'ancient Balkan hatred' and the policy that should be pursued.

This case points more generally to the way in which classical texts take on an intertextual life of their own. What is drawn upon is not, then, the text itself but a story about what the text says; *Black Lamb and Grey Falcon* was constructed as pro-Serbian, and this reading of West's political affinities was lifted into the present to argue that her book supported a Western policy of inaction in Bosnia in the 1990s, although this was (as chapter 8 shows) a rather limited reading of the original book. These readings occur not simply because people do not read the original, but because their readings are made through the discursive constructions already in place and through established interpretations of the work in question. Although at a meta-theoretical level, no intertextual link or re-reading will ever fully reproduce the original and multiple readings are always possible, one can still argue that at the more specific level of concrete analysis not all readings are equally valid. As chapter 3 argues, one *can* say something decisively about the construction of identity and policy within a given text. One should therefore undertake an intertextual reading which analyzes: first, how identity and policy are articulated within the original text; second, how the construction of identity and policy of the original text is represented in later re-readings; and third, how the original and its re-readings compare (Figure 4.1). The aim of this three-step reading is not simply to decide whether re-readings misinterpret the original, but to identify the potential span between the original and its interpreters, to investigate the possibility of competing re-readings, and to provide an understanding of why and how contemporary discourses work to influence readings of older or non-policy texts.

Three intertextual models and their research agendas

Foreign policy analysis has usually drawn on policy texts which stipulate official policy or chronicle its parliamentary or bureaucratic genesis and implementation, but an intertextual approach suggests the inclusion of a wider body of texts. Official foreign policy discourse is the discourse through which

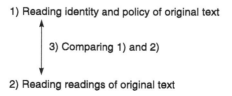

Figure 4.1 Intertextuality as a three-step reading process.

state action is legitimized, and thus under any circumstances crucial for understanding political and social relations within and beyond state boundaries. Adopting official discourse as the analytical point of departure offers a useful tangent between discourse analysis and more conventional forms of foreign policy analysis, and it provides a point of demarcation for a structured account of how to define the analytical, empirical, and methodological focus of one's research project. Official discourse should, however, be situated inside a larger intertextual web that traces intertextual references to other texts, thereby bringing in sources that are constructed either as supporting influences or as texts in need of repudiation. This implies that while an organizational starting point in official discourse might seem rather conservative, it is simultaneously pointing to the inclusion of a multitude of texts and genres, including journalistic reportage, academic analysis, travel writing, autobiography, or even fiction and popular culture. Expanding the focus beyond official discourse to a wider set of actors and media, the list of potential sources and genres grow even longer. Starting with official foreign policy and moving toward a wider conception of public debate, three research models for conducting intertextual analysis can be suggested.

The first model (model 1) is directly based in official foreign policy discourse and centers on political leaders with official authority to sanction the foreign policies pursued as well as those with central roles in executing these policies, for instance high-ranked military staff, senior civil servants (including diplomats and mediators), and heads of international institutions. It identifies the texts produced by these actors, including speeches, political debates, interviews, articles, and books, as well as the texts which have had an intertextual influence on their discourse. The goals of a model 1 study are to carefully investigate the constructions of identity within official discourse, to analyze the way in which intertextual links stabilize this discourse, and to examine how official discourse encounters criticism. Three more specific methodological guidelines can also be presented: first, official policy texts might be either single-authored, as in speeches, articles, and books, or might be produced in dialogue with political opponents or journalists; second, intertextual references may be made either in support of a proposed policy or in response to critical events or contestations of the official policy; third, one might identify intertextual links as they are made explicitly by political leaders or as secondary sources argue them, thereby creating a story of intertextual influence which further heightens the intertextual salience of the text quoted.

Adopting these guidelines calls forth a variety of genres: from direct links to popular culture, as in the influence of Tom Clancy's novels on Vice President Quayle and Secretary of Defense Weinberger (Der Derian 1992: 195), to secondary sources creating stories of influence, as when John F. Kennedy was said to have been heavily influenced during the Cuban Missile Crisis by Barbara Tuchman's account of the outbreak of World War I in *Guns of August* (Der Derian 1992: 174), or popular academic works such as Samuel Huntington's *The Clash of Civilizations*, which was reported as being 'fashionable in America's foreign policy establishment' (Walker 1997c). Religious texts can be an intertextual influence, as in George W. Bush's recurring invocations of the Bible, and media texts are intertextually linked when responded to by political leaders, as was the case with Roy Gutman's 1992 Bosnia reports in *Newsday* or the 2004 prison scandal at Abu Ghraib, triggered by photographs broadcast by CBS News' '60 Minutes II.'

Foreign policy memoirs by leading politicians, diplomats, advisors, and military personnel constitute a particular venue for policy leaders to construct themselves and their policies in a favorable light; memoirs are obviously well suited for constructing legacies, but they are also important for the reading of the present and the future. Memoirs might be seen as providing guidance for later conflicts, as when Richard Holbrooke's *To End a War* (on the Bosnian Peace Accord) was read as a lesson on how to engage Milosevic in Kosovo in 1999, or they might be part of a heated foreign policy debate, as with *Against All Enemies: Inside America's War on Terror* by Richard A. Clarke, a former White House counter-terrorism chief (Clarke 2004), which offered ample criticism of—and produced heated responses from—the Bush administration in 2004. Memoirs are also written in an attempt to 'clear the past for the future' as with Hillary Rodham Clinton's *Writing History* (Clinton H.R. 2003), which was met by huge media attention and widely believed to help prepare her for the 2008 Democratic presidential nomination. Or memoirs might be an integral part of an election campaign, as in the 2004 American presidential race, where the timing of Clinton's memoir (Clinton W.J. 2004) was considered crucial to John Kerry's campaign (Rutenberg and Kirkpatrick 2004).

The second intertextual research model (model 2) broadens the analytical scope beyond official discourse and its intertextual links to consider the major actors and arenas within a wider foreign policy debate. The most prominent discourses to consider are those of the political oppositional parties, the media, and corporate institutions. This facilitates analysis of the discursive and political hegemony a governmental position enjoys and thereby of its room for maneuver. It also provides a good indication of how official discourse might change, either through a discursive adjustment made by the present government or were there a change in the government itself. Oppositional political discourse can be investigated through the policy statements made by oppositional parties and influential individual politicians as well as their contributions to the public debate. A particularly useful site for studying oppositional discourses is, however, parliamentary debates as these bring out longer statements within a context of public contestation. The inclusion of the media further deepens the assessment of official discursive hegemony as well as the relationship between the political and the media more broadly, in particular in cases where official discourse has not incorporated or responded to potentially critical reports. Media texts fall in different categories depending on their official and explicitly political status. One can distinguish between editorials/official statements, field reporting opinion pieces, and debate written/spoken by outside sources. The relationship between these types of media texts is itself a topic worthy of analysis: do field reporting and editorial policy differ or align? Which critical opinions are given space within major media outlets? The inclusion of opinion and debate material implies that prominent public academics might be included in model 2 studies if they manage to write texts that are repeatedly quoted and discussed. Corporate institutions, including employers' associations, trade unions, large firms, powerful NGOs, and in some cases the armed forces, can also come into model 2 focus when they are major voices in foreign policy debates, for instance in the area of trade and economic integration. A particularly noteworthy type of text arises from public campaigns undertaken by institutions to influence either government or the outcome of elections or referenda. As in model 1, it is possible to expand a model 2 study along the intertextual dimension to identify and analyze those texts that are repeatedly constituted as significant sources.

The actors and institutions of model 2 are all considered major players within the broader political debate and they are all explicitly concerned with foreign policy. Moving into model 3, the scope of analysis is expanded to include material not explicitly engaging official policy discourse (model 3A), or which is concerned with policy but has a marginal status (model 3B). Model 3A brings in representations of foreign policy issues as they are articulated within 'high' as well as 'popular' culture and relates them to articulations within official foreign policy discourse.[2] Analysis investigates whether popular representations reproduce or contest those of official discourse and how representations travel between the spheres of entertainment and politics (Shapiro 1990, 1997). Studies of popular culture include film, fiction, television, computer games, photography, and comic books. It analyzes, for instance, how a particular region, country, or people is cinematically represented (Iordanova 2001) or how espionage is treated within popular fiction (Der Derian 1992). Linking popular culture and official foreign policy, one might compare the construction of 'Mexicans' within American cinema and television series with the way in which US foreign policy has constructed 'Mexicans' and approached the question of Mexican immigration, illegal border crossings, and assimilation in the United States. Crucially, from a political point of view a popular culture construction of 'Mexicans' as different from and inferior to 'Anglo-Americans' provides a set of widely circulated identities around which an anti-immigration policy can legitimate itself. Or, to give another example, one might locate an analysis of official American policies on gays in the military inside an account of how homosexuals are constructed within popular media.[3]

Poststructuralist analysis has often focused on popular culture, but analyses of 'high culture' might be equally valid (and the definition of 'popular' should be extensive and historically situated) in showing, for example, how music, poetry, painting, architecture, and literature have been employed in constructing national and civilizational identities. Travel writing in particular has been an important genre for communicating the construction of 'foreign places and people' to the Western public since the eighteenth century and has been employed by a large variety of professions: by merchants or emissaries; pirates and buccaneers; missionaries; explorers; warriors and Spanish Conquistadores; ambassadors; scientists (botanists, geologists) and engineers; and not least, tourists, from the European Grand Tours of the seventeenth century to the backpacking of the present day (Adams 1983; Pratt 1992). Turning to the present, travelogues and memoirs by regular soldiers make up a commercially popular genre that speaks to foreign policy issues without being explicitly analytical (Turnipseed 2003; Swofford 2003).

Model 3A points to the importance of widely available representations, but less widely dispersed discourses might also be worthy of analysis in model 3B studies as these might intersect with and influence dominant representations in subtle ways and hence become important for the future. Iver B. Neumann, for instance, has traced the Russian debates on Europe and shown how new ideas usually appear in marginal publications and later make their way into the center of debate and the vocabulary of the state (Neumann 1996a: 195). NGOs which do not hold the discursive power associated with model 2 are also potential model 3B actors to consider. Early re-articulations of identity that open political space might be found within the cultural sphere, hence combining models 3A and 3B, as was the case in Slovenia in the 1980s, where the first contestations of the communist Yugoslav project were articulated by 'deconstructionist' groups in music, performance, and the visual arts (Hansen 1996). One might also find satirical television and radio that address contested political issues (Rutenberg 2004).

Keeping a space open for a possible inclusion of marginal actors and discourses becomes salient when analyzing where resistance and future re-articulations might occur, particularly in the cases of authoritarian regimes that do not allow for the public debate that would be identified within model 2, or in cases where governmental discourse has successfully hegemonized the political and media discourses of model 2. The marginal status of texts within model 3B makes it, however, difficult to identify exactly where texts should be found, especially in non-democratic societies, and it is therefore important that model 3B studies are followed by detailed knowledge of the case in question. Students and scholars of IR might have a particular interest in the relationship between official discourse, the wider political debate, and academic analysis, and the last might also be included as a marginal discourse and an object of study within model 3B.

The three intertextual research models (Table 4.2) are structured along a decreasing link to official foreign policy discourse. Does this mean that model 1 is more important than the two others, or that models 1 and 2 should always be privileged over model 3? The answer is no. The ambition of discourse analysis is not only to understand official discourse, and the texts and representations which have directly impacted it, but also to analyze how this discourse is presented as legitimate in relation to the larger public and how it is reproduced or contested across the variety of political sites and genres reflected in different ways by models 2 and 3.

Table 4.2 Intertextual research models

	Model 1	Model 2	Model 3A	Model 3B
Analytical focus	Official discourse: Heads of states Governments Senior civil servants High ranked military Heads of international institutions Official statements by international institutions	Wider foreign policy debate: Political opposition The media Corporate institutions	Cultural representations: Popular culture High culture	Marginal political discourses: Social movements Illegal associations Academics NGOs
Object of analysis	Official texts Direct and secondary intertextual links Supportive texts Critical texts	Political texts Parliamentary debates Speeches, statements Media texts Editorials Field reporting Opinion—debate Corporate institutions Public campaigns Recurring intertextual links	Film, fiction, television, computer games, photography, comics, music, poetry, painting, architecture, travel writing, autobiography	Marginal newspapers, websites, books, pamphlets Academic analysis
Goal of analysis	The stabilization of official discourse through intertextual links The response of official discourse to critical discourses	The hegemony of official discourse The likely transformation of official discourse The internal stability of media discourses	Sedimentation or reproduction of identities in cultural representations	Resistance in non-democratic regimes Dissent in cases of models 1 and 2 hegemony Academic debates

Constructing authority: power, knowledge, and narrativity

Theorizing foreign policy as intertextually constituted through a larger body of texts points to the importance of *genre*; to understanding texts not as identical in their rhetorical structures but as having a particular 'rationale [that] shapes the schematic structure of the discourse and influences and constrains choice of content and style' (Swales 1990: 58). There are certain traits and conventions that are expected when authors write within a particular genre, for example: that academic scientific analysis addresses an issue as truthfully as possible and that the emotional experiences of the author are not part of the analysis; that politicians will construct themselves as forceful leaders and as socially responsible; and that journalism is built on verifiable sources, not on fictional accounts. There is, however, no consensus on how to define genre within discourse analysis or linguistics. Some, like Norman Fairclough, locate it with social practices such as advertising and interviewing, while others, like Julia Kristeva, defines it through the form of the text, such as a short story, a letter, or a speech (Fairclough 1995: 56; Kristeva 1980: 83). For our purpose, a more substantial division based in part on a particular set of activities and in part on an inclination toward a particular form of knowledge production is most useful. More specifically, foreign policy texts fall into the main genres of policy documents, journalism, academic writing, and literary non-fiction (writings that are constituted primarily as non-fiction, but deploy a series of literary or narrative techniques). These distinctions, although rough, point to crucial differences in how texts establish not only identities and foreign policies, and also in how they construct authority and employ forms of knowledge.[4]

To introduce genre into foreign policy discourse analysis is not to define an alternative set of discourses built on genres. Some discourse analyses, such as Norman Fairclough's, are organized along genre-based distinctions, speaking for instance of 'political discourses,' 'media discourses,' or 'cinematic discourse,' but for a politically centered discourse analysis it is more useful to maintain a concept of discourses as defined by *substantial* articulations of identity and policy (Fairclough 1995, 2001; Chouliaraki and Fairclough 1999). This facilitates a study of how discourses engage each other on substantial political issues, in that foreign policy debates are concerned with a similar issue across multiple genres. Analytically, the *basic discourses* of a debate structure the political and substantial positions and divisions, whereas *intertextual models* identify the locations of different discourses in relations to official discourse and other sites of opinion and debate.

The majority of this book is focused on policy texts, journalism, academic analysis, and on two forms of literary non-fiction: travel writing and memoir.[5] This focus is in part due to considerations of space: to fully theorize fiction and popular culture would require a thorough consideration of visual and interactive forms of representation that goes beyond the boundaries of this book. This book's case study, the Western debate on Bosnia was, furthermore, a powerful illustration of the potential importance of travel writing and memoir for foreign policy debate, while fiction and popular culture failed to have a similar intertextual influence on official foreign policy discourse. This raises two questions. First, was the Bosnia debate a unique example of the importance of literary non-fiction? The answer here is that there are good reasons to assume that the Bosnian case has parallels. Travel writing and autobiography are genres with huge commercial success that generate widespread attention and sales, despite these works' questionable academic status.[6] Tracing the history of memoirs and travel writing, they have, furthermore, long historical connections to the field of international politics. Second, are there other genres or sub-genres that should be included in future studies of foreign policy debates? A relevant addition would be biography, or there could be a more explicit focus on popular science, that is books and magazines that construct themselves with academic authority but are written for a wider audience. Perhaps most challenging, however, would be to embrace religious texts as a genre which has been powerfully politically employed in recent years and which defies conventional epistemological distinctions between fact and fiction, and between verification and faith.

Foreign policy texts might differ in how much emphasis they devote to the elaboration of either identity or policy; they also, obviously, differ in their connection with the formal institutions of foreign policymaking. Importantly, however, they all strive to establish themselves as having the *authority* to speak about a particular foreign policy issue. Yet, different genres employ different modalities of authority: the authority of a president of a nation giving a foreign policy speech differs from that of an academic expert interviewed on primetime news, which differs from that of a travel writer chronicling the political culture of a place and its people. All genres construct *knowledge* as important for the authority of a text, its author and its foreign policy discourse, but to be knowledgeable about a foreign policy issue is a position that can be constructed in a number of different ways. Knowledge might be constituted through objective forms of fact-finding or through subjective and personal encounters; through historiographic readings of long civilizational structures or abstract models of balance of power; through the explicit invocation of the voice and emotion of an author or the detachment of a distanced observer; through bestowing importance on cultural artifacts and traditions; or through a universal utilitarian subjectivity. Knowledge, if seen as a discursively constituted and mobilized modality within foreign policy debates and texts, is thus much broader than the causal positivism advocated by social scientists. To understand why texts that from an academic point of view are sorely lacking in factual content, causal reasoning, and historical accuracy and which nevertheless become influential within foreign policy debates requires a consideration of non-scientific, subjective, and narrative forms of writing.

Subjective and narrative forms of knowledge will be considered more thoroughly below, but it should be noted first that while modalities of authority are connected with different forms of knowledge, authority is not constituted through knowledge alone. For politicians to have authority is not only a matter of claiming knowledge—about a conflict, national interests, or strategic capabilities—they must also have the ability to *take responsibility and deploy power*. As chapter 2 lays out, policy speech in general, and security discourse in particular, constructs its authors or speaking agents through a dual logic of power and responsibility. Governing politicians have the institutional power to define foreign policy, and their ability to deploy power is discursively mobilized in encounters with enemies as well as allies. But politicians also have a responsibility regarding their body politics, especially in the face of 'imminent danger,' even if this implies making sacrifices on the part of the national collective. When confronting critical foreign policy issues, politicians will therefore often emphasize their ability to lead, to 'provide leadership' and to act with 'force and determination,' and they will stress the 'obligation' bestowed upon them to guard national and societal interests. Authoritarian systems and liberal democracies alike might furthermore deploy a construction of 'obligation' that accentuates the educational and superior skills of the governing leaders: not only are they privy to more extensive, and potentially classified, information, but they also have a vision of the common good and its long-term interests that the public lacks.

There are large differences between and within the genres of journalism and academic writing, but they do (to a larger extent than policy texts and literary non-fiction) construct authority solely around the provision of knowledge. The modality of authority for foreign policy journalism and academic writing—at least within liberal democracies—is to provide information and knowledge that is not implicated in, or written with concern for those with political and financial power. This, of course, is not to say that this adequately represents how the media or the academic world actually operate; rather that the discourse through which these genres construct their authority is one where the separation of knowledge from power is constituted as crucial and where diversions from this separation have to be legitimized through extreme securitizations and constructions of existential threats and dangers.

Turning to literary non-fiction, authority is constructed not only through knowledgeable access to foreign places or secret meetings, but also through literary, poetic, and narrative skills and techniques. What makes for a good memoir or a travelogue is not simply what the author might have experienced and therefore has verifiable knowledge of, but rather his or her ability to entertain: to make foreign places come alive, to make personal experiences exotic or universal. The invocation of an 'I' sets travel writing and memoir aside from most academic writings, and certainly from scientific ones, in that it brings a human subject to the foreground, which facilitates a more intimate relationship between author and reader. The vivid travel narrative seeks to describe the cold of the Himalayas and the sun of Sahara, to give the reader the sensation of traveling without leaving the room. Memoirs can weave a story of the importance of 'lived life,' dramatize the extraordinary achievements of the writer, and narrate experiences with which the reader can identify. As John Hawkesworth wrote in the late eighteenth century, the first-person format 'would, by bringing the Adventurer and the Reader nearer together … more strongly excite interest, and consequently afford more entertainment' (quoted from Pratt 1992: 235–6).[7] It offers the possibility of entertainment, identification, and intimacy under the (more or less accurate) disguise of information while dispensing with the demand for documentation and statistical validity of traditional academic analysis (Shapiro 1988: 55).

Beyond objectivity: narrative knowledge and literary non-fiction

The most striking difference between scientific and factual forms of knowledge on the one hand and narrative and subjective ones on the other is how the two situate the author within the text. Scientific and factual knowledge stems from a text's ability to demonstrate the existence of pertinent facts, from a positivist model's capacity for adequately accounting for causal effects within a body of data, or from a historiographic scrutiny of archival material. There are many important differences between empiricist fact-finding, abstract causal social science, and historiographic forms of knowledge, not least between the general aspirations of rationalist social science and carefully contextualized historical analysis, but they all converge on presenting knowledge which is verifiable, representative, and could be replicated by others had they access to the same sources. As a result, knowledge is usually presented through the impersonal third person, which 'is used in order to imply an objective level that will connect the study to a scientific, knowledge-validating code' (Shapiro 1988: 66). Narrative and subjective forms of knowledge, by contrast, construct authority through the personal encounters and experiences the author has been privy to, and through writing the first-person 'I' explicitly into the text. Its knowledge is intimately tied to the subjective trajectories of the author, and 'anchors what is being expressed in the sensory experience, judgment, agency, or desires of the human subjects' (Pratt 1992: 76). Accidental encounters with roadside strangers, nameless but imbued with narrative and cultural significance, form the stable of many travelogues; memoirs will describe encounters long in the past and private conversations and personal ruminations that cannot be verified, reproduced, or said to be representative beyond the author's own claims. These are observations which do not constitute a proper data set, nor can they be the basis for causal, scientific analysis.

The importance of personal and subjective forms of knowledge is immediately present in the genres of travelogues and memoir, genres that are constituted as non-fiction in that they are supposedly about 'real travels' and 'real lives' rather than fictitious ones, but which nevertheless appropriate a series of literary means that bring to the fore the narrative and poetic aspects of writing as well as the 'writing of Self and Others.' At first the two genres might differ in that travel writing is more about 'writing the Others' and memoir more about 'writing the Self,' but there is significant overlap, particularly perhaps in the case of foreign policy. Travel writing is usually written in first person and employed to reflect on the development of the Self, and foreign policy memoir usually involve a fair amount of traveling, whether as a politician, diplomat, or member of the military. Most foreign policy literary non-fiction draws on elements of both travel writing and memoir, in writing personal as well as collective identities.

Treating travel writing and memoir as literary non-fiction highlights their ambiguous position between scientific knowledge and 'pure fiction.' The history of travel writing shows that travels and expeditions have been intimately connected with the birth of modern science, from Herodotus who 'knew personally all of the Mediterranean lands, especially Egypt, interviewed other travelers, checked sources, related anecdotes, included myths' to the botanists and colonial travel writers of the eighteenth and nineteenth centuries (Adams 1983: 46; Pratt 1992). Yet, this scientific genesis has been accompanied, since the modern travel narrative of Marco Polo's *Book of Marvels* from the early fourteenth century, by writings where supernatural beings and fictitious characters were mixed with the 'real' (Todorov 1995: 61–2). Travel writing as a genre thus balances between science on the one hand, and autobiography on the other (Todorov 1995: 68), between fact and fiction, although the fictitious often seeks to masquerade as fact (Holland and Huggan 1998: xi). Specific authors blend these two components in different ways, and particular epochs privilege certain mixtures, but it is the combination of empiricist claims to factual knowledge and the aesthetic pleasures of a narration of 'subjective inquiry,' of 'anecdote and analysis,' which is the knowledge form as well as the narrative attraction of this genre (Holland and Huggan 1998: 9–11). Even twentieth-century travel writing that presents itself as factual often employs elements of literary freedom, for instance in narrating several trips as though they were one, in changing the time and places of particular encounters, and in recounting dialogues word by word to an extent beyond any human mnemonic capacity.

Turning to memoir this might at first appear to be a factual genre where 'most readers still expect autobiographers to be making a good faith effort to tell the truth as they see it' (Bjorklund 1998: 27). Readers of political memoirs presume the account will be truthful insofar as the author is not consciously presenting false information, and relevant material is addressed even if it compromises the author. Readers expect to gain access to closed negotiations, private meetings, and secret discussions, or to get a 'raw and truthful' account of what war is really like 'in the field.' But not only is this a personalized— and subjective—account of events, it is also one where facts are interspersed with 'the author's candid opinions of others' (Bjorklund 1998: 31). It would, however, be impossible for any memoirist or travel writer to give a complete account of everything that has ever happened in one's life or on a travel, and literary non-fiction is therefore dependent not only on the author's truthfulness and memory but also on the author's selection of what is most important. Autobiographers, argues Bjorklund, 'select "events" and "facts" from their lives that fit into a comprehensible narrative' (Bjorklund 1998: 17), thereby making autobiography, in Philip Roth's words, 'probably the most manipulative of all literary forms' (quoted from Bjorklund 1998: 159). The key distinction between memoir on the one hand and history as an academic discipline on the other is thus not simply one of facts, but the personal selection of personal facts as the epistemological basis within memoir; the privilege of the anecdotal over the systematic; and the discursive construction of these facts within a modality of knowledge that is centered on the explicit invocation of the 'I.'[8]

Eakin argues that the importance of selection implies that a narrative structure needs to be employed (Eakin 1992: 193–4). This structure not only helps select events, it also narrates and constructs 'the I' of the autobiographer. Scholars working in the field of autobiography therefore distinguish analytically between 'the recollecting self' and 'the recollected self,' the 'one who writes' and the 'one being written' (Eakin 1992: 183). The construction of the Self inside memoir usually employs two narrative figures: *formative experiences* and *retrospection*. Looking back upon the life narrated, the author will single out certain moments and experiences as formative for the Self: points of realization or dramatic events that transform the author and his or her perception of destiny, identity, meaning, and purpose in life. A formative experience might be constructed as instantaneously transforming, but it might also be written as formative in hindsight; it might be employed at the beginning of a memoir to preface a crucial later development—Holbrooke for example opens his memoir with a youthful backpacking visit to Sarajevo—or it might be a moment of realization at the end of a narrative, as in Rebecca West's *Black Lamb and Grey Falcon*, which makes all previous encounters fall into place.[9] The formative experience is in both cases a narrative and structuring device, deployed by an author who is writing in the present; the author knows what the effects of an early experience is going to be, or how to write a narrative so that a later experience becomes a satisfying solution to the events preceding it. Formative experiences are, in other words, always narrated from a retrospective vantage point, even if the memoir is written in the present tense and in a chronological form (Eakin 1992: 179). Retrospection might in addition be explicitly employed as a narrative device when the author comments on earlier experiences, for instance indicating that 'had I known this at the time I would have acted differently' or 'this was the moment at which I began to realize that things might go really wrong.'

Employing formative experiences and retrospection, the writing of the Self usually seeks to conform to a set of (discursively constituted) qualities. Very generally, argues Bjorklund, is the wish 'to persuade readers that they possess desirable characteristics through either the content or, less obviously, through the construction of the narrative' (Bjorklund 1998: 21). What constitutes desirable characteristics is dependent upon the social and historical context of the author, but surveying the past 200 years of American autobiography, Bjorklund finds that six qualities stand out: modesty, honesty, an interesting life, a desire to appear well-educated, a sense of humor and irony, and showing 'commendable emotions such as love and compassion' (Bjorklund 1998: 22–37). These qualities are then employed in autobiographies of the nineteenth century in two proto-typical narratives of the Self: the dominant one of religious conversion and a competing one of self-development (Bjorklund 1998). Extrapolating these two models to a more general level, which is useful for our specific case of political memoirs, one can identify a *narrative of conversion*, where the Self undergoes a religious, spiritual, or cultural conversion from a fallen, barren, evil existence to a truer, better, deeper one; 'the oldest continuous tradition of autobiographical writing' argues Eakin (Eakin 1992: 78). The *narrative of self-development*, on the other hand, is one which often chronicles the rise of the successful self-made businessman. Here the narrative plot is not one of submitting the fallible Self to a higher, divine power; rather, in accordance with scientific and evolutionary theories, it is one of developing mental or moral qualities, importantly amongst them education and discipline (Bjorklund 1998: 66–88; Eakin 1992: 78). The Self of this narrative undergoes a development, and might experience what was labeled 'turning points,' but it does not experience the radical transformation of the 'converted Self' and the narrative is thus one of refinement or success (Bjorklund 1998: 77).[10] Looking specifically to the genre of foreign policy memoir, what is of interest is not only what new information memoir might uncover, but how it might be employed to constitute the Self and legitimize past foreign policies, thereby granting future legitimacy to particular constructions of identity and policies.[11] Or, alternatively, how a retrospective revision of the policy pursued is set within a narrative of conversion.

The narration of the Self within subjective forms of knowledge introduces an epistemological emphasis on personal encounters. It is through the traveling and memorializing Self that Others are encountered, both in their personal, individual identities and in their collective ones. *Personal encounters* are selected among a series of possibilities, and although often presented as anecdotal or coincidental they become emblematic for larger, general constructions of identity; as 'typical of Bosnian Serbs,' or of 'Turks' or 'Scandinavians.' A person is not simply encountered as a freestanding individual, but is situated and constructed inside a larger discourse of collective identities. Different narrative techniques might be employed to write forth this collective identity: an account of 'what Scandinavians are' might be presented early in the text and the 'Scandinavianess' of subsequent 'Scandinavians' assessed in accordance therewith, or the author might select particular elements and give them a paradigmatic status by repeatedly presenting encounters with, for instance, 'drunken Balkan men,' in effect establishing a collective drunken male Balkan identity.

The construction of personal encounters in literary non-fiction is always situated within a simultaneous construction of collective identity, but collective identity might also be an explicit epistemological concern produced through a *cultural hermeneutic*. The Self does not only encounter individuals, it also encounters a set of objects and habits which are articulated as indicative of a place or a people. Aspects singled out might include architecture, food, landscapes, literature, music, paintings, churches, interior design, and clothing; not as simple observations, but as expressions of political identities and cultures. Cultural artifacts and landscapes, for instance, are thus seen as representations of deeper identities. One can know a country through understanding its architecture, literary tradition, or food, and it is in turn through these artifacts and anthropomorphized landscapes that identity is being reproduced.

The epistemological investment in personal encounters and cultural hermeneutics creates an important difference between literary non-fiction and other forms of writing. But it should also be noted that subjective forms of personalized knowledge are often combined with other forms of knowledge in discussions of structural and historical factors, of philosophical principles and general political, cultural, and religious questions, perhaps even, theories of IR (Eakin 1992: 120). It is thus precisely in the intersection between the mobilization of traditional academic forms of epistemic authority—to know the history of a place, Clausewitz's theory of warfare, or the schisms within the Orthodox church—and the personal authority of lived, narrated presence that the commercial and political popularity of travel writing and memoir should be found. And as literary non-fiction tends to combine several forms of knowledge, there are also appropriations of subjective and narrative forms of knowledge within other genres. Journalism and travel writing collaborate frequently as magazines and newspapers are used as venues for articles to be published as book-length travelogues later. Field reporting might appropriate the personal encounter as an epistemological and narrative strategy, as in Michael Herr's groundbreaking impressionistic *Dispatches,* which chronicled the life of 'the grunts,' the everyday soldiers, during the Vietnam War (Herr 1977). Politicians frequently mobilize 'autobiographical speech,' for instance in accounting for their 'life story,' and hence their political righteousness and trustworthiness, for instance in President Bush's narrative of conversion to evangelical Christian, or in 2004 presidential candidate John Kerry's construction of his service during the Vietnam War as a formative experience (Hansen 2005). Politicians might also emphasize personal encounters with emblematic individuals that shaped their understanding of and policy toward a particular issue.[12]

In conclusion, it should be stressed that narrative and subjective forms of knowledge are not in and of themselves more conservative, progressive, or feminist than other forms of knowledge and writing (Stec 1997: 140). Subjective forms of knowledge can be used to destabilize established constructions of collective identity, but they might also be appropriated to reproduce collective narratives that discipline and distance the Other. They hold distinct possibilities and dangers when mobilized in a political context, as do all other forms of writing, but the key to analysis, as well as to political practice, is to understand their distinct form, authority, and attraction.

5 Research designs
Asking questions and choosing texts

At the heart of foreign policy research should be an engagement with politically pertinent issues, but 'reality' is always larger than the number of questions one can ask of it; to formulate a research project is therefore inevitably to make a series of choices. For poststructuralist discourse analysis, the central choices concern whether one should study official foreign policy discourse or expand the scope to include the political opposition, the media, and marginal discourses; whether one should examine the foreign policy discourse of one Self or of multiple Selves; whether one should select one particular moment or a longer historical development; whether one should study one event or issue or a multiplicity; and, finally, which material should be selected as the foundation for and object of analysis. Making these choices might sometimes appear as if produced by the case itself. If there is heated debate it would be reasonable to analyze competing discourses; if the media has propelled governmental discursive changes, it appears commonsensical to include both discourses; and if a country or an institution has undergone radical change, it would seem logical to trace this transformation through an analysis of the discourses before and after the historical turning point. But rarely, if ever, does a case present itself 'beyond any reasonable choice'; there will always be a process of selecting agents of discourse as well as the material to be drawn upon. Even official foreign policy discourse is articulated through a multitude of sources, ranging from official speeches, press statements, parliamentary debates, and interviews, and going beyond official discourse to the intertextual references made within it; the choices expand exponentially.

This chapter builds on the theoretical framework of the first four chapters and turns to the more concrete methodological issues involved in selecting research questions and building research designs. In short, it discusses how discourse analysis can be 'put to work.' The first section begins with a discussion of the research questions produced by the three intertextual models developed in chapter 4 and continues by combining these models with decisions along three substantive dimensions: first, whether to focus on one Self or multiple Selves; second, whether to make a study of a particular moment or analyze a longer historical development; and third, whether to examine one foreign policy event or compare foreign policy discourses across a larger number of events. The second section turns to the selection of textual material and argues for the inclusion of historical as well as contemporary texts—where the contemporary is defined as the time of one's study—and of key texts that constitute intertextual reference points, as well as general material that enables an identification of the most common discursive constructions. The third section links the first two by presenting the design and textual material adopted in the case study to be pursued in the second part of the book, the Western debate on Bosnia.

Developing research designs

Chapter 4 developed three intertextual models (Table 4.2) structured around official foreign policy discourse. The first model (model 1) had official discourse and the intertextual links made within it as its analytical focus; the second model (model 2) broadened the scope of analysis to include the wider media debate, oppositional political parties, and corporate groups; and the third model extended the analysis even further through studies of popular culture (model 3A) and marginal political discourses (model 3B). Taken as a whole, these intertextual models provide a structured view of different locations for political debate, different types of actors, and different forms of genre, and they produce two prominent sets of research questions. The first set concerns the type of links articulated in official foreign policy discourse and asks to what extent links to oppositional discourses and critical texts and authors are being made. This question seeks to determine the extent to which official discourse deems it necessary to counter critical discourses, as well as the responsiveness and political or media strategy of governments more broadly. The study of the links of official foreign policy discourse also implies a concern with the political articulation of texts from journalism, academic writing, popular culture, and literary non-fiction and thereby the way in which the authority and knowledge forms of other genres are mobilized by policy speech and writing.

The second set of research questions moves from the links established within official discourse to the choice of a particular intertextual model. The further the scope is broadened from model 1 to models 2, 3A, and 3B, the higher the likelihood that the analysis will be able to capture discourses that contest and challenge official foreign policy discourse. A study built on a model 1 research design would only be able to detect oppositional discourses insofar as these were explicitly responded to in official discourse, and this study would as a consequence be unable to fully assess the degree of stability official discourse enjoys within the wider political and public sphere. The choice of intertextual model therefore has consequences for what can be concluded about discursive stability: the more models included, the stronger the foundation for assessing the hegemony of official discourse.

The three intertextual models produce a set of important research questions and structure the choice of analytical focus, but they do not decide which substantial questions should be pursued or provide a full account of how concrete research designs should be established. To help produce a complete research design one needs, therefore, to couple the intertextual models with choices along three additional dimensions: first, whether one or multiple Selves are examined; second, whether one makes a study of one particular moment or a longer historical development; and third, whether the analysis is based on one event or multiple events. Methodologically, the intertextual models and the three additional dimensions form the basic structure of discourse analytical research design, as shown in Figure 5.1. This research design illustrates that discourse analysis entails a comparative dimension insofar as it studies the articulation of a foreign policy issue across a series of Selves, over time, or through a series of events. Critics of poststructuralism often assert that it lacks a comparative perspective, but the only non-comparative research project would in fact be one that takes a single Self and examines its articulation toward one event within official discourse only (Katzenstein *et al.* 1998: 676–7). There are situations where such non-comparative projects might be warranted, but most research designs would involve some element of comparison. It would, however, be difficult to imagine a research design that incorporated *all* intertextual models and studied a multitude of Selves through a large number of events located across a long historical span. Choices do, in short, always have to be made, and they have to be made for all four dimensions.

Going through the dimensions of Selves, temporal perspective, and events in more detail, the *choice of Selves*—or how many states, nations, or other foreign policy subjects one wishes to examine—can result in just one being selected, as in David Campbell's study of American security policy, or in Iver B. Neumann's analysis of Russian debates on Europe (Campbell 1992; Neumann 1996a). Expanding the number of Selves, one possibility is to construct a comparative research design around different Selves' responses to the same event or policy issue. European integration, for instance, can be subjected to a comparative study of national discourses on 'Europe' and European integration, or one might compare the responses to the war against Iraq in 2003 (Hansen and Wæver 2002; Jachtenfuchs, Diez and Jung 1998; Marcussen *et al.* 1999; Wæver 1990). The discourses of multiple Selves need not, however,

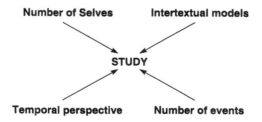

Figure 5.1 Research design for discourse analysis.

address issues set at the same moment in time. Studies of EU enlargement might, for instance, compare the discourses of prospective members of different rounds of enlargement to investigate whether the transformations within the EU from the 1980s onwards have had a discursive impact.

Choosing which Selves to compare can be a tricky problem. One possibility is to include all Selves, but this will often not be practically viable as discourse analysis requires linguistic as well as general knowledge of the Selves under study. Designing the comparative focus is, in this case, not so much a question of whether a selection is 'wrong' but whether it is politically and analytically pregnant. Political pregnancy is tied to questions of (discursively constituted) influence, a study of NATO's transformation would, for instance, be hard pressed to avoid an inclusion of American discourses, and analyses of the future of European integration would normally include France and Germany. The politically and analytically pregnant are further connected in that studies can select Selves based on what is the most common discourse or on what are the most radical ones. A study of, for example, the discourse on abortion within the EU might choose the states with the most frequently adopted policy closest to an aggregated average, or alternatively it might select the most radical cases of pro- and anti-abortion. The first analysis would show the most common constructions of national, religious, and gendered identities, whereas the latter would identify the discursive and political span within the EU.

The comparative study of Selves addressing the same foreign policy issue or event constitutes one 'multiple Self option.' Another possibility is a *discursive encounter*; rather than comparing Selves, the study contrasts the discourse of the Self with the Other's 'counter-construction' of Self and Other. Linking back to the discussion of state identity in chapter 3, the Self is constituted through the delineation of Others, and the Other can be articulated as superior, inferior, or equal. It might be constituted as threatening, but it might also be an ally, a stranger, or an underdeveloped subject in need of help. Most discourse analysis within and beyond International Relations (IR) has examined the construction of a national or a regional, usually Western or European, Self and thereby the discourse the Other has to address if engaging the West (Said 1978; Campbell 1992; Wolff 1994). These studies do not, however, address the discourses *of* the Other: how the Other constructs itself as well as the opposing 'West.' Studying the discourses of both Self and Other—which then becomes multiple Selves when viewed from the inside of the Other—is significant in that it provides knowledge of the discursive and political room of maneuver of foreign policy issues. For instance, knowing how the EU's construction of 'Turkey' and 'its' European identity is encountered by Turkish discourses on 'Europe,' 'Turkey,' and 'Islam' provides an understanding of how the EU's discourse might be received by Turkish politicians and media and hence its impact on the possible trajectory of EU enlargement (Oguzlu 2003; Rumelili 2004: 44–5; Buzan and Diez 1999; Neumann and Welsh 1991; Neumann 1999).

Discursive encounters inevitably evolve around constructions of inferiority and superiority and hence a particular distribution of discursive and political power. The encounter between the EU and Turkey, for example, does not take place between two equally powerful parties, not only is it the EU which defines the political and financial measures that Turkey needs to adopt, the EU also constitutes the discursive structures to which Turkey has to respond. This does not, however, imply that Turkey is without possibilities for maneuver. Turkish political leaders have appropriated the EU's 'political values' discourse, which constitutes membership as possible insofar as Turkey complies with the political and economic demands of the EU, and they have constructed Turkey as a bridge between Europe and the Middle East, as 'a major contribution to the dialogue and harmony of civilizations within the EU and beyond' (Republic of Turkey, Ministry of Foreign Affairs, 2004).

This discussion might suggest that studies should always incorporate discursive encounters, but this might not always be possible. The choice between a discursive encounter on the one hand and a single-Self or a comparative-Selves study on the other is influenced by pragmatic questions of linguistic abilities in that one usually needs to know the language of the Self as well as the encountered Other and questions of access to material documenting the discourse of the Other.[1] More substantially, a single-Self study can be the better choice when there is insufficient engagement to produce an encounter; when there is no clearly identifiable Other and hence no counter-discourse to study; or when there is such a discrepancy in the Self's ability to lay out discourse and policy for the Other that the Other's ability to respond is neutralized.

Multiple-Selves studies have a comparative complexity that might seem to position single-Self studies as less ambitious or interesting. This, however, is not necessarily the case as the Self is not as 'single' as the term might lead one to believe. Referring back to chapters 2 and 3, one should remember that the discourses of the Self are trying to stabilize the Self's identity, yet that this is an inherently unstable and often contested project produced and reproduced through foreign policy discourse. Taking the 'not so single Self' and locating it within the other three dimensions of the discourse analytical research design in Figure 5.1, the transformations and contestations within the Self become even more outstanding. Moving from official discourse to competing ones in intertextual models 2 and 3, one is likely to find re-articulations of the official national Self. The number and magnitude of these re-articulations usually increase when the Self is not a national one but a regional or civilizational one, such as 'the West' or 'the Balkans.' As will be argued in more detail in the second part of this book, the 'West' of the Western debate on Bosnia was articulated differently within European and American discourses, and differently by pro- and anti-interventionist positions. Situating the constitution of the Self within a longer historical perspective, previously important representations that have been marginalized by contemporary discourse are usually uncovered, further complicating the singularity of the Self.

Turning from the choice of Selves to the question of the *temporal perspective*, foreign policy can be studied as it addresses events either at one particular moment or through a longer historical analysis. Starting with the study of a single moment, the moment chosen will often have a striking character and be the subject of intense political concern. Much of poststructuralist discourse analysis has focused on policy discourses responding to such striking moments as conflicts and wars, but discourse analysis might also be applied to less politically conspicuous events, events which illustrate the daily practices of reproduction and transformation. Discourse analysis can, for instance, be used when studying how identities are 'implemented' and put into concrete negotiated practice, for instance by international institutions and local populations. Western male peacekeepers can, for example, be seen as situated within a set of discursive demands—formed by the armed forces, politicians and media discourse as well as by popular culture—that constructs 'military masculinity,' 'impartiality and protectionism,' as well as 'proper sexual conduct' (Higate and Henry 2004). The research question then becomes that of how the deployed peacekeepers construct and 'implement' their own discourse and how it is situated inside the web of the discursive demands confronting them. Single-moment studies might also gain in complexity by being coupled to expansions along the other dimensions of the research design: they might be analyzed through multiple Selves or within intertextual models 2 and 3.

Studies of more than one moment range from comparisons of a smaller number of events to extensive historical analysis that traces the evolution of identities across centuries. Studies of 'comparative moments' evolve around a smaller number of clearly defined points in time which are tied to particular foreign policy events. One might, for instance, compare American discourses on Iraq during the Gulf Wars in 1991 and 2003, where the moments selected have the Self (America) and the Other (Saddam Hussein's Iraq) as elements in common. A study of British discourses on Bosnia in 1992–5 and American discourses on Iraq in 2003–4 would by contrast lack a comparative connection, and while they would perhaps be valuable studies in and of themselves they would not generate additional new knowledge.

One might argue that wars such as the ones in the Gulf are, by their very nature, of such political importance that studying them requires no further justification. Danish EU referenda are, to take another example, of such importance to Danish foreign policy that the debates surrounding them constitute crucial moments worthy of comparison. But not all foreign policy events have a similarly striking political saliency—the selection of moments should therefore also be analytically driven by changes in important political structures or institutions. To take the example of the two Gulf wars; important 'variables'—the international structure and American security discourse—had changed between the early 1990s and the early twenty-first century. In 1990–1 the global structure was still in the aftermath of the collapse of the Soviet Union and American security discourse did not envision territorial threats to the United States. By 2003 the United States had emerged as the unrivalled unipolar state and the events of September 11, 2001 had brought terrorism and a deterritorialized subject attacking American soil into American security discourse. To take another example, one might study British discourses on Bosnia, Kosovo, and Iraq to investigate the potential impact of the change in government from Major to Blair between Bosnia and Kosovo, and the impact of September 11 from Kosovo to Iraq.

There are no fixed rules as to the number of moments that should be chosen in a comparative-moments study, but one should ensure that moments are not so far apart in time that making comparisons become difficult or holds little information. Comparing national discourses on Europe in 1850 and 2005 might provide an interesting snapshot, but it would leave the question of how discourses develop between 1850 and 2005 unanswered.

Research designs focused on comparative moments are valuable for generating knowledge of discursive changes—or repetition—across well defined moments, usually rather close in time. But research designs can also be based on longer historical analysis that traces the evolution of discourse and identity over a series of closely knit moments. While there is a comparative aspect to this research design in that it studies changes over time, it is less explicitly concerned with comparison itself and more with understanding the formation of identities. Campbell's study of the United States from the time of Columbus's 'discovery' onwards, across a multitude of periods, events, and issues, is a case in point (Campbell 1992). The analytical—and political—value of historical studies is that they provide detailed insights into the structures of present national and civilizational identities, hence show how deeply rooted particular aspects of current identities are. Historical studies have a further genealogical and critical potential in that they trace how previously important representations have been silenced and written out of the discourse of the present. The Balkans, for instance, is articulated as a radically different Other by post-1920 Western discourse, but a historical discourse analysis shows that it was constituted in much less radical terms by nineteenth and early twentieth century discourses. Historical genealogies effectively argue that present 'objective' identities are in fact contested, contestable, and hence politically decided.

As historical developments are analyzed over perhaps hundreds of years, one needs to select certain events and periods as more important than others. There is thus a comparative aspect to historical studies, although it is less emphasized than in analyses of comparative moments. Similarly, a study of one moment usually also involves some identification of 'sub-moments' or periods. The study of the Western Bosnia debate in the second part of this book is, for instance, defined as one moment, but analyzed through seven periods, characterized by heightened political, military, and media activity. There is, linking back to chapter 3, also a historical aspect to single-event and comparative-moments studies in that they should identify the basic discourse(s) of the foreign policy debate under study; and basic discourses, it was argued, are often centered around representations of identities with particular conceptual histories.

Turning to the final dimension, the *number of events*, the term 'event' is itself rather broadly defined. It includes a policy issue, for instance European integration after the Maastricht Treaty, as well as what would commonly be understood as an event, such as a war. One should note also that events will often be studied through analysis of 'events within events'; the Western debate on Bosnia for instance is defined as one event for the purpose of building a research design, but the analysis of this event will itself trace the discursive construction of events such as Srebrenica.

The issue of the number of events to be chosen has already been touched upon in the discussion of the temporal dimension: if one event is chosen, it is logically set within a temporal one-moment study. Shifting the focus to multiple event studies, these are constructed along two dimensions. First, events might be located at different times but related by issue, one might for instance compare the British responses to the wars in Bosnia in 1992–5 and Kosovo in 1998–9, two events related by their location in the former Yugoslavia and 'the Balkans.' Second, events might be related by time in a comparison of the discursive construction of multiple issues within the same period. For instance, Campbell's study of American post-Cold War security discourses identified two events within the same period: the war on drugs and the construction of Japan as a threat to US security. Or, to take another example, one might analyze the Danish construction of European integration and immigration to investigate the links between discourses on the 'European Other' and the 'immigrant Other,' thereby generating important knowledge of the discourses of national identity.[2] The analytical advantage of multiple events studies is that a comparison across time allows for an identification of patterns of transformations and reproduction while a comparison of issues located within the same temporal horizon generates knowledge of the discourses of the Self across politically pertinent areas.

The four dimensions of poststructuralist research design are summed up in Figure 5.2, which shows the key options within each dimension. It is through the combination of choices along all dimensions that a concrete study is produced and two examples of poststructuralist analysis should be briefly discussed to illustrate the model's application.

The formulation of one's research design will often begin with a choice on the 'number of Selves' or the 'number of events' dimension as these point most explicitly to substantial political questions. David Campbell's 1992 analysis of American foreign and security policies, *Writing Security* (Campbell 1992), defines itself as a single-Self study and as a study of official discourse; that is, an intertextual model 1 (Figure 5.3). These two choices are then combined with ambitious decisions along the temporal perspective as the historical foundation of present American foreign policy discourse is traced from Columbus into the early 1990s. The number of events incorporated is also impressive as the constitution of religious, racial, gendered, and political Others are traced across time and diverse Others are compared within the same period, making this a 'multiple events related by issue' as well as a 'multiple events related by time' study.

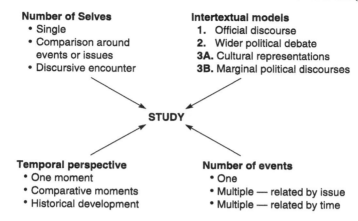

Figure 5.2 Elaborated research design for discourse analysis.

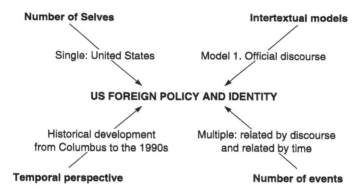

Figure 5.3 The research design for David Campbell's *Writing Security*.

It might seem as if poststructuralist discourse analysis is always generated by a focus on Selves or on a particular event, but research designs can also be built around political practices or concepts. Cynthia Weber's study of the importance of intervention for the principle of state sovereignty, *Simulating Sovereignty* (Weber 1995), is a case in point. Making intervention the primary object of analysis, Weber's research design is formulated as a 'multiple events related by issue' study, where 'issue' is the practice of intervention (Figure 5.4). Six events are chosen: two interventions by the Concert of Europe, two by the Wilson administration, and two by the United States/the Reagan–Bush administrations, and they are set within an intertextual model 1. In terms of the 'temporal perspective,' this implies a three-comparative-moments study. Turning to the 'number of Selves' dimension, this entails a comparison of three Selves— or two Selves if the American administrations are seen as instantiations of 'America'—engaging in events of a similar issue, namely intervention. There

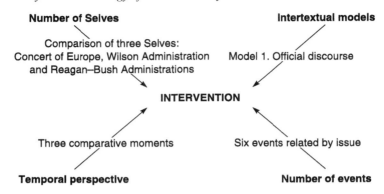

Figure 5.4 The research design for Cynthia Weber's *Simulating Sovereignty*.

is, however, a commonality between the three/two Selves: they are all relevant for understanding the articulation of the principle of intervention by Western sovereign territorial states from the early nineteenth century and until the end of the twentieth century. Hence one might argue that underpinning Weber's comparisons is a Western single Self that makes the issue-oriented comparison analytically and politically poignant.

Making textual selections: key texts and general material

Research design defines the focus of study through choices along the dimensions of intertextuality, Self, time, and events, but on what basis should the selection of concrete textual material for discourse analysis be made? In short, what should be read?

As a general methodological principle, material should be chosen in accordance with two sets of considerations. First, the majority of texts should be taken from the time under study, but historical material that traces the genealogy of the dominant representations should also be included. Second, the body of texts should include key texts that are frequently quoted and function as nodes within the intertextual web of debate, as well as a larger body of general material that provides the basis for a more quantitative identification of the dominant discourses. Combining these sets of textual considerations produces a 2 × 2 textual selection matrix (Table 5.1).

Before discussing the selection choices of each of the four categories of text, it should be stressed that poststructuralist discourse analysis gives epistemological and methodological priority to the study of primary texts; that is, for instance, presidential statements, speeches, and interviews in the case of official foreign policy; parliamentary debates in the case of the political debate; and reportage and editorials in the study of the wider media discourse. This does not, however, imply that what are normally referred to as secondary sources—discussions of primary texts and broader presentations of a foreign

Table 5.1 Textual selection matrix

| Material | Temporal location | |
	Time of study	Historical material
General material	Three criteria • Clear articulations • Widely read and attended to • Formal authority	• Conceptual histories
Key texts	• Primary reading of broader set of sources • Digital search engines	• Conceptual histories • Quoted in contemporary debates • Re-published

policy issue—have no place within poststructuralist discourse analysis. First, conceptual histories or genealogies will, when available, provide important knowledge of the sedimentation of current representations as well as a critical means through which the so-called objectivity and naturalness of these representations can be contested. Second, secondary material might itself become primary material, either by being key texts repeatedly quoted in official discourse or wider public debate or within intertextual model 3B as exemplars of academic discourse. This in turn implies that the status of a text can be primary in some cases and secondary in others. Samuel Huntington's *The Clash of Civilizations?*, for instance, is a secondary text as far as an analysis of the West's policy toward the Balkans is concerned, but its prominent intertextual status made it a primary text for debates on the 'clash of civilizations' (Huntington 1993, 1996). Third, and not least, the writing of good discourse analysis of primary texts requires knowledge of the case in question, and knowledge comes, in part, from reading standard works on the history, processes, events, and debates constituting a foreign policy phenomenon. A discourse analysis that lacks this epistemological foundation would in all likelihood make rather self-evident conclusions; for instance, that 'NATO constituted its Cold War identity through the Soviet Other.' Furthermore, this use of secondary sources does not prevent one from subjecting them to discourse analysis at a later stage of the research process.

The emphasis in discourse analysis on the importance of language makes knowledge of a particular language and its codes essential. Translations might sometimes be a worthy alternative to studies of original texts, but one should be conscious of the importance of this being a translation. Alternatively one should shift the focus of analysis to texts that were aimed at an international, usually English-speaking, audience; for instance, texts written for international institutions, foreign governments, and an English-language media.

Language is not, furthermore, only a linguistic capability, it is also a social epistemology composed by a set of linked codes. This implies that a particular concept, 'the people' for example, does not necessarily articulate the same political meaning in all contexts, and so without knowledge of a key political vocabulary and its conceptual history one would be unable to identify the precise contextualized constitution of meaning. One should as a consequence always be hesitant about making discourse analysis of places whose linguistic and epistemological codes one has no knowledge of, particularly perhaps in cases of authoritarian systems that restrict free speech and where official discursive codes have been vigorously enforced.

Returning to the selection of textual material, as outlined in Table 5.1, the historical material might be conceptual histories or critical genealogies, such as Said's *Orientalism*, which trace the dominant and marginal discourses of different periods through readings of key texts as well as a larger body of general material (Said 1978). These works should be read through the theoretical lens of chapter 3 to identify a smaller number of historical discourses based on competing articulations of spatial, temporal, and ethical identity as well as constitutions of the Other and its relationship to the Self. These historical discourses are of importance for defining the basic discourses within the primary study as well as for contesting the construction of history within contemporary debates.

Methodologically, it is problematic to rely upon secondary sources, but making a full primary analysis of the development of a concept or identity across perhaps several centuries will usually be too demanding. Reliability can, however, be improved in two ways. First, by including, when possible, more than one conceptual history. Second, by selecting the most significant key texts, subjecting them to a primary reading, and comparing this reading with the one of the conceptual history. This brings primary analysis into the study and provides an indication of the analytical angle and quality of the conceptual history being used. Looking specifically at historical key texts, these will usually be evident from historical works, but they will also often be widely quoted within contemporary debates and re-published.[3] The mobilization of historical key texts within contemporary debate makes it possible to identify texts that are not referred to by standard historical works, either because these works are more focused on literary sources and less on policy documents of relevance to foreign policy debates or because the history of texts and concepts is constantly rewritten. Some historical texts might therefore become subjects of concern and debate within the present, even though they had a less striking status when they were first published.

Moving from historical material to the material situated at the time of one's study, the identification of key texts is often rather easily made from a broader reading of policy speeches, media coverage, commentary, and, with some delay, academic analysis. Prominent and explicit cases of intertextuality can also be traced by using digital search engines, such as LexisNexis and ProQuest, which check the number of references to a given author within (mostly Western) newspapers, journals, and magazines.

The most difficult questions regarding textual selection appear in the case of contemporary general material—or, in a parallel situation, in the cases of historical discourses for which there are no conceptual histories—within intertextual models 1 and 2. Here, texts should be selected that meet the following three criteria: they are characterized by the clear articulation of identities and policies; they are widely read and attended to; and they have the formal authority to define a political position. The three criteria have different analytical and methodological strengths: the clear articulation makes it easier to apply the discourse analysis of chapters 2 and 3; the widely read criteria ensures that texts have a central role in defining dominant discourses; and the formal authority criteria signals the importance of status and power. Key texts by definition already meet the second requirement—to be widely read and attended to—and they might also meet one or both of the other two. The shift from key texts to general material implies, however, a shift from considering the status of *single* texts to *types* of texts.

Turning to the three criteria in more detail, some types of text, for example State of the Union addresses by American presidents, meet all three criteria: they set out clear constructions of identity and policy; they are widely attended to by other politicians, the public and by governments throughout the world; and they are articulated by a formal political authority. Other types of text might score high on one or two of the criteria, but low for the others. For instance, parliamentary debates on foreign policy issues might, as in the cases of British and American debates on Bosnia, articulate clear identities as well as policies and those speaking are elected politicians with the formal authority of a political party, an electoral platform, and a constituency, yet these debates may or may not be widely read and attended to. Another important example of policy texts that score high on one criteria and low on others is legislation and official authoritative text from international organizations, such as resolutions, statements, and communiqués. These texts score high on formal authority, and might in some cases also be highly attended to, as in the case of the EU's constitutional treaties, but they are often not very explicit in their articulation of identities as the documents are the products of negotiations between many actors and their (socially constructed) interests. The absence of explicit identity constructions within legal documents and resolutions means that these types of text should be coupled with texts more directly articulating identities to produce a 'full discourse,' for instance parliamentary debates, debates within international institutions, or statements by heads of states and prominent politicians on the meaning and importance of the adopted legislation and resolutions. Policy texts in general are usually characterized by an inverse relation between the degree of formality and the degree of sharpness with which identity is constructed: the more formal the text and its institutional location, the more implicit and circumscribed the constructions of identities are likely to be.[4] Although not a form of text typically included in poststructuralist discourse analysis, it is also possible to integrate one's own interviews (Der Derian 2001). One should, however, be conscious of the particular textual form of the interview—a text that is constituted through interaction and dialogue rather than monologue—and the role of the discourse analyst in producing it (Chouliaraki 2000).

For media texts within intertextual model 2, the third criterion, formal political authority, is by definition irrelevant, with the exception of government-controlled media. Examining media texts on their own, there is, however, important differences between the two dominant types of text, field reporting, and editorials, in that the latter constitute the authoritative political voice and are usually rather explicit as far as identity and policy are articulated. Field reporting from conflict zones abroad, or powerful capitals, is by contrast less explicit in articulating identities and policies (Fairclough 1995; Chouliaraki and Fairclough 1999). Media texts that are widely read and responded to might include a particular form of journalism, for instance battlefield reportage, or it might be based on a particular newsagent, for example a newspaper with national distribution, or a particular program, such as CBS's '60 Minutes' or ABC's 'Nightline.' In addition to reportage and editorials, the media might also provide space for opinion and commentary by a host of writers, including academics. Opinion texts are usually very explicit in terms of identity and policy, but as media outlets separate themselves from opinion pieces' stances, their formal authority is even less than that of field reports.

The exact composition of a body of general material should always be contextualized. Material that might score high in one national, regional, or local context might not necessarily do so in another, and institutions or media that were prominent at one point in time might recede from their central location as other forums and outlets become more important. The US Senate Foreign Relations Committee, for example, does not hold the power to influence public debate that it did in the late 1960s (Rosenbaum 2004). It is also advisable to include several types of text to insure that both texts with a high degree of formal authority and texts with explicit articulations of identity and policy are included. This further allows for a comparison between different types of texts, for instance whether the editorial line of a newspaper is reiterated by the field reports from the conflict covered or whether there are subtle differences in their articulation of the identities involved.

Table 5.2 summarizes the selection criteria that apply to common types of general material located at the time of a study.

Having decided which types of text should form the basis of study, the remaining question is how much should be read. This, clearly, is a difficult question for poststructuralist discourse analysis: it does not adopt a quantitative methodology and hence cannot retort to statistical significance as a measure for how many texts should be selected, but it does want to make claims to having identified and analyzed the dominant discourses within a particular intertextual model. It would be impossible to define a particular number of texts as a general standard; for one thing, there is a difference between an MA thesis, a PhD dissertation, a monograph, and an academic article, and hence what can reasonably be expected. More substantially, one

Table 5.2 Criteria of selection and common types of general material

	Criteria		
Type of text	*Clear articulations*	*Widely read and attended to*	*Formal authority*
Presidential addresses	Yes	Yes	Yes
Parliamentary debates	Yes	Variable	Yes
Legislation, communiqués	No	Variable	Yes
Field reporting	No	Variable	No
Editorials	Yes	Variable	No[a]
Opinions	Yes	Variable	No

Note
[a] Formal authority within media discourse.

might couple the selection of texts to a timeline that identifies periods of higher levels of political and media activity. Selecting material around these periods of heightened activity is more manageable and it provides a structure for an analysis of change, or, adversely, of how discourses reproduce themselves in the face of criticism, developments 'on the ground,' and new 'factual evidence.' Once a timeline and a decision on the relevant types of policy and media texts have been made, databases such as LexisNexis and ProQuest can be used to select media texts, and different types of policy texts can be accessed through the websites of most international institutions, governments, parliaments and presidential libraries.

The discussion of general material has evolved around intertextual models 1 and 2, but the same basic principles can be applied in studies of popular culture in model 3A. Here, key texts would have been widely read or watched and influenced a genre of popular culture, for instance as in the case of *Apocalypse Now* in the cinematic representation of the Vietnam War. General material should be selected with a particular view to commercial success as well as critical reception. Turning to model 3B, marginal discourses are by their very nature difficult to find, particularly when speaking of social movements and illicit organizations. In these cases, it will often be a matter of selecting any material that might be available. Academic analysis was also included in model 3B, and the focus would here be on those authors and approaches who have engaged most explicitly with a particular foreign policy issue.

The Western debate on Bosnia: a detailed research design

The detailed case study pursued in the second part of this book—the Western response to the war in Bosnia—was chosen, as described in chapter 1, because it allows for an illustration and further discussion of many of the key theoretical arguments of chapters 2 to 4: it was a war constituted through radical as well as non-radical representations of the Other; it showed the importance of historical discourses and temporal representations for contemporary debate; it brought forth transformations in the construction of identity as well as policy; it pointed to discursive and political splits within the Western Self; and it exemplified the importance of journalism, travel writing, and memoir for foreign policy debate.

Locating this study within the research design of Figure 5.2, the study took an event—the Bosnian war—and analyzed it from the outbreak of the war in early 1992 until its conclusion with the Dayton Accord in the fall of 1995. The longevity of the war and the complex developments within it implied, however, that a timeline was constructed of seven periods, each of which contained important events. Concerning the selection of Selves, the starting-point was the single Western Self, but the debate within the West also evolved around West European and American Selves, and the analysis therefore eventually had a 'multiple Selves' component. The analytical focus on the Western constructions of the war implied, however, that a study of the discursive encounters between the West and 'the Balkans' was not undertaken. These substantial choices were situated within a combination of intertextual models 1, 2, and 3B. American and British official discourses were studied, as were the discourses of the political opposition within the US Senate and the British House of Commons. The wider media debate, located within model 2, was covered through the incorporation of three American and three British newspapers, and academic discourses of model 3B included neorealism, classical realism, feminism, and poststructuralism. The intertextual links made within official foreign policy discourse as well as the wider media discourse identified key texts from journalism, popular academic writing, travel writing, and memoir. The research design for this study is summarized in Figure 5.5.

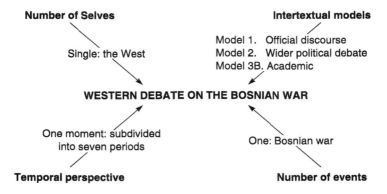

Figure 5.5 The research design for the Western debate on the Bosnian war.

To summarize the practical execution of the research project, the first element is the construction of the basic discourses (chapter 6), which are then used as structuring devices in chapters 7 to 9. Applying the methodological guidelines described in chapter 3 and reading the majority of the material discussed in chapters 7 to 9, two basic discourses are identified: a Balkan discourse and a Genocide discourse.[5] The Balkan discourse employed a spatial and temporal representation of the war as a product of 'the Balkans' and the political and literary history of this concept is therefore laid out. It is shown that the 1990s construction of 'the ancient hatreds Balkans' is in fact a particular twentieth century conception, and that this conception has been preceded by two other discourses, a Romantic discourse and a civilizational discourse, both of which constructed 'the Balkans' in much less inferior terms. The three historical discourses and the two contemporary basic discourses are read through their articulations of spatial, temporal, and ethical identity, their degree of radicalization of the Other, and their linkage of identity and policy, and it is argued that while there is a clear lineage between the Balkan discourse and the post-1920 Balkanization discourse, the links between the Genocide discourse and the Romantic and civilizational discourses are more complex and intersect with the temporal and ethical post-Holocaust discourse on 'genocide.' The textual material used for identifying the historical discourses consist of a mixture of secondary and primary sources. Maria Todorova's *Imagining the Balkans* and Vesna Goldsworthy's *Inventing Ruritania* provide excellent and complementary studies of the history of the concept of the Balkans, the former lays out the Balkanization discourse in particular, and the latter offers pertinent analysis of the Romantic construction of the nineteenth century (Todorova 1997; Goldsworthy 1998). These two works do not, however, take much notice of a third discourse, on the transformability of 'Balkan civilization,' which is traced through primary material, particularly the Carnegie Commission's *Report of the International Commission To Inquire into the Causes and Conduct of the Balkan Wars* (Carnegie Endowment for International Peace 1914), as well as other studies of the importance of Enlightenment civilizational thinking for Western engagements with the surrounding world.

Having established the basic discourses and the historical discourses from which contemporary debate has developed, chapter 7 is focused on official as well as oppositional discourse tracing events and transformations as well as the central points of contestations. The dominant political division ran between West European countries with peacekeepers on the ground on the one hand and the United States who did not provide ground troops on the other, and the chapter is therefore structured as a comparison between these two discourses. On the one hand, the dominant Western European discourse rearticulated the Balkan discourse to construct a 'humanitarian responsibility' but situated this within a construction of the war as one between three 'Balkan parties.' The Bush and Clinton administrations on the other hand shifted between a Balkan discourse and a re-articulation of the Genocide discourse that argued a more active Western intervention on behalf of the Bosnian government. Within the Western European group, the study devotes particular attention to the British discourse, as this country contributed the second largest number of troops and was the one most reluctant to break with the Balkan discourse and hence the country furthest apart from the political and discursive stance of the United States. Official discourses were formed in the face of domestic political opposition and media criticism and the analysis points to the most prominent instances of these criticisms.

Analytically, chapter 7 is located at the level of general discourse, and to ensure that the main political and media representations were identified a systematic reading of a larger body of policy and media texts was conducted. The wider policy texts included the main debates on Bosnia in the British House of Commons and the US Senate. In the British case, the governmental position was covered through a combination of these debates and the media texts below; the central politicians articulating official policy were the Secretaries of State for Defence and for Foreign and Commonwealth Affairs, while John Major, the Prime Minister, was making relatively few statements on Bosnia. The United States has a presidential political system and the debates in the Senate—where Democrats were offering fierce criticism of Clinton's policy—needed therefore to be coupled with analysis of George H. Bush's and Clinton's major statements on Bosnia. Since the first months of Clinton's presidency were significant for constituting the structure of the American position, all of his statements on Bosnia from February to June 1993 were read. For the remainder of the war, statements were examined at times when criticism of Clinton's policy was particularly fierce, usually in response to events in Bosnia. These statements were identified through the *Public Papers of the Presidents of the United States*.

The media was systematically studied through the selection of three American newspapers, *The New York Times*, *Washington Post*, *LA Times*, and three British ones, *The Times*, *The Guardian*, and *The Independent*. It would have been extremely time-consuming to read all articles on Bosnia for the full three and a half year period, and the textual selection was therefore based on the construction of the timeline that identified seven periods around which political and media activity was particularly fierce. For each period, twenty British and twenty American articles were selected that featured 'Bosnia' in the title, and the selection was centered on reportage with the inclusion of some opinion pieces, undertaken to include the longest articles available, and balance between field and home reporting. In addition to these 280 articles, the editorials on Bosnia for the full course of the war were included.[6]

Chapters 8 and 9 switch the analytical strategy from general policy and media discourse to situate particular key texts within this landscape. This implies simultaneously that links are made to the genres of memoir and travel writing and that more marginal discourses are brought in.[7] The two chapters are furthermore organized to pursue variations on the two basic discourses, the Balkan discourse and the Genocide discourse. This mode of organization has the advantage of being focused on the political differences within the debate, but it should be noted that other organizational strategies might have been chosen: the analysis could have been structured around genre, around the division between Europe and the United States, or chronologically around the seven periods of the timeline.

Chapter 8 traces the Balkan discourse, and begins with a reading of Robert D. Kaplan's *Balkan Ghosts*, a travelogue and a key text within the American debate, and it analyzes how and why this book was read as having particular policy implications. The chapter then turns to Kaplan's primary intertextual reference, Rebecca West's *Black Lamb and Grey Falcon*, a book which itself is widely cited within the 1990s debate as supporting a pro-Serbian policy. The third part of the chapter pursues an important conceptual intertextual link within the Bosnia debate, namely the one of 'civilizations,' which is articulated prominently by Robert D. Kaplan and Rebecca West, and also by Samuel Huntington in his 'clash of civilizations' thesis, another key text. The influential classical realist George F. Kennan, who wrote a much-read introduction to the 1993 re-publication of the Carnegie Commission's *Report of the International Commission To Inquire into the Causes and Conduct of the Balkan Wars*, also articulated the concept of 'civilization' to important political effects (Kennan 1993). Finally, the realist–civilizational–Balkan discourse thematic of Huntington and Kennan is contrasted with a central discourse within IR, the neo-realist writings of Mearsheimer, Posen, and van Evera.

Chapter 9 turns from the Balkan discourse and its modifications and variations to the criticism thereof within the Genocide discourse. The chapter begins with a thorough analysis of the first key text within this discourse, Roy Gutman's investigative reporting from 1992 collected in *A Witness to Genocide* (Gutman 1993). The next section turns to three main variations on the Genocide discourse, which illustrate the modification of three different elements of the basic discourse's identity construction: the 'European responsibility for Genocide' splits 'the West' into radically different 'European' and 'American' parts; the Balkanizing Serbia discourse radicalizes the construction of Serbia; and the Gendering Genocide discourse shifts the identity construction from a national to a gendered optic through an articulation of a 'Balkan patriarchy.' These discourses were articulated within American media and academic circles and were thus located in part within the wider media debate of model 2 and in part as marginal discourses within model 3B. Continuing the discussion of academic analysis, David Campbell's poststructuralist reading of the Western response to the Bosnian war is read through the lens of the basic discourses. The last part of the chapter turns to the memoirs, and key texts, of the two most prominent negotiators, David Owen and Richard Holbrooke, and their responses to the Genocide discourse criticism fielded against them.

Table 5.3 Textual material for analysis of the Western debate on the Bosnian war

| | Temporal location | |
Material	Time of study	Historical material
General	American presidential statements US Senate debates British House of Commons debates 280 articles from six British and US newspapers All editorials from 1992 to 1995 with Bosnia in the title Academic analysis: neorealism, classical realism, feminism, and poststructuralism	Conceptual histories: Goldsworthy and Todorova Civilizational discourse
Key texts	Robert D. Kaplan: *Balkan Ghosts* Samuel Huntington: *Clash of Civilizations* Roy Gutman: *Witness to Genocide* David Owen: *Balkan Odyssey* Richard Holbrooke: *To End a War*	Rebecca West: *Black Lamb and Grey Falcon* Carnegie Endowment: *Report of the International Commission* (1914)

Table 5.3 summarizes the textual material used for the analysis of the Western debate on the Bosnian war in terms of the textual selection matrix categories identified in Table 5.1.

Part II

A discourse analysis of the Western debate on the Bosnian war

6 The basic discourses in the Western debate over Bosnia

The first part of the analysis of the Western debate on the Bosnian war consists of the construction of the debate's basic discourses. Basic discourses provide, as argued in chapter 3, an analytical perspective that facilitates a structured analysis of how discourses are formed and engage each other within a foreign policy debate. They identify the main convectors of discussion by asking how competing discourses articulate the relationship between Self and Other through the deployment of spatial, temporal, and ethical identities and how they couple identity and policy. Basic discourses are based on readings of a large number of texts, preferably spanning a wide set of genres, including policy speeches and interviews, journalistic reporting and editorials, academic analysis, and literary non-fiction, to ensure that the basic discourses identified have a dispersion throughout the wider debate. But one should keep in mind, as argued in chapter 3, that basic discourses are *analytical* constructions and that texts referred to when composing a basic discourse might not be in complete concordance with the ideal-type basic discourse. For instance, a text might be used as an example of the articulation of a basic discourse's construction of 'the West' but may also make a particular construction of 'America' which further complicates 'the West' into a discursive variation. This underlines that basic discourses are located at a fairly general level of debate and that the detailed readings of discursive variations, for instance of divisions within 'the West,' constitutes the next step of the analysis; this is the subject of later chapters.

Basic discourses offer 'ideal-type' constructions of the spatial, temporal, and ethical dimensions of identity discussed in chapter 3, and their articulation of degrees of Otherness and difference. Chapter 3 also suggested that basic discourses are identified around explicit articulations of key representations of identity, and constructed using the following methodological criteria: basic discourses should construct radically different Others and Selves, both as concerns the degree of Otherness and the spatial, temporal, and ethical articulations of identity; they should argue very different policies to be pursued; at least one might be argued as an initial position, while the other(s) will be argued in response to and in criticism of this position; and past constructions of key representations of identity are likely to have an influence on how present constructions are articulated, and these earlier constructions might be identified through a structured reading of relevant conceptual histories.

Drawing on these guidelines, the first discovery in the debate on Bosnia was the frequent spatial construction of the war as 'Balkan,' as indicated for instance by the large number of books published with 'Balkan' titles. *Balkan Ghosts* pointed to the return of 'the Balkans' ancient passions and intractable hatreds' (Kaplan 1993a: back of the cover on the 1994 Vintage edition), *Balkan Odyssey* referred to the long and exhausting path trodden by the Bosnian parties as well as by David Owen himself (Owen 1995), *Balkan Babel* alluded to the futile attempt to build a tower of Babel embracing the various national and/or ethnic groups of Yugoslavia and their tongues (Ramet 1996), and *Balkan Tragedy* underlined loss and devastation (Woodward 1995). There were books which situated the war in the context of the previous Balkan wars by identifying the current one as the third, as in *The Fall of Yugoslavia: The Third Balkan War* (Glenny 1996 [1992]), or the first and the second Balkan wars as 'the other' Balkan wars, as in the reprinting of a Carnegie Endowment Inquiry from 1914 as *The Other Balkan Wars* (Carnegie Endowment for International Peace 1993). 'The Balkans' was used to locate the war in relation to Europe in *Europe's Backyard War: The War in the Balkans* (Almond 1994) and as a partly deconstructive device turned against the West, as in *The Balkanization of the West: The Confluence of Postmodernism and Postcommunism* (Mestrovic 1994) and *Genocide After Emotion: The Postemotional Balkan War* (Mestrovic 1996).

Out of this spatial demarcation grew one basic discourse, the Balkan discourse, which constructed 'the Balkans' as violent, tribal, hating, and backward, and as having embodied this Otherness for hundreds if not thousands of years. This confluence of spatial and temporal identity implied that 'the Balkans' would be unable to break these patterns and progress toward more civilized and Western forms of behavior, and the West had therefore neither the practical capacity nor any moral responsibility for intervening and bringing the war to a halt.

However, as reports of Bosnian Serbian atrocities reached the Western media, a counter discourse began to form. This basic discourse centered on the construction of the war as 'genocide,' thereby challenging the spatial, temporal, and ethical dimensions of the Balkan discourse and its 'policy of inaction.' Where the Balkan discourse read temporality and ethicality through a spatial location, the Genocide discourse read identity through the absolute ethical responsibility invoked by the articulation of 'genocide' and it rearticulated the Balkan discourse's construction of a uniform 'Balkan' space of 'three factions' by separating a multicultural and democratic 'Bosnian victim' from a 'Serbian aggressor.'

The concept and identity of 'the Balkans' is thus important for both basic discourses, for the Balkan discourse it is the central spatial and temporal reference through which the war is constructed, and for the Genocide discourse it is this construction which has to be battled. It is also a representation with a conceptual history that goes beyond its mobilization within the debates of the early 1990s, although its history is both briefer and more multi-faceted than its contemporary usage indicates. There is a strong link between the current construction of 'the Balkans' as violent, barbaric, and backward to the discourse on 'Balkanization' which developed after World War I, but two other historical discourses which break with this negative construction did in fact precede it: one which read 'the Balkans' through a Romantic construction of the struggling Slavs of the Ottoman Empire and one which constructed 'the Balkans' as a 'young client of civilization,' with the capacity for change and for whom the West held a responsibility. The history of the concept of 'the Balkans' and the history implied *in* the concept are, in other words, two different and non-converging phenomena.

This chapter begins with the conceptual history of 'the Balkans,' drawing out three dominant nineteenth and early twentieth century constructions which articulated very different spatial, temporal, and ethical identities. These constructions point, incidentally, to Self–Other constellations of relevance beyond the Bosnian/Balkan case in that they are instantiations of more widespread Western discourses of Romanticism and 'the exotic'; of civilization and development; and of radical Othering, distance, and fear. Bringing out the historical constructions of 'the Balkans' has critical importance for showing that the concept in question is not as solid and its attribution of identities not nearly as inevitable as the current Balkan discourse claims. It shows that this articulation is not an innocent and informative representation of 'Balkan history' but a production and reproduction of a particular construction of identity which should be challenged through counter-readings of older material and discourses. After these critical, historical readings, the chapter returns to the two basic discourses and analyzes in more detail how these discourses articulate spatial, temporal, and ethical identity, how they construct difference or Otherness, how they link identity and policy, and how they draw upon and rearticulate the conceptual histories of the first part of the chapter.

'The Balkans' of the nineteenth and early twentieth centuries

'The Balkans' started out as referring to the mountain chain running across Bulgaria from east to west, apparently chosen by the German geographer August Zeune in 1808 because it was common practice to name a region after a prominent mountain range (Todorova 1997: 25). The word 'balkan' had entered the peninsula with the Ottoman Turks, who used it to denote 'mountain,' linking it to specific locations by adding names or adjectives, and the area south of the Bulgarian mountains identified by Zeune had already been the subject of a variety of names. Some alluded to the medieval or classical heritage of particular states or regions, such as the 'Hellenic peninsula' or the 'Byzantine peninsula'; some applied ethnic markers, as in 'Greek peninsula' or 'South-Slavic peninsula'; to the Ottomans it was 'Rumeli,' meaning 'land of the Romans'; and, most common until the Congress of Berlin in 1878 were names which pointed to the Turkish/Ottoman presence, as in 'European Turkey,' 'Turkey in Europe,' 'European Ottoman Empire,' and the 'European Levant' (Todorova 1997: 26–7). Gradually gaining the terminological upper hand during the latter part of the nineteenth century, it was not until the turn of the twentieth century, right before the 'Balkan' wars in 1912 and 1913, that 'the Balkans' became the standard concept (Todorova 1997: 27; Todorova: 1994: 462–4). Although 'the Balkans' eventually became the common designation, it is not surprising that names like 'Turkey in Europe,' pointing to the Ottoman influence, were more common until late in the nineteenth century.[1] These names described not only the geopolitical reality—that Bulgaria, Serbia, Montenegro, and Albania were part of the Ottoman Empire but not seen as belonging to Turkey proper—but also the symbolic location of these lands as situated somewhere between 'Europe' and 'the Orient.'[2] There was a difference between 'Turkey' and the Balkan peninsula, in that the latter was seen as 'in Europe' and Turkey not, but the Turkish imprint also meant that the culture and identity of the South Slavs, Greeks, and Romanians were not constructed as self-evidently 'European.'

When the concept of 'the Balkans' was initially coined, it referred to an Ottoman-influenced area smaller than the current twentieth century usage, and it reflected the political division between the Ottoman and the Habsburg empires. The decay of the former led to the recognition of Serbia, Montenegro, and Bulgaria at the Congress of Berlin in 1878, and the pan-Slavic Illyrian movement inside the Austrian–Hungarian Empire, which began in Croatia but found a sound following in Slovenia as well, gained force from the 1830s onwards (Banac 1984: 75–9; Rogel 1994; Bennett 1995: 22–8). As World War I dealt its death blow to the Habsburg Empire, and Yugoslavia was formed in its aftermath, 'the Balkans' came to identify the whole of the peninsula, including usually Yugoslavia, Bulgaria, Romania, Greece, and, sometimes, Hungary. The boundaries, though, were still fuzzy, as Traian Stoianovich, student of Ferdinand Braudel and author of *A Study in Balkan Civilization*, dryly stated 'The subjects of our study are the *Balkans* and *civilization*. Both require definition. The term "Balkans" lacks precision' (Stoianovich 1967: 3).[3]

The location of 'the Balkans' between 'Europe' and 'the Orient' has led to a certain ambiguity or flexibility in its identity, an ambiguity which has been differently resolved at different times and by competing discourses. Metaphorically, this has lead to the construction of 'the Balkans' by the countries in its midst, as a borderline, a gate, a bridge, a crossroad, and a frontier (Goldsworthy 1998: 7; Bakic-Hayden and Hayden 1992; Hansen 1996). For the West, this liminal identity has been the subject of a set of intersecting concerns and debates since the nineteenth century. The process of ascribing meaning to the Balkans was one which clearly highlighted the questions of identity and history, not least the importance of religion and the history of classical Greece, and which also involved the confrontations between arguments based on geopolitical concerns for European stability and those based on the suppressed Christian subjects and the Western responsibility for their plight. These discourses all ascribed identity to the spatial construction of 'the Balkans,' but they provided different constructions of its temporal identity, its degree of difference from 'the West' and 'Europe,' its attractions and dangers, as well as the ethical responsibility 'the West' held for its past, present, and future.

'Byronic Balkan': romanticism and the nineteenth century

The Western construction of 'the Balkans' was until the end of the nineteenth century largely built around texts on specific countries rather than on the entire Balkan region. Greece in particular was brought to the attention of the Western world by Byron's romantic writings, and they were later reinforced by 'the vogue of philhellenism that swept over Europe in the 1820s' (Todorova 1997: 62; see also Goldsworthy 1998: 15). Goldsworthy argues that Byron's 'Balkan,' which drew on more general traits within European Romanticism, provided 'the template which subsequent generations of writers felt obliged to follow or dispute' (Goldsworthy 1998: 14). It was, one might say, the first dominant discourse through which rearticulations and attacks needed to be made.

This 'Byronic Balkan' situated 'the Balkans' between East and West, as 'simultaneously familiar and distant,' as a place influenced by the rule of the Ottomans, yet with a distinct identity owing to its classical Hellenic past (Goldsworthy 1998: 19). The relationship between classical past and contemporary identity was far from simple: Byron was both 'seduced by and uneasy with his Oriental subject,' Greece had adopted many traits of Oriental culture which made it attractive yet conjured up the danger that classical Hellas and the heart of European civilization would be irredeemably lost to the East (Goldsworthy 1998: 20; Hertzfeld 1987). This temporal split in Greek/Balkan identity between present Orientalism and past civilizational glory could be articulated in two directions, depending on how far on the route to Orientalization Greece was deemed to have slid. Byron opted for a pro-Balkan and pro-redemption discourse, whereas much philhellenism of the nineteenth century were to become too disappointed with modern Greece to continue its political support (Todorova 1997: 62).

But the importance of past civilization was not limited to a consideration of classical Hellas and contemporary Greece, but extended to the question of the Byzantine Empire, which had preceded the Ottomans. The Byzantine Empire, centered in Constantinople, was the successor to the Eastern part of the Roman Empire, Greek-speaking, and based on a missionary belief in Orthodox Christianity. The Balkan Slavs converted to Orthodox Christianity, but the relationship between Constantinople and the Balkan Slavs was sometimes tenuous, being as they were not at the center of the empire, and they occasionally both wanted to and succeeded in gaining control over 'their' lands (Watson 1992: 111). For the Byronic Balkan discourse, the Byzantine heritage added another liminal identity component to the Balkan mix: dominated by the Greek and home of Orthodox Christianity, the Byzantine was different from Western and Catholic Europe, but importantly still closer to the West than the Islamic Ottomans. For the Byronic Balkan discourse, as well as for a series of later writers, the (largely) Christian identity of the Balkans was essential not only in constructing similarity between Europe and 'the Balkans' but also in representing 'the Balkans' as 'the guardians at the gate,' or later as 'liberators' (Goldsworthy 1998: 8). They had protected 'Europe' from the wider expansion of 'the Turks,' kept Christianity alive during the Ottoman occupation, and managed to expel the Turks from the region in the latter part of the nineteenth century.[4]

These 'liberators' and 'protectors' were furthermore read through a Romanticist optic, which intertwined landscapes and people in producing an 'essential Balkans' of the mountains and their 'rural,' 'tribal,' and 'unpolluted' people. To constitute 'the rural' as the privileged essence of 'the people' was, as Goldsworthy points out, in line with the wider European Romanticist tradition, and 'the mountain peoples of the Balkans, "the martial races," akin to their fellow highlanders in Scotland or British India, seemed more attractive as a poetic subject than the more prosperous inhabitants of the lowlands who ineptly aped the West' (Goldsworthy 1998: 23). The Romantic vocabulary emphasized the heroic, wild, proud, and brave—and occasionally also what was seen as the mysticism of the Orthodox church—and the poetic blood letting of writers such as Shelley and Tennyson was in celebration of the independent, irrepressible, and passionate Balkan peoples fighting the oppression of the Turks (Goldsworthy 1998: 24–5 and 34–5). The construction of 'passion' as a central—and attractive—element of Balkan identity was later underlined by Stoianovich, who claimed that the Balkan propensity for violence was vastly overrated, but that the Balkan peoples were highly emotional and characterized by 'impulsiveness and especially the ease with which they can pass from one emotion to its opposite even in our own time. Joy gives way to tears and lamentations, the tearing of hair, and the beating of breasts, and tears and lamentations yield to rejoicing' (Stoianovich 1967: 59–60).

According to the Romantic discourse, 'the Balkans' should not try to emulate the West. It was the individual particularity of nations which should be protected and the extreme and exotic which made the Other attractive, not its proto-Westernness (Allcock 1991: 189). 'The Balkans' was to be liberated so its people could live freely in accordance with their individual, honorable identities, not so they could become like the West. Yet, while this discourse constructed 'the Balkans' in positive and attractive terms, it was nevertheless a subject constructed through the discourse of the West. 'The Balkans' did not, in other words, have the right to define 'its' identity or to embark on a route of Westernizing transformation, at least not without disturbing its privileged Romantic position.

Byron famously lost his life in the Greek war for independence and the question of whether Europe was to take political and military responsibility for the Balkans came to the fore again later in the century, when William E. Gladstone, the opposition leader and former Prime Minister, argued that Britain had an obligation to come to the assistance of Bulgaria against Turkey. His *Bulgarian Horrors and the Question of the East*, published in 1876, sold 200,000 copies within less than a month and sparked a major debate with Benjamin Disraeli, the Prime Minister, who 'saw earlier uprisings of Greeks and Albanians against the Turks as "a provincial, rather miserable throwback to barbarism," and tended to dismiss the Bulgarian atrocities as grossly exaggerated' (Goldsworthy 1998: 29). The Gladstone–Disraeli dispute over the Balkans was significant not only in bringing forth Gladstone's persecuted Christian Bulgarians versus Disraeli's 'barbaric' Balkan, but in linking constructions of identity with European responsibility and foreign policy.[5]

The 'Byronic Balkan' put 'the Balkans' on the European map, but this conceptualization was not uncontested, in particular as the nineteenth century came to a close. The fear of Balkan instability and its potential for drawing the rest of Europe into a larger war was looming on the horizon. 'Byronic Balkan' is important, however, not because it has been transferred timelessly through history, but because it constituted the basic representation from which other constructions would develop and argue. It thematized the difference between 'Europe' and 'Balkan,' a distinct, brave, heroic, fighting Balkan, the importance of past civilizations and empires, and the question of Western responsibility, whether for individual countries, or, later on, the stability of the region as a whole.

Balkan Enlightenment: 'young clients of civilization'

The Romanticist discourse was not, however, the only discourse of the late nineteenth and early twentieth century. It was accompanied by a parallel discourse centered on the progressive development of non-European civilizations, including the one in the Balkans. This discourse was less dominant in travel writing and literary works, but played an important role in more political-oriented documents, such as the report by the Carnegie Commission, *Report of the International Commission To Inquire into the Causes and Conduct of the Balkan Wars*, published in 1914.[6] It was, like the Romantic discourse, part of a larger tradition of European political thought, in this case eighteenth and nineteenth century Enlightenment thinking centered on the concept of civilization (Wolff 1994). This concept was first used in its modern form in the latter part of the eighteenth century and it was closely linked to the growing belief in the rational and experimental sciences which emphasized the idea and method of factual classification at all conceivable levels, including the one of human societies.[7] However, as Lucien Febvre notes, these facts did not present themselves unmediated to the observer but were classified according to 'an absolute concept of a single, coherent, human civilization' and not a 'relative concept of highly particularised and sharply individualised ethnic or historical civilizations' (Febvre 1930: 232).[8] The belief in universal civilization made people 'confident that such civilization, in which we participate, which we propagate, benefit from and popularise, bestows on us all a certain value, prestige, and dignity' and it was informed by a utopian, but nevertheless Western-based, standard as that which the world should and could progress toward (Febvre 1930: 220). Surely, not all cultures or peoples had reached the standard of civilization? Indeed, Europeans were normally the only ones who embodied or came close to the universal ideal, but non-Europeans had the capacity for transformation. They might be backward, but this was merely because of a temporal delay, not because they held fundamentally different ontological identities that blocked them from inclusion in a universal civilizational project. This in turn implied a Western responsibility for helping— sometimes forcing—other civilizations onto the path of the civilized world, as this was in their own best interest (Todorov 1992).

The idea of one universal civilization was challenged between 1780 and 1830, when a relativization was coined through the term 'state of civilization' which then developed into the plural 'civilizations.' Amongst the first to argue the pluralist position were Vico and Herder (the latter a key founder of German national Romanticism) who held that civilizations were distinct and that they could only be understood on their own terms. Because each civilization's values were thus equally objective and sensible, they could not be arranged in a spatial or temporal hierarchy with Western civilization at the top, nor should one attempt to force the merger of different civilizations (Berlin 1990: 79).

The history of the concept of civilization has continued to evolve as a debate between a universal tradition and a pluralist one and their different political and normative beliefs. The Carnegie Commission, dispatched by the recently founded Carnegie Endowment to investigate the atrocities of the first and second Balkan wars, located themselves within the universalistic perspective of 'the civilised world.'[9] Their understanding was of a world composed of several civilizations, but only one—the European and American— was truly civilized, and their report is a textbook example of an optimistic Enlightenment construction of civilizational politics, where civilization is seen as a state of moral, economic, and political culture, accessible to other non-civilized peoples, in this case the Balkans. Compared with the civilized world, Balkan people had not yet 'obtained the stability of character found in older civilizations' nor the 'synthesis of moral and social forces embodied in laws and institutions giving stability of character, forming public sentiment, and making for security' (Carnegie Endowment for International Peace 1914: 267, 271). Yet this inferiority and backwardness stemmed not from any essential flaws or radically different identity but from their long separation from Europe: 'No one knew anything of them, no one said anything about them' wrote de Constant, the chairman of the Commission. He continued: 'These peoples, mingled in an inextricable confusion of languages and religions, of antagonistic race and nationality ... are not less good or less gifted than other people in Europe and America. Those who seem the worst among them have simply lived longer in slavery or destitution. They are martyrs rather than culprits' (de Constant 1914: 3). As in Byronic Romanticism, there was thus moral support for the plight of the Christian Slavs living 'under the Turkish yoke' who had been 'martyrs' in the protection of Europe.

In spite of its general commitment to the abolition of war, the Carnegie Commission was therefore in support of the first Balkan war as this was a war of independence, a 'supreme protest against violence, and generally the protest of the weak against the strong,' and 'for this reason it was glorious and popular throughout the civilized world' (de Constant 1914: 4). The second Balkan war, on the other hand, was a sad and deplorable one as it took place between the former Balkan allies, with Bulgaria on the one side and Greece and Serbia on the other. Surveying the battlefields of the wars in 1912 and 1913, the Commission chronicled the brutality of warfare through 400 intensely detailed pages, but they did not construct these findings as evidence of any particular emotional propensity for violence that set the Balkans aside from the West. Any traces of Ottoman influence were amenable to the forces of transcendence and progress, and there was no 'essential Balkan identity' but rather a temporarily blocked and impoverished subject in need of guidance, education, and support. It was argued by the Russian Paul Milioukov, the main architect behind the report, that the Treaty of Berlin had disturbed 'the way of the normal development of the highly national conception of an alliance between the Balkan peoples, has turned it aside from its true aim, that of preparing the way for federation; and by informing it with an alien egoism and mania have delayed its development and brought it prematurely to an end' (Carnegie Endowment for International Peace 1914: 40). Granted that the ties between Bulgaria and Russia had been close, and Milioukov's call for a Balkan alliance might echo larger Russian geopolitical aspirations, one should nevertheless note the construction of Balkan warfare not as a product of essential Balkan identities but as constituted through a mixture of great power interventions and the poverty and oppression inflicted by the Ottoman Empire. Yet, writing after the end of the second Balkan war and with little sense of the pending World War I, the Commission was more concerned with post-war reconstruction than questions of intervention and it suggested a policy of economic and political transformation through free-trade liberalism, which was believed to generate societal wealth and prevent violent conflicts. It also encouraged civilizing the individual through personal hygiene and the orderliness of public space.[10]

The spread of civilization to the Balkans would transform it in accordance with the political and economic standards of Western modernity, and with this belief in the superiority of the West came a firm insistence on the responsibility of Europe:

> these unhappy Balkan States have been up to the present, the victims of
> European division much more than of their own faults. If Europe had sin-
> cerely wished to help them in the past thirty years, she would have given

them what makes the life in a country, that is, railways, tramways, roads, telegraphs and telephones, and in addition, schools. Once these fertile countries were linked to the rest of Europe, and connected like the rest of Europe, they would of themselves become peaceful by means of commerce and trade and industry, enriching themselves in spite of their inextricable divisions. Europe has chosen to make them ruined belligerents, rather than *young clients of civilization*, but it is not yet too late to repair this long error.

(de Constant 1914: 8; emphasis added)

But de Constant found serious faults in Europe's willingness to take on her civilizing mission. 'Europe Divided and her Demoralizing Action in the Balkans' would, in his view, have been the most proper title of the report, although, he added: 'taking it all round this might have been unjust' (de Constant 1914: 19).

The civilizational and the Romantic discourse have points of divergence as well as convergence. The former constructs the Balkans as underdeveloped yet with the capacity to transform in the image of Western/universal civilization, while the latter celebrates the vitality and heroism of the 'unpolluted' Balkan nations that should not be destroyed by Westernization. Both, however, construct the time of the Ottoman Empire as a brave struggle for independence, and both discourses articulate a Western responsibility for assisting 'the Balkans,' whether on its road to civilizational development or in a liberation of the Romantic Slavic peoples.[11] These complex constructions of difference, attraction, and responsibility were, however, absorbed into a discourse of 'Balkanization' after World War I, a discourse which radicalized the difference between 'the Balkans' and 'the West,' constituted it as an alien and dangerous Other, and absolved 'the West' of any moral or geopolitical responsibility for its development. It is this concept of 'the Balkans,' rather than its two predecessors, which achieved twentieth century hegemonic status and was mobilized by the Balkan discourse of the 1990s.

Post-World War I: Balkanization, violence, and 'barbaric Balkan'

The negative rearticulation of 'the Balkans' was succinctly expressed through the term 'Balkanization,' first used by journalist Paul Scott Mowrer in 1921; it referred to 'the creation, in a region of hopelessly mixed races, of a medley of small states with more or less backward populations, economically and financially weak, covetous, intriguing, afraid, a continual prey to the machinations of the great powers, and to the violent promptings of their own passion' (quoted from Todorova 1997: 34). Unpacking this dense and emblematic quote, it links the construction of a highly inferior and negative construction of 'Balkan peoples' as weak, covetous, intriguing, and afraid with their propensity for violence and passion to the region's geopolitical ability to become a cataclysmic part of European great power politics, thereby triggering wider wars. 'Balkanization' combines, in John McManner's nice phrase, 'inner fragmentation and outer accessibility' (quoted from Der Derian 1992: 146). However, 'Violence as the leitmotiv of the Balkans was, strictly speaking, a post-Balkan wars phenomenon,' and it was one which both drew upon and radically transformed the previous discursive terrain (Todorova 1997: 122). It took the construction of the Romantic, heroic, fighting subject and turned the celebration of the passion and vitality of 'the Balkans' one hundred and eighty degrees, to constitute 'passion' not in positive terms but as a negative sign of violence, barbarism, irrationality, and backwardness. A discursive move which illustrates, as stressed in chapter 3, the importance of situating the analysis of signs (here 'passion') inside their larger web of linkages and differentiations. Romanticism had constituted a 'Balkan subject' with elements of identity with the other heroic 'unpolluted peoples' of the Scottish mountains, and the Christian cause at the heart of Balkan liberation also spun a link of identity between 'Europe' and 'the Balkans.' The Balkanization discourse, on the other hand, made an unambiguous distinction between 'the West' and 'the Balkans': there were no traits of identity between the two and 'the Balkans' was incapable of change. The question of change also brought forth an affinity with the civilizational discourse which had argued that 'the Balkans' was underdeveloped by the standards of universal/Western civilization. But civilizational discourse articulated 'backwardness' as a stage to be passed on the road to evolutionary social, political, and financial progress, whereas the Balkanization discourse constructed it not as a phase which could be improved and rectified but as an essential temporal identity.

The Balkan discourse's construction of a temporally arrested and ontologically inferior Balkan identity was furthermore situated inside a reading of the history of 'the Balkans' which reinforced this identity and absolved 'the West' of any of the responsibilities argued by the first two discourses. The discourses of the nineteenth century had constructed the Ottoman period as a time of heroic struggle and the Ottoman Empire as the harbinger of economic, cultural, and political destitution for which 'Europe' and 'the West' had to assume responsibility, but the Balkanization discourse shifted the legacy of the Ottoman Empire onto the identity and responsibility of the 'Balkan subject' itself. The earlier discourses constructed 'the Balkans' as influenced by yet fundamentally separate from the Ottomans, while the Balkanization discourse constructed Balkan identity as a product of the Ottomans thereby pushing 'the Balkans' out of its in-between location toward the East in an 'Orientializing' move (Goldsworthy 1998: 5).[12] The rearticulation of Ottoman history not only 'explained' the inferior and radically different identity of 'the Balkans,' it also reinforced the construction of an absent Western ethical responsibility. The West was no longer seen as having benefited from the 'Balkan bulwark' against the East, nor were there any Romantic or civilizational traits of identity between 'the West' and the 'Balkan subject' which called forth moral responsibility for the prosperity and safety of 'the Balkans.' There was nothing 'the West' could do to change these alien and violent peoples, and attempting to do so would only draw it into a dangerous morass of disastrous consequences.

The Balkans had been at the center of Western attention for the first two decades of the twentieth century, but with the rise of Nazism, Italian fascism, and Soviet Communism, the focus of the 1930s moved elsewhere. The dominant conception of the Balkans that had crystallized was, however, of the region as barbaric, alien, and dangerous. As Joseph S. Roucek argued in 1948, 'For many years the word "Balkans" has been used derogatively with the implication of corruption, disorder, and anarchy' (Roucek 1948: 2).[13] The Cold War 'overlaid' the political and conceptual dynamics of 'the Balkans' and made it part of the Communist and Eastern Other, with Greece and Turkey returning to their classical ambiguous roles, but the breakdown of communism and the dissolution of the Warsaw Pact brought back the concept of Balkanization as a synonym for instability, even before the wars in the former Yugoslavia put 'the Balkans' squarely at the center of Western foreign policy debate (Der Derian 1992: 141–69; Wæver 1995: 72–5; Todorova 1997: 136).[14]

The principal characteristics of the three historical Balkan discourses are summarized in Table 6.1.

The Balkan discourse

The Balkan discourse of the 1990s has a striking continuity with the Balkanization discourse as it reads the identity of the Bosnian war, its causes, participants and the role of 'the West,' through an articulation of this as a 'Balkan war' driven by violence, barbarism, and ancient intra-Balkan hatred stretching back hundreds of years (Todorova 1994: 461; Iordanova 2001: 40–1). The spatial and temporal Otherness of 'the Balkans' is emphasized through articulations of, in the words of British Secretary of State for Defence, Michael Portillo, 'the barbarism in the Balkans' (Portillo, *Hansard*, July 19, 1995, column 1741), its 'tribal past' (Kennan 1993: 11), its 'psychologically

Table 6.1 Historical discourses on 'the Balkans'

| Discourse | Identity | | |
	Degrees of Otherness	Temporal identity of 'the Balkans'	Western responsibility
Byronic Balkan	Different and admired	Remain different	Assist in independence
Balkan civilization	Different and underdeveloped	Transformable	Civilizing mission
Balkanization	Radical Other and threatening	Incapable of change	None

closed, tribal nature' (Kaplan 1993a: 16), and its ensuing insusceptibility to 'reason' (Cohen 1994). The linkage of the tribal, barbaric, hateful, and unreasonable situates 'the Balkans' as radically different from the modern, Western world of the nation, order, civilization, and reason. This construction of backward temporal Otherness is further radicalized by a second temporal move, which constitutes this uncivilized violent, hateful, and barbaric Balkan identity as 'ancient.' Warren Zimmerman, the last American ambassador to Yugoslavia, argued for example that the wars of the former Yugoslavia were 'a throwback to the ancient bandit traditions of the Balkans,' a leading article in *The Guardian* spoke of 'ancient flames of negative passion and hatred,' and Michael Dobbs of *The Washington Post* wrote of a 'fratricidal war based on ancient nationalist hatreds' (Zimmermann 1996: 152; Dobbs 1995; *The Guardian* 1992). President George H. Bush called it 'a complex, convoluted conflict that grows out of age-old animosities. The blood of innocents is being spilled over century-old feuds' (Bush 1992a), and influential Republican senator John McCain described it as 'a conflict which has been going on in the Balkans for hundreds of years' (McCain S1204010, 102nd Congress, August 10, 1992). Linking in with the importance of the Ottoman and Byzantine empires articulated by the Balkanization discourse, this Balkan 'salient of non-European civilization' has 'very deep historical roots,' stretching back to the 'Turkish domination' and 'Byzantine penetration' (Kennan 1993: 12–13).[15] Or, in a variation on the civilizational theme (which echoes Huntingtonian clashes), it is Bosnia's location on 'the historic geopolitical fault line between Byzantium and Rome' which constitutes the long temporal lens through which the war should be read (Dobbs 1995). With the brutal violent continuity in place, the relatively peaceful co-existence of the nationalities of the second Yugoslavia during the Cold War had to be constructed as an anomaly, as something which broke the pattern of 'normal' Balkan behavior. This was accomplished by arguing that communism 'on the inside' and the bipolar division of Europe 'on the outside' 'suppressed' or 'froze' the 'true' identity of the Balkans. As argued by President George H. Bush, 'the collapse of communism has thrown open a Pandora's box of ancient ethnic hatreds, resentment, and even revenge' (quoted from Lytle 1992: 308; see also Gati 1992: 64–5).

The temporal longevity of an identity does not in and of itself preclude change, as illustrated by the civilizational discourse's construction of 'backward Balkan' as produced through centuries of Turkish exploitation and Western ignorance yet with the capacity for transformation. But the Balkan discourse's articulation of the 'ancient' roots of 'Balkan conflicts' is situated inside a simultaneous construction of the ontology of Balkan identity as incapable of change. This incapacity is crucial for the constitution of difference between 'Europe' and 'the Balkans,' in particular as the discourse seeks to explain World War II and Nazi Germany without it destabilizing the fundamental difference between a violent, barbaric, and large-scale war producing 'Balkans,' on the one hand, and a civilized, rational, and peaceful 'Europe' on the other. A double discursive move attempts to stabilize this weak spot within the discourse. First, World War II is constituted as a product of 'German Nazism,' as a phenomenon 'in' Europe but not 'of' Europe and thereby not an inherent flaw within Western identity but an alien influence. Second, the discourse articulates 'the West' as capable of learning, of progressing, and solving conflicts through reason and calculation rather than through hatred and passion, and thus as moving beyond the forces which created World War II.

The Balkan discourse draws upon and reproduces the Balkanization discourse's construction of 'the Balkans' as violent, passionate, and backward, but the articulation of the 'ancient roots' of the contemporary conflict constitutes a further accentuation of temporal longevity. The Balkanization discourse of the early twentieth century was formed in the wake of the Balkan wars and the onset of World War I, wars that evolved around the south Slavic nations and the fraying Ottoman and Habsburg empires. The Otherness of the Balkans was at that time constituted through its violent, backward, and passionate identity and its ability to engage great powers in its local struggles. But while conflict was an essential feature of 'the Balkans,' it was not necessarily the same conflict played out over and over again, in no small part because the main line of conflict, the one between 'the Balkans' and the Turks and the Ottoman Empire, had lost its salient status. In the Balkan discourse of the 1990s, the 'ancient roots' accentuate a temporality that was not similarly emphasized in the 1920s, yet the discourse is silent about the historicity of the concept itself. 'The Balkans' is, as laid out above, a much more recent concept than the 'Balkan discourse' would indicate, and its ancestors, such as 'Turkey in Europe,' show that it was centered on the southern part of the peninsula. Croatia and Slovenia, on the other hand, were only incorporated through their post-World War I inclusion in Yugoslavia, and 'the Balkans' of the 1920s was, in short, centered further south than the northern republics of Slovenia and Croatia, where the first wars of the 1990s took place. While the remainder of the twentieth century brought fierce and bloody conflict between Croats and Serbs, it was not on this conflict, nor on an intra-Slavic conflict in Bosnia, that the concept of 'Balkanization' was originally built.

The articulation of the spatial and temporal Otherness of the Balkans as the representational lens through which the Bosnian war should be understood drew upon another ethical and political component of the Balkanization discourse: the fear of European great power entrapment. 'In 1914, a single act in an unimportant country—the assassination of Austrian Archduke Franz Ferdinand in Sarajevo—spread to become a continent-wide conflict. An admittedly lesser, though similar, risk exists today,' warned former Secretary of State, James A. Baker III (Baker 1995).[16] Or as Charles Gati, a former advisor to the Department of State, argued in *Foreign Affairs*: 'with the old hatreds and ancient feuds so much in evidence, it seems as if little of significance has changed. The worlds of Sarajevo 1992 and Sarajevo 1914 suffer from the same disease' (Gati 1992: 71).

After 1914, the 'treacherous terrain' and the history of the fighting skills of the Yugoslavs, tying down German forces during World War II, were articulated to further emphasize the dangers of intervening in 'Balkan warfare.' Linking in with other historical analogies, particularly the American experiences of 'Vietnam' and 'Beirut,' and later 'Mogadishu,' 'the West' was warned of the dangers of attempting to intervene to solve local or civil wars (Ó Tuathail 1996a). Not only was it dangerous to intervene, in that it might draw great powers into a wider war of their own, as in 1914, or lead to the loss of lives and credibility, as in the 'morass' or 'quagmire' of 'Vietnam,' but there was also, as evidenced by the articulation of the 'ancient roots' of the conflict, nothing 'the West' could fundamentally do. The temporal construction of 'the Balkans' as locked into repetitive violence implied that there was no hope that 'the West' might be able to impose a solution from the outside—nor was there any likely possibility that the region might turn itself into a more civilized, stable and peaceful place.

The construction of 'the Balkans' as incapable of change and with the capacity of entrapping the West functioned to legitimize a Western policy of inaction. But as accounts of the warfare surfaced in Western media, the Balkan discourse had to engage in a debate on whether 'ethnic cleansing' and 'genocide' warranted Western intervention. Here 'the Balkan discourse' made a double move. First, it homogenized 'the inside' of 'the Balkans' by constituting the subjectivity of anyone involved in the war in Bosnia as one of being 'Balkan,' more specifically as 'parties' or 'warring factions.' This construction implied that there was no particular differentiation between the identity and political values of the Bosnian Serbs and the Bosnian government, and therefore there were no particular links between 'Bosnia' and 'the West.' Second, the 'Balkan discourse' argued that although the Serbs and the Bosnian Serbs had committed most of the atrocities and the war was a 'tragedy,' neither of the 'parties' were blameless. 'Recent atrocities between Croats and Muslims show that the Serbs are not the sole perpetrators in this war' (Doder 1993: 23). As the first general in command of the UN forces in Bosnia, the Canadian Lewis MacKenzie told the House Armed Service Committee in Washington after his removal: 'Dealing with Bosnia is a bit like dealing with three serial killers—one has killed fifteen, one has killed ten, one has killed five. Do we help the one who has only killed five?' (quoted from Bennett 1995: 194). The Serbian conduct, while perhaps amounting to ethnic cleansing, did not, it was argued, amount to 'genocide': 'the attempt to eradicate a people' (Cohen 1993). 'It is bad enough that Muslims are being forced from their home, for territorial readjustment. But it is not the same as genocide. This is a fight over turf' (Steel 1992: 15). It should be acknowledged, furthermore, that 'the Serbs have legitimate interests like anyone else' (Doder 1993: 23). The dual construction of the war as 'less than genocide' and of 'Bosnia' as composed of 'parties' with a fundamentally similar 'Balkan identity' situated the war as something for which the West bore no ethical responsibility. Responsibility was instead shifted onto 'the parties' themselves.

According to Les Aspin, US Secretary of Defense from 1993 to 1994: 'Ultimately, however, the Bosnian parties themselves must be the ones that make peace. Neither NATO nor any other outside entity can force the parties to the dispute to make peace against their will' (Les Aspin 1994: 4). This construction created a space where each 'party' was responsible regardless of what the actions of the 'other parties' might be, a 'party' which had to make accommodations even in the face of violations of previous agreements and the potentially extraordinary demands of the other side.

The articulation of a set of identities which prevented the possibility of Western responsibility from arising did not imply that responsibility was wholly absent from the discourse, but rather that it was situated inside a classical national discourse that articulated it as enacted by political leaders toward their own citizenry and armed forces. In the words of Senator McCain: 'our first obligation is to the young men and women who serve in our military who are the ones who will be sent into this quagmire. We must not use them in political or military experiments. We must not risk them unless our military experts are fully convinced that our actions will succeed' (McCain S12041, 102nd Congress, August 10, 1992). This articulation constituted those reluctant to intervene in Bosnia not as subjects devoid of care and ethical responsibility, as some of their critics might argue, but as preoccupied with their responsibility for the safety of 'our troops' and the feasibility of their potential missions.

Having created a discursive space unencumbered by any responsibility toward the Bosnian war (Figure 6.1), the foreign policy question of Western engagement was situated inside a classical security discourse of 'national interests' and 'military and strategic feasibility.' 'The relevant question is,' argued *The New York Times*, 'whether the United States has a strong enough interest in the outcome of the Bosnian conflict to risk its troops in ground

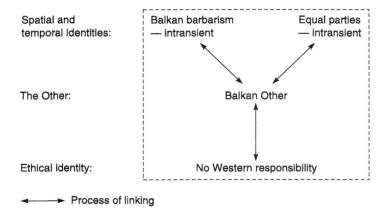

Figure 6.1 The Balkan discourse.

combat. In the view of this page, it does not' (*The New York Times* 1995). Having created a discursive space which framed the question of which policy to pursue through a consideration of Western 'strategic interests,' the key debate within the Balkan discourse was whether there was a threat of the conflict spilling over into neighboring countries, and thereby a need for containing it, for example by placing monitors in Macedonia, supporting international mediation, and by applying pressure on Serbia through a series of sanctions.

The Genocide discourse

The stability of the Balkan discourse is built on a firm articulation of spatial and temporal difference between 'the Balkans' and 'the West,' but this stability can only be upheld as long as the representation of the warfare as 'genocide' can be avoided. To characterize the Serbian conduct toward the 'Bosnian' or 'Muslim Bosnian' population as 'genocide' was to inscribe it in a political discourse that brought forth a longer history of human and legal responsibility.[17] The Convention on the Prevention and Punishment of the Crime of Genocide, drafted in New York in 1948, defines genocide in Article II as:

> any of the following acts committed with intent to destroy, in whole or in part, a national, ethnical, racial or religious group, as such: (a) Killing members of the group; (b) Causing serious bodily or mental harm to members of the group; (c) Deliberately inflicting on the group conditions of life calculated to bring about its physical destruction in whole or in part; (d) Imposing measures intended to prevent births within the group; (e) Forcibly transferring children of the group to another group.

The Convention also obligates its signatories to prevent and punish genocide 'whether committed in time of peace or in time of war' (Article I). However, while the Genocide Convention is a legal document with a particular standing within international law, it is not, from a discourse analytical perspective, its legal status as much as its political mobilization which is in focus. The articulation of a situation as 'genocide' imposes not only a legal obligation but also constructs an ethical responsibility through a mobilization of the tremendous human sufferings inflicted on a people exposed to genocide. A 'genocide' constitutes the exceptional, that which goes beyond even the atrocities of 'normal warfare,' and 'one' cannot respond passively to a 'genocide' knowing what happened in Auschwitz, the pinnacle of the genocide discourse, or later in Srebrenica or Rwanda. Yet, as there are no objective measures given by the Genocide Convention—how many does it take to destroy a group 'in part'?—it will in most cases be a matter of political debate whether to characterize a situation as 'genocide' and, if this usage is adopted, what foreign policy to undertake in response. The Western debate on Bosnia showed that adopting a representation of 'genocide' was a powerful discursive move which radically changed the construction of ethical, spatial, and temporal identities within the Balkan discourse, but that it was also a point of contestation whether what was happening was 'a genocide' or something of a lesser magnitude.

The Genocide discourse's clearest immediate challenge to the Balkan discourse took place at the level of ethical responsibility. 'The world,' in the words of US Senator Cranston, 'should not stand by when genocide is undertaken in any part of this world' (S12029, 102nd Congress, August 10, 1992) and *The New York Times* concurred that America and Europe 'have a moral and legal duty to prevent genocide' (*The New York Times* 1992). The articulation of Bosnian Serb warfare as 'genocide' instituted a fundamental Western ethical responsibility for acting in defense of the Bosnian government and population, and 'the West' could not reconcile its identity as civilized and humane with taking a passive stance (Miles 1994). The construction of 'Bosnia' in terms of genocide constituted it within a realm beyond and above that of 'normal warfare' and it warranted action '*on purely moral grounds*' (Mestrovic 1994: 126).[18] But not only did the Genocide discourse construct a fundamental ethical imperative, which overrode the national security discourse's national interests and strategic feasibility, it sought to incorporate 'strategic interests' into its discourse. Confronting 'genocide' would, it was argued, converge with 'strategic interests' by hindering the spread of the conflict beyond the borders of Bosnia, Yugoslavia, and the Balkans; it would prevent the alienation of Muslims in the Balkans, Europe, and elsewhere; and it would function as a deterrent against other leaders who pondered the use of genocidal strategies.[19] As summarized by Senator Lieberman: 'we have something on the line in what is happening in Bosnia today. Our moral strength, our strategic interest, and ultimately our security. Because when we turn away, turn our backs on the acts that are occurring in that country today that we have seen with our own eyes, we diminish ourselves, we diminish the security in which we and our families want to live' (S12038, 102nd Congress, August 10, 1992). This fusion of irrevocable responsibility and strategic interests strove to prevent a choice between the two, a choice that would make the discourse susceptible to the Balkan discourse's articulation of 'domestic responsibility' toward troops and citizenry.

The construction of 'Western responsibility' was pursued not only through an incorporation of a traditional security discourse of interests, but through a radical rearticulation of the spatial and temporal identities of the 'Balkan discourse.' The shift from 'warfare' to 'genocide' implied that the uniform construction of 'equal parties' of the Balkan discourse was replaced by a construction of 'Bosnians' as 'victims' who were not responsible for the outcome of the war or its conclusion.[20] The editors of *The New Republic* stated that 'there have been too many platitudes about the responsibility of "all factions" for the war. This lazy language is an escape hatch through which outside powers flee their responsibility' (reprinted in Mousavizadeh 1996a: 162). Lifting 'Bosnia' out of the Balkanized spatial and temporal construction of the

Other and separating it from 'Serbia,' it was argued that 'Bosnia' embodied multiculturalism and tolerance, that it was a 'model of what a multi-ethnic society in the Balkans could be,' and that besieged Sarajevo in particular was 'a city as cosmopolitan as any in the West' (Burns 1992; Kupchan 1995). This constructed 'Bosnia' as an exemplar of a multicultural, tolerant, and cosmopolitan 'West,' thereby breaking with all of the previous historical discourses' constitution of 'the Balkans' as different from 'the West' while simultaneously articulating 'multiculturalism' as a political ideal—and reality—for 'the Balkans' and 'the West.'[21] This in turn created further support for Western action: not only was 'Bosnia' a victim of genocide, it was a country whose identity was similar to, in some cases even superior to, the one of 'the West.' 'What,' argued Charles A. Kupchan, a former staff member of the National Security Council under the Clinton administration, 'is left of the Western democracies if they are no longer willing to defend civic society in the heart of Europe?' (Kupchan 1995). 'Bosnia' hence was relocated from its place in an Orientialized 'Balkan' in 'the far corner of Europe' to Europe's geographical and cultural 'heart.' Or from the editor of a collection of *The New Republic* articles on Bosnia, 'If we would not intervene there—on the border between East and West and in the heart of Europe, with force and with determination, on the side of the victim—then nothing the West had ever said about the lessons of appeasement would mean anything' (Mousavizadeh 1996b: xii).

The failure of the West to take on the ethical and political obligation evoked by 'genocide' and 'multiculturalism' implied that the identity of 'the West' had itself been tainted. Bogdan Denitch called it 'the responsibility and complicity of the West in the slow murder of Bosnia' (Denitch 1994), Kupchan, 'the rot of the West,' and this failure destabilized the construction of 'the West' as spatially, temporally, and morally distinct from 'the uncivilized' world (Kupchan 1995; Magas 1993: xx; Mestrovic 1994: 39; Rieff 1996: 10). 'The West,' in short, had shown itself incapable of enacting its identity, thereby undermining its privileged position. This coupling of 'genocide' and 'multiculturalism' reinforced the support for an interventionist policy, but it also constituted a point at which the discourse became vulnerable to destabilization as it raised the question whether all 'genocides' were worthy of actions, or if only those involving 'multicultural identities' were (particularly) worthy ones, and if so, if that did not amount to another Western privileging of identities constructed in its own image.

Having separated 'Bosnia' from 'the Balkans' and reconstituted the war from one of 'factions' and 'parties' to 'multicultural victim' and 'aggressor,' the remaining question is how the 'Serbian subject' was constituted.[22] Here the Genocide discourse argued that the Serbian and Bosnian Serbian populations had been manipulated by 'a discrete faction of Serbian nationalists' and 'politicians who saw profit in unleashing forces' thereby breaking fundamentally with the Balkan discourse's construction of violence, barbarism, hatred, and irrationality (Mousavizadeh 1996a: 162; Burns 1992).[23] The Serbian subject was reconstituted through a separation of genocidal leaders and manipulated population, with the latter as the victims of the propaganda of the former. 'The Serbs' as a general, popular subject is perhaps not at a similar level of sophistication and cosmopolitan insights as the 'Bosnians,' in particular the ones of Sarajevo, but they are a subject with an educational potential and a modernist receptivity to non-nationalistic, non-Balkanized politics once their current leaders are removed. This, in turn, implied that this discourse rather than 'Balkanizing the Serbs' had echoes of the civilizational discourse of the late nineteenth century, which constructed 'the Balkans' as currently backward and uneducated.

The Genocide discourse (Figure 6.2) had a call for action and responsibility built right into its center, and it read spatial and temporal identities through this ethical lens. Yet, as the next chapter shows, there was very little consensus within the West as to what concrete policies should follow from this 'genocidal imperative.' 'Genocide,' on the one hand, created a politically demanding space, yet, as genocide discourses were articulated within concrete debates, they were coupled to policies as different as the dispatching of humanitarian assistance, military intervention—including air strikes—in defense of the Bosnian government, and a lifting of the arms embargo imposed on the republics of the former Yugoslavia.

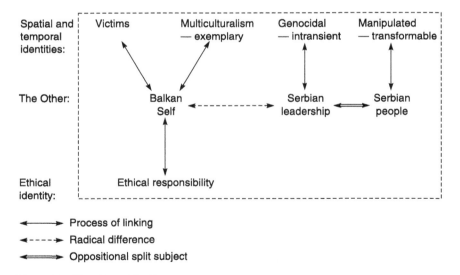

Figure 6.2 The Genocide discourse.

7 Humanitarian responsibility versus 'lift and strike'

Tracing trans-Atlantic policy discourses

The two basic discourses, the Balkan discourse and the Genocide discourse, articulate radically different constructions of spatial, temporal, and ethical identity and they create very different scopes for Western policy. The Balkan discourse constructs the Western choice of policy as linked to whether there are 'Western strategic interests' that warrant an intervention, whereas the Genocide discourse articulates a demand for a policy that stops or rectifies the Bosnian Serbian genocidal actions against the Bosnians or Bosnian Muslims. Yet, as the concrete policy debates unfolded, this picture of ideal-type discourses and their associated policies of intervention was often complicated by discourses which created more complex constructions of the identities of 'the Balkans,' 'Bosnia,' and 'the West' and which raised and debated specific concerns related to 'military feasibility.' Variations of the Balkan discourse might as a consequence lead to extensive interventions in the conflict, while the Genocide discourse is paradoxically not necessarily followed by calls for Western ground troop military intervention.

This chapter analyzes how the main policy discourses within the West evolved from 1992 to 1995, how the two basic discourses were employed and elaborated into more complex variations, how they legitimated competing policies, and how they sought to stabilize both their representations of identity and the link between identities and policy. Tracing the evolution of discursive constructions over time involves, as discussed in chapter 2, an examination of how key events are responded to by official foreign policy discourse. These events do not exist in and of themselves, but are constituted as events by governing political bodies, oppositional parties and groups, international institutions, and the news media, yet once established they have the potential to destabilize existing discourses. Official foreign policy discourses might respond to key events by rearticulating their constructions of identity and the ensuing foreign policy; they might acknowledge the importance of these events but articulate them as in accordance with the discourse already in place; or they might try to pass by the events in silence.

Key events can be used methodologically to establish a timeline that identifies when main events occurred and central policies were either adopted or defended. Working with a case study that stretches over a longer period of time, a timeline identifies periods of heightened activity, where the density of events is greater. In the case of the Western Bosnia debate, key events were predominantly linked with developments on the ground in Bosnia and the negotiation of a series of peace plans sponsored by the international community. The key periods identified in a timeline might subsequently be used methodologically as critical instances when examining a discourse's stability over time. For instance, since the Balkan discourse constructs all parties as 'equal,' analysis should ask how this discourse confronts the critical instances where reliable and extensive reports of Serbian or Bosnian Serb atrocities questioned this construction.

This chapter begins with a timeline of the key events of the war and the Western policy responses thereto. Looking at the competing representations of the war, the identities involved, and the policies which should be adopted, it is obvious that the main discursive division ran between the West European countries with peacekeeping forces on the ground on the one hand and the United States, which was adamant about not deploying troops, on the other. This chapter therefore turns first to the West European discourse of humanitarian responsibility, as exemplified by the British government. This discourse both modified and reinforced elements of the Balkan discourse and its resilience in the face of key events and media criticism is documented and explained. The chapter continues with an analysis of the American positions, starting with President George H. Bush and continuing with President Clinton. The first four months of Clinton's presidency showed a vacillation between a Balkan discourse and a modified Genocide discourse, but the West European rejection of the American policy of 'lift and strike' brought a move toward the former discourse. Both American Presidents faced strong political opposition, and a study of the mobilization of the Genocide discourse within the US Senate is therefore included.

A timeline of key events: developments on the ground and the policy responses of the West

The prelude to war and the cleansings of 1992: humanitarian peacekeeping and mediation

The war in Bosnia was in large part a product of the general break-up of Yugoslavia, a process that was actualized by Slovenian and Croatian secessionism in June 1991 but which was related to a multiplicity of factors, including the expanding power base of Milosevic and his promotion of Serbian nationalism in the 1980s, the financial difficulties of Yugoslavia, and the crumbling of bipolarity (Banac 1992; Ramet 1996; Woodward 1995). The war in Slovenia was over almost before the West could produce a response, the Yugoslav People's Army (JNA) withdrew after ten days and about twenty Slovenian casualties to concentrate its energies on Croatia, whose population was one third Serbian. The American foreign policy agenda was preoccupied with the break-up of the Soviet Union following the coup against Gorbachev in August 1991 and the 1991 Gulf war, and the Bush administration therefore left the scene largely to the Europeans. Jacques Poos, Luxemburg's foreign minister and a member of the troika leading the EC, famously declared that 'The hour of Europe has dawned' as the EC took the lead in setting up the Badinter Commission, which should assess human rights standards as a requirement for EC recognition and in brokering a peace accord under the helm of Lord Carrington (Silber and Little 1997: 159). It became clear over the summer and early fall of 1991 that Slovenia and Croatia would not agree to a looser form of Yugoslav confederation, and Bosnia and Macedonia were as a consequence confronting the choices of staying inside a Serbian-dominated Yugoslavia or seeking independence. Both republics chose the latter, the Bosnian presidency after a vote on 20 December 1991, where the Serbs on the presidency voted against. On January 9, 1992 the Bosnian Serbs 'retaliated' by declaring their own Serbian Republic of Bosnia-Herzegovina and pronouncing it a part of the Yugoslavian federation (Silber and Little 1997: 218). The subsequent referendum on Bosnian independence, which was stipulated by the Badinter Commission as a precondition for EC recognition, gave overwhelming support for independence but was boycotted by the Serbs.

Bosnia was recognized by the EC and the United States on April 6, 1992, and war broke out two days later when JNA began shelling the Bosnian town of Zvornik. Fighting escalated rapidly over the next couple of months and into the summer. A UN weapons embargo on the whole of Yugoslavia had been in effect since September 1991, and since the resources of JNA had been expropriated overwhelmingly by the Serbian side, the Bosnian government found itself at a serious disadvantage. Most of the Serbs' territorial gains were made within the first months of the war. In mid-June 1.1 million people had been displaced, and by the end of 1992 almost 2 million—about half of the pre-war population—were refugees (Silber and Little 1997: 252). On July 19 the Serbian/Bosnian Serb camps in Bosnia were described by Roy Gutman in *Newsday*, and Penny Marshall produced a television report for ITN on the camp Omarska in early August which showed pictures of emaciated prisoners behind barbed wire (Gutman 1993; Campbell 2002a and 2002b; Ó Tuathail 1996b). The documentation of four large camps, Omarska, Trnopolje, Manjace, and Keraterm, put pressure on Western governments to stop what became known as 'ethnic cleansing,' and the British government—who held the EC presidency—convened the London Conference in August on behalf of the EC and the UN (Silber and Little 1997: 252). This conference agreed on a framework for peace talks to be set up in Geneva, and the Serbs conceded to letting the UN monitor their heavy weapons around Sarajevo, Bihac, Gorazde, and Jajce within a week and to withdraw from an undefined part of their territory (Silber and Little 1997: 260; Simms 2001: 261). Cyrus Vance functioned as the UN-appointed mediator, and at the end of the conference Lord Owen was appointed as the new EC mediator, replacing Lord Carrington.

In late June the UN had secured an opening of the airport in Sarajevo. The city was under siege and faced a humanitarian crisis due to lack of food and medication, and on September 14 UN Security Council Resolution 776 declared the deployment of peacekeepers to Bosnia by extending UNPROFOR (the UN Protection Force) from Croatia to Bosnia. UNPROFOR would become the largest peacekeeping operation ever undertaken by the UN, growing into 40,000 men and women by the end of 1994 and drawing troops primarily from West European NATO-members, with France and Britain as the biggest contributors (Roberts 1995: 401; Ramet 1996: 247). The mandate of the force was, despite its deployment in a war zone, within the peacekeeping tradition: the force should not engage in fighting but, as the mandate put it, 'ensure a peaceful political settlement' (UN Security Council Resolution 743 of February 1992). The major task of the force was the delivery of—and the protection of the delivery of—humanitarian aid, which required 'the permission of the dominant forces in the area, in many cases the Bosnian Serbs' (Roberts 1995: 402). The deployment of peacekeepers on the ground implied that the troop-contributing countries became highly skeptical of the adoption of use of force, in particular air strikes, as this might threaten the security of their lightly armed forces.

The Vance–Owen Peace Plan and the 'Safe Areas'

Although Bosnia was not a key priority of the George H. Bush administration, it did become an issue in the American election campaign in 1992, in particular as the stories of detention camps broke over the summer. Presidential candidate Clinton had advocated the use of air strikes and the lifting of the weapons embargo imposed on the Bosnian government, a policy known as 'lift and strike,' but when he came into office in 1993 he found that the West European policy of humanitarian peacekeeping and mediation put significant restrictions on which policies could be adopted, in particular on the possibility of reaching a Western approval of 'lift and strike.'

The Vance–Owen Peace Plan, the first major attempt to bring a solution to the war, was presented in January 1993 and unconditionally supported by the foreign ministers of the EC (Daalder 2000: 11). The Vance–Owen plan envisaged ten 'areas,' three of which would be dominated by the Bosnian Serbs, three by the Bosnian Muslims, two by the Croats, one by a mixed Croatian–Muslim constellation, and one, Sarajevo, which would be the shared capital (Silber and Little 1997: 276). The territorial distribution gave roughly 40 percent to the Serbs, and 30 percent each to the Muslims and Croats. With the Bosnian Croats making up only about 17 percent of the pre-war population, and with 'areas' adjourning Croatia proper, they were the obvious beneficiaries of the plan and signed up to it immediately (Silber and Little 1997: 277). The Bosnian Serbs comprised 30 percent of the pre-war population, but were now in control of 70 percent of the territory and they were not allocated continuous territory or territory that was fully linked to Serbia. The Bosnian

Muslims, on their part, had to relinquish the idea of Bosnia as a multi-ethnic, territorially unified entity. The Clinton administration considered the plan to reward the ethnic cleansing carried out by the Bosnian Serbs/Serbs as well as strategically unenforceable, but its European support prevented an outright American rejection (Daalder 2000: 10–11).

March and April 1993 were hectic months. The Bosnian Serbs laid siege to the Muslim enclave of Srebrenica, a town swollen with refugees from areas which had previously been ethnically cleansed. The Serbs were imposing a ban on aid convoys and reports from British doctors working for the WHO told of people dying of hunger. UN Force Commander Philippe Morillon was also informed by the Muslim/Bosnian defenders of Srebrenica that they were running out of ammunition and that they would be unable to defend the town against a Serbian offensive (Silber and Little 1997: 266). Morillon took it upon himself to bring a convoy into Srebrenica, where he found himself blocked in by hundreds of women and children, unable to leave until he had promised to end the Serbian assaults. Pictures from Srebrenica were broadcast worldwide on March 18, strengthening the calls for Western action, and on March 25 Izetbegovic reluctantly signed up to the Vance–Owen plan. But Serbian attacks on Srebrenica intensified, culminating in an artillery attack on April 12 which killed 56 people in less than an hour, some of them children playing soccer in a school yard (Silber and Little 1997: 269). Four days later, the UN Security Council passed resolution 819, which declared Srebrenica a 'safe area,' 'free from any armed attack or any other hostile act' and Morillon announced that an attack on Srebrenica would constitute 'a declaration of war against the entire world' (quoted from Silber and Little 1997: 275). In Washington, advisors, including chief-of-staff Colin Powell, moved toward 'lift and strike,' and the Secretary of State, Warren Christopher, went to Europe in early May to seek support for this policy as the deadline for the signing of the Vance–Owen plan was running out. The Europeans, however, were not convinced: 'lift and strike' would bring peacekeepers in harms way and jeopardize the humanitarian mission; air strikes were furthermore not believed to be strategically significant if not coupled with a deployment of ground troops, and Clinton was adamant that deployment of American ground troops was *not* an option.

The Bosnian Serb parliament announced a referendum on the Vance–Owen plan, to take place on May 15–16, but this was largely interpreted as a tactical way of delaying the Serbian rejection. On May 6, five other enclaves were added to the list of 'safe areas': Sarajevo, Tuzla, Bihac, Zepa, and Gorazde. However, the requested number of additional troops, 34,000, was not matched by contributing countries as only 7,000 were added to the enforcement of the safe areas resolution (Silber and Little 1997: 275). By mid-May, the Bosnian Serbs had formally turned down the Vance–Owen plan and the Bosnian Croats and Bosnian government forces/Bosnian Muslims had fallen into war with one another. On May 22 the Joint Action Plan, signed by the United States, Russia, Spain, Britain, and France, expressed willingness to protect the safe areas with force, to establish a war-crimes tribunal, to monitor the border between Bosnia and Serbia to secure the latter's compliance with the embargo on the Bosnian Serbs, and to increase the presence in Kosovo and Macedonia in an attempt to contain the spread of the conflict (Daalder 2000: 19).

The Contact Group, Serbian shelling, and NATO hostages

The key events of the next two years were predominantly related to reports of Serbian atrocities, particularly toward the safe areas, and a series of peace plans, none of which were approved by all three parties. Taken chronologically, July 1993 brought renewed reports of a humanitarian disaster in Sarajevo, as shelling prevented food from reaching the city. This brought a brief revitalization of Clinton's attempt to get European support for 'lift and strike,' and NATO's Secretary General Wörner stated on August 2 that 'the alliance had decided to prepare for "stronger measures, including air strikes," to be used if "the strangulation of Sarajevo continues"' (quoted from Secretary General of the UN 1999: 29). But another statement a week later retracted from this position and reaffirmed the so-called 'dual UN–NATO key': that all use of air power should be approved by the UN Secretary General as well as by the UNPROFOR Force Commander and the NATO Commander-in-Chief of Allied Forces South. The dual key system was generally considered to make the adoption of air strikes a cumbersome process and Britain had been a key factor in insisting that it be upheld (Daalder 2000: 22). Still, the heightened threat of air strikes made the Bosnian Serbs abandon key positions in the mountains above Sarajevo, and Izetbegovic, who had withdrawn from the peace negotiations in protest against the Serbian shelling, returned to the process. The British warship HMS *Invincible* gave its name to the next plan, also known as the 'Union of Three Republics Peace Plan,' which presented some movement toward adjoining territories, but the safe areas in eastern Bosnia, Srebrenica, and Zepa, which were allocated to the Bosnian government, were also highly desired by the Bosnian Serbs, who suggested an exchange of these areas for territory around Sarajevo. The Bosnian assembly rejected this offer, and subsequently also rejected the *Invincible* Peace Plan on September 29. The plan's main components were incorporated into the EU-sponsored Action Plan presented in December 1993, which collapsed in January 1994 (Silber and Little 1997: 306; Secretary General of the UN 1999: 30–1).

The next major massacre to capture the Western news media and mobilize international activity came on February 5, 1994, when a mortar round exploded in the open market of Sarajevo killing 68 people, mostly civilians, and wounding over 200 others. The Secretary General of the UN sought Security Council support for NATO air strikes against Bosnian Serb positions in and around Sarajevo, but Michael Rose, the British UNPROFOR commander, opposed this move, suggesting that the mortar might have been fired from the Bosnian government side, a claim that was later refuted. Rose leaned on the British government to support a ceasefire, which included the establishment of a 20-kilometer weapons-exclusion zone within 10 days or else the use of air strikes would be initiated, conditions to which the Bosnian Serbs complied. Meanwhile, the US-brokered Washington Agreement ended the Croat–Muslim front that had opened after the fall of the Vance–Owen Plan the year before.

In April 1994 the negotiation framework was reconfigured, with the formation of the Contact Group, which consisted of the United States, Russia, Britain, Germany, and France and which sidelined the EU/UN negotiators Owen and Stoltenberg. The Contact Group's peace plan, proposed in July 1994, was, however, rejected by the Bosnian Serbs. April also brought intense Serbian attacks on the safe area of Gorazde, and on April 10 American F-16s successfully hit an artillery command facility and attacked a tank and two armored personnel vehicles (Secretary General of the UN 1999: 34). In response, on April 14 about 150 UN personnel were taken hostage by Bosnian Serb forces. They were released only after the UN agreed to end 'combat air patrols over Gorazde.' The next round of heavy fighting came in the fall of 1994, when Serbian attacks on the safe area of Bihac were followed by air strikes against the Serbian controlled Udbina airfield in Croatia. NATO had wished to take out the entire facility, but UNPROFOR insisted that only the airstrip be bombed.

By the end of 1994 the Bosnian Serbs and the Bosnian government had signed a ceasefire intended to last for four months, but intense fighting resumed in early April 1995. The new UNPROFOR commander, Rupert Smith, was, however, more forceful than his predecessor in arguing for the use of air strikes against the Bosnian Serbs; now objections came from the Special Representative of the UN Secretary General, Yasushi Akashi, and the Force Commander, Bernard Janvier. On May 22 Bosnian Serbs seized two pieces of heavy weaponry from a UN collection point, and Bosnian government forces withdrew weapons in return. Rupert Smith threatened both sides with air strikes unless weapons were returned within 24 hours. As the Bosnian Serbs failed to comply, six NATO aircraft attacked two Bosnian Serbian munitions bunkers outside the Serbian parliamentary town of Pale. In retaliation, the Bosnian Serbs stepped up the attacks on other parts of Bosnia, including a shelling of the safe area of Tuzla, which led to 71 fatalities and close to 200 wounded. NATO responded with further bombardments of the facility in Pale, and Bosnian Serbs answered by taking more than 370 UN peacekeepers hostage, tying some of them to militarily strategic sites to prevent further NATO bombardment. Not wanting to risk the lives of UN peacekeepers or escalate the confrontation, UN and NATO refrained from additional air strikes and the hostages were released between June 2 and June 18. France and Britain were concerned, however, for the safety of their troops and created the Rapid Reaction Force, composed of two heavily armed brigades.

Srebrenica, Deliberate Force, and the Dayton Peace Accord

Retrospectively, the years between the fall of Vance–Owen plan and the events of June 1995 were characterized by successive peace negotiations, rejected plans, Bosnian Serb atrocities, UNPROFOR soldiers being taken as hostages, and UN reluctance to adopt air strikes against the Bosnian Serbs. What significantly changed this pattern of events and brought the United States to the head of the military and political process was the massacre in the safe area of Srebrenica. Srebrenica was protected by lightly armed Dutch peacekeepers, who were unable to prevent the Serbian conquest of the enclave on July 11, 1995. The Bosnian Serbs subsequently deported about 5,000 women, children, and elderly on July 12, and executed more than 7,000 Bosnian men and boys, either in the town of Bratunica (to which many were transported) or along the route to Tuzla (which was traveled by a column of between 12,000 to 15,000 Bosnian Muslim men trying to escape Srebrenica). Survivors began arriving in Tuzla on July 17 and the news media reported their stories of summary executions, which in turn put further pressure on the UN, NATO, and the international community.[1]

The reports from Srebrenica and the fall of another safe area, Zepa, fortified Western resolve. France pushed for a stronger military defense of the safe areas, Clinton concurred, and the traditional reluctance of the UK was eventually overpowered. Briefly thereafter, and to the surprise of most Western commentators, the Croatian government forces launched Operation Storm, which drove the Croatian Serbs from the Krajina region which they had held since 1991. Richard Holbrooke, who had become the head of the US negotiating team, urged the UN to relocate its personnel from places that would make them easy hostages should the Serbs wish to retaliate against future air strikes. A Bosnian Serb attack on the Sarajevo marketplace on August 28 resulted in 37 dead and about 90 injured, and UNPROFOR and NATO commanders agreed that the conditions for commencing air strikes against Bosnian Serb positions were met (Secretary General of the UN 1999: 94–5).

NATO's Operation Deliberate Force flew around 3,500 sorties, hitting more than 60 targets between August 30 and September 21 (Secretary General of the UN 1999: 98; NATO 2002). Holbrooke's team simultaneously conducted a hectic shuttle diplomacy, which paved the way for peace negotiations on the Wright-Patterson Air Force Base in Dayton, Ohio. These negotiations were concluded with the Dayton Accord on November 21, signed in Paris on December 14. The Dayton Accord created continuous territories, giving 51 percent to the Federation of Bosnians/Bosnian Muslims and Bosnian Croats on the one hand, and 49 percent to the Serbian Republic on the other. It created a political structure with a rather weak federal level and it situated the four remaining safe areas of Bihac, Tuzla, Sarajevo, and Gorazde within the Bosnian Federation, while the Bosnian Serbs retained the areas of Srebrenica and Zepa which they had overrun in July. The implementation of the Accord was divided into a military and a civilian annex, and the former was undertaken by NATO in a historically unprecedented 'out of area' operation that amounted to 60,000 troops, one third of whom were American. The ending of the war did not, however, put an end to debates over the merits and faults of the West, nor was there agreement on how to evaluate the Dayton Accord: some saw it as nothing short of condoning ethnic cleansing and genocide, whereas others argued it was the only peace that could be achieved.

Summing up developments from the beginning of the war in 1992 until the ratification of the Dayton Accord in 1995, a timeline can be constructed around the following periods, which signify increased military, political, and media activity. These periods were, as described in chapter 5, used for selecting empirical material and for studying discursive stability.

1   March 6 to May 29, 1992: the prelude to and beginning of the war.
2   July 19 to September 20, 1992: the revelations of camps and ethnic cleansing, the London Conference, the extension of UNPROFOR to Bosnia.
3   February 1 to May 22, 1993: the presentation of the Vance–Owen Peace Plan and the creation of safe areas.
4   February 5 to April 30, 1994: massacre in Sarajevo, Serbian attacks on Gorazde, NATO bombings, and 150 UN personnel taken hostage.
5   May 20 to June 30, 1995: NATO's bombing of Bosnian Serbian munitions bunkers in Pale, Serbian attack on Tuzla with 71 casualties, more NATO bombardments, and 370 UN personnel taken hostage.
6   July 1 to September 16, 1995: the fall of Srebrenica and Zepa, massacre in Sarajevo, and Operation Deliberate Force.
7   November 10 to December 20, 1995: the conclusion of the Dayton Accord.

The humanitarianism of Western Europe

The central Western policy from the outbreak of war and until Operation Deliberate Force was to combine a peacekeeping operation aimed at alleviating the 'humanitarian crisis' with the negotiation of a political solution that all three parties would accept. The central political actors undertaking and defending this policy were the troop-contributing countries, France and the UK being the largest among them, and the EC/EU and UN mediators and special representatives. Since the British government was the most reluctant to adopt more aggressive policies, including the American 'lift and strike,' and was the strongest defender of 'humanitarianism' it was an exemplary case of how the Western policy of mediation and peacekeeping was legitimized.[2] The dominant discourse within which this policy was situated articulated key elements of the Balkan discourse, but complicated this discourse through a construction of a 'humanitarian responsibility' for the victims of the conflict. This discourse proved itself remarkably resilient, even in the face of the critical events of repeated Bosnian Serb/Serbian atrocities and the Bosnian Serbs' rejections of the Vance–Owen and the Contact Group peace plans.

Reproducing the Balkan discourse

The continuity between the West European discourse and the Balkan discourse was clear in the use of representations that emphasized the Balkan spatiality of the conflict and the temporal identity of 'ancient hatred' that was blocking 'the Balkans' from transforming and progressing (Silber and Little 1997: 254). The war was linked to 'the fault lines that run through that part of Europe today, as they have for centuries' (Hurd, *Hansard*, May 9, 1995, column 583), and it was making 'the civilized world' 'appalled by the barbarism in the Balkans' (Portillo, *Hansard*, July 19, 1995, column 1743). Douglas Hurd, Secretary of State for Foreign Affairs, stated that 'Once old hatreds have been aroused, they are hard to put to sleep again' and that the Bosnian war belonged to a group of wars which were 'usually civil wars simmering with centuries of mutual hatred, sustained by people with no will for peace' (*Hansard*, September 25, 1992, column 125; quoted from Simms 2001: 23). Policy texts articulated the distinct spatial and temporal identity of 'the Balkans,' but even more frequently adopted the political spatiality of the Balkan discourse which constructed the war as taking place between 'equal parties' (Conversi 1996: 245; Simms 2001). The Serbs had committed most of the atrocities, but this did not fundamentally change the construction of the war as taking place between three sides who were parties to a 'civil war.' 'No side has,' argues Hurd, two weeks after the Serbian attack on Srebrenica which killed 56 people in April 1993, 'the monopoly on evil. This is not a war with saints or heroes' (*Hansard*, April 29, 1993, column 1167). This representation was reiterated in the responding speech by John Cunningham, the Labour Party's shadow minister, who stated that, 'The reality is that among the political leaders as well as among the military leaders in Bosnia there are no innocents. They all bear a grave responsibility for continuing the slaughter in the way they do' (*Hansard*, April 29, 1993, column 1178).

With these constructions of spatiality and temporality, it would come as no surprise to find an articulation of the Balkan discourse's construction of responsibility as resting with 'the parties' themselves. In Douglas Hurd's words, 'The UN cannot just stay in the Balkans for ever to pick up the bits and save people from the consequences of their own actions.' And, 'we can point the parties toward the negotiating table, but only they can decide when to sit down and talk seriously about peace' (*Hansard*, May 5, 1995, columns 587–8). After the massacre at Srebrenica in July 1995, Michael Portillo, Secretary of Defence, argued that 'The time is now ripe for decisions, for the warring factions to contemplate the stark reality of the withdrawal of the UN' (*Hansard*, July 19, 1995, column 1746). Turning to the Labour Party, Cunningham argued that 'there will have to be a political solution to the situation in Bosnia. Sooner or later people will have to accept that they cannot go on slaughtering each other but will have to come to terms with living together as neighbours, peacefully and in harmony or at least without resorting to the violence of the past few months' (*Hansard*, April 29, 1993, column 1183).[3]

With the articulation of 'the responsibility of the parties' came, furthermore, the construction of a political space which privileged 'national interests' and 'domestic responsibility.' 'We could not agree to action which would put British forces at serious risk,' argued Hurd, who continued that 'it is not a British interest, and it would only be a pretence, to suppose that we can intervene and sort out every tragedy which captures people's attention and sympathy ... Decisions cannot be based either on false analogies or on a desire to achieve better headlines tomorrow than today. That is particularly true when those decisions affect human life, and more especially still when the lives are those of British service men or civilians' (*Hansard*, April 29, 1993, columns 1174 and 1176). The Balkan discourse opened, as argued in chapter 6, for Western actions in Bosnia, but these were to be carried out because there were national or Western interests at risk, not because of a moral concern for Bosnia. Portillo argued that 'There has been from the start a serious risk that this conflict could degenerate into a regional war, setting light to the Balkans and bringing into play highly dangerous international forces. The west has a vital interest in containing the conflict,' but, he continued, the deployed peacekeeping forces should not be seen as taking sides in a war: 'we are not in Bosnia to fight a war; we are there to save lives ... Our forces are equipped not to make war but to move among the local population bringing food and medicine and confidence and security wherever we are able to do so' (*Hansard*, July 19, 1995, column 1741). One should not therefore become 'an army of occupation' or 'combatants on behalf of the Muslim or any other community' (Hurd, *Hansard*, April 29, 1993, columns 1168 and 1173).

The split responsibility of humanitarianism

The West European policy discourse did not, however, slavishly reproduce the Balkan discourse but modified it through the articulation of a 'humanitarian responsibility' for the 'victims of the conflict.' Counterfactually, it would have seemed rather unlikely—and an unstable discourse—had an unmodified Balkan discourse with its limited scope for Western intervention been mobilized to legitimize the deployment of a large peacekeeping force working under rather dangerous conditions. Justifying British participation in UNPROFOR in September 1992, Hurd declared it 'a humanitarian task to help cope with a humanitarian disaster,' and eight months later he stated that 'our troops are in Bosnia for a humanitarian purpose and we do not intend to convert them into an army of occupation or an army fighting to impose a particular solution on the problem by force' (*Hansard*, September 25, 1992, column 123; *Hansard*, April 29, 1993, column 1168). 'Humanitarianism' was thus not to be confused with a military engagement in the conflict itself; the troops were in Bosnia to protect civilians from starving and to enforce the embargo and sanctions against the former Yugoslavia, and their presence might help stabilize the situation in such a way that a 'political settlement' between 'all parties' could be reached. Deployment of UNPROFOR soldiers on the ground was separate from a 'military intervention,' which was constituted as 'not an option' (Hurd, *Hansard*, April 29, 1993, column 1168).

The construction of a humanitarian mission, of 'saving lives and relieving hunger,' meant that the Western governments and the UN could represent themselves as acting in response to the media reports of Serbian atrocities which appeared from the summer of 1992 (Hurd, *Hansard*, May 9, 1995, column 584). Governments were concerned with their national interests, but they were not disconnected from larger moral concerns about human suffering. This discourse of humanitarian responsibility reproduced the distinction between the 'war-torn Balkans' and the 'civilized West' from the Balkan discourse, but it incorporated elements of older normative and civilizational discourses, which constructed 'Western civilization' as having a moral responsibility for the suffering and backwardness of the Other. This 'humanitarian responsibility' had reverberations for the construction of spatial identities as the insertion of a 'humanitarian responsibility' complicated the 'equal parties' of the Balkan discourse. The main discursive move of the humanitarian responsibility discourse was to introduce 'civilians' as 'innocent victims' opposed to the 'leaders' of 'the parties': 'The innocents are women and children, elderly people, civilians and non-combatants, the hapless victims of the civil strife that their political and military leaders continue to inflict on them' (Cunningham, *Hansard*, April 29, 1993, column 1178). This 'humanitarian responsibility' for 'civilians' modified the original Balkan discourse by introducing a 'dual subject': 'Bosnia' was no longer comprised solely by 'parties,' but by a juxtaposed constellation of 'parties' and 'civilians,' of 'responsible leaders' and 'innocent victims.' In the analytical terminology of linking and differentiation, as laid out in chapter 3, this implied a linking of 'civilian,' 'victim,' and 'innocent' which was radically differentiated and dichotomously juxtaposed to a linking of 'leaders,' 'agents,' and 'responsible.' It further implied that 'Balkanness' was constituted as a trait of the leaders whereas the 'innocent civilians' were ambiguously located as both produced by 'the Balkans' and as distinct from its leaders (Figure 7.1). Compared with the Genocide discourse's articulation of 'Bosnian victims' as embedded within a multicultural, tolerant, and liberal democratic 'Bosnia,' the 'innocent civilian victims' of the humanitarian responsibility discourse are political blank slates. They have no particular national or political identity, nor are they imbued with an explicit civilizational potential that the West might have a responsibility for actualizing. The 'civilian victims' are, in short, produced simply through their negative difference to their 'Balkan leaders.' The splitting of the 'Balkan' subject into 'leaders' and 'civilians' implies furthermore that responsibility was divided into a Western humanitarian responsibility and a Balkan political responsibility in that the 'Balkan leaders' were the ones who uniformly and exclusively held responsibility for the war itself.

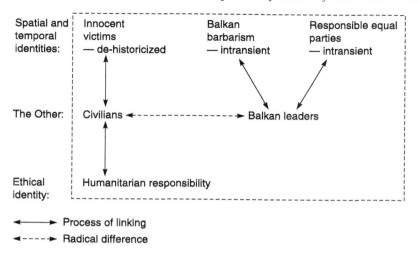

Figure 7.1 The humanitarian responsibility discourse.

Taking a closer analytical look at the stability of the dual 'Bosnian subject,' the first important observation is that the introduction of 'civilians' complicates the 'Balkan subject,' but that it also constructs a dichotomy between the 'parties': those who are military or politically engaged, and the 'civilians,' who are constituted precisely by their non-political-military status. The boundary between these two subjects implies that by taking action—even in the attempt of finding a peaceful solution to the conflict—a subject is automatically moved from the privileged 'innocent' space of 'the civilian' to 'the political parties,' and as a consequence is no longer embraced by the responsibility of the West. In short, the humanitarian responsibility discourse constitutes responsibility as applicable to a passive subject only. As 'leaders' have been constituted as those with agency, yet also as responsible for the warfare, there is no real possibility for incorporating 'civilian agency': how 'civilians' were trying not only to stay alive, but seeking to influence the outcome of the war, either by supporting 'their leaders,' by creating civil society networks, or by mobilizing the intervention of 'the international community.' An incorporation of such 'civilian agency' would complicate the construction of a sharp division between 'leaders' and 'victims,' and it would more importantly destabilize the separation between Western humanitarian responsibility and Balkan political responsibility that the humanitarian discourse strives to uphold. If 'civilians' are no longer passive 'victims,' but agents working with a political goal, then taking on responsibility for 'civilians' becomes a much more encompassing endeavor than offering 'humanitarian assistance,' and the separation between 'apolitical, civilian victims' and 'political, responsible leaders' is destabilized.

While the humanitarian discourse promises an ethical responsibility toward a Bosnian subject it is a subject that is constituted in depoliticized terms. The Balkan discourse constructed, as argued in chapter 6, the spatial and temporal identities of the war in such a manner that its background and trajectory and the status and actions of particular groups and agents were subsumed and cancelled in a reading of the war as caused by 'ancient' forces beyond the political control or responsibility of the West.

The humanitarian responsibility discourse might at first seem to offer a more politically sensitive account that separates between 'leaders' and 'civilians,' but the dichotomy of 'leaders' and 'civilians' is set in a space with no historicity or political account of how these 'civilian victims' were produced. 'Civilian victims' are constituted without any political or national signification, there are no 'Bosnian victims,' or 'Muslim victims,' but simply 'civilian victims,' forming an equally uniform subject as 'the parties' of the Balkan discourse. The absence of a political account implies that 'responsibility for the civilians/victims' falls back upon 'the leaders' of the Balkan discourse: 'the leaders' are the ones who have brought on the war, and who are preventing its conclusion. The pressure on and responsibility of 'the leaders' is as a consequence reinforced: not only are they responsible for 'the war' they are also responsible for 'the slaughter' of their own populations. While the responsibility of 'the West' is thus on the one hand expanded in the move from a Balkan discourse to a humanitarian responsibility discourse, it is on the other hand fundamentally patrolled: the West takes on a humanitarian responsibility for the 'victims,' but these are constituted as produced by their 'political and military leaders,' not by any political history or Western (in)actions.

The humanitarian responsibility discourse constructs a discursive position which seeks to accommodate the media pressure arising from the summer of 1992, but which modifies rather than breaks with the Balkan discourse. Western responsibility is only extended to an 'innocent civilian victim' produced by the 'Balkan leaders,' who in turn are responsible for the production of 'the victims' the West is trying to save. This is not to argue that there was no difference between the Balkan discourse and the humanitarian responsibility discourse, that there was not 'victims' from all political, ethnic, national and religious 'groups,' or that UNPROFOR did not save the lives of concrete individuals, but rather that the responsibility of the humanitarian responsibility discourse was circumscribed in its articulation of ethical responsibility and in important ways reproduced central elements of the Balkan discourse.

Understanding the stability of the humanitarian responsibility discourse

The discourse of humanitarian responsibility proved itself remarkably resilient throughout the war and it was even supported by the shadow ministers of the Labour Party for the majority of the period.[4]

The quotes above are drawn largely from British debates following such significant events as the uncovering of Serbian-run camps in July and August

1992, the artillery attack on Srebrenica and the fall of the Vance–Owen Peace Plan due to Serbian rejection in April 1993, and the massacres at the fall of Srebrenica in July 1995: all critical instances that one might presume would have challenged the construction of the parties as 'equal.' The challenge arising from these events was further reinforced by the media's critical stance toward the government's construction of 'equal parties' and its rejection of a more robust military intervention. *The Independent* wrote on August 15, 1992, that 'The Muslims have, after all, suffered far the worst from the brutal policy of ethnic "cleansing," practiced most ruthlessly by the Serbs,' and that 'For the past year Western policy has been hopelessly indecisive and reactive' (*The Independent* 1992). *The Guardian* ended its editorial on April 6, 1993 by asking 'How, why, have we failed so dismally to save Bosnia?' *The Times* argued that 'Bosnians are paying a terrible price for Europe's vacillation more than a year ago, when preventive action could have stopped the fighting from breaking out,' and *The Independent* pointed to 'the deep sense of collective shame that is building up among the people of this country as they watch the atrocities in Bosnia unfold' (*The Guardian* 1993b; *The Times* 1993; *The Independent* 1993b). Turning to July, 1995, two years later, similarly critical notes are struck by *The Times*, speaking of 'The miserable record of solemn pledges unfulfilled, of piecemeal improvisation, of ultimatums found to be nine parts bluff' (*The Times* 1995a). And, moving past the conclusion of the Dayton Accord, *The Independent* looked back on 'a war that has shamed Europe' (*The Independent* 1995).[5]

The critical stance of the media indicates that there *was* a pressure on the British government to defend its construction of the Bosnian war as well as its policy of peacekeeping and political mediation.[6] How then was this policy defended in the face of Serbian atrocities, Bosnian Serb unwillingness to accept peace plans and the media's reporting of this to the wider public? Drawing on the analysis of the humanitarian responsibility discourse above, the mobilization of three discursive strategies can be identified. First, the construction of 'equal parties,' even if rearticulated into a split between 'leaders' and 'victims,' is remarkably internally stable as far as countering atrocities and transgressions, even if these are committed overwhelmingly by one party. For example, after the fall of Srebrenica in July 1995 it was argued by Portillo that 'No faction is blameless' and that 'All sides have been guilty of slaughter, rape and other atrocities' (Portillo, *Hansard*, July 19, 1995, column 1740). The uniform spatiality through which 'parties,' 'leaders,' and 'warfare' is read implies that any constitution of 'atrocities' as 'Serbian,' 'Muslim,' or 'Croatian' is overwritten by their location inside the uniform spatiality of 'Balkan' and 'parties.' The more atrocities are identified, even if committed by one 'party,' the stronger the support for the construction of this as a 'non-Western' and 'barbaric' war. The split subjectivity of 'leaders' and 'victims' does not change this dynamic, but reads 'atrocities' through the lens of the 'barbaric' nature of 'the leaders,' and a heightened need for Western humanitarian assistance to 'the victims.'

The second discursive strategy for countering criticism was to articulate concern for the 'international responsibility towards civilian victims' and the 'domestic responsibility towards our troops' and couple them to assessments of military feasibility. The central claim was that a lifting of the arms embargo and a more sustained use of air strikes would be militarily insufficient and endanger both peacekeepers and humanitarian delivery. 'I know of no Government,' argued Hurd in May 1995, 'whose military experts think that the use of air power could swing the balance of advantage in the mountains of Bosnia. Equally, if the arms embargo were lifted, the fighting would at least continue and, most of us now think, escalate' (Hurd, *Hansard*, May 9, 1995, column 583). It was repeatedly argued that the Serbs had outstanding military skills, especially for guerrilla warfare in the mountains of Bosnia, and that during World War II the German forces found them almost impossible to subdue (Simms 2001: 223–72). As the repeated insistence on a 'political settlement' showed, the British government was adamant in its rejection of more-aggressive military strategies. 'Continued fighting' might change the battlefield in favor of the Bosnian government, but it would also produce more victims, thereby aggravating the 'humanitarian crisis' the West was trying to solve; and it would also, particularly if supported by Western air strikes, put UNPROFOR troops at risk. 'Lift and strike' would therefore compromise *both* the responsibility toward the uniform 'Bosnian victims' and the responsibility toward 'the national troops.' And since the discourse had effectively eradicated any potential political responsibility toward the Bosnian government, there was no concern for the adverse effects of the embargo on the Bosnian 'parties.' While the current policy was thus constituted as honoring and uniting international and domestic responsibility, it was also explicitly stated, for instance when Bosnian Serbs took hostages in 1994, that 'national responsibility' held the ultimate prerogative, and that 'further fighting' might necessitate a withdrawal of UNPROFOR.

The third component of the discursive defense of the stability of the humanitarian responsibility discourse was to construct the politicians speaking as having knowledge and authority and assuming leadership and responsibility. Politicians were constructing themselves as knowledgeable in discussions of military feasibility either in the case of Hurd, as relying upon 'experts,' or through historical analogies; as Simms polemically puts it, through 'quaint and repetitive reference to the military experience of MPs, however irrelevant' (Simms 2001: 282). But perhaps more striking than these mobilizations of knowledge was the construction of politicians as assuming the 'political responsibility' for 'leadership and action,' a responsibility setting them aside from the media and the broader public. Hurd stated that 'Many more people inside and outside the House, faced daily with the horror of Yugoslavia as presented in the press and on television, say that something must be done but are not specific about it. *We* must be specific in government and in the House' (*Hansard*, September 25, 1992, column 119, emphasis added). A similar position, although now less generous toward the 'wider public/people,' is argued in April 1993, when Hurd stated that one cannot 'intervene and sort out every tragedy which captures people's attention and sympathy. I have never found the phrase "something must be done" to be a phrase which carries any conviction in places such as the House or the Government where people have to take decisions' (*Hansard*, April 29, 1993, column 1176). Robin Cook, then the Labour Party's shadow minister for foreign affairs, chimes in by mobilizing the knowledge/authority of the traveler's 'personal encounters.' He describes a visit to the British troops in the safe area of Gorazde, who had 'good morale and the sense of a rewarding job being done with commitment. That sense of satisfaction comes from the troops knowing rather better than some of the media over here what they had achieved. It is worth repeating that' (*Hansard*, May 9, 1995, column 594). The discursive effect of these constructions of knowledgeable and responsible politicians is not only to differentiate the former from the media and the general public, but to situate their foreign policy decisions inside a realm of superior reflection and difficulty that in and of itself bestows legitimacy upon their decisions.

Accommodating American leadership

How then was American leadership and the adoption of NATO air strikes in 1995 accommodated by the humanitarian responsibility discourse? Did this undermine the construction of 'equal parties' in so far as the campaign was in support of the Bosnian government, and did it indicate, as argued by *The Times*, that 'this was a war that could be halted only when mediation was backed by effective firepower?' (*The Times* 1995b). The Labour Party's shadow minister Robin Cook argued that 'Had the international community shown the same resolve two years ago, tens of thousands of Bosnians might not have lost their lives, and hundreds of thousands of refugees might not have lost their homes. Until today, Bosnia has represented the failure of international intervention' (*Hansard*, November 22, 1995, column 662). The response of the Conservative government was to create as much continuity with the previous discourse as possible and to portray the policy of the past three and a half years not as a failure but a humanitarian success, a successful containment of the conflict, and as a precondition for the Dayton Accord. Secretary of State for Foreign Affairs Malcolm Rifkind argued that 'Yes, there have been massive disappointments, but I believe that the extent to which the international community saved many hundreds of thousands of lives prevented the conflict from spreading elsewhere in the Balkans and helped to provide the framework that has led to the peace settlement … I can think of no comparable past conflict in which the international community has been able to achieve so much. The fact that we did not achieve nearly as much as we would all have liked is not evidence of failure; it just shows how painful and difficult the task is' (*Hansard*, November 22, 1995, column 662). Responsibility was therefore still firmly located with 'the parties': 'the prime responsibility for the time that it has taken for the war to come to a conclusion must lie with the combatants' (Rifkind, *Hansard*, November 22, 1995, column 663). As a consequence, the British government was vague on the response if a party were to breach the Dayton Accord—'the whole weight of the international community would seek to ensure that it respected the treaties into which it had voluntarily entered'—and on the question of how to create a 'better balance between the armaments possessed by the different warring factions.' Here the stance was to encourage a reduction in Bosnian Serb capabilities rather than an increase in the level of the Bosnian-Croatian Federation, as stipulated as a possibility in the Dayton Accord (Rifkind, *Hansard*, November 22, 1995, column 666; Portillo, *Hansard*, December 12, 1995, columns 844–5).

The responsibility for maintaining the peace and rebuilding Bosnia was therefore still, as during the war, located with the three 'parties,' yet there was one slight change in the discourse insofar as the 'parties' were paralleled by an articulation of 'the people.' 'The people' integrates 'leaders' and 'civilians,' it is less radicalized than the 'leaders' and has more capacity for agency than 'the victims,' but it is still a uniform 'Bosnian/Balkan' subject. 'It is critical,' argues Portillo, 'that the people of Bosnia and Herzegovina should understand that, after a certain period, if there is to be peace in their country, peace must be generated from within; it cannot perpetually be imposed from outside' (*Hansard*, December 12, 1995, column 841). This uniform 'people' is also projected back in time, with Portillo arguing that 'ultimately the people of that area have to love peace more than they love war for the peace to succeed' (*Hansard*, December 12, 1995, column 843). The 'war loving peoples of the Balkans' have to prove to the West that 'they' are willing to mend their ways, and if not fundamentally transform their identity at the very least realize the futility of 'their' propensity for violence. The continuity with the Balkan discourse's construction of 'Balkan warfare' and 'uniform parties/peoples' is thus in the end upheld.

Unity in diversity: the American debate on 'lift and strike'

The analysis of the British debate reveals a remarkable continuity within governmental discourse as well as an opposition, which is largely supportive of this discourse, especially during the first years of the war. The media's criticism is acknowledged but incorporated through an articulation of the 'domestic responsibility' to the British troops, the humanitarian responsibility toward the 'civilian victims,' and the military infeasibility of a pro-Bosnian intervention, whether in the form of air strikes, a lifting of the arms embargo, or the deployment of ground troops.

Turning to American official discourse and political debate, the picture is much more complex. The analysis will therefore trace more discontinuities and criticism than in the British case. Not only is the Bosnian war spanned by two administrations and a Presidential campaign, it is also characterized by changes within Clinton's presidency, which moved from appropriations of central elements of the Genocide discourse to the Balkan discourse within the span of a few months. Clinton was also confronted by a much more significant opposition than was the British government, the US Senate held major debates on Bosnia where prominent Democratic senators, such as Joseph Biden, Carl Levin, and Joseph Lieberman, as well as influential Republicans Robert Dole, John McCain, and later Secretary of Defense in the second Clinton administration William Cohen, expressed thorough criticism. This opposition culminated in the adoption of the Bosnia and Herzegovina Self-Defense Act of 1995 by the Senate on July 26, 1995 and the House of Representatives on August 1, which stipulated a unilateral American lifting of the arms embargo imposed on the Bosnian government, a bill vetoed by Clinton on August 11. This critical oppositional policy discourse articulated significant elements of the Genocide discourse, but tried to reconcile this representation with an unwillingness to commit American ground forces.

Genocide contra Balkan hatreds—the discursive terrain of 1992

The Bush administration was less concerned with Bosnia than were the European governments, in particular those with troops on the ground, but Bush's discourse nevertheless shared many of the traits of the West European humanitarian responsibility discourse. The war was a 'complex, convoluted conflict that grows out of age-old animosities,' the Balkans 'a troubled region' ridden by 'century-old feuds,' and as a consequence 'an enduring solution cannot be imposed by force from outside on unwilling participants.' As in the humanitarian responsibility discourse, this spatial and temporal 'Balkan' reading of the conflict was coupled to the need for a 'mission of mercy' that would bring assistance to 'the people of Bosnia,' the 'innocent children, women and men' (Bush 1992a). The concerns for regional stability implied that the containment of the conflict was a necessary, if not, perhaps, a 'vital interest.' Bush even touched upon the representation of 'genocide' in early August 1992, arguing that 'The world cannot shed its horror at the prospect of concentration camps. The shocking brutality of genocide in World War II in those concentration camps are burning memories for all of us.' His response, however, was limited to pointing to the need for humanitarian assistance, to looking forward to the London Conference, and to supporting sanctions against Serbia (Bush 1992b). As in the West European debate, this is a discourse which seeks to construct its speaker as compassionate, yet simultaneously avoid any articulations which could support calls for more robust military interventions, in particular for the deployment of American ground troops.

Turning to the wider American debate, Bush's discourse is trying to steer between more radical articulations of the Balkan discourse as well as the Genocide discourse, discourses which argued that the United States had even less of a responsibility than the one constituted by Bush, or that the ethical imperative of 'genocide' warranted stronger Western, and if need be unilateral American, action. These two discourses were, for example, articulated in a major debate in the Senate in August 1992 on the 'Authorization of Multilateral

Action in Bosnia-Hercegovina,' a resolution which urged the President to convene the UN Security Council to have it authorize the use of multilateral force. The Balkan discourse was articulated through constructions of warfare as 'going on in the Balkans for hundreds of years' (McCain S12040, 102nd Congress, August 10, 1992), as built on the 'fault line' of the Habsburg Empire, and as taking place 'in one lightly inhabited part of the world' (Wallop S12026, 102nd Congress, August 10, 1992). The American version of the Balkan discourse combined the construction of 'Balkan' spatial and temporal identity with the articulation of previous American experiences in 'Vietnam' and 'Beirut' to constitute Bosnia as a dangerous 'foreign involvement' in a 'far away place' with no clear American national interests and no comprehensible military strategy. To McCain, who had spent five years as a prisoner of war in Vietnam, the sponsors of the resolution were propagating 'exactly the same kind of vague rhetoric we heard in 1965'; to take military action, in his view, requires that there are 'US national interests at stake' and that there is a 'a reasonable expectation of success,' neither of which were met by 'Bosnia' (S12040, 102nd Congress, August 10, 1992). These representations drew upon a dual fear of entrapment, the classical 'Balkan entrapment' of World War I and the 'US entrapment in foreign conflicts' that conjured the 'quagmire' of Vietnam, of being 'sucked into' guerrilla warfare, peacekeeping, and the subsequent American human and symbolic losses (Ó Tuathail 1996a; Ramet 1994). Speaking to the question of American interests, Wallop argued that there was no threat of the war spreading beyond the former Yugoslavia and that humanitarian interests or 'an emotional sense of outrage' did not justify the use of military force (S12024, 102nd Congress, August 10, 1992). Although feeling 'terrible about this tragedy,' McCain invoked the importance of balancing calls for action with a politician's necessary understanding of 'domestic responsibility;' that 'our first obligation is to the young men and women who serve in our military who are the ones who will be sent into this quagmire' (S12041, 102nd Congress, August 10, 1992).

The key political message of the American Balkan discourse is its reiterated warnings against a policy of American military intervention that would either explicitly commit or more incrementally draw the United States into a ground troop deployment. Those arguing within it would in most cases express support for a negotiated settlement and humanitarian aid, but the strongest imperative of the Balkan discourse was to caution against the future specter of ground troops, and to warn of the slippery slope that might lead to this policy if the dangers of 'the Balkans' and of interventions in 'guerrilla wars' were not taken seriously. If European countries thought their interests were at risk, they could act, but they should always be fully aware that America would not help them implement their interventionist policies or come to their rescue.

Turning to the other side of the discursive spectrum, the debate in the Senate shows, in contrast to the British debate, explicit mobilizations of 'genocide' and the ensuing demand for international action: 'The polite term for what is happening in Bosnia-Hercegovina is ethnic cleansing. I believe a more accurate term is genocide. The world should not stand by when genocide is undertaken in any part of this world' (Cranston S12029, 102nd Congress, August 10, 1992; see also Specter S12032, 102nd Congress, August 10, 1992). The lesson of Nazi Germany and the appeasement of the 1930s are also articulated in references to the 'chilling resemblance' between the atrocities of the Serbian forces and 'the Nazi "final solution"' (Pell S12024, 102nd Congress, August 10, 1992), or the 'Nazi-like games' of the Serbs (DeConcini S12030, 102nd Congress, August 10, 1992). In the words of Levin, 'We have seen death camps and have seen genocides in Europe this century. We have had enough. If the United Nations will not act in this situation, in an area which could easily spread into another broad war in Europe, when will it act?' (S12033, 102nd Congress, August 10, 1992). The West and America have therefore a moral obligation as well as a strategic interest in countering Serbian/Bosnian Serb aggression; 'genocide are of concern to the world and cannot be tolerated,' argues Cranston (S12029, 102nd Congress, August 10, 1992). There is also a danger of the conflict spreading beyond the borders of Yugoslavia; 'We should not forget that World War I sprang from an assassination of Archduke Ferdinand in Sarajevo, the very city whose plight now concerns us' (Cranston S12029, 102nd Congress, August 10, 1992). But rather than articulate this historical analogue as a caution for entrapment, as in the Balkan discourse, the lesson is to understand that 'what seems to be a faraway conflict not of great interest or concern to us [will be] spreading until it becomes a conflagration that engulfs us.' It is thus absence of action, not intervention, which endangers the West (Cranston S12029, 102nd Congress, August 10, 1992). World War II is mobilized as an analogy in a similar fashion by Lieberman, who points to how American reluctance to engage leads to 'paying a much dearer price, certainly, in the blood of Americans' (S12038, 102nd Congress, August 10, 1992). Action is necessitated by a 'risk to our own national interest,' but also by a moral responsibility 'If our country and the world has advanced in any respect since World War II, it has been by the addition of a moral component to our foreign policy that obligates us to respond to situations exactly like this' (DeConcini S12030, 102nd Congress, August 10, 1992). A position seconded by Specter, who argues that 'it is plain to see that the United States has very significant security interests in Western Europe, but I also feel that this action is justified entirely on moral grounds to stop crimes against humanity' (S12033, 102nd Congress, August 10, 1992).

Considering the references to Nazi-Germany, the mobilization of moral outrage, national interests, and the dangers of appeasement and non-intervention, the policy implications of this discourse may, however, seem fairly meek. The goal of the resolution is not, argues DeConcini, 'to take a side on the civil war but to be sure that humanitarian aid is delivered and that the camps are inspected' (S12030, 102nd Congress, August 10, 1992; repeated by Levin 12033, 102nd Congress, August 10, 1992). More radically, Lieberman advocates a lifting of the arms embargo to give the disadvantaged Bosnian government forces 'a fair fight'—a call which was to be repeatedly argued in the Senate through the next almost three years—but, crucially in terms of staking out the limits of interventionism, he clarified that 'I think everyone on the floor here will agree in this debate that we do not want American ground forces engaged in civil war there' (S12038, 102nd Congress, August 10, 1992). Although advocating from opposing ends of the discursive identity spectrum, the Balkan discourse and the Genocide discourse therefore agreed on rejecting a policy involving American ground troops.

These articulations of the war as a 'genocide' drew on the basic Genocide discourse, not least in its attempt to combine ethical and strategic reasoning, yet this was a discourse which articulated a more simple construction of identities than did the ideal-type Genocide discourse. First, it was not very concerned with the multi-ethnic or multicultural identity of Bosnia and hence did not explicitly articulate 'Bosnia' as a 'Western Self.'[7] Second, the discourse strove to mobilize the West to act in Bosnia, but the 'failure of the West,' another central element of the Genocide discourse, had not yet been firmly established.[8] The discovery of a 'simpler' discourse than the one established as the basic discourse might lead to a consideration of whether this simpler version rather than the more elaborate one laid out in chapter 6 should have been opted for as 'the' basic discourse. Since basic discourses function as analytical building blocks from which the complexity of a foreign policy debate can be mapped, it might be argued that the simpler version should have been chosen as the basic discourse. But, taking the methodological guideline that basic discourses should construct radically different Others and Selves into account, it is seen that the more complex Genocide discourse articulates a bigger difference to the Balkan discourse than the simpler 1992 US Senate version: the former fills in the content of the 'Bosnian' identity as 'multicultural,' which makes for a larger difference to the Otherness of the Balkan discourse than the 'blank Bosnian spot' of the 1992 discourse; and the constitution of 'Western failure' implies a larger difference to the Balkan discourse's refusal of Western responsibility, that the 1992 Genocide discourse's construction of the West as simply responsible for stopping 'genocide.' Basic discourses are, furthermore, supposed to span a larger array of genres and types of texts, and the multicultural identity of 'Bosnia' and the 'failure of the West' were key components of the journalistic and academic articulations of the Genocide discourse, which are discussed in chapter 9.

Clinton's vacillations—or the dangers of ambiguous discourse

After his victory in the Presidential election of 1992, Bill Clinton stepped into the discursive Bosnian terrain in earnest. As a Presidential candidate, he had argued on several occasions for an American policy that would stop atrocities committed by the Serbs and the Bosnian Serbs; and those supporting a Genocide discourse were hoping that Clinton would steer America toward a more proactive and more pro-Bosnian course. The Vance–Owen plan had just been presented as Clinton came into office and from his first statements in early February, he expressed concern for the fate of the Bosnian Muslims under Vance–Owen, 'the United States at the present time is reluctant to impose an agreement on the parties to which they do not agree, especially when the Bosnian Muslims might be left at a severe disadvantage if the agreement is not undertaken in good faith by the other parties and cannot be enforced externally' (Clinton 1993a). The announcement of his new Bosnia policy on February 10 declared his commitment to the enforcement of an accepted peace plan, but he was equally clear in upholding the 'policy maxim' of 1992 that the United States would not commit ground troops. Clinton wanted to prevent that 'the terrible principle of *ethnic cleansing* will be validated,' an articulation that spoke to the Genocide discourse while not going as far as adopting the more demanding term of 'genocide,' and he wanted to prevent the spread of the conflict, yet one should 'Never forget, it's no accident that World War I started in this area. There are *ancient ethnic hatreds* that have consumed people and led to horrible abuses' (Clinton 1993b; emphasis added).

This ambiguous articulation of the war as, on the one hand, 'ethnic cleansing' which identifies a perpetrator and constructs an American moral responsibility for intervening, and, on the other hand, as based on the 'ancient hatred' of a violent and barbaric 'Balkan' is continuously found during the first months of Clinton's presidency. On April 16: 'we have an interest in standing up against the principle of ethnic cleansing ... this could play itself out in other parts of the world' (Clinton 1993d). Although the Holocaust was on a 'whole different level,' what goes on in Bosnia is still 'abhorrent,' and in a revision of his 'Balkan reading' from early February, Bosnia is now an 'area where people of different ethnic groups live side by side for so long together' (Clinton 1993e). Yet Clinton leans toward the Balkan discourse, later arguing that 'The United States is not, should not, become involved as a partisan in a war' (Clinton 1993e). The duality of the administration's discourse was also evidenced in the statements by Secretary of State Warren Christopher, who spoke close to a 'Genocide' representation on February 10, stating that 'Serbian ethnic cleansing has been pursued through mass murders, systematic beatings, and the rapes of Muslims and others, prolonged shellings of innocents in Sarajevo and elsewhere, forced displacements of entire villages, inhumane treatment of prisoners in detention camps.' And, he continued, Bosnia 'tests what wisdom we have gathered from this bloody century, and it measures our resolve to take early concerted action against systematic ethnic persecution.' Yet, on March 28, he argued on CBS News within a Balkan discourse that: 'It's really a tragic problem. The hatred between all three groups—the Bosnians and the Serbs and the Croatians—is almost unbelievable. It's almost terrifying, and it's centuries old. That really is a problem from hell. And I think that the United States is doing all we can to try to deal with that problem ... The United States simply doesn't have the means to make people in that region of the world like each other' (quoted from Friedman 1993).[9]

Clinton's attempt to incorporate representations from both the Balkan and the Genocide discourses, representations which constitute opposing spatial and temporal identities as well as very different American responsibilities, led to the criticism that he was 'all over the place in terms of policy toward Bosnia,' that he was vacillating between the two discourses (Dan Rather in Clinton 1993c; Dobbs 1995; Ó Tuathail 1996a; Holbrooke 1998). Discourse analysis assumes that politicians are striving to articulate internally consistent discourses, but there is no guarantee that this will always be the case in practice. Such inconsistency is, however, often seized upon by other politicians, the media, and commentators, in particular during a heated political debate, and it was therefore highly unlikely that Clinton would be able to maintain his ambivalent discursive position.[10] One might also read his internally unstable discourse as a way of keeping his policy doors open while the acceptance of the Vance–Owen plan was being negotiated: Clinton was adamant that deployment of ground troops was 'the option I have never ruled in,' but that all other options were open (Clinton 1993d); that a Serb rejection should be followed by giving 'the Bosnians a means to at least defend themselves' (Clinton 1993c); that one should not underestimate the difficulties involved in intervening in Bosnia, 'Remember, in the Second War, Hitler sent tens of thousands of soldiers to that area and never was successful in subduing it, and they had people on the ground' (Clinton 1993f); and that American policy had to be based on a multilateral framework (Clinton 1993d). The need for intervention was, in short, matched by an articulation of three components hindering any easy enactment of this policy: the difficulties of the Balkans, the concern for the West Europeans, and the American lesson of Vietnam.

When Christopher returned from his unsuccessful European tour in early May 1993 it was not surprising to find that the combination of discursive instability, significant events (the fall of the Vance–Owen plan and the failure to garner European support for 'lift and strike'), and limited policy options (no American ground troops) was followed by a shift within Clinton's discourse to settle more consistently with the Balkan discourse and to downgrade the possibility of 'lift and strike.' This Balkan turn was expressed on May 7 when Clinton told reporters that 'these fights between the Serbs and the Bosnian Muslims and the Croats, they go back so many centuries' (Clinton 1993g). On May 12 Clinton argues that 'Those folks have been fighting each other for a long time,' and 'Our policy is not to do what we did in Vietnam, which was to get in and fight with one side in a civil war to assure a military victory' (Clinton 1993h), and 'We don't want our people in there basically in a shooting gallery' (Clinton 1993j). This unwillingness to get engaged on 'one of the sides,' or with 'one of the belligerents,' and the difficulty of forcing 'everybody to fall in line overnight for people who have been fighting each other for centuries' is reiterated on May 14, where the multilateral necessity and the European location of the conflict are emphasized: 'the United States must act with our allies, especially because Bosnia is in the heart of

Europe, and the Europeans are there' (Clinton 1993i). The construction of the 'Europeans' as blocking for 'lift and strike' stabilized Clinton's discourse insofar as this constituted him as restrained in his choices: 'Bosnia' was not a case that should threaten the unity and stability of trans-Atlantic relations. But the articulation of being blocked by 'Europe' and 'multilateralism' should also be treated with some caution in that it might lend itself to a critical construction of Clinton as incapable of action and leadership. As the President of the world's only superpower, there was a limit to how constrained and incapacitated Clinton could present himself to be.

Once established in May–June 1993, this discourse did not generate the demands for American action that the Genocide discourse, or even the ambiguous discourse of the first months of Clinton's presidency, had done and it proved itself almost as stable as the Western humanitarian responsibility discourse. The critical case of the Sarajevo massacre on February 5, 1994 was, for instance, incorporated within the Balkan discourse by Clinton arguing that 'Until those folks get tired of killing each other over there, bad things will continue to happen. And sooner or later they're going to have to decide that it's in their interest to let their children grow up in a world free of war' (Clinton 1994a). This construction of a uniform 'Balkan they,' rather than a separation between aggressors and attacked, is repeated two days later in his statement that 'Somehow the people of Bosnia must decide that it is not worth the continuation of killing each other … Surely, surely in the wake of the horror last weekend, the parties will be able to, with a little support from the rest of us, reach an agreement that all can live with and honor' (Clinton 1994b). The uniformity of 'the parties' is inscribed into a discourse that abhors the 'horror,' but which is silent about the history of the war and the repeated atrocities committed by the Bosnian Serbs.

Nor did the critical events of Spring 1995, including the deaths of 71 people in the massacre in Tuzla, bring any significant discursive or political shifts. Two speeches in the immediate aftermath reiterated the construction of the war as based on 'age-old conflicts rooted in ethnic, racial, and religious hatred,' and as 'fueled by ancient, bloody divisions between Bosnian Serbs, Muslims, and Croats' (Clinton 1995a; Clinton 1995b). Clinton argued that the United States had done anything it could, short of ground troops, 'to help prevent the multiethnic Bosnian state from being destroyed and to minimize the loss of life and the ethnic cleansing,' but one should 'remember that the Balkans are a troubling area and that it was trouble in the Balkans that sparked World War I' and that 'we can't completely solve all the world's problems.' In a striking defense of Western policy, it is noted that 'the casualties have dropped from 130,000 in 1992 to about 2,500 in 1994, still tragic but dramatically reduced. And all of this has been accomplished without any involvement of American ground forces in combat or peacekeeping missions' (Clinton 1995b). The construction of this 'reduction' as an 'accomplishment'— rather than as a failure to prevent so many deaths in a population of 4.35 million—is perhaps one of the most jarring examples of Clinton's Balkan discourse. While Clinton's turn to the Balkan discourse brought more internal stability to his Bosnian policy, it was also, not surprisingly, a turn which invigorated the domestic criticism based on a Genocide discourse.

'Lift and strike' and a 'fair fight'

Clinton's argument that the Europeans would not support 'lift and strike' and his repeated insistence on the necessity of multilateral action did not convince the critical American voices speaking within the Genocide discourse. As the war went on, multiple bills were proposed in the Senate calling for a unilateral lifting of the embargo and for adopting air strikes; and support for these policies was echoed by editorials and commentators. This oppositional discourse continued to construct the war in terms of 'genocide,' but it was equally adamant that the United States should not dispatch ground troops. The full basic Genocide discourse, which articulated the multicultural and multiethnic identity of 'Bosnia' and the failure of 'the West' was argued by strong proponents of lifting the embargo, most prominently perhaps Joseph Biden and Joseph Lieberman. Biden argued in August 1993, under the telling title 'Sarajevo on the Abyss: The Fatal Moment Before Bosnia's Tragedy and The West's Shame are Complete,' that 'the West' had 'orchestrated its institutions in a symphony of evasion,' been 'accomplices in a calculated act of negligence' and that its tolerance of the atrocities 'represents a historic abdication of responsibility.' The construction of the multiethnic character of the Bosnian government and its 'powerful, ennobling principle of multiethnic harmony' further added to the need for defending Bosnia (S10251, 103rd Congress, August 3, 1993). These constructions were reiterated in May 1994, where Biden raised both the multiethnic character of Sarajevo and the failure of 'the West': 'Decades from now, historians will reflect on the Bosnian tragedy and wonder what compelled Western leaders to stand inert in the face of a challenge that so clearly threatened Western interests and Western values' (S5608, 103rd Congress, May 12, 1994). Senator Lieberman also took issue with the construction of ancient hatred in pointing to 'Bosnia as a multicultural society' and the 'failure of the civilized world to take action to stop the aggression' (S258, 103rd Congress, January 27, 1994).[11]

To articulate an instance as a 'genocide' is, as laid out in chapter 6, to constitute a legal, political, and moral obligation, an irrevocable imperative that cannot be pushed aside but must be acted on, and 'genocide' is, as a consequence, a representation which is never adopted lightly by politicians with decision-making capacity. To construct the Bosnian war as a 'genocide' therefore put significant discursive pressure on the policy which should be undertaken, not least when America was constructed as having 'a special history and a special understanding for the plight of the Bosnian people' and as carrying 'the burden of world leadership' (Dole S5416, 103rd Congress, May 10, 1994). To lift the embargo was to 'protect America's strategic interests and to uphold our principles; to be true to our moral traditions which have always distinguished this country' (Lieberman S5424, 103rd Congress, May 10, 1994). But how was the ethical imperative of 'genocide,' the strategic interests in Bosnia, and the American superior military and moral authority reconciled with the American Genocide discourse's refusal to send ground troops? Which discursive strategies were employed to help stabilize this seemingly unstable construction of ethical responsibility and military might on the one hand with deferral of a fully committed action on the other?

One strategy was to qualify the moral and strategic interests established by the Genocide discourse. Senator Lieberman constructed the war in Bosnia as a 'genocide' and the United States as having 'strategic and moral interests,' yet these were subsequently qualified by the rhetorical question: are these interests 'enough to justify sending American soldiers to fight in Bosnia? My answer is no.'[12] Not explicating *why* genocide was not 'enough' of a moral interest or obligation, Lieberman reframed the moral question as whether a people who 'want to fight' to protect themselves should not be allowed to do that (Lieberman S5424, 103rd Congress, May 10, 1994). This construction of the Bosnians as 'wanting to fight' and the justice of a 'fair fight' constituted a much repeated linchpin of the American Genocide 'lift and strike' discourse. This construction rearticulated responsibility and located it ambiguously with 'the West' as well as with Bosnian government forces. The West and America were responsible for creating better military and strategic conditions for the Bosnian army, but they were not responsible for fighting the war itself, or ultimately for rectifying 'genocide' (Dole S5416, 103rd Congress, August 10, 1994; *The New York Times* 1994c).

The American Genocide 'lift and strike' discourse (Figure 7.2) sought to stabilize this narrowing of American responsibility by arguing that the 'fair fight' was the policy called for by the 'Bosnians,' who were not asking for 'the American cavalry riding over the hill to save them. They are not asking for that. They have soldiers—their own—and what they want is the arms with which to fight their battles' (Lieberman S5621, 103rd Congress, May 12, 1994). 'They do not want American forces' (Dole S5622, 103rd Congress, May 12, 1994). The analytical point here is not the historical validity of this claim—clearly the Bosnian government was at this point of the war acutely aware that under no circumstances was Clinton going to send American ground troops, and that a lifting of the embargo might be the only realistic alternative—but the production of the 'Bosnians' as a subject capable of undertaking its own defense. The Bosnian leadership is, furthermore, constituted as the legitimate voice of the 'Bosnian people.' 'We ought,' argued Lieberman, 'to listen to the words of the democratically elected leaders of Bosnia as to what is best for the Bosnian people' (Lieberman S5621, 103rd Congress, May 12, 1994). Where the humanitarian responsibility discourse constituted its (circumscribed) responsibility toward a 'civilian' subject in need of assistance because of the actions of 'its' leaders, it is precisely those leaders who have the capacity to make legitimate

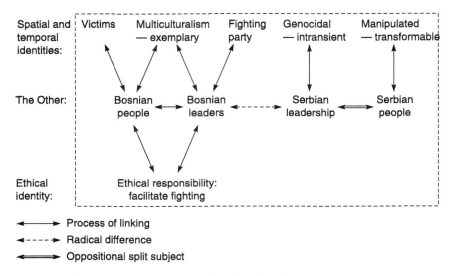

Process of linking

Radical difference

Oppositional split subject

Figure 7.2 The American Genocide 'lift and strike' discourse.

decisions within the American Genocide 'lift and strike' discourse. As these leaders are bestowed with political agency and legitimacy, they hold the right to take the 'humanitarian chance' that lifting the embargo will aggravate the situation for the civilian population. The construction of the 'fair fight' as the legitimate response to 'genocide' is also supported by an optimistic view of the embargo's impact, that 'it is not too late' (Dole S5419, 103rd Congress, August 10, 1994). That it will, indeed, produce a Bosnian government army that is not only putting up a 'fair fight' but which can reclaim lost territory, defend its citizens, and give the Serbs the incentive to negotiate in earnest.

The articulation of the 'fair fight' as a response to genocide is clearly aimed at countering the Balkan discourse's conjuring of the fears of Balkan and Vietnam entrapments and loss of American life. The 'no ground troops' imperative was constituted as so discursively dominant that the American Genocide 'lift and strike' discourse was forced to accommodate to this discursive constraint, yet doing so by constituting the 'Bosnians' as parts in a 'fair fight' reconfigured the subjectivity of the 'victims' of the basic Genocide discourse. 'Victims of genocide' cannot take on the responsibility for their own defense but are dependent upon the ethical imperative's actualization in the Other coming to their rescue and protection. An armed part in a 'fair fight' is not, by contrast, a 'victim' dependent upon the agency of Others, but is responsible for its own survival—as well as ultimately for a potential defeat. To see the Bosnian government defeated in a 'fair fight' was indeed the unstable 'silent spot' that the American Genocide 'lift and strike' discourse could not address as this would expose either the need for American ground troops or the discourse's inability to acknowledge the full ethical responsibility of its 'genocide' representation.

Bringing back America: responsibility and an 'honorable peace'

The massacre in Srebrenica, the attacks on Sarajevo in August 1995, and the repeated Congressional calls for the lifting of the arms embargo put 'Bosnia' at the top of Clinton's foreign policy agenda. The air strikes of Operation Deliberate Force challenged Serbian positions on the ground, and Holbrooke's diplomacy ultimately culminated in the Dayton Accord, the enforcement of which called for 20,000 American troops. The most significant accommodations within Clinton's discourse was to move away from the 'ancient hatred' construction of Balkan temporal identity—on September 23 he claims that Bosnia is a place where 'Muslims, Serbs, and Croats had lived together peacefully for centuries' (Clinton 1995e) and in November he turns to 'the mosques and churches of Sarajevo' as 'a shining symbol of multiethnic tolerance' (Clinton 1995g)—while retaining a spatial construction of the 'parties' and 'warring ethnic groups.' NATO's bombing campaign is constituted as 'the right response to the savagery in Sarajevo' (Clinton 1995c) and an honoring of 'our commitment to protect Sarajevo' because 'We cannot allow more innocent civilians and children to die there' (Clinton 1995d). But these articulations of 'innocent victims' of savage war are simultaneously linked to a repeated insistence that the war should be solved not on the battlefield but at the negotiating table. This emphasis on negotiations brings forth the spatial identity of 'equal parties' from the Balkan discourse: 'We can't force peace on the parties; only they themselves can make it. That's why I have refused to let American ground troops become combatants in Bosnia. But we can press the parties to resolve their differences at the bargaining table and not on the battlefield' (Clinton 1995e). And, after the conclusion of the Dayton Accord, Clinton is adamant in making the distinction between deploying ground troops to a war and the enforcement of an agreed peace accord. He is also careful to point out that American soldiers will be well prepared, that they 'will fight fire with fire, and then some' (Clinton 1995g). In an attempt to constitute his Bosnia policy as continuous, he argues furthermore that he has been in favor of American participation in the implementation of an agreement for 'more than two and a half years now' (Clinton 1995f). Congress in turn gave their approval of the deployment, although several cautioned against sending ground troops and Robert Dole complained that 'If we had our way, we would have lifted the embargo and we would not be talking about sending troops' (S18550, 104th Congress, December 13, 1995).

The articulations of 'parties' and 'negotiations' imply, as discussed earlier in this chapter, that the responsibility for a conclusion of the war rests not with 'the West' but with 'the parties,' who have to negotiate in good faith and compromise. If one 'party' is constructed as morally and politically separate from the others, as in the Genocide discourse, it becomes difficult, if not impossible, to maintain that this 'party' must subject itself to a process of mediation and compromise. Were the Bosnian war a 'genocide' it would be immoral to design a process of 'compromise' to which 'the Bosnians' should comply as the demand of the discourse is an unconditional restoration of 'Bosnian' authority and the simultaneous surrender of the 'Serbs/Bosnian Serbs.' Therefore, the responsibility for entering into an agreement still rests in Clinton's discourse, as in the unmodified Balkan discourse and the humanitarian responsibility discourse, with 'the parties' and their leaders, and there is no discursive demand for stronger, unilateral, military intervention were negotiations to break down. The construction of 'the parties' as 'negotiating' is also significant for countering criticism of the Dayton Accord as being unfair to the Bosnians/Muslim Bosnians: 'the Bosnians' have a democratic and legitimate leadership which functions as a responsible agent capable of making its own decisions. Hence, if 'Bosnians' agree to a settlement it is by its very nature legitimate as it is concluded between 'warring factions' who have 'agreed to put down their guns' (Clinton 1995g). This discursive construction avoids, however, the question whether the Bosnian government had any real alternatives to accepting the Dayton Accord.

The disappearance of 'ethnic hatred' from Clinton's discourse constituted one modification during the second half of 1995. Another modification came through a heightened articulation of the importance of American leadership— 'it became clear that Europe alone could not end the conflict'—of taking on 'the responsibilities of leadership,' and of being 'freedom's greatest champion' and the embodiment of 'an idea that has become the ideal for billions of people throughout the world' (Clinton 1995g). The articulation of the special identity of America functioned not only to constitute America as powerful, but as acting in accordance with the responsibility of its identity. The necessity that the Dayton Accord is implemented is furthermore supported by a construction of national interests which intersect with analogies of World Wars I and II: 'Securing peace in Bosnia will also help to build a free and stable Europe. Bosnia lies at the very heart of Europe, next door to many of its fragile new democracies and some of our closest allies. Generations of Americans have understood that Europe's freedom and Europe's stability is vital to our own national security. That's why we fought two wars in Europe' (Clinton 1995g). This, however, also raises the question why the United States, and Clinton in particular, did not act earlier. The response is a reiteration of the centrality of the 'parties,' 'American ground troops should not fight a war in Bosnia because the United States could not force peace on Bosnia's warring ethnic groups,' and Clinton returns to the 'European veto' of the previous years, underlining how difficult this was for him personally: 'it's hard for us when we're the strongest country in the world, when other countries are—don't do what we think they should do ... that was very hard for me' (Clinton 1995d). In the end, Clinton does not fundamentally revise or excuse the policy responses and discourses of the first three years of his presidency.

Western policy discourses and analytical conclusions

The main purpose of this chapter was to map the dominant Western foreign policy discourses on the Bosnian war. It was quickly established that the central political rift ran between American discourses on the one hand and West European ones on the other. Britain was one of the largest contributors to UNPROFOR and its government adopted the position furthest away from America's, and it was therefore chosen as the primary West European case study. Locating the analysis of this chapter within the theoretical framework of the first four chapters and the research design of chapter 5, this chapter was concerned with the official and oppositional foreign policy discourses. To establish the larger discursive field within which these political discourses were situated, media discourse was drawn upon as well. Theoretically, the chapter pursued two themes: first, the argument, presented in chapter 2, that foreign policy discourses are constituted through non-causal linkages between constructions of identity and policy, and that discourses seek to present these identity–policy constellations as internally as well as externally stable, as 'the' legitimate and efficient response to a given situation. Set in a dynamic perspective, these identity–policy constellations confront a series of challenges: from events on the ground as they are articulated by the media and oppositional political forces and from the policies of other international actors. These challenges lead official discourse to accommodate its identity– policy constellation through an adjustment of identity or policy, or of both; or by arguing that these challenges are indeed accounted for, or perhaps support the discourse already in place; or, by trying to silence the challenges at hand, hoping that the eye of the media storm moves elsewhere.

The second theoretical theme pursued by this chapter is also related to the question of stability, more precisely to the argument that discourses always seek to reach closure and stability but that there are always elements of ambiguity, openness, or blank spots which a discourse has to leave in silence to present itself as stable. Taking this general theoretical point to the study of foreign policy discourses, these ambiguous or blank spots might appear as a discourse is seeking to reconcile its articulation of multiple identities, or as it tries to account for events and policy formulations within a particular construction of identity. It is the aim of discourse analysis to trace where these ambiguities are located—to ask, in other words, which questions a discourse cannot ask or answer.

These two theoretical themes were pursued simultaneously in this chapter as the key analytical tool of basic discourses was employed to identify the structured mobilization of identities within the Western debate. Two basic discourses, the Balkan discourse and the Genocide discourse, were laid out in chapter 6, and the analysis in this chapter shows that these were appropriated and modified into important variations as governments confronted events in Bosnia, domestic media criticism and, in the American case, domestic political opposition.

Integrating these theoretical and analytical themes, the first important conclusion to be drawn from this chapter is that there were significant differences between the British and the American cases. The former showed a governmental articulation of a Balkan discourse which was modified into a humanitarian responsibility discourse whose key discursive move was to separate the 'equal parties' of the Balkan discourse into 'Balkan leaders' and 'civilian victims' and to take Western responsibility for the latter, while situating political responsibility exclusively with the uniform 'Balkan leaders.' This discourse legitimized the deployment of a peacekeeping force as necessary for the delivery of humanitarian assistance, but it drew simultaneously a sharp boundary against direct military intervention in support of the Bosnian government. This discourse was remarkably resilient in its strategy of incorporation, as even dramatic events such as the massacres in Sarajevo, Tuzla, and Srebrenica were constructed as in concordance with the humanitarian responsibility discourse's dual Bosnian subjects: the construction of uniform 'Balkan leaders' read atrocities as 'Balkan' rather than as caused by particular political or national groups. Hence more 'atrocities' became evidence of the violence, irresponsibility, and barbarism of 'the Balkans,' rather than being military or political actions that would force the West to take sides. The 'civilian victims' were equally depoliticized in that they were constituted without political designations or history—a political history that might, again, have destabilized the construction of 'all as equals' and their protection as secured through Western peacekeeping rather than military intervention. The key blank spot of the humanitarian responsibility discourse is thus located precisely with the political and historical background to the conflict: the discourse cannot ask how 'victims' have been produced without resorting to a depoliticized and dehistoricized Balkan identity. The splitting of responsibility into a Western humanitarian responsibility for 'civilian victims' and a Balkan political responsibility for 'the war' was further mobilized in countering American demands for 'lift and strike.' Not only would lift and strike be unable to produce the military and strategic results the Americans envisioned—it was, in other words, unfeasible and unrealistic—it would endanger peacekeepers and thereby directly and indirectly endanger the 'civilian Bosnian population' also. The official British discourse was not only resilient in its defense of its policy–identity constellation, it was also widely supported by the political opposition within the Labour Party.

Turning to the American case, the picture is a radically different one. The stability of British governmental discourse is contrasted to a replacement of George H. Bush with Bill Clinton in early 1993, which brought a discursive shift from a humanitarian responsibility discourse without any commitment of American peacekeepers to an ambiguous simultaneous articulation of the Genocide discourse and the Balkan discourse. These discourses were never fused but ran as unstable dual tracks through the first four months of Clinton's presidency; as instability increased, a choice was necessitated to bring the policy–identity constellation into line. The American case showed a much stronger discursive opposition to official discourse, but a striking American policy consensus on never to dispatch American ground troops to a warring Bosnia was shared by both Presidents, the Senate and Congress, and the majority of the news media. This consensus in conjunction with the European rejection of 'lift and strike' pushed Clinton toward the Balkan discourse. As massive criticism was raised over the years, the Balkan discourse was not, however, Clinton's only discursive strategy for incorporating events in Bosnia. His articulation of the Balkan discourse was coupled with a mobilization of the external constraints imposed by 'the Europeans': multilateral action was a necessity and 'lift and strike' could not be undertaken in defiance of Western European countries with troops on the ground. This external constraint needed, however, to be articulated with some discursive caution to avoid a construction of the American President as disempowered, hence the unstable blank spot of Clinton's discourse lay in incorporating criticism without compromising the construction of 'America,' and his own presidency, as 'capable of taking the lead.'

The fluctuation of Clinton's discourse was matched by another important difference between the American and the British cases: while British political opposition was largely in support of the governmental discourse, the American political scene was characterized by much fiercer opposition. Massive criticism was voiced throughout the conflict by an American Genocide 'lift and strike' discourse, which modified the basic Genocide discourse by splitting the 'Bosnian' subject into 'leaders' and 'Bosnians,' a move which facilitated a construction of 'Bosnian leaders' as 'fighting parties.' This articulation was essential for legitimizing the ethical blank spot of the American Genocide 'lift and strike' discourse: the articulation of 'genocide' creates an ethical imperative that cannot be excused or qualified and hence a demand for actions that prevent and rectify it. American politicians speaking within the Genocide 'lift and strike' discourse were adamant, however, that ground troops should not be deployed, and their policy–identity constellation needed therefore to be protected from this policy option. The construction of the 'Bosnian leaders' as 'wanting to fight' was an important attempt to create stability and close the blank spot of the discourse's ethical responsibility, in that these leaders had the right to make decisions (including potentially compromising the humanitarian situation of the general 'Bosnian population'), and to argue that they did not need foreign troops but only 'lift and strike.' Discursive stability was furthermore sought through an assessment of military strategy and feasibility which differed dramatically from the policy dictum of the British debate: 'lift and strike' was seen as both enforceable *and* capable of making a difference for the course of the war.

8 Writing the past, predicting the future

Travelers, realism, and the politics of civilization

Having established the official discourses of American and British governments, their political opposition as well as the media criticism fielded against them, chapters 8 and 9 shift the theoretical and methodological focus and pursue an analysis of the intertextual web spun within the debate on Bosnia. The analytical use of basic discourses from chapters 6 and 7 is retained in that chapter 8 is devoted to texts which articulate the Balkan discourse or variations thereof, and chapter 9 is concerned with texts set within the Genocide discourse and its modifications. Drawing upon the theory of intertextuality presented in chapter 4, chapter 8 identifies the key Balkan discourse texts which have been constituted as influential within official foreign policymaking or which have been highly discussed and referred to within the larger media, public, and academic debates. Using the vocabulary of intertextual models, this chapter thus pursues the main intertextual links constituted within intertextual models 1 and 2. Having identified these texts, the analytical ambition of this chapter is to subject them to a double reading: to analyze the way in which key texts were read and constructed within the debate and to conduct a primary reading of the texts themselves.

These readings produce in turn a series of research questions: first and foremost whether the general consensus on how a particular text should be read concord with the primary readings suggested here. The process through which texts are given political meaning within a foreign policy debate becomes particularly central when the key texts in question are not explicitly concerned with foreign policy; are historical texts from an earlier and different political context; or are located within the non-traditional policy genres of literary non-fiction or fiction. These three situations are all characterized by an interpretive deficit in that those employing these key texts need to add policy to a non-policy text, add the contemporary to a historical text, or add factuality to a narrative and subjective genre. Reading the readings of key texts, this chapter points out how texts that are constituted within the debate as clear cases of the Balkan discourse are indeed more complex, that rather than slavishly reproduce the Balkan discourse they articulate modifications and variations. Such 'misreadings' appear to be particularly likely when the key texts in question have a high interpretative deficit: the two most important key texts within the Balkan discourse were travelogues and hence of a narrative, subjective genre, one of them did not explicitly discuss policy and the other was written in the second half of the 1930s.

Interpretative deficits might provide some explanation of why texts are read in ways that simplify their articulations of Bosnian/Balkan identities and ensuing policy options, but why is it that a simple Balkan discourse reading often prevailed over other possible readings? The analysis below draws upon the theoretical arguments laid out in chapter 4 and argues that these readings occurred in part because texts are read through the main categories of the debate itself. Since the Balkan discourse had a prominent, in some contexts even a dominant, status, it was the interpretive lens through which key texts were read. Hence these texts were later constituted as supporting the Balkan discourse that had structured how they were read in the first place. It is therefore important, particularly when working with texts from an earlier period, or with current texts which draw upon past works, to situate readings within a conceptual history of the identity in question, in this case the Balkans. Drawing upon the history of the concept of the Balkans laid out in chapter 6, this chapter shows how the nineteenth century Romantic and civilizational discourses which were marginalized by the post-1920s Balkanization discourse were indeed at play in key texts, but that these discourses were overlooked by the readings of the 1990s.

The construction of the intertextual web of Balkan discourses begins with Robert D. Kaplan's *Balkan Ghosts* (Kaplan 1993a), which became famous for having made Clinton abandon his policy of 'lift and strike' in May 1993 and for moving into a Balkan discourse of ancient hatred (Drew 1994: 157–8; Owen 1995: 161–2; Dobbs 1995; Ringle 2002). This account and high-profile reviews—*The New York Times* chose it as one of the best books of the year—made *Balkan Ghosts* the most quoted book within the American Bosnia debate, even though it never explicitly broached the question of which policy the West should pursue. Kaplan's strongest intertextual reference for the Yugoslavian leg of his journey was another legendary travelogue, Rebecca West's *Black Lamb and Grey Falcon: A Journey through Yugoslavia* (1941), a book, which is said to have had a wide impact on two generations of British and American policymakers, journalists, diplomats, and readers. It was, argues Brian Hall, the most dominant secondary source among British and American journalists covering the war (Holbrooke 1998: 22; Simms 2001: 179; Hall 1996: 76; Conversi 1996: 252; Schweizer 2002: 2). Moving closer to West's intertextual construction, she is either uncritically celebrated or disparaged for her alleged pro-Serbianism, but a reading which emphasizes her use of narrative forms of knowledge as well as her appropriation of a nineteenth century Romantic representation of the Balkans shows that *Black Lamb and Grey Falcon* is more complex than indicated by these standard readings.

The last part of this chapter broadens the intertextual focus from key texts, which are identified through direct quotes or widespread accounts of their use, to the conceptual intertextuality that stemmed from *Balkan Ghosts* and

Black Lamb and Grey Falcon. The first conceptual intertextuality was established through the concept of 'civilization' which was articulated within *Black Lamb and Grey Falcon* as well as *Balkan Ghosts.* 'Civilization' was linked, firstly, to Samuel P. Huntington's influential article and book on 'The Clash of Civilizations' which were key texts within the general foreign policy debate of the 1990s. Huntington argued that post-Cold War dynamics were produced by irreconcilable cultural and religious civilizations, where the Islamic one was particularly prone to conflicts (Huntington 1993, 1996). This thesis gained widespread media attention and struck a chord with decision-makers in Washington, in spite of there being substantial academic criticism leveled against it (Walker 1997a, 1997b; Buzan 1997; Walt 1997). The simultaneity of the Bosnian war and Huntington's writings, and the implication of the 'Islamic civilization' in the 'Bosnian Muslims' turned the Bosnian war into a prominent and much discussed example of Huntington's thesis on civilizational alignment and Western interventionism. The second civilizational text linked to the Balkan discourse was by the classical realist and architect of Cold War containment, George F. Kennan, who introduced the 1993 reprinting of the classical travel report on the first and the second Balkan wars, the Carnegie Commission's *Report of the International Commission To Inquire into the Causes and Conduct of the Balkan Wars* (Kennan 1993; Carnegie Endowment for International Peace 1914). This report was mobilized when James R. Schlesinger, former Secretary of Defense under the Nixon and Ford administrations, testified to the Senate Armed Services Committee suggesting that the Committee considered the report, which 'reads just as if it were written yesterday, with regard to the rivalries among these ethnic groups.' As a consequence, 'there's no settlement that they can—no permanent settlement that they can aspire to' (quoted in Clines 1995). Kennan's reading resonates with Schlesinger's warnings and the Balkan discourse, although a closer reading of the report, which was presented in chapter 6, locates it as an example of the civilizational Enlightenment discourse rather than the Balkanization discourse.

The second conceptual intertextuality within the Balkan discourse was through 'ancient hatred,' a catchphrase which figured prominently in *Balkan Ghosts.* As the 'ancient hatred' thesis allegedly traveled from Kaplan to Clinton, it was argued that neorealism articulated a similar reading of the Bosnian war, but the analysis shows that neorealists explicitly rejected 'ancient hatred' in favor of a more ambiguous construction of identities as modern yet incapable of change.

Balkan Ghosts and the power of intertextual constructions

The common account of *Balkan Ghosts* is that it changed Clinton's policy from an active promotion of 'lift and strike' to a passive policy of containment and that the book 'recapitulated the ancient-ethnic-hatreds version of contemporary Bosnian history' (Rieff 1996: 256; Owen 1995: 162). Yet, a closer reading set within the longer tradition of Western discourses on the Balkans, as laid out in chapter 6, reveals a slightly more complex articulation of 'the Balkans' in that *Balkan Ghosts* blends the basic Balkan discourse with elements of the Romantic discourse on the exotic and passionate peoples of the Balkans. Furthermore, while *Balkan Ghosts* is alleged to have had more influence on American policy toward Bosnia than any other single text, it is also a book which is remarkably devoid of any policy advice—how come then that it would be such an influence on Clinton?, and was a passive policy of containment the only lesson Clinton could have drawn from Kaplan's writings?

Hatred and Romanticism: Kaplan's construction of Balkan identity

The construction of Balkan identity in *Balkan Ghosts* unfolds in keeping with the genre of travel writing through the account of a journey from Austria to Yugoslavia, Romania, Bulgaria, and Greece, a spatial and temporal narrative structure that allows Kaplan to mix the use of personal encounters and comments on cultural artifacts and habits with general historical and political analysis. These two forms of knowledge, the personal and the historiographic, are effectively mobilized as each others validation: personal encounters are constructed as evidence of the general accounts of Yugoslav and Balkan history, while people are simultaneously explained through reference to historiographic claims. Going through the Yugoslavian part of the journey, the specific epistemological lens through which Kaplan reads history, places, and people is Rebecca West's *Black Lamb and Grey Falcon*, a book which Kaplan coyly declares 'had already capsulized the situation in Serbia, in the rest of former Yugoslavia, and in the other Balkan states for the 1990s' (Kaplan 1993a: 32). Reading Kaplan through West, which is discussed in more detail in the next section, one finds glimpses of Orthodox and Byzantine Romanticism interspersed with articulations of the Balkan discourse.

Combining the epistemological layers of narrated experiential and historiographic knowledge, there are multiple articulations of the spatial and temporal construction of Balkan identity as 'ancient hatred.' The book's back cover points to 'the Balkans' ancient passions and intractable hatreds,' the Balkans is ruled by passion not by reason, and its people are of a 'psychologically closed, tribal nature' (Kaplan 1993a: 16, 59). More specifically, 'Bosnia is rural, isolated, and full of suspicions and hatred,' and while Sarajevo is a 'sophisticated urban center,' 'the villages all around were full of savage hatreds, leavened by poverty and alcoholism' (Kaplan 1993a: 22). Even Nazism 'can claim Balkan origins' as the Balkans is a place where 'men have been isolated by poverty and ethnic rivalry, dooming them to hate' (Kaplan 1993a: xxiii).

The chapters on Yugoslavia are, taking the genre of travelogue into account, rather sparse on casual encounters with 'ordinary people,' but the foreignness of 'the Balkans' is reinforced by a narration of Kaplan's experiences with people on the train from Austria to Slovenia, and on the bus from Zagreb to

Prishtina. He notices that 'As everywhere in Yugoslavia, pornographic magazines were ubiquitous,' and he finds himself amongst drinking and shouting men with 'grimy fingernails' whose 'breath reeked of alcohol,' despite the Muslim decent of the Albanian bus passengers (Kaplan 1993a: xxvi, 41). 'Never,' writes Kaplan, 'have I felt that way among Muslims, except in a war zone' (Kaplan 1993a: 41). These observations might seem straightforwardly empirical, but their selection amongst many others involves a narrative choice of how to introduce and explain the 'foreignness' of the Balkans to an uninformed Western (predominantly American) audience.[1] To single out 'drunkenness' and 'pornography' as signifying 'Balkan men' relies upon this being a valuable way of separating 'the Balkans' from 'the West.'[2] Put differently, if there were drunken men and pornographic magazines on every American train and bus there would be little point in mentioning these as distinctive of *Balkan* travel: alcohol and pornography signify the lack of civility, the crudeness, and immoderation of 'the Balkans' as opposed to the civil, sober, and developed Kaplan/'West.' The disapproving construction of the 'pornographic Balkan' relies furthermore on an agreement between Kaplan and his (American) reader on how to judge pornography.[3]

The importance of temporarily situated identity is implicit in the articulation of 'ancient hatred,' but it is also illustrated by the subtitle of *Balkan Ghosts: A Journey Through History*. It is a journey through Balkan history, but it is also, for the Western reader, a story about the importance of time. Kaplan presents extensive accounts of Balkan and Yugoslavian history, stretching from the medieval origins of Croatia and Serbia to the wars of the twentieth century, but with the exception of a brief account of Milosevic's trip to Kosovo Polje in 1987 which stirred up Serbian nationalism, there is little discussion of the political developments inside Yugoslavia in the 1980s. Not only is historical knowledge constituted as important for understanding current conflicts, Balkan history is seen as repetitive and thereby as the key to predicting future events. This constitution of 'the past as present' is further produced through Kaplan's employment of Rebecca West as a lens through which to understand the present and by always asking people about the past, because 'Only in this way could the present become comprehensible' (Kaplan 1993a: xxi). Milovan Djilas, a prominent dissident intellectual imprisoned under Tito, 'was always right ... His technique was a simple one for an East European, but a difficult one for an American: he seemed to ignore the daily newspapers and think purely historically' (Kaplan 1993a: 74). As a consequence, 'Politics in Yugoslavia perfectly mirrors the process of history and is thus more predictable than most people think' (Kaplan 1993a: 8). This understanding of history as repetitious is reinforced by the Balkan belief that 'history is not viewed as tracing a chronological progression, as it is in the West. Instead, history jumps around and moves in circles; and where history is perceived in such a way, myths take root' (Kaplan 1993a: 58). Writings from the beginning and the middle of the twentieth century are thus not bound by their historical context, but adequate sources to a timeless, historically entrapped 'Balkan.' History is given, determined and determining, not mobilized by political actors within particular discourses to particular political ends and hence open to change.

These passages show Kaplan's appropriation of the spatial and temporal identities of the Balkan discourse; appropriations which have been duly noted within the Western debate. It has, however, been overlooked how *Balkan Ghosts* simultaneously reflects the nineteenth century Romantic discourse on the Balkans, a discourse which was strongly mobilized by his intertextual guide, Rebecca West, in her celebration of the Orthodox and Byzantine influences on the southern parts of Yugoslavia. When Kaplan traces West's fondness for Orthodox iconography to the Church of the Apostles, at the Serb monastery of Pec, he asks the reader whether the saints, apostles, medieval kings, and archbishops that adorn the church constitute superstition or idolatry. He answers, rhetorically, that asking this very question 'would be a Western mind talking' (Kaplan 1993a: xvi). In the Balkans, the distinction between superstition and idolatry is irrelevant, blurred in a morass of 'dogma, mysticism, and savage beauty' (Kaplan 1993a: xvii). Arriving at a Serb monastery in Kosovo, he examines another painting, this time in a chapel of John the Baptist, to which he remarks that 'No Western artist—no product of the Italian Renaissance—could approach this obscure fourteenth-century Serbo-Byzantine master's ability to understand, and thus render, the Baptist of St. Mark's Gospel' (Kaplan 1993a: 29). Catholicism and Orthodoxy are not just different beliefs, haphazardly distributed, but indicative of the more fundamental schism between Western rationality and Eastern mysticism: 'While Western religions emphasize ideas and deeds, Eastern religions emphasize beauty and magic' (Kaplan 1993a: 25). This emphasis on religious belief—as opposed for instance to modern political and financial grievances—also leads Kaplan to declare that 'Were it not originally for religion, there would be little basis for Serb-Croat enmity' and hence to create a civilizational politics (discussed further below) (Kaplan 1993a: 25). It is a familiar trope of the Romantic traveler to lament the modernization of his or her subject, and leaving Austrian Klagenfurt for Slovenia Kaplan declares that he has to go to the Balkans fast because 'Soon, whether in the late 1990s or in the decades following, the entire canvas would go dull, as it already had in Klagenfurt' (Kaplan 1993a: xxvii). For all the ancient hatreds, drunken screaming men, and incomprehensible Orthodox paintings, Kaplan, like most Western self-professed adventures, is sad to envision his subject tamed and dulled.

This construction of a fundamental difference between the Orthodox and the Western, with the Westerner fascinated by the strange magic and mysticism of the Balkans, draws strongly on the Romantic discourse of the nineteenth century. But Kaplan's Romanticism comes out not only in the construction of his (inherited) object, but also in his Romanticizing of his intertextual interlocutor, Rebecca West. He declares that he 'would rather have lost my passport and money than my heavily thumbed and annotated copy of *Black Lamb and Grey Falcon*' (Kaplan 1993a: 8) and that

It was no coincidence that *Black Lamb and Grey Falcon* begins in Zagreb, focuses on Yugoslavia, and is written by a woman: such a book almost had to be all of these things. The fussiness and creativity of an accomplished cook and embroiderer, combined with the earthly sensitivities of a countrywoman and soon-to-be grandmother, were undoubtedly necessary characteristics to enable Dame Rebecca to reel in the thoughts, passions, and national histories of Europe and Asia, and to remake them into a coherent, morally focused tapestry

(Kaplan 1993a: 7–8)

Cooking and embroidery, traditional female chores, and the organic connection to the soil and procreation constitute Rebecca West inside a traditional conservative Romantic representation of women as homely and organically connected to the natural world. West's thoughts were, exclaims Kaplan, 'more passionate and exacting than any male writer's could ever be' (Kaplan 1993a: 8; Elshtain 1981; Yuval-Davis 1997). Rebecca West and Yugoslavia are thus linked through a dual Romantic construction: West could understand the Balkans because of her 'fussy,' 'earthly,' 'sensitive,' and 'passionate' female character, precisely because these romantic and irrational traits were those of the Balkans itself. This deployment of gendered identities within Kaplan's discourse constitutes an ambiguously gendered 'Balkan' split between drunken men and romanticized women, but it also presents Kaplan as doubly excluded: from the reprehensible Balkan masculinity he observes from a frightened Western distance as well as from the heralded Romantic femininity to which he can only gain access through his reverend Rebecca West.

The politics of absence and the civilizational corrective

To situate *Balkan Ghosts* within the policy debate on Bosnia is no simple matter. On the one hand the book depicts itself as a 'political travelogue' and argues that travel writing is 'a technique to explore history, art, and politics in the liveliest fashion possible' (Kaplan 1993a: back cover and ix). Yet there is, as already pointed out, no discussion of Western policy toward the wars in the former Yugoslavia in *Balkan Ghosts*. In fact, Kaplan does not even seem to journey through Bosnia as he moves directly from Zagreb to the Serbian monasteries in Kosovo (Kaplan 1993a: 30). So, how does one account for the political reading that allegedly caused Clinton to adopt a Balkan discourse and a policy of American inaction? This story of Clinton's reading and subsequent policy shift should be situated inside the analysis from chapter 7, which showed that Clinton articulated an ambiguous combination of the Balkan discourse and the Genocide discourse during the first four months of his presidency. His statement at the unveiling of his administration's new Bosnia policy on February 10, 1993, allegedly before reading *Balkan Ghosts*, included, for instance, a prominent articulation of the war as linked to 'ancient ethnic hatred' (Clinton 1993b). It is thus more accurate to describe

Clinton's discourse as undergoing a shift in emphasis upon the dual failure of the Vance–Owen plan and 'lift and strike' than to portray it as a dramatic change. This in turn is not to say that *Balkan Ghosts* might not have had an impact on Clinton, but it would be one of reinforcing a discourse already partially in play rather than of bringing about an entire shift. It might also be argued that *Balkan Ghosts* fitted with a likely discursive change given that the policy of 'lift and strike' was very unlikely to garner European support and that Clinton's discourse was internally unstable. Opting for a discourse, which solved internal instability by moving in the direction of the Genocide discourse, would have increased the pressure for 'lift and strike,' thereby alienating the European allies, and Clinton was therefore likely to take a Balkan discourse route with or without the reading of *Balkan Ghosts*.

These are good reasons for questioning the story of *Balkan Ghosts*'s dramatic effect on policy, but the power of the story is precisely from an intertextual perspective that it helped to constitute *Balkan Ghosts* as a prominent text within the debate. The story of Clinton reading it made it a key text regardless of the actual impact the book might indeed have had on Clinton's discourse, and by 2002 it had sold more than 300,000 copies (Ringle 2002). This constituted *Balkan Ghosts* as an exemplar of the Balkan discourse and in support of a policy of Western disinterest regardless of the book's more complex articulation of Balkanization and Romanticism and its lack of policy advice. *Balkan Ghosts* was, in intertextual terms, read through its alleged impact on Clinton: Kaplan is said to have changed Clinton's discourse, yet this discursive shift is indeed read back upon *Balkan Ghosts* to inform the reading of the identity constructions within *Balkan Ghosts* itself.

If the meaning of *Balkan Ghosts* has been intertextually formed through the story of Clinton's reading and the general importance of the Balkan discourse, was American abandonment of an active policy then a reasonable policy lesson to draw from Kaplan's book? Kaplan himself was, according to later interviews, 'dismayed,' and in an article in *The New Republic* in August 1993 he did in fact adopt a much more proactive policy position (Ringle 2002; Kaplan 1993b). Kaplan argued that

> The Balkans—the fault line between east and west since Roman-Byzantine days—is the strategic heart of the world. It is the place where the vectors of conflict in the Middle East, the Caucasus and the towns and cities of Germany intersect. In an era of civilization clash, defending the Muslim enclaves of Bosnia and making them a showcase of multiethnic peace and free markets will be the equivalent of defending and making a showcase out of Berlin after World War II. Europe is being defined not by Maastricht, but by what will occur in the Balkans.
>
> (Kaplan 1993b: 16)

This article echoes the split between Eastern and Western Christianity that played a crucial role in the Romantic articulations of the Orthodox Balkans within *Balkan Ghosts*, but the Romanticist vocabulary is now overshadowed by elements from the basic Genocide discourse in that the Bosnian Muslims are constituted as 'the most Westernized and sophisticated citizens of their region,' with the *Realpolitik*-identity argument that the fall of Bosnia would spur fundamentalism in the Middle East with severe consequences for Clinton's 'real' Middle East policy (Kaplan 1993b: 16). 'What it [the Clinton administration] fails to realize is that the Balkan region—except for the cold war era—*is* the Middle East' (Kaplan 1993b: 16).

Kaplan appears at the end of the day to have employed almost all of the discourses available: constructions of ancient hatreds and Romantic Orthodoxy are mixed with the Westernized and multi-ethnic Muslim Bosnians to form a discourse that is too incoherent to produce any clear construction of identity. If the Bosnian Muslims are the 'most Westernized' of the Balkan people, then a group/nation/civilization is not determined by its religion or region; people, even Balkan people, can change—for better or worse—and history is no longer the predictable key to the present, as argued within *Balkan Ghosts*. But these inconsistencies and the ensuing difficulty of deducing any clear policy from Kaplan's Balkan writings have not subtracted from his popularity as a policy analyst or, for that matter, the political attractions of the genre of travel writing. Riding on the waves of *Balkan Ghosts*, Kaplan's next book on anarchy and Africa, *The Ends of the Earth*, built on his famous 'The Coming Anarchy' article in *The Atlantic Monthly*, reinforced Kaplan's reputation and made him an influence on American decision-makers and 'almost predictive as to where US national attention will focus next' (Grau no date; Ringle 2002).

Reading Rebecca West: pro-Serbianism reassessed

Kaplan's celebration of Rebecca West's *Black Lamb and Grey Falcon* might have further boosted this book's central intertextual location within the debate on Bosnia, but Kaplan's intertextual homage was also indicative of the influence of West's work over the past fifty years.[4] *Black Lamb and Grey Falcon* was first published in two volumes in 1940 and 1941, republished in 1994 as a Penguin Twentieth-Century Classics edition and sold, according to Brian Hall, 21,000 copies in the United States alone from 1993 to 1996 (Hall 1996: 76).[5] The influence of West on generations of readers, diplomats, and policymakers, as well as on the journalists covering the wars of the 1990s, has been frequently noted, but there is no consensus on how to read West's construction of Yugoslavian and Balkan identities or how these constructions have impacted Western policy. One group lauds it, like Kaplan, as 'the masterpiece of travel literature in our century,' 'the book to read on the Balkans'; and even David Rieff, who was highly critical of Kaplan and the Western unwillingness to intervene in defense of the Bosnian government, calls it one of 'the great travel books of the interwar period' (Wolfe 1971: 25–6; Rollyson 1996: 215; Rieff 1996: 47).[6] But these voices are countered by those who argue that *Black Lamb and Grey Falcon* espouses a blatantly pro-Serbian position that has translated into Western policy and underpinned an unwillingness to confront the Serbs in Bosnia. Richard Holbrooke found Rebecca West's impact so significant that he labeled one of his five explanations of the Western policy toward the wars in Yugoslavia 'Bad History, or The Rebecca West Factor,' arguing that West's 'openly pro-Serb attitudes and her view that the Muslims were racially inferior had influenced two generations of readers and policy makers' and supported the 'ancient hatreds' thesis (Holbrooke 1998: 22). Daniele Conversi argued that in Britain 'thanks to the works of Rebecca West and many others, Serbophilia was conveniently "balanced" by equivalent doses of Croato-phobia' and Brendan Simms describes it as 'a rabidly Serbophile travelogue' making 'the rounds of the UN headquarters at Sarajevo with a label warning "UNPROFOR use only"' (Conversi 1996: 255; Simms 2001: 179).[7]

The analysis of *Black Lamb and Grey Falcon* below engages these competing readings by discussing how West constructs identities through an epistemological strategy that combines personal and cultural encounters with historical analysis of civilizational structures and philosophical mediations on human nature. This reading argues that West's Romantic construction of the Yugoslav peoples, in particular of those with a Byzantine and Orthodox history, should caution against an account of *Black Lamb and Grey Falcon* as an unproblematic historical, cultural, or political analysis of Yugoslavia, whether for the 1930s or the 1990s. But the construction of West as espousing a pro-Serbian position is equally questionable insofar as other Yugoslav peoples were embraced by a Romanticizing prose and the polluting Habsburg influence on the northern Slavs to be transcended. It is, as a consequence, impossible to deduce any simple foreign policy advice for the 1990s from *Black Lamb and Grey Falcon*.[8]

Traveling Yugoslavia: romantic bodies and cultural aesthetics

The genre of travelogue opens, as described in chapter 4, for the use of fictitious narrative strategies, and West makes good use of this literary freedom. *Black Lamb and Grey Falcon* is constructed as a 1937 journey from Salzburg, through Croatia, Dalmatia, Bosnia, Serbia, Macedonia, Kosovo (called 'old Serbia'), and Montenegro, before returning to Zagreb; but West inserted material from two other journeys, from her first trip to Yugoslavia in 1936, which is noted in her narrative but with a different content, and from a later unmentioned journey in 1938. The appropriation of events and material from all three trips in a narrative structure focused on one journey not only brings a simpler narrative structure but also provides West with an 'intermediary position' between Yugoslavia on the one hand and the West on the other in that the previous trip in 1936 grants her a knowledge that her accompanying husband, who takes the narrative place of the 'Western newcomer,' does not have.[9] It also allows her to use her own previous ignorance of the Balkans as a means of creating a bond with her reader, who presumably—at least in 1941—did not know much about the region either. Her point of departure resonates closely with the post-World War I construction of 'Balkan violence': 'Violence was, indeed, all I knew of the Balkans: all I knew of the South Slavs,' and pondering the inadequacy of this view she declares that 'I must have been wholly mistaken in my acceptance of the popular legend regarding the Balkans' (West 1941: 21).

Setting out from Saltzburg, the train is dominated by a German party of four travelers who prepare the stage for recurring reflections on the looming threat of Hitler's Nazi Germany and West's negative ruminations on the contributions of German and Habsburg culture. West declares her inability to ever reach an understanding of Germans, an inability contrasted to her happy exclamation when arriving in Zagreb that 'I was among people I could understand' (West 1941: 35, 38). The welcoming committee immediately introduces the complexities of Croat–Serb relations: there is Constantine, their guide and companion through most of the journey, a Serb government official, of Jewish descent but a member of the Orthodox Church; Valetta, a Croat lecturer and Roman Catholic from Dalmatia; and Marko a journalist from Croatia. Laying out the political differences between the two Croats, one is an ardent federalist and proponent of an autonomous Croatia, the other a strong believer in a unified Yugoslavia, West nevertheless decides that 'they are all different and they are all the same' (West 1941: 43). As she later argues, 'it's precisely because there are so many different peoples that Yugoslavia is so interesting. So many of these peoples have remarkable qualities, and it is fascinating to see whether they can be organized into an orderly state' (West 1941: 662).

West speaks derisively in the prologue of those English travelers who returned with 'a pet Balkan people' and her narrative balances throughout between pointing to national differences and Slavic similarities that unite the Yugoslavs, even when they escape the Yugoslavs themselves (West 1941: 20). West believed in one political state and destiny for the Yugoslavs, if not in a Yugoslav nation, but she was also at pains to point out how different imperial histories complicated the manifestation of a shared Slavic identity. The history of the Byzantine, Ottoman, and Habsburg empires had produced 'two kinds of Slavs,' there were 'the *inheritors* of the Byzantine tradition' and there were those who 'had been *incorporated* in the Western bourgeois system by Austrian influence' (West 1941: 603–4, emphasis added). The construction of the Byzantine Slavs as the truly Slavic did not imply that Croatians were completely without their historical merits: they played a decisive role in defending Vienna against the Turks in 1683, but they had been 'diluted by the German poison' and 'weakened by Austrian influence as by a profound malady' (West 1941: 63–4, 89, 122, 216).[10] These metaphors indicate, however, that Croatia could be cured and regain its true Slavic strength. The cure appeared to require Croatian recognition of the cultural superiority of the Byzantine Slavs—not only the Serbs, but the Macedonians and the

Montenegrins—and a Croatian gratitude toward the sacrifices Serbia had made for the whole of Yugoslavia. West was not ignorant of Croatian drives toward independence, but she also saw an independent Croatia as a military-political impossibility: with the looming Italian and German threats, the only chance of Croatian survival would be inside a strong Yugoslav state (West 1941: 606). West, however, never offers a deeper analysis of why Croatian nationalism was formed. The Serbian King Alexander had unsuccessfully tried to console Croatian criticism of Serbian dominance, while Matchek, the Croatian independence leader, had argued in favor of an unrealistic Croatian independence. West finds the King's imprisoning of Matchek, dispatch of abusing Serbian police to Croatia, and abolishment of democratic representation if not to be applauded, then understandable under the circumstances.[11]

West was adamant that her book should be considered not only a travel story but also a serious historiographic account of Yugoslavia, a 'complete explanation of the course of history,' and she combined civilizational analysis with individualistic historical explanations focused on the personal abilities of royalty, generals, and governments (quoted from Rollyson 1996: 206). However, of equal or more importance for the construction of identities were the narration of West's personal and cultural encounters. These encounters generally constituted the Other as magnetically different: as strange but speaking to a wilder, more passionate nature that the author could not find at home. The Yugoslav Other is different, yet someone West understands and who in turn makes West understand and recognize herself. But as in the Romantic tradition, it is West's continuous attribution of thoughts and meaning, in particular to the rural and heroic poor, rather than the Other's own speech, which brings the Other into being. Adopting a technique of zooming in on a particular human being, she or he becomes the vehicle for West's elaborations on general cultural, political, and religious identities, whether it is through West's construction of a silent being or her account of a constructed dialogue.[12]

West's personal encounters show the brilliance of Yugoslav intellectuals and artists, who conversed thoughtfully and skilfully in English, French, Russian, and German and who are no less sophisticated than their Western colleagues. Constantine has a particular status as a revered traveling companion; he is a government official, but he is also a Serb-Jewish poet and constituted as the struggling voice of the noblest ideas behind the Yugoslav project.[13] The complexity of his Slavic and Jewish heritage is brought out when Gerda, his German wife, joins them half way through the book. Gerda, the clear villain of the journey, takes the unenviable role of the German Other. Not only does she symbolize the looming Nazi Germany—it is 'of enormous importance to calculate how many Gerdas there are in the world, and whether they are likely to combine for any purpose' (West 1941: 801)—she displays her Germanic nature on all possible occasions. She is in constant search for things German, she forces them to Franztal, a town of German descendants and liver sausages, the only place and food that West truly dislikes, while espousing a litany of insults to Slavic culture (West 1941: 446–98). She has no care for others and their needs, and she is oblivious to what goes on around her, epitomized in her ruining of West's beloved Orthodox Easter in Ochrid, Macedonia (West 1941: 722). Most important, perhaps, is that she successfully dismantles Constantine's self-confidence, making him feel that, being a Jew, there must be something wrong with him.

These intellectual and urbane characters provide rich testimony to the validation of the Balkans, but the most emblematic encounters appear nevertheless as within the Romantic tradition, with the heroic and authentic rural poor. Since the charge against West of being pro-Serbian is so commonly held, one might begin a brief account of her personal encounters with her celebration of the beauty and masculinity of the men on the Dalmatian coast. West admires a particularly stunning group that was 'beautiful, with thick, straight, fair hair and bronze skins and high cheekbones pulling the flesh up from their large mouths, with broad chests and long legs springing from arched feet. These were men, they could beget children on women, they could shape certain kinds of materials for purposes that made them masters of their worlds' (West 1941: 208). Travel writing has a long tradition of eroticizing its object, yet what is interesting here is West's (uncritical) appropriation of a traditional male gaze, but West was also occasionally taken by female Dalmatian beauties, who were 'lovely as primroses in a wood' (West 1941: 262). This construction of both men and women as physically appealing is not only making an aesthetic point. West adopted, as Brian Hall has argued, an almost medieval logic of representation which argued a direct correspondence between peoples' physical appearance and their character (Hall 1996: 79). Beauty was a sign not of genetic fortune but of being a good and pious person, and for West to put emphasis on the good looks of the Dalmatian Yugoslavs was not only to make observations on prevalent bone structures, height, and skin color, but also to argue that these people had superior qualities.

A similar representational power was bestowed upon cultural artifacts. *Black Lamb and Grey Falcon* is packed with descriptions of architecture, music, houses, frescos, paintings, clothing, embroidery, and food and wine, recorded not simply as observations but as expressions of a culture's identity. One can read many of a nation's qualities from its cultural objects and practices; the frescos at the church in Dechani in Old Serbia show, for example, 'a coincidence between national expansion and a flowering of creative art' (West 1941: 984; Wolfe 1971: 25). But it is also through cultural objects and practices that an identity is reproduced. 'A tradition is not a material entity that can survive apart from any human agency. It can live only by a people's power to grasp its structure, and to answer to the warmth of its fires' (West 1941: 784). The reproductive loop that ties creative expression and identity together is combined with West's romantic preference for pure national/Slavic cultures and she does not approve of the 'pollution' or 'cultural perversion' of

Slavic culture by foreign sources, whether of Austrian, Italian, or Turkish descent (West 1941: 94). It is a sign of weakness when Western culture is mistakenly privileged over local, Slavic, and Byzantine culture, a weakness more frequently found in Croatia, whose long subjugation by the Habsburgs made it susceptible to this fallacy of judgment.

As significant as the meetings with the Northern Yugoslavs were, it is, however, when West reaches Macedonia, Serbia, and Montenegro that her most formative and paradigmatic encounters occur. Two women are granted particular significance, first in a Romantic construction of a peasant woman at Orthodox Eastern mass in Macedonia 'who was the very essence of Macedonia, who was exactly what I had come back to see' (West 1941: 637). This essence reverberates with a Romantic articulation of the Turkish repression and the construction of the heroic, brave, and authentic subject. This woman, 'had two possessions which any Western woman might envy. She had strength, the terrible stony strength of Macedonia; she was begotten and born of stocks who could mock all bullets save those which went through the heart, who could outlive the winters when they were driven into the mountains, who could survive malaria and plague, who could reach old age on a diet of bread and paprika' (West 1941: 638). This narration of the stoic, silent suffering Slav was reflected in another paradigmatic encounter, this time with a Montenegrin mountain woman. This woman's approach to her grueling life constitutes her as 'the answer' to West's 'doubts' (West 1941: 1012). West's celebration of the stoic approach to the hardship of life in Southern Yugoslavia is culturally reflected in her fondness for embroidery. The movement of the yarn and the weaving of the thread provided an appropriate symbol for the care which went into the cultural reproduction of identity, a process which showed women's cultural defense and their preservation of the 'memory of Byzantium and the Serbian Empire,' a struggle not matched by the northern parts of Yugoslavia (West 1941: 784).

West's Romanticism is, in sum, more intensely applied to the Byzantine subject—which could, but need not, be Serb—and her disparaging of the Austrian influence on the northern part of Yugoslavia is accompanied by an equally derisive account of the Turkish people as 'a people who tire easily' and as so 'destitute of speculative instinct that they have no word for "interesting" in their language' (West 1941: 649, 749).[14] The Muslims of Bosnia are, however, not seen as Turks but as of the same Slavic stock as the other Yugoslavs (West 1941: 309). Their ancestors, the Bogomils, had been declared heretic by the Pope, and had in the face of violent prosecution—understandably to West—accepted the Turkish offer of protection. To the Bogomils, argues West, this felt like 'a concession no greater than they would have made had they submitted to the Roman Catholic Church' (West 1941: 303). The Bosnian Muslims were not, in short, of a different racial or ethnic identity than the other Slavs, but had made a pragmatic decision that helped them survive.

The politics of sacrifice and the 1990s

West's constructions of civilizational history and her narration of personal and cultural encounters were set, finally, inside her larger philosophical belief that humans are caught in a constant struggle between good and evil.

> Only part of us is sane: only part of us loves pleasure and the longer day of happiness, wants to live to our nineties and die in peace, in a house that we built, that shall shelter those who come after us. The other half of us is nearly mad. It prefers the disagreeable to the agreeable, loves pain and its darker night despair, and wants to die in a catastrophe that will set back life to its beginnings and leave nothing of our house save its blackened foundations.
>
> (West 1941: 1102)

This dualistic view was based on her readings of Manichaeism, Freud's theory of Eros and Thanatos, and Saint Augustine who had installed in Western thought 'this repulsive pretense that pain is the proper price of any good thing' (West 1941: 827; Hall 1996: 77; Orel 1986: 84–5).[15]

The human drive toward sacrifice was narratively epitomized in the story of the black lamb, prominently mentioned in the title of the book, a *formative experience* which made the events of the previous 800 pages fall into place and which provided the launching pad for West's international politics.[16] The black lamb is encountered in Macedonia, where a group of Gypsies are enacting a fertility ritual on a large rock on Sheep's Field. When West arrives it is morning, but numerous animals had been slaughtered during the night; the rock is covered by wool strands, all drenched in blood and grease. 'The spectacle was extremely disgusting,' yet 'the place had enormous authority. It was the body of our death, it was the seed of the sin that is in us, it was the forge where the sword was wrought that shall slay us' (West 1941: 823). West watches a young gypsy slice the throat of a black lamb in gratitude to the rock for having brought his wife a child, but the rock is a 'huge and dirty lie,' a symbol of the forces of darkness, and the mistaken belief in violence and sacrifice as the necessary path to life and love (West 1941: 826). Yet, it is also an illustration of the struggle to come to terms with the heritage from Saint Augustine onwards: 'A part of us is enamoured by the rock and tells us that we should not reject it, that it is solemn and mystical and only the shallow deny the value of sacrifice' (West 1941: 831).

The significance of the dangerous attractions of sacrifice is repeated in the poem of the grey falcon, which makes up the second part of the book's title. Saint Elijah appears in the shape of a grey falcon at the famous battle on the plains of Kosovo in 1389 and offers the Serbian Prince Lazar the choice of a victory against the Turks and an earthly kingdom or of losing the battle but gaining a heavenly kingdom. Lazar chooses the latter, bringing on five hundred years of Turkish slavery; a choice, argues West, that she does not believe in: 'I do not believe that any man can procure his own salvation by refusing to save millions of people from miserable slavery' (West 1941: 911). Furthermore, she argues, this poem speaks to the fallacies of pacifism: 'what the pacifist really wants to be is defeated' (West 1941: 911). The story of the grey falcon shows Lazar willingly adopting the role of the black lamb, and it speaks to the power of bloody sacrifice, not as the one sacrificing but as the one being sacrificed. The black lamb makes the deceptive claim that 'by making a gift to death one will receive a gift of life,' but the grey falcon is equally deceptive in its claim that by giving the gift of earthly life and future generational doom, one will be divinely rewarded (West 1941: 914).

Bringing the two stories together has as many repercussions for West's analysis of Western Europe as it has for the history and rituals of Yugoslavia. Constructing a politically pregnant narrative of the 1930s and 1940s, the story of the lamb and Lazar is also the story of the Western peace movement, whose belief in pacifism as a means of countering fascism and Nazism is seen as intellectually vacuous and politically dangerous. It is the story of Chamberlain's appeasement of Hitler in Munich, where 'we had exchanged the role of priest for the role of the lamb, and therefore we forgot that we were not performing the chief moral obligation of humanity, which is to protect the works of love' (West 1941: 915). Facing a Yugoslavia which 'swore it meant to live,' England, France, and America simply 'turned away, for what lived disgusted them; they wanted a blanched world, without blood, given over to defeat' (West 1941: 1103). The West had a responsibility to counter Italy and Germany, and it had a responsibility for the fall of Yugoslavia.

But as seductive and historically embedded the logic of self-sacrifice might be, it is nevertheless possible, argues West, to break free of its reins, not to resume the role of the pagan priest, but to counter the forces of darkness. This involves making choices, of knowing the difference between good and evil and when to fight. The Yugoslavs, led by King Peter, showed the power of the good by defying the Nazi offer of surrender, putting themselves in the line of attack because they knew that 'if a state based on love bows to the will of a state based on hatred without making the uttermost resistance it passes into the category of the other in the real world' (West 1941: 1146). Although Belgrade was bombed to pieces and Yugoslavia invaded, at the time of West's writing, in early 1941, there was still fighting in the mountains, and the Yugoslav army managed to drain German resources, inspiring hope all over Europe (West 1941: 1147–9). The Serbian ability to kick its 'Kosovo syndrome' led West to pray that she, and the West as a whole, could 'behave like a Serb' (West 1941: 1126).

The sum of West's construction of Yugoslav/Balkan identities and her international politics were more complex than simply pro-Serbian and anti-Croat (Glendinning 1987: 155) or 'inspired by hatred' (Anzulovic 1999: 171). This in turn makes it difficult, if not impossible, to extract any clear foreign policy prescription for the 1990s. Brian Hall suggests that West might have applied the black lamb analogy to the Bosnian Serbs, seeing their actions justified by their unwillingness to be the sacrificial lamb, but other readings might be equally possible (Hall 1996: 82). First, because Nazi Germany and fascist Italy were to be opposed not simply because they were German or Italian but because they were Nazi and fascist and set on destroying freedom, love, dignity, and light. To argue that West would side with Serbia and the Bosnian Serbs regardless of the political values they were promoting would be to disregard her politics in favor of a purely nationalistic reading. Second, West's historiography put significant emphasis on particular individual rulers, and she was highly critical of many Serbian leaders. She would, as a consequence, presumably have taken the character and actions of Milosevic into account and, given her aversion to communism, treated him critically. It is hard to see those values West cherished among the Serbs—their Byzantine mysticism, their democratic predilection—reflected in Milosevic's career and persona, and it is not impossible that West would have seen him as a squanderer of Yugoslavia and a cynical manipulator of Serbian myths and traditions. While West was feeling most at home in southern Yugoslavia, Macedonia not least, she was also taken by the country as a whole, by the ambition of providing a south Slav homeland, and she might not have judged favorably those leaders, Milosevic included, who abused the possibilities of keeping Yugoslavia together. West's pro-interventionist policy, and her repeated insistence that the West holds a responsibility for the safety of the Balkans discord, finally, with the anti-interventionism of the Balkan discourse of the 1990s. To see West as against intervention is Bosnia is thus possible only if her book is read as pro-Serbian to the detriment of any other concerns and identities.

Conceptual intertextuality: 'civilizations' and 'ancient hatred'

Balkan Ghosts and *Black Lamb and Grey Falcon* stand out as the key texts within the intertextual web of the Western Bosnia debate: they have been linked directly to policy, they are frequently quoted, and they are popular bestsellers. As mentioned above, *Balkan Ghosts* makes numerous *direct intertextual links* to Rebecca West's *Black Lamb and Grey Falcon*, but it is also part of an intertextual analysis to trace the *conceptual links* established within a debate. The last part of this chapter presents the main conceptual links produced by Kaplan and West and discusses the texts that are brought into the intertextual web of the Balkan discourse through these linkages. Texts will, as argued in chapter 3, always articulate a longer series of concepts and identities, in particular if they are book-length and engaged with numerous places and themes, like *Balkan Ghosts* and *Black Lamb and Grey Falcon*. When deciding which concepts to 'read out' of works such as Kaplan's and West's, the key texts themselves, as well as the debate as a whole, should be considered.

Adopting this methodological principle, two concepts stand out from *Balkan Ghosts*, *Black Lamb and Grey Falcon,* and the debate of the 1990s: 'civilization' and 'ancient hatred.' 'Civilization' is articulated most explicitly by Rebecca West, who, as argued above, adopted a civilizational view of history. *Balkan Ghosts* is less explicit, but the book's reliance on *Black Lamb and Grey Falcon* implies a strong implicit civilizational focus centered on the schism between the Byzantine and the Orthodox on the one hand, and Rome and the Catholic on the other; between the Ottomans on the one hand and the Habsburgs on the other. Kaplan's article in *The New Republic* brought, as shown above, this implicit civilizational focus into full force. 'Civilizations' gained furthermore a central location within the foreign policy debates of the 1990s. The most prominent articulation was made by Huntington, whose *Foreign Affairs* article 'The Clash of Civilizations?' from 1993 gained instant foreign policy fame—and was applauded in Kaplan's *New Republic* article for 'describing what I have long felt'—a fame nurtured by the publication of *The Clash of Civilizations and the Remaking of World Order* in 1996 (Kaplan 1993b) (Figure 8.1).[17]

While Huntington presented civilizations as the new dynamic structuring post-Cold War relations, it was, indeed, a concept with a long history within the field of International Relations (IR). Chapter 6 showed, for instance, how a civilizational discourse played a prominent role within the Western construction of 'the Balkans' during the nineteenth and early twentieth centuries. One of the primary texts used in the presentation of this discourse was the Carnegie Commission's *Report of the International Commission To Inquire into the Causes and Conduct of the Balkan Wars*, published in 1914, and it is not surprising to see the civilizational optic reproduced in George F. Kennan's introduction to the republication of this report in 1993.

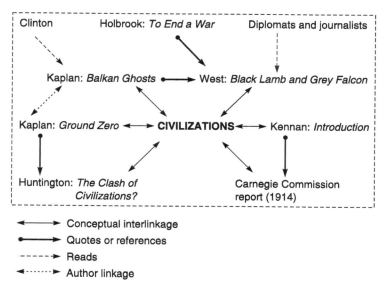

Figure 8.1 The intertextuality of civilizations in the Balkan discourse.

'Ancient hatred' was the second concept, or catchphrase, which stood out as a point of conceptual interlinkage. This concept was, however, articulated only within *Balkan Ghosts*. This, again, is not too surprising considering, as argued in chapter 6, that 'ancient hatred' was a concept that first appeared within the debate of the 1990s where it radicalized the construction of temporal identity of the 1920s Balkanization discourse. Keeping in mind the analysis of *Black Lamb and Grey Falcon* it would, furthermore, not have been a concept Rebecca West would have been likely to subscribe to had she had the possibility. Her strong invocation of Slavic unity and her belief in the necessity of a common Yugoslav state were at odds with seeing the Yugoslav peoples as caught in ancient and non-transformable hatred. 'Ancient hatred' became, however, the catchphrase of the Balkan discourse of the 1990s. Not only did it have a prominent place within *Balkan Ghosts*, it was also quoted by politicians, most noticeably perhaps Bill Clinton, on numerous occasions, as shown in chapter 7. The conceptual intertextuality of 'ancient hatred' that is pursued in this chapter is, however, one of particular interest to the field of IR in that it brings in neorealist analysis of the war in Bosnia. As 'ancient hatred' gained its catchphrase status, it was argued that neorealists adopted this reading of the war in Bosnia. But as the analysis below shows, this was not an adequate account of neorealists such as John Mearsheimer and Barry Posen who implicitly and explicitly rejected this representation. Hence there is a conceptual interlinkage between 'ancient hatred' and 'readings of Mearsheimer' and then to 'Mearsheimer' and 'neorealism' (Figure 8.2) rather than directly between 'ancient hatred' and 'neorealism.'

Bosnia and the clash of civilizations

Self-consciously staging his analysis as the 'X'-article of the post-Cold War era, Huntington argued in 1993 that the world was now composed of irreconcilable

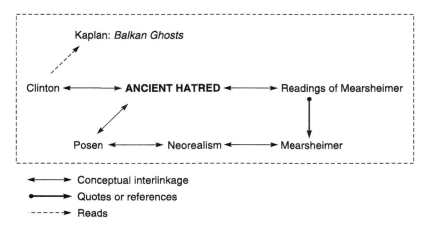

Figure 8.2 The intertextuality of ancient hatred in the Balkan discourse.

cultural and religious civilizations, where the Islamic one in particular was prone to conflicts. Relying explicitly on the work by Ferdinand Braudel and the *Annales* school, Huntington identified civilizations as the largest form of cultural community and as determined primarily by religion. This in turn lead him to identify the following contemporary civilizations: Sinic, Japanese, Hindu, Islamic, Western, Orthodox, Latin American, and, possibly, African.[18] Writing from a pluralist concept of civilization, Huntington argued that the idea of a singular civilization—even if built on Western standards—had to be discarded in favor of civilizations in the plural, not only because the idea of a universal civilization was unfounded empirically, but also because it was dangerous politically (Huntington 1996: 41). Yet, while Huntington's theoretical optic was one of civilizations, and while he argued that the structuration of international conflicts—and thus the route to their solution—followed a civilizational logic, he was also adamant that the actors were states, not civilizations.

As states were the ones who act they were also ascribed primary responsibility for the maintenance of world order: 'The avoidance of global wars of civilisations requires that core states take responsibility for maintaining order within their civilisation; refrain, except in most unusual circumstances, from intervening militarily in conflicts in other civilisations; and jointly attempt to prevent and mediate local fault line wars between groups from their respective civilisations' (Huntington 1997: 142). While this vision requires a minimum of understanding at the level of the leading states there is no vision of dialogue leading to inter-civilizational commonality. Responsibility becomes, as a consequence, a matter of maintaining the *system* itself as well as of protecting one's own citizenry. Hence, there is no possibility that states, minorities, or individuals of other civilizations might be one's responsibility, nor is there necessarily a responsibility to intervene in wars involving one's own civilization.

It is a precondition for Huntington's pluralist—almost relativist—definition of civilization that civilizations are truly distinct from one another and that each civilization enjoys a high degree of uniformity on the inside. If civilizations do not hold a distinct identity, the claim that they cannot be reconciled is challenged, as is the rejection of bonds with and responsibility for entities inside other civilizations. Within this logic of civilizational thinking, threats might stem from external as well as from internal sources. Externally, other civilizations might seek to expand their cultural and territorial domains; internally, threats arise when forces try to import values which are alien to the original civilization. As a consequence of this dual conception of threats, Huntington is not only concerned with threats arising from the Islamic world; he is, in fact, most passionate when debating the state of American civilization. Huntington agrees with James Kurth that the *real* clash is whether America will conquer the 'siren calls of multiculturalism' (Huntington 1996: 307; Huntington 2004).

Huntington's work was not devoted exclusively to the wars in Yugoslavia, but the Bosnian war figured as a prominent example of his thesis. First, because of the important role Huntington accorded Islamic civilization; and second, because it was the key illustration of one of Huntington's core hypotheses: that fault-line conflicts between different civilizations would be more violent and more dominant than conflicts within civilizations.[19] According to Huntington's categorization of civilizations, the Bosnian war took place between three different ones: the Western Christian, the Orthodox, and the Islamic (Huntington 1996: 288). Furthermore, the Bosnian war was the only conflict occurring directly on the fault line between the Western and the Islamic civilizations, and was the only case which illustrated the global as well as the local character of the clash of civilizations: 'While at the macro or global level of world politics the primary clash of civilizations is between the West and the rest, at the micro or local level it is between Islam and the others' (Huntington 1996: 212, 255). The analysis of the Bosnian war was thus de-Balkanized in that there was no particular 'Balkan identity' or 'Balkan civilization' that united 'the parties,' but Huntington nevertheless echoed two of the traditional Western fears of the Balkans: the fear of entrapment and the fear of the 'Balkan Oriental,' in this case as transferred onto the Bosnian Muslims. The association of the Bosnian Muslims with Islam—the key threat to civilizational world order as shown by Huntington's claim that Islam has 'bloody borders'—was made even as Huntington acknowledged that civilizational/religious consciousness converged around the religious fault lines of the Western Christian, Orthodox, and Islamic civilizations as a *product* of the on-going conflict—especially in the case of the Muslim identity of the Bosnian Muslims—not as its *cause* (Huntington 1996: 269). This difference between identity as product and as cause pointed to an important instability within Huntington's discourse: civilizations were, on the one hand, treated as entities with essential identities and hence as the explanatory variable of post-Cold War conflicts. Yet, on the other hand, if civilizational identity appeared only as the outcome of other processes, for instance wars, it was not essential, not explanatory, and importantly, dependent on political agency (Buzan 1997; Walt 1997).

This ambiguous articulation of civilizations was not reflected in Huntington's policy advice, which adopted an essentialist conception of civilization and coupled it with a realist insistence on national interests and the rejection of an ethical foreign policy. His view was straightforward and driven by his aversion to inter-civilizational conflict: the West should avoid involvement in the Bosnian war (Buk-Swienty 1996). As a consequence, Huntington was also a strong critic of the American Genocide discourse's support for the Bosnian Muslims, which he labeled a 'noncivilization anomaly' explained by the Bosnians successfully 'wrapping themselves in the victim guise' while 'American idealism, moralism, humanitarian instincts, naivete, and ignorance concerning the Balkans thus led them to be pro-Bosnian and anti-Serb' (Huntington 1996: 281, 290, 296). As these heated remarks show, Huntington sided with a policy reading based on civilizations which had already hardened their boundaries and content, not with the prevention of an Islamification of Bosnia or with a conception of Western responsibility.[20]

Situating Huntington's articulation of Bosnian/Balkan identities and his policy of non-intervention within the web of the Balkan discourse, one finds similarities as well as modifications. Huntington's explicit rejection of a morally based foreign policy in favor of a policy based on American civilizational interests concords with the Balkan discourse's construction of a foreign policy space unencumbered by any Western ethical responsibility toward Bosnia. Following Huntington's line of reasoning, the civilizational candidate for support would have been the Christian Bosnian Croats, but they were the smaller group of the three and aligned with the Bosnian Muslims for the majority of the war, two reasons which might have contributed to his assessment of Western interests as not sufficiently involved to warrant intervention in 'defense of the West.' And, a potential engagement, even in defense of the West, would always have to be balanced against the dangers of intervening.

The similarities between Huntington's and the basic Balkan discourse's articulation of ethical identity and policy advice were not fully mirrored, however, in their constructions of spatial and temporal identities. Huntington's primary lens was not, as in the Balkan discourse, with the construction of a particular Balkan identity but with the general spatial identity of 'civilization' and the particularities of individual civilizations, in this case the identity of and the meeting between Western Christianity, Eastern Orthodoxy, and Islam. 'Civilizations' have a certain temporal ambiguity in that they have long historical roots, but these are also actualized, and in some cases radicalized, by the end of the Cold War. Hence, there is no 'ancient hatred' or eternal Balkan to Huntington's reading, but rather a particular construction of a rapidly growing and radicalizing Islamic civilization. This construction of an 'Islamic Other' rather than a uniform 'Balkan Other'—and the articulation of 'multiculturalism' as a threat to civilizations in general and to the Western/American one in particular—was often pointed to in debates on Western policy as a reason why the West did not intervene in defense of the Bosnian government. But, as is discussed in chapter 10, the 'Islamic Other' was almost always a discursive figure mentioned by those within a Genocide discourse who argued that the West did not intervene because of a (misplaced) fear of Islam. Voices like Huntington's, who explicitly based an anti-interventionist policy on the Islamic identity of the Bosnian government, were indeed few and far between.

Balkan civilization as Byzantine legacy

Turning from Huntington to his 'X' predecessor, George F. Kennan, one finds a civilizational discourse closer to the Balkan discourse insofar as Kennan's articulation of spatial identity is 'Balkan civilization,' not the Balkans as the stage for the meeting of several Huntingtonian civilizational identities. Kennan wrote the introduction to the republication in 1993 of the Carnegie Commission's *Report of the International Commission To Inquire into the Causes and Conduct of the Balkan Wars* (Carnegie Endowment for International Peace

1914), and in addition to his prominent classical realist credentials he had two particular qualifications related to the focus on 'Balkan civilization' of the old report. First, Kennan was known for his analysis of the Soviet Union and the formulation of the doctrine of Cold War containment in his 'Mr. X' article in 1947, and a civilizational optic was indeed the driving logic behind this analysis. The distinction between history, culture, and civilization on the one hand, and ideology on the other enabled a division between the Russian people and the Communists—between 'the people' and 'the leaders'—and the hope that the former would rebel against the Party thereby leading the Soviet Union onto a new and more prosperous and peaceful path (Kennan 1947: 586, 577; Harper 1994: 167). Kennan's positive view of Russian/Soviet change, as well as his recommendation of an uncompromising strategy of containment, was thus built on two moves: that civilization was more basic than ideology; and that Russian civilization was enough at odds with Communism that a change could be triggered.

Kennan's second qualification was linked specifically to the former Yugoslavia, which had been his last Foreign Service assignment and remembered as 'one of the richest, most pleasant, and most rewarding of the personal experiences of a Foreign Service life' (Kennan 1972: 269). The account of this experience in Kennan's memoir resonated furthermore with a Romantic construction of Balkan passion:

> One had to believe that under all this charm and hospitality there lay a relatively low threshold of potential brutality. Still, one could not help but like these people and respond to them. They were, for the most part, strong, simple people, proud but dignified, initially suspicious but always responsive to courteous approach. One readily believed that even in their brutalities they were passionate, courageous and sincere—not cynical or cowardly or sneaky.
>
> (Kennan 1972: 272)

Like Rebecca West and many other Western travelers before him, Kennan was both intrigued by and attracted to the simple, yet passionate, Balkan Romantic Other.

Turning to Kennan's reading of the Carnegie Report from 1914, the personal encounters and the mobilization of experiential knowledge are marginalized by an analysis of the long historical roots of the Balkan conflicts, in particular of the legacy of the Ottoman and Byzantine empires. Despite the changes in weaponry and communications which have occurred over the course of the twentieth century, Kennan declares the similarities between the Balkan Wars of 1912–13 and the ones of the 1990s to be more significant: these changes are located at the level of technology, the similarities at the much more important level of civilization (Kennan 1993: 9). To understand the wars of the 1990s one has therefore to examine the civilizational roots of the conflict, which go back to the 'penetration' of the Balkans by the Byzantine

Empire (Kennan 1993: 13). The separation from Europe meant that the Balkans missed 'three centuries of immensely significant development in the civilization of the remainder of the European continent' (Kennan 1993: 13). The result is that:

> What we are up against is the sad fact that developments of those earlier ages, not only those of the Turkish domination but of earlier ones as well, had the effect of thrusting into the southeastern reaches of the European continent a salient of non-European civilization that has continued to the present day to preserve many of its non-European characteristics, including some that fit even less with the world of today than they did with the world of eighty years ago.
>
> (Kennan 1993: 13)

Balkan civilization is perhaps not entirely non-European, or at least not as non-European as the civilization further East, but it is nevertheless radically different from 'Europe.' Non-European influence on the Balkans has created a brutal and violent form of nationalism which draws 'on deeper traits of character inherited, presumably, from a distant tribal past: a tendency to view the outsider, generally, with dark suspicion, and to see the political-military opponent, in particular, as a fearful and implacable enemy to be rendered harmless only by total and unpitying destruction' (Kennan 1993: 11). This conceptualization of the Balkans as a uniform civilization which due to an Ottoman presence has acquired a non-Western propensity for brutality and violence reiterates both the Balkanization discourse that formed in the 1920s and the Balkan discourse of the 1990s. This spatial articulation of 'the Balkans' as located inside a non-European space is produced through a temporal articulation that repeats the double Othering of the Balkan discourse: the Balkans are barbaric and backward and they are—as evidenced by the commonalities between 1912–13 and the 1990s—unable to transform.

This Balkan Other is, as in the Balkan discourse, combined with an articulation of ethical identity that constructs all 'parties' as responsible for the war and hence leaves the West in a political space unencumbered by moral considerations. A potential Western intervention should be based not on moral concerns related to the Balkans or the Bosnians but on the consequences the war might have for European and Western security. It is Kennan's assessment that both Europe and the international community have an interest in solving, or at least containing, the conflict because of the threats to European stability it entails, in particular if the fighting spreads to Macedonia, but this is primarily Europe's problem, not America's (Kennan 1993: 16). This strategic assessment of European security does not, however, imply a fuller, ethical commitment to finding a solution to the conflict. As Kennan writes from inside the Balkan discourse: 'it is clear that no one—no particular country and no group of countries—wants, or should be expected, to occupy the distracted Balkan region, to subdue its excited peoples and to hold them in order until they can calm down and begin to look at their problems in a more orderly way' (Kennan 1993: 14). Such a 'calming down' is, however, hard to envision on the basis of Kennan's own analysis as it would require a transformation of the very identity of the Balkan civilization itself.

Kennan's civilizational reading of the Bosnian war is in sum a good illustration of the basic Balkan discourse. This articulation of 'Balkan civilization' and the intertextual linkage to the Carnegie report from 1914 stand as conceptual and textual testimonies to the intractability of Balkan wars and the futility of Western intervention. But this discourse is not, however, without historical and textual instabilities as three sets of such instabilities can be identified. The first instability evolved around Kennan's construction of the wars of the 1990s as a civilizational replica of the Balkan wars in 1912–13. The first Balkan wars described by the Carnegie Commission were products of the declining power of the Turkish state and involved Serbia, Greece, Montenegro, and Bulgaria; the ones of the 1990s were situated on the boundary between the old Ottoman and Habsburg empires and they involved Slovenia-Serbia, Croatia-Serbia, and in Bosnia: Croats, Serbs and Bosnians/Bosnian Muslims. The political entities involved in the two wars were not the same and hence had not fought each other for centuries. They did not share a civilizational history but could be traced back to two different civilizational ancestors. For Kennan to constitute 'a' 'salient of non-European civilization' which was responsible for 'the' fighting of the 1990s is hence to conflate two sets of actors and civilizational dynamics. This historical inaccuracy is not explicitly acknowledged by Kennan, and it is textually stabilized through the articulation of a uniform 'Balkan civilization' that is applied to both sets of wars. The wars of 1912–13 and the Bosnian war of the early 1990s are seen as both explained by and evidence of 'the Balkans.'

Reading Kennan's account of the civilizational history of 'the Balkans' through the intertextual lenses of Robert D. Kaplan and Rebecca West, one finds a second important instability. This one is not so much a historical inaccuracy as a silencing of the distinction between the Byzantine and the Ottoman empires. To Kennan, the identity and problems of the Balkans have their 'very deep historical roots' in not only the 'Turkish domination' but also the 'Byzantine penetration' of the Balkans (Kennan 1993: 13). As the analysis of *Black Lamb and Grey Falcon* and *Balkan Ghosts* showed, there is a long Western tradition of making a crucial distinction between the Christian Orthodox civilization of Byzantium on the one hand and the Islamic one of the Ottoman empire on the other. The Romantic tradition argued that Byzantine civilization survived and vitalized generations of South Slavic people in the Balkans, not that it was the alien 'penetrator,' as Kennan would have it. That Byzantium was the organic civilizational ancestor to modern Slavic culture and that it underpinned the fight for independence from the repressive Ottoman Empire. The point is not that Romanticism was right, that 'the Balkans' were and are the sole products of an esteemed Byzantine civilization distinct from and superior to the Ottoman one, but rather that

Kennan silences this Romantic tradition and the distinctive historical trajectory that the Byzantine Empire did indeed have. To bring up this distinctiveness would destabilize Kennan's construction of an unbroken uniform 'Balkan civilization,' it would destabilize his articulation of 'the Balkans' as radically Other by bringing in the Christian heritage of the Orthodox Balkan, and it would, finally, question a timeless Balkan identity by installing a temporal civilizational identity produced through, and hence open to, change.

The third textual instability is that even if one were to accept that the Carnegie report from 1914 provides important insights into the Bosnian war of the 1990s, the lesson is by no means necessarily the continuity established by Kennan's reading. In fact, the report is, as argued in chapter 6, not a historical predecessor to the Balkan discourse but a central example of the competing civilizational Enlightenment discourse which constructed 'the Balkans' as victims of European neglect and transformable clients of civilization. The Carnegie Commission believed that documenting the horrors of war and bringing them to the attention of the Western world would produce action and responsibility, and they believed in the possibility of individual and collective change. For Kennan to take this report and construct it as a testimony to the Otherness and inevitability of the Balkans is to silence the articulation of identities and the policy advocacy of the report itself. It is to present the historical facts documented within the report as in support of the Balkan discourse and to transform a discursive challenger into an ally.

Reading the ancient hatred of neorealism

Kennan did not explicitly invoke the Balkan discourse catchphrase of 'ancient hatred,' but his formulations of a 'distant tribal past' and 'total and unpitying destruction' struck a similar chord. 'Ancient hatred' was the second concept which figured prominently within both *Balkan Ghosts* and the Western Bosnia-debate as a whole, and this conceptual intertextuality brought forth readings of neorealists, most prominently John Mearsheimer, as subscribing to an 'ancient hatred' thesis. Crawford and Lipschutz located Mearsheimer in the group of people who explained the Bosnian conflict as an ethnic conflict, 'rooted in ancient hatred' (Crawford and Lipschutz 1997: 135 and 158), and Campbell argued that the assumptions Mearsheimer made underpinned the ancient hatred thesis (Campbell 1996b: 172). But turning to neorealist writings one finds, in spite of Mearsheimer's 1992 statement at the American Political Science Association Convention that 'Because of Bosnia I am a realist,' that neorealists explicitly refute the 'ancient hatred' thesis as a 'folk theory' (Mearsheimer quoted from Lapid and Kratochwil 1996: 125n6; Posen 1993b: 80). As a 'folk theory' rather than a scientific or historical explanation, the ancient hatred thesis was problematic because 'The claim that newly released, age-old antipathies account for this violence fails to explain the considerable variance in observable intergroup relations' (Posen 1993a: 27). Posen argued that 'Serbs and Croats both have a terrifying oral history of each other's behavior. This history goes back hundreds of years, although intense Croat–Serb conflict is only about 125 years old,' but that the structural explanation for the conflict should be sought in the security dilemma which makes states as well as groups within collapsing multiethnic empires, such as Yugoslavia, compete for security (Posen 1993a: 36; Van Evera 1994). Multiethnic states, or 'empires,' fall apart because different ethnic or national groups find each other's identity to be a threat, and Posen concluded that this perception was caused by 'the primitive military capabilities they [Serbs and Croats] could field and the terrible record of their historical relationship' (Posen 1993a: 42).

To construct the Bosnian war within the realist theory of the security dilemma is to take it out of its particular 'Balkan location' and to situate it within a general neorealist ontology of the state. This ontology constructs the state as rational to the extent that it is driven by its need for security and relative capabilities and it is therefore susceptible to the logic of the balance of power. Individuals or groups who do not abide by this logic will be punished by the system through a mechanism of adaptation and selection. This neorealist state is modeled on Waltz's utilitarian individual and microeconomic analysis, and it is an ontology of the individual/state as calculating, not hating. War in the Balkans cannot thus be explained through 'ancient ethnic hatred' but has to be based on the security assessments of reasoning entities.[21]

This neorealist discourse appears at first to break fundamentally with the Balkan discourse: there is no particular Balkan identity which explains the war in Bosnia and there is no unique violent history which sets 'the Balkans' apart from the rest of the (realist) world. The wars in the former Yugoslavia appear, rather, to vindicate general realist dynamics: war is always a possibility and states, nations, or ethnic groups will always compete for security and power. But there are also important elements of commonality between neorealism and the Balkan discourse insofar as the former retains the political spatial identity of 'three groups.' The three national groups are not founded in ancient hatred, but they are nevertheless seen as distinct to such an extent that they cannot live within the same state and Bosnia should as a consequence be divided into three contiguous territories: a Bosnian-Muslim, a Croatian-Bosnian, and a Serbian-Bosnian; where the latter two should be free to join Croatia and Serbia proper (Mearsheimer and Pape 1993). The Dayton Accord in 1995 was accordingly criticized for not separating the Bosnian Muslims and the Bosnian Croats into two self-governing entities, and it was predicted that this would make the Accord fundamentally unstable (Mearsheimer and Van Evera 1995). A division into three 'national' groups was necessary because the idea of a unified Bosnia was an illusion, because the forces of nationalism had created too deep divisions between the three groups, and because the Croats and the Serbs wanted to unite with their 'homestates.' This policy of partitioning was taken even further by Kaufmann, who argued that the international community 'must facilitate and protect populations movements to create true national homelands' (Kaufmann 1996: 137).

Having stated contiguous and distinct national entities as their political solution, neorealists were not opposed to Western help in its implementation. Crucially, the Balkan discourse's repudiation of Western moral responsibility for the war is maintained, 'What John Kennedy said of Vietnam should apply to the Muslims: "In the final analysis it is their war",' but Western interests were sufficiently at stake that an active policy should be pursued (Mearsheimer and Pape 1993: 23). Mearsheimer and Pape argued, for instance, in 1993 in favor of a 'lift and strike and training' of the Bosnian government forces led by the United States and with the involvement of NATO (Mearsheimer and Pape 1993: 24–5). Once the three groups had been divided and Bosnia had become an independent Muslim state/entity, the West should restore the balance of power by rearming the Muslims to the level where they could defend themselves but without giving them 'enough offensive capability to lead them to try to take lost territory' (Mearsheimer and Pape 1993: 24–5).

Situating this policy advice within the previous analysis of how the two basic discourses made very different demands on Western policy toward Bosnia, one might be struck by a neorealist variation of the Balkan discourse which calls for a 'lift and strike' policy. The Balkan discourse constructed a policy space where decisions were made through a consideration of Western interests—which were generally thought to be limited—while calls for 'lift and strike' policies have so far been encountered within the American variation of the Genocide discourse. How should one interpret this policy convergence between a neorealist variation of the Balkan discourse and a variation of the Genocide discourse? A first empirical-political observation is that this convergence is a testimony to the widespread support for a policy of 'lift and strike' within the American debate. 'Lift and strike' was argued as *the* alternative by Clinton's critics, but it was also the boundary at which interventionism stopped as no sustained demands were made for deploying American ground troops to Bosnia. Second, this convergence shows that while basic discourses articulate a series of identities to which policy should respond, it is not the case that they delineate only one policy option: the Balkan discourse constructed a political space where Western policy is unencumbered by ethical concerns and hence is based on a calculation of Western interests; the Genocide discourse demanded, to the contrary, that the West ensured a termination or rectification of genocidal actions. Yet, how these political spaces and demands were translated into specific policies depended on a series of assessments of whether and when interests were threatened and of the effects of policies on countering genocide. Third, the convergence between neorealism and the American Genocide discourse shows that while basic discourses articulate positions that are far from each other, this is a distance which might be bridged as discursive variations develop. The analysis in chapter 7 shows that the American modification of the Genocide discourse made an ambiguous rearticulation of the absolute ethical demand that flowed from the genocide representation, and neorealism took the ancient hatred spatial and temporal identity out of the Balkan discourse. The two discursive variations modified the basic discourses in ways which brought their constructions of identity and their ensuing delineation of policy closer together.

The neorealist articulation of identities and policy modifies the Balkan discourse by making it possible that conflicts in Bosnia can be alleviated through an alignment of identity and territory. There is, in Balkan discourse terminology, a way out of the recurring violence and hatred of the Balkans. But there is also an important continuity between the Balkan discourse and neorealism in that the latter reiterates the impossibility of peaceful multiethnic and multicultural Balkan societies (Campbell 1998a). This impossibility was echoed in the statement that any attempt to keep Bosnia together was bound to create more instability and reflected 'a dogmatic American faith that other multiethnic societies can harmonize themselves, that ethnic groups elsewhere can learn to live together as America's immigrants have' (Mearsheimer and Van Evera 1995: 21). This was a critical remark intended to repudiate the Genocide discourse's construction of 'Bosnia' as a multicultural and tolerant society replicating the (ideal of the) liberal West, but it also pointed to an instability at the center of the neorealist discourse: if some countries—that is, privileged Western ones—are able to unite across national and ethnic differences, why aren't others? Either there must be a particular identity that makes this an impossibility in Bosnia, in which case the Balkan discourse's construction of an intransient Balkan subject is retained, or if it is a possibility then neorealism's rejection of a unified, multicultural Bosnia is destabilized. This instability implies that even though neorealist discourse explicitly refutes the ancient hatred of the Balkan discourse, it cannot fundamentally break with its construction of the 'parties' as self-contained entities doomed to repeat their antagonistic views of each other, nor can it account for the formation of these 'parties' without simultaneously destabilizing its own abstract claim about the impossibility of 'their' reconciliation and integration.

Intertextual conclusions and Balkan discourse variations

This chapter has two main aims: to show how an intertextual analysis can be constructed and to show how the Balkan discourse was articulated, rearticulated, and modified across a series of texts. The intertextual analysis focused on those Balkan discourse texts which had reached key textual status within intertextual models 1 and 2, which had been either directly quoted by top politicians, established as having made a significant impact on top politicians, or been of central importance for a broader set of politicians, journalists, and diplomats. Adopting these criteria, two texts stood out: *Balkan Ghosts* by Robert D. Kaplan and *Black Lamb and Grey Falcon* by Rebecca West. These cases of direct intertextuality were subjected to readings that analyzed the interpretations of these texts within the debate and compared them to primary analysis of the texts in question. Both texts are travelogues and appropriate this genre's dominant forms of knowledge and narrative techniques and both texts have an interpretative deficit: *Balkan Ghosts* abstained from any policy advice and *Black Lamb and Grey Falcon* was written in the late 1930s. To use these texts within the debate of the 1990s required therefore significant interpretation, and the analysis showed that there are more complex readings available than those commonly made. It was argued more specifically that both key texts employed a Romantic discourse which modified the standard reading of *Balkan Ghosts* as a straightforward Balkan discourse and *Black Lamb and Grey Falcon* as either a neutral guide to Yugoslavia or an uncompromising proponent of pro-Serbian policies.

Broadening the intertextual analysis from cases of direct intertextuality to conceptual intertextuality, the analysis took the readings of the two key texts, located them within the general Western debate on Bosnia, and identified two central concepts: 'civilizations' and 'ancient hatred.' Tracing 'civilizations' within this intertextual web brought in analysis of Samuel Huntington's 'The Clash of Civilizations?,' a key text within the larger foreign policy debate of the 1990s and Kennan's 'Introduction' to the republication of the Carnegie Commission's report on the Balkan wars of 1912–13. The analysis pointed to internal textual instabilities and it argued that Kennan made direct intertextual links to the 1914 Carnegie Report, but that he read it as supporting a Balkanization discourse rather than the civilizational Enlightenment discourse that was originally advocated by the report.

This dissonance between Kennan's discourse and the discourse of the original Carnegie report, as well as the mobilization of the Romantic discourse in *Balkan Ghosts* and *Black Lamb and Grey Falcon*, show the analytical and political value of the historical discourses presented in chapter 6. The civilizational and the Romantic discourses were dominant before the Balkanization discourse gained its prominent status in the 1920s. They were subsequently marginalized, but they might still influence contemporary writing, as in *Balkan Ghosts*, or be silenced, as in Kennan's, with significant political effects.

The second conceptual intertextuality within the Balkan discourse went through the concept of 'ancient hatred,' articulated prominently by *Balkan Ghosts*, and the analysis showed how readings of neorealism as espousing this concept should be qualified insofar as neorealists explicitly rejected ancient hatred's analytical validity. The discussion of neorealism does show, however, that writers such as Mearsheimer and Posen articulated Bosnian identities as incapable of change.

These intertextual readings simultaneously analyzed the mobilization and modification of the basic Balkan discourse and discussed how specific policies were formed within this discourse. All of the texts, from *Balkan Ghosts* to neorealism, have been interpreted by other texts as examples of the Balkan discourse, and hence in support of a policy of Western inaction. Going through the texts themselves, the analytical picture became, however, more complex, as shown by Table 8.1. *Balkan Ghosts* articulated a mixture of the Balkan discourse and the Romantic discourse of the nineteenth century, and its complete absence of policy discussion made it difficult to deduce any definitive advice. *Black Lamb and Grey Falcon* entailed a similar ambiguity; its

Table 8.1 Balkan discourse variations

Text	Identities	Policy
Kaplan: *Balkan Ghosts*	Balkan discourse and Romanticism	Not explicit
West: *Black Lamb and Grey Falcon*	Slavic Romanticism	Hard to deduce
Huntington: *The Clash of Civilizations*	Balkan discourse's ethical identity and the Islamic Other	Non-intervention
Kennan: 'Introduction'	Balkan discourse	European prevention of spill-over
Neorealism	De-Balkanization and essential national identities	'Lift and strike' and partitioning

dominant discursive construction of Yugoslavia was one of Slavic unity and a general Romanticism, in particular of the Byzantine Slavs, rather than a Balkanization discourse. West's belief in a unified Yugoslavia and her strong adversity to communism made it therefore impossible to read her as in support of any specific contemporary Western policy. Huntington's civilizational discourse was, by contrast, explicit in terms of policy, and advised strongly against Western intervention. The similarities between Huntington's construction of ethical identity and that of the Balkan discourse were, however, countered by his articulation of spatial and temporal identity, which modified the ancient hatred of a uniform 'Balkan' identity into a particular civilizational optic centered on the threat of an Islamic Other. Kennan, on the other hand, turned out as a clear illustration of the basic Balkan discourse articulated through the concept of civilization. Here, the policy advice was one of European containment of the conflict to prevent its spill-over into neighboring countries, particularly Macedonia. Neorealism, finally, was often read as an advocate of the Balkan discourse but did in fact de-Balkanize the conflict. Taking the furthest step toward an active Western policy so far, neorealists coupled this modification of the Balkan discourse with an advocacy of a policy of 'lift and strike' and the creation of a balance of power between the three separate—and separated—groups.

9 The failure of the West?

The evolution of the Genocide discourse and the ethics of inaction

The previous chapters show that the Balkan discourse played a prominent role within American and British policies toward the Bosnian war. President Clinton constructed the war as one of ancient hatred, and the British government's discourse of humanitarian responsibility modified the basic Balkan discourse by separating Balkan leaders from innocent civilians. The Genocide discourse was, in contrast, much less prominently mobilized; it did not, with the exception of Clinton's ambiguous usage during the first four months of his presidency, find its way into Western governmental discourse. This, as chapter 7 lays out, did not mean that it was without political significance: the Bosnian war was a hotly contested foreign policy issue during Clinton's first term and an influential bipartisan opposition in the US Senate adopted an American Genocide discourse that sought to pressure Clinton toward a policy of 'lift and strike.' Turning to Western Europe, the humanitarian responsibility discourse was articulated in response to media coverage and public criticism which adopted significant elements of the Genocide discourse.

This chapter turns to a closer analysis of the Genocide discourse and the challenges it produced for Western governments. A study of the genesis, dissemination, and policy implications of the Genocide discourse provides a contrast to the analysis of the Balkan discourse in chapter 8, as well as the possibility of pursuing three theoretical themes from the first part of the book: the mobilization and importance of different genre for foreign policy discourse, the development of discursive variations that incorporate elements of the 'opposing' basic discourse, and the process through which policy is linked with representations of identity.

Comparing the intertextual web of the Genocide discourse with the one of the Balkan discourse, there is one text, or rather a collection of texts, which stands out as particularly central, namely Roy Gutman's reporting from 1992. Gutman's writings in *Newsday* gained the Pulitzer Prize and were subsequently published in 1993, together with a lengthy introduction, in the monograph *A Witness to Genocide: The First Inside Account of the Horrors of 'Ethnic Cleansing' in Bosnia*. The analysis of *A Witness to Genocide* in the first part of this chapter brings in the genre of investigative journalism and highlights its insistence on the importance of verifiable facts. It also makes the theoretical and empirical point that 'facts' do not in and of themselves produce a particular policy that governments are forced to undertake. This is shown by reading Gutman's 'factual reporting' from 1992 through his introduction to *A Witness to Genocide*, which retrospectively and painstakingly argues that the West failed by not adopting the pro-Bosnian interventionist policy that Gutman saw as immanent in his reporting. *A Witness to Genocide* is not only a continuously quoted key text within the Genocide discourse, it is also a good example of the basic Genocide discourse: it articulates the war as a genocide, 'Bosnia' as a multicultural identity, and 'the West' as morally responsible yet failing to honor this ethical demand. In keeping with the American Genocide discourse, Gutman delineates the policy response that flows from his Genocide representation as one of 'lift and strike.'

The second part of the chapter turns from Gutman's exemplary Genocide discourse to three variations, identified methodologically from political commentary, editorials, and academic writing. Two of these variations have elements in common with the Balkan discourse and they illustrate the way in which identity constructions are interwoven and mobilized within foreign policy debates. The first variation draws upon the American Genocide discourse on 'lift and strike' described in chapter 7, and it accentuates the difference between American and European policies to articulate a fundamental split within the identity of 'the West.' The second discourse, 'Balkanizing Serbia,' articulates a variation of the identity of 'Serbia' by constructing it as a uniform 'Balkanized Serbian Other' whose identity mirrors closely the general 'Balkan Other' of the Balkan discourse. The third variation, 'Gendering Genocide,' maintains the representation of the war as one of genocide, but it reads it through a radical feminist lens that articulates a masculine Balkan identity quite similar to the one of the 'Balkan Other,' but splits this Other into two, radically opposed 'men' and 'women.' This raises the question whether the last two discourses should be understood as variations of the Balkan discourse rather than the Genocide discourse, and more generally how one should understand variations that mix elements of multiple basic discourses.

The third part of the chapter is devoted to the most extensive post-structuralist analysis of the Bosnian war, David Campbell's *National Deconstruction: Violence, Identity, and Justice in Bosnia*. *National Deconstruction*'s poststructuralism locates it at a similar level of discourse analysis as *Security as Practice*, but reading it for this chapter as 'any other text' it is argued that Campbell privileges the Genocide discourse while simultaneously criticizing its understanding of multiculturalism as ensured by ethnic co-existence. *National Deconstruction* is also noteworthy for its refusal of a policy of 'lift and strike' in favor of granting Western support to alternative media and NGOs.

The last part of the chapter turns from the Genocide discourse's critique of the West and its negotiators to the memoirs of the two most prominent ones: David Owen's *Balkan Odyssey* and Richard Holbrooke's *To End a War*. Both authors trace their transformation from staunch critics of Western policies to the structural impartiality of the negotiator, and both adopt a powerful use of narrative forms of knowledge—the writing of personal encounters, retrospection, and formative experiences—in their legitimation of the autobiographical Self, the difficulties of 'the Balkans,' and the constrained policy choices before them.

A Witness to Genocide: from reporting facts to advocating policy

Where Kaplan's *Balkan Ghosts* was the most frequently quoted testimony to the ancient hatreds of the Balkans, Gutman's reporting became an equally cited exemplar of the Genocide discourse. Gutman had fielded reports from the former Yugoslavia from November 1991, and he was the first Western reporter to enter the camp Manjaca, described in a report on July 19, 1992, and to bring eyewitness accounts of Omarska on August 2, 1992 (Gutman 1993: 28). Despite *Newsday* being, in Gutman's own words, 'a tabloid with a circulation of more than 800,000 in Long Island and metropolitan New York,' his reports became renown throughout the Western world, leading to a wave of media interest, including a report from the British TV news organization ITN, lead by Penny Marshall who entered Omarska and Trnopolje in early August. A worldwide circulation of pictures of emaciated prisoners kept behind barbed wire ensued (Campbell 2002a, 2002b). Returning to Bosnia in mid-September 1992, Gutman discovered that 360 reporters had visited Serb-controlled Bosnia since his August 2 report (Gutman 1993: xiv).

If Kaplan's and Gutman's books share a status as key texts within their respective basic discourses, their temporal and epistemological focuses could hardly be more different. Where *Balkan Ghosts* draws upon narrative and subjective forms of knowledge and is set in a temporal space prior to the Bosnian war, a war it does not try to document or analyze, *A Witness to Genocide* is an illustrative example of investigative journalism. As Gutman sums up in the book's 'Author's Notes': 'the story was of such dimensions and seriousness that every element had to be sourced, using eyewitnesses or official statements, and that photos were essential to establish instant credibility. Every theory I developed about the events and those responsible should be potentially falsifiable—that is, structured in a way that if it was wrong, it could be so proven' (Gutman 1993: xii). Key reports, in particular the long 'follow up' report from a visit to Omarska in mid-October, discuss explicitly the validity of different sources: 'Omarska kept no records, making it extremely difficult to determine exactly how many died' and the estimated number of deaths is therefore based on 'eyewitness accounts of daily killings by three former detainees who spoke in separate interviews. It does not reflect other, possibly duplicate, first-person reports of mass execution or disappearances; if it did, the toll could easily be twice as high' (Gutman 1993: 90–1). The authority of Gutman's accounts is thus built on the provision of reliable, falsifiable, factual knowledge, of uncovering what 'actually happened' in Bosnia, and this allows him to counter the charge 'that the news media have "hyped" the story, that is, overdramatized it. The judgment is based on ignorance. The facts are there, painstakingly unearthed. The accounts speak for themselves' (Gutman 1993: xvi). But regardless of how empirically well-founded Gutman's reports were, to engage in foreign policy debates implies, as argued in chapter 2, that facts have to be attributed meaning: discourses have to 'explain the facts,' construct the identities of those involved, and, crucially, generate a policy response. As the lengthy and far more politically explicit 'Introduction' to *A Witness to Genocide*, published in 1993, illustrates, although 'the facts might have been there' they did not generate the Western policy response that Gutman had imagined his reporting entailed.

Turning to the discursive articulation of Gutman's facts, his reports of early August 1992 presented detailed eyewitness accounts of the conditions in the camps in Northern Bosnia. Prisoners told of being held without 'sanitation, adequate food, exercise or access to the outside world,' of 10 to 15 prisoners being executed by armed guards every few days, of Serbs slitting victims' throats, of bodies with genitalia and noses cut off, of women being gang raped, of extensive beatings and torture, and of prisoners being ordered to perform sex acts on other prisoners (Gutman 1993: 44, 51, 56–9). One prisoner, who was held for a week in the camp, reports that 35 to 40 men had died after being beaten while he was there; based on assessments from other prisoners he thought there were around 8,000 inmates at the camp, and the Bosnian State Commission on War Crimes is quoted as having estimated the number at 11,000 (Gutman 1993: 46). Other reports describe what became known as 'ethnic cleansing,' the terror and murders which forced people to leave their homes, creating hundreds of thousands of refugees. The camps are described as 'concentration camps' at Omarska, Brcko, and Kereterm, and as 'detention camps' at Trnopolje (Gutman 1993: 84–5). These camp representations, in particular the one of 'concentration camp,' implied an analogy with Nazi Germany, an analogy that was reinforced by the statement that human rights abuses were 'exploding to a dimension unseen in Europe since the Nazi Third Reich,' the phrase of the 'Kristallnacht for the Bosnian Muslims,' and the description from witnesses of 'executions, mass deportations in closed freight cars, forced marches and a regime of starvation and abandonment to the elements' (Gutman 1993: 29, 80).

The articulation of 'concentration camps' and the analogies to the Nazi Holocaust pointed to an articulation of the war as a 'genocide,' explicitly highlighted in the title of the book. The construction of Bosnia as a 'genuine melting pot' and Sarajevo as a 'testimony to centuries of civilized multiethnic coexistence,' 'the perfect example of a multiethnic city' and a 'sanctuary of tolerance in the Balkans' further locates Gutman within the basic Genocide discourse as far as 'Bosnian identity' is concerned (Gutman 1993: xix, 16, 80). The articulation of 'genocide,' the construction of Bosnian identity and the European location of the war, established, as argued in chapter 6, an ethical imperative that 'those watching' should act. This call for action is also stylistically employed in Gutman's use of direct quotes formed as questions, first to Gutman, but later to the reader; for instance, when a Muslim man, Aga, describes his losses of family, job, and property, asking 'You can only imagine if this happened to your family. How would you act?' (Gutman 1993: 136).

The first reports from July and August do not make explicit calls for Western intervention, but a policy demand grows during the fall and into 1993 as Gutman finds that the West fails to take on its responsibility and counter the genocides. The Bush administration is criticized for staying inside the Balkan discourse by engaging 'in a series of calculated evasions. Calling the war against Bosnia "a blood feud" and "a complex, convoluted conflict that grows out of age-old animosities",' and for not demanding the closure of the camps but only for the International Red Cross to gain access (Gutman 1993: xxxi).[1] The identity of Bosnia as 'a European nation' making 'a unique contribution to Western civilization based on the practice of multiethnic coexistence' meant that 'principles were at stake,' but Bush's aides, not least the State Department's 'Belgrade Mafia,' comprising Lawrence Eagleburger among others, avoided responsibility by labeling the war 'a civil war in which all sides were to blame and [that] all sides were crazy' (Gutman 1993: xxviii, xxxi, xxxv). Gutman speculates that his discovery of the camps was possible only because of Western disinterest—'Since when in the age of spy satellites does a reporter come up with such a scoop?'—and that governments were avoiding the genocide representation 'because it would force them to come up with a policy response' (Gutman 1993: xiii, xiv). This in turn implies that the Western policy of peacekeeping and humanitarian assistance is seen as 'another case of inadequate humanitarian "Band-Aids" that have no impact on the war itself' (Gutman 1993: 126–7).

The West's moral and political failure is underscored by its 'acquiescence' in Milosevic's actions, its borrowing of the construction of 'moral equivalence' from Karadzic and its opting for a 'hypocritical middle ground' (Gutman 1993: xxviii–xxix, xxiv, xxx). As in the articulation of the Genocide discourse in the US Senate, Gutman sees a lifting of the arms embargo as a feasible and decisive military response: 'the situation did not require a Western ground intervention, but Bosnia did need weapons to offset the immense Serb advantage and a guarantee of support against cross-border intervention by Serbia .... Britain and France refused to reconsider the arms ban. Thus the West abandoned Bosnia and consigned victory to the "ethnic cleansers"' (Gutman 1993: 179). Europe had a particular responsibility for the failed Western policy, but the United States also had to confront the fact that its passivity had prevented the West as a whole from taking on its moral responsibility (Gutman 1993: xl, 178). Being a journalist, and particularly in reporting mostly from the ground in Bosnia, Gutman is not as concerned with questions of military feasibility as the US Senators, but he shares their view of 'lift and strike' as a policy that is enforceable in spite of European protests and which would change the distribution of power in Bosnia and rectify the losses of the Bosnian government forces. But as in the discourse in the Senate, the full ethical imperative of genocide is left unanswered: Gutman's discourse is dependent on the success of 'lift and strike' and the question of whether the West should adopt a full-scale military intervention in defense of the Bosnian government should 'lift and strike' fail is deferred.

Variations on Genocide: Europe, Serbia, and gender

The confluence between *A Witness to Genocide* and American congressional 'lift and strike' discourse was no coincidence: Gutman, and prominent journalistic reports following in his footsteps, provided politicians with news about Bosnian warfare, with evidence of camps, ethnic cleansing and mass rapes, which destabilized Western beliefs in a steady and non-violent transformation of post-communist Eastern Europe and a benign liberal new world order. Journalists on the ground not only provided factual information, but were also in effect pressuring their editors, governments, and citizens to engage, explain, and prevent further atrocities in Bosnia. Chapter 7 described the pressure applied by the Genocide discourse on British and American politicians, and Roy Gutman was certainly not alone in chastising the West for its inadequacies. Looking to the American debate, journalists, academics, and former policy advisors employed powerful metaphors: Charles A. Kupchan, a staff member of the National Security Council in 1993 and later a professor at Georgetown University, spoke about 'the rot of the West'; Bogdan Denitch, a professor at the City University of New York, called it the 'responsibility and complicity of the West in the slow murder of Bosnia'; and according to David Rieff, one of the most prominent journalists writing on Bosnia and the author of *Bosnia Slaughterhouse*, Bosnia had shown 'the bankruptcy of every European security institution' (Kupchan 1995; Denitch 1994; Rieff 1996: 22).

As the Balkan discourse was rearticulated into a series of variations, so was the Genocide discourse. The scope for discursive variations within the latter discourse was significant, not least because a multitude of subjects were constituted through the basic discourse and because the policy space articulated by the basic discourse was simultaneously highly ethically demanding yet loosely defined and heavily contested.[2] The most significant subjects of the Genocide discourse were: the multicultural 'Bosnia,' an identity which implied the acknowledgment of different national groups as well as their simultaneous identity within a multicultural subject; the 'Serbian subject' split between genocidal leaders and manipulated people; and 'the West' whose liberal and democratic identity forged an identity with 'Bosnia,' but where its failure to prevent genocide implied a self-critical destabilization of its superior, civilized identity. These subjects, 'Bosnia,' 'Serbia,' and 'the West,' were at the center of three variations that also articulated more distinct Western policies within the broader and ethically demanding space of 'genocide.'

European responsibility for Genocide

The first variation constitutes less of a break with previously encountered discourses than the other two in that it develops from the American Genocide discourse on 'lift and strike' laid out in chapter 7. The latter discourse argued that the West, and the United States, had a responsibility for countering genocide while ambiguously separating responsibility as residing with 'the West' as well as the Bosnian government as a party in a 'fair fight.' The policy through which responsibility should be enacted was 'lift and strike,' a policy constituted as morally warranted and strategically feasible and decisive. The European rejection of this policy lead to a massive criticism of 'Europe,' and the variation which developed accentuated the differences within the West to constitute it as split between two identities, 'Europe' and 'America.' This discourse, *European responsibility for Genocide*, worked on the difference between these two parts of the West in a discursive maneuver that wove together past and present identities: America and Europe had different histories and, importantly, different relationships with multiculturalism and difference. David Rieff stated in *Bosnia Slaughterhouse* that 'Bosnia was and always will be a just cause. It should have been the West's cause. To have intervened on the side of Bosnia would have been self-defense, not charity. America, for all its fissures, is still the most successful multicultural society in history. And the Western European countries are becoming multiracial and multiethnic. If they are *lucky*, they will become multicultural as well' (Rieff 1996: 10). Leon Wieseltier, the literary editor of *The New Republic*, argued even more strongly that: 'there is no such place as "the West." There is Europe and there is America, and they are distinct chapters in the history of decency. Consider the European tradition of nationalist thought. There is no vision of heterogeneity in that tradition, there is only the anxiety (an admirable one, too) about minorities; but the anxiety about minorities is just a scruple of homogeneity. Its premise is still that otherness is a problem' (Wieseltier, October 25, 1993, in Mousavizadeh 1996a: 139–40).

The American experience with and capacity for difference implies that multiculturalism, in Bosnia and America, is constituted, in opposition to Huntington's civilizational discourse, as a privileged sign. The difference between European and American pasts is one of the eradication of difference versus making it a foundational identity, and 'Europe's' inability to protect tolerance, difference, and multiculturalism in Bosnia is constituted as evidence of the continued resilience of its past identity. Or, in the words of Leon Wieseltier, 'For this much, therefore, Slobodan Milosevic has my thanks: he has exposed Europe for what it really is, which is the part of the civilized world that is second to none in its horror of otherness' (in Mousavizadeh 1996a: 138). As this variation grew out of the general American Genocide discourse on 'lift and strike,' one could also find it echoed by politicians; such as Senator Joseph Biden, who stated that 'I can't even begin to express my anger for a European policy that's now asking us to participate in what amounts to a codification of a Serbian victory' (quoted in Owen 1995: 164). *The Los Angeles Times* held that 'Americans are not wrong to criticize the moral truancy of the Bush Administration, but the larger failure is surely that of the Europeans. Empty gesture has followed empty gesture in a parade whose bitterly clear intent has been to avoid responsibility.' What is lacking is not the means, but the 'courage and the will to lead. What is hideously on display is a political rottenness at the European core' (*Los Angeles Times* 1992).[3]

The implications of the splitting of 'the West' for the constitution of responsibility were complex: America's privileged identity and its affinity with the Bosnian one made it responsible for countering genocide, yet the unwillingness of the Europeans to adopt a policy of 'lift and strike'—the policy continuously maintained as the boundary of American interventionism—implied that America was prevented from enacting its responsibility. Europe as a consequence became doubly responsible: for its inability to prevent atrocities in Bosnia and for its blockage of the American enactment of its responsibility. American identity was as a consequence stabilized as privileged, in its past as well as its present. This, however, did not mean that the Bush and Clinton administrations were absolved of all responsibility for the war in Bosnia. As was argued in chapter 7, while Clinton was pointing to the European allies as blocking his ability to conduct a policy of 'lift and strike,' he needed simultaneously to guard himself against accusations that he, as the leader of the world's only superpower, was unable to exercise force and leadership. Hence the point of the European responsibility for Genocide discourse was not to agree with Clinton that Europe made stronger action in Bosnia impossible, but rather to argue that Clinton's administration used this as an alibi, that 'It was because the divergence between Europe and the United States was not properly understood that there arose the mistaken notion that the United States could not act except together with Europe. There were many who believed that something should be done, but that the Europeans should do it; but they may as well have believed that nothing should be done. And so nothing was done' (Wieseltier 1993: 140). Responsibility was in sum conferred onto the European subject insofar as fundamental questions of ethical action and identity were concerned, but a second order (ir)responsibility was attributed to the two American presidents through their incapacity or unwillingness to understand 'Europe' and its limitations. In terms of European responsibility for Genocide's own policy suggestions, 'lift and strike' was usually advocated as the best option, which in turn implied that the discourse left a similar unaddressed blank spot, as did the general American Genocide discourse on 'lift and strike.'[4]

Balkanizing Serbia

The second variation on the basic Genocide discourse, *Balkanizing Serbia*, rearticulates the identity of the Serbian subject from a split subject to a uniform 'Balkan Other.' 'Serbia' proper as well as the 'Bosnian Serbs' played an important role within the Genocide discourse in that the constitution of distinct national groups and the attribution of agency thereto was at the center of the discourse's break with the Balkan discourse and its undifferentiated 'Balkan parties.' The Serbian and Bosnian Serbian leadership were deemed responsible for genocide, but the simultaneous constitution of 'Bosnia' as multicultural, as composed of people of Serbian, Croatian, Muslim, and mixed ethnicity, was intertwined with a demarcation of the difference between Serbian leaders and the Serbian people. 'Bosnia' could, in short, only be multicultural if inclusive of 'Serbians.' What is at the discursive and political center of the Genocide discourse is predominantly the Serbian elite, but the constitution of a popular Serbian subject who is manipulated, and vulnerable to manipulation, yet with a transformative and civilizational potential, plays an important role in stabilizing the construction of identities within the Genocide discourse (Rieff 1996; Lewis 1995).

The constitution of a split between leaders and people has played a prominent role in the legitimation of Western interventions since the early nineteenth century. States have argued that transgressions of sovereignty were undertaken not (only) out of consideration for their own national interests, but in the defense of 'the people' of the country subjected to intervention, and the Genocide discourse draws upon this tradition insofar as it locates a protoliberal desire in the 'Serbian subject' (Weber 1995). This constitution of identity implies in turn that combating Serbian and Bosnian Serbian forces can be legitimated not only as a prerequisite for Bosnian survival, but ultimately as in the interest of the Serbian people as well.[5] However, as this constitution of the 'Serbian people' takes place through a Western discourse it is also one which locates agency outside of this Serbian subject. The Serbian people have been manipulated and do not have the capacity to make independent decisions. This absence of agency implies that it cannot be held responsible for the policies of, or indeed its support of, its 'own' regime.[6] To make this point is not to say that many Serbs did not confront Milosevic's regime or that the latter did not conduct extensive propaganda campaigns seeking to boost a nationalist Serbian sentiment, but rather that responsibility as well as agency ultimately falls upon Serbian leaders and the Western Self.

This articulation of the Serbian subject is fundamentally transformed in the Balkanizing Serbia discourse, which erases the distinction between leaders and people in the articulation of a uniform Serbian identity. 'Serbia' in this discourse is very similar, if not identical, to the construction of 'the Balkans' within the Balkan discourse (Sadkovich 1996: 290). The Balkanizing Serbia discourse holds that Serbian nationalism was of a fundamentally different kind than the 'normal' Western and Central European ones. Beverly Allen argues in *Rape warfare: The Hidden Genocide in Bosnia-Herzegovina and Croatia* that it 'advocate[s] vengeance,' and 'derive[s] from the blood-cloudy mists of extremist Serb nationalist legend' of which the most important element is 'the Chetnik cult of the knife' (Allen 1996: 16, 42, 79–81). This identity sets Serbia aside from the civilized world, and as a prominent example of the barbarity of Serbian warfare their use of wartime rape to cause forced impregnation constitutes a unique 'invention' in the history of warfare. To establish a comparable point of reference for Serb identity, 'not even the Nazis managed to invent a way to turn the biological process of gestation into a weapon of annihilation'

(Allen 1996: 91). Following the articulation of Western responsibility within the Genocide discourse, the fact that 'even one person has been subjected to such treatment should be enough to guarantee immediate and effective intervention to stop it,' and humanitarian intervention was not sufficient to guarantee the security of Bosnia nor of the Bosnian women (Allen 1996: 66, 138). Ultimately, the Western unwillingness to muster the prescribed military intervention resulted in a negative assessment of the West: 'Lack of intervention to stop the genocide is a clear sign of the crisis, if not the end, of the moral and ethical systems upon which Western democratic institutions have historically been based' (Allen 1996: 135).

The substitution of the dual Serbian subject of the Genocide discourse for a single, uniform one might at first seem to make for a less complicated discourse, but the introduction of the primitive, knife-wielding, blood thirsty Balkan-Serbian Other creates new discursive instabilities. If 'Serbia' is a violent, barbaric, Balkan subject, how is it to be reconciled with the construction of 'multicultural Bosnians,' a 'multi-construction' that includes or promises to include Bosnian Serbs? Not only is the construction of a 'multicultural Bosnia' dependent on the participation of multiple cultures, it is also predicated upon these participants being liberal political subjects who subscribe to democracy, tolerance, reason, and compassion, at both the collective and the individual levels. The Serbian subject of the Balkanizing Serbia discourse clearly breaks with these preconditions as it is barbaric, rampant, violent, and irrational. This discourse dissolves the liberal individual into a nationalist collectivity with none of the capacity for civilizational change and resistance that the basic Genocide discourse held out as a temporal possibility for the Serbian people. This implies that while it is the Serbian subject which is most conspicuously rearticulated within the Balkanizing Serbia discourse, it is a rearticulation with destabilizing ramifications for the Bosnian subject who cannot maintain its multicultural liberal identity. And the constitution of the Balkanized Serbia has consequences for the liberal West as well: it is the Western liberal democratic tradition which is constituted as the demarcation between 'the West' and 'Bosnia' on the one hand and 'Serbia' on the other, but the construction of the latter as an indiscriminant nationalist collectivity with no room for individual civic traits or transformations dissolves the very Western liberal individuality that the Balkanizing Serbia discourse is trying to protect. To construct Serbia as a totalizing Balkan Other is, in short, to read it through the same logic of identity that the Western liberal tradition has (ideally) transgressed.

These internal instabilities helped push *Balkanizing Serbia* toward the margins of the discursive terrain of the Western Bosnia debate. While there were many texts which constructed Serbia as Balkan, these constructions took place predominantly within a Balkan discourse, not within a Genocide discourse with its articulation of Bosnia as multicultural. Of the extensive body of material read for this book, Balkanizing Serbia is only articulated in parts by Beverly Allen's *Rape warfare* (Allen 1996). Yet, despite being an empirically marginal discourse, Balkanizing Serbia is analytically noteworthy in that it shows the possible appropriation of elements from two basic discourses—the representation of the war as a genocide and the identities of Bosnia and the West from the Genocide discourse, and the construction of Serbia as a radical Other from the Balkan discourse—and how this produces an internally unstable discourse. Balkanizing Serbia also raises the important theoretical question of how basic discourses should be defined and their boundaries drawn. As argued in chapter 6, the basic Genocide discourse was defined as articulating a split Serbian identity rather than a Balkanized one: first because Balkanizing Serbia was less frequently argued, and second because the split Serbian identity of the Genocide discourse provided more of a distance to the other basic discourse than would a Balkanized construction. Based on the analysis above, a third reason should now be added: the coupling of a multicultural construction of Bosnia with a Balkanized Serbia creates more internal instability than does the constitution of identities within the basic Genocide discourse, pushing a discourse toward one of the two basic forms.

A final analytical question that arises from the case of Balkanizing Serbia is whether this discourse should be read as a variation of the Balkan discourse rather than the Genocide discourse. The abstract theoretical answer is that insofar as a discourse is a hybrid of two basic discourses, it could in principle be read as a variation of both. But the articulation of the war as a genocide, rather than a Balkan war between equal parties, and the subsequent constitution of Bosnia as multicultural imply that Balkanizing Serbia shares more discursive terrain with the Genocide discourse than with the Balkan one.

Gendering Genocide

The third variation on the Genocide discourse, *Gendering Genocide*, was also a discourse that articulated elements from both basic discourses. Although marginal, this discourse was theoretically and empirically remarkable in that it shifted from the political-cultural-national-ethnic terrain shared by all of the previous discourses to a construction of identities as gendered. Substituting national for gendered identities, the Bosnian war was read as taking place between a patriarchal, nationalist leadership on the one hand and a threatened body of women on the other (Denich 1995: 69). Bette Denich held that 'Serbian *Chetniks* and Croatian *Ustasha* were resurrected from World War II, while the Muslim Green Berets represented a new wave of Islamic fundamentalism. But under their opposing symbols and flags, these fighters were akin in their goals and methods. Young men turned into warriors, and in this particular kind of ethnic war, they attacked not only the opposing warriors of the other side, but entire populations of the "other" ethnicity who inhabited contested territory' (Denich 1995: 67). The consequences for women were that 'whatever their ethnic and religious background, and in whatever fighting zone they happen to find themselves, [they] have been thrust against their will into another identity' (Brownmiller 1994: 180).

The discovery of mass rapes in Bosnia played a prominent role in the media coverage of the war and contributed to making Bosnia, and in particular the question of gendered warfare, a topic of numerous feminist analyses (Gutman 1993; Stiglmayer 1994a; Denich 1995; Hansen 2001a; Morokvasic 1998; Rodgers 1998; Stanley 1999; Zarkov 1995).[7] Feminists argued that the Bosnian rapes were part of a military strategy, and that they were also an identity producing practice that reinforced the national and gendered identity of the 'Bosnian nation' and Bosnian 'women/men.' They separated 'women' from 'men,' and 'Bosnians' from 'Serbs,' and attributed superior and inferior gendered and national identities upon these subjects (Zalewski 1995: 355; Stiglmayer 1994b: 85; Ramet 1996: 284; Butler 1990: 33). The rapes highlighted the importance of gender at the same time as they invested the two national communities with particular constructions of feminine and masculine identity. Through raping 'the other nation's women' the goal was to install a disempowered masculinity within the nation's men, as illustrated by the Serbian idea that an impregnated woman was a passive container carrying a child of the rapist's nationality (Stiglmayer 1994b: 119, 122, 140, 142; Nikolic-Ristanovic 1996: 201; see also Yuval-Davis 1997: 29).

Embracing those who advocated a radical feminist discourse, Gendering Genocide argued that men who engaged in warfare, even if fighting on opposing sides, shared an understanding of practices such as rape, prostitution, pornography, and sexual murder 'as an excess of passion in peace or the spoils of victory in war, or as the liberties, civil or otherwise, of their perpetrators' (MacKinnon 1994: 185; Brownmiller 1975: 31–40).[8] This reading of gendered warfare concurred with elements of the Balkan discourse; George F. Kennan, for instance, had pointed to the pervasiveness of rape in earlier Balkan wars, that 'Woe betided the man of military age, or the woman of "enemy" national identity, who were found alive in the conquered village. Rape was ubiquitous, sometimes murderous' (Kennan 1993: 10). The difference between Kennan's reading and that of the radical feminist was, however, that Kennan's realism took rape to be a deplorable, yet expectable, corollary of war, while the latter deemed it an unacceptable gendered security problem.

To Gendering Genocide's view of patriarchy as a universal structure negatively influencing women's lives was often added an account of the particularity of Balkan patriarchy. Denich held that 'Male perpetrators appropriated women simultaneously as objects of sexual violence and as symbols in a contest with rival males that replicated the traditional forms of *Balkan patriarchy*, in which men's inability to protect "their" women and to control their sexual and procreative powers is perceived as a critical symptom of weakness' (Denich 1995: 68, emphasis added; Denich 1974, 1994; Brownmiller 1994: 180; Morokvasic 1998: 68). Making pornography a pervasive feature of Yugoslavia and attributing causal power thereto, MacKinnon argued that 'The saturation of what was Yugoslavia with pornography upon the dissolution of communism—pornography that was largely controlled by Serbs, who had the power—has created a population of men prepared to experience sexual pleasure in torturing and killing women' (MacKinnon 1994: 192). As in Kaplan's narration of 'pornographic Yugoslavia,' described in chapter 8, this articulation of 'pornographic men' relies upon the reader's normative view of pornography as a trait of the Other, whether masculine, Balkan or both.

The combination of genocide, rape, and (Balkan) patriarchy made the Genocide discourse ambiguous in its calls for political action: the existence of a radically threatening situation demanded intervention in defense of women, but specifying the form intervention should take was complicated for two reasons. First, if aggressive male behavior was a corollary to all military action, one would have to be critical of Western military intervention, even where its explicit goal was to stop rape. This reservation was echoed in MacKinnon's comment that UN peacekeeping troops had been accused of rape (MacKinnon 1994: 185). Second, as pointed out by Stanley, many women who called attention to the rapes had a background in peace movements and tended to take a more anti-militaristic attitude to foreign policy (Stanley 1999: 99).

Turning more critically to the constitution of identities within Gendering Genocide, the radical feminist understanding of patriarchy in general, and the one of the Balkans in particular, often relied upon an essentialist understanding of rape as built upon a masculine biological drive (Elshtain 1981: 207–8). The separation between 'patriarchic men' and 'female victims' implied that 'Balkan women' were constituted not only as non-violent and non-combatants but also as essentially different from men, and this construction of women as the peaceful nurturing core of the nation reverberated with a Romantic conservative discourse that radical feminists would normally seek to distance themselves from. This essentialist discourse relied upon a construction of 'women' as separate from the military and political masculine leadership. As the superior status of 'victims' within the humanitarian responsibility discourse was dependent on their dislocation from the realm of politics, so was the privilege bestowed upon women as a uniform collective identity. This idealized construction of 'women' implied that destabilizing cases where women acted in a manner that showed their connection with, and reproduction of, national security practices and discourses were downplayed. Gendering Genocide was also destabilized by the majority of the raped women, who spoke within a *national* Genocide discourse, promoting Western military intervention, rather than a radical feminist Gendering Genocide discourse. The radical feminist response to these destabilizations was usually to leave them in silence.

As in the case of Balkanizing Serbia, the Gendering Genocide discourse can be read as articulating elements from both the Genocide discourse and the Balkan discourse. The construction of Balkan patriarchy mirrors key element of the Balkan discourse insofar as both discourses articulate an aggressive, violent, and barbaric Balkan. But the deferral of this 'Balkan' onto the masculine part of the split-gendered Balkan subject, and the adamant call for Western action, imply that the Gendering Genocide discourse is most appropriately read as a variation of the Genocide discourse. The convergence of the Balkan discourse and the Gendering Genocide discourse can, however, also be employed in a reading which analyzes the former's articulation of Balkan and Western identities and its reluctant interventionism through the gendered identities of the latter. The Balkan discourse's construction of the Balkans as violent, passionate, hostile, barbaric, and war-prone is an identity which resonates with stereotypical accounts of aggressive masculinity, and this articulation of gendered identities is employed with significant effects. The analysis of Robert D. Kaplan's *Balkan Ghosts* presented in chapter 8 showed how drunken and pornographic men were significant demarcations of Balkan identity, and for Kennan to argue that rape and barbaric masculinity are ubiquitous in the history of the Balkans it to make a differentiation between 'threatening men' and 'vulnerable women.' This implies that the uniform Balkan subject of the Balkan discourse is in fact split into two gendered identities, 'Balkan men' and 'Balkan women,' and that this destabilizes the construction of the Balkans as an undifferentiated violent, aggressive, and barbaric whole. To acknowledge 'vulnerable women' as victims of 'the Balkans' rather than as accomplices would, however, further destabilize the Balkan discourse's refusal of any ethical responsibility toward the Bosnian war. If women, the defining sign of vulnerability, cannot be protected, does this not expose the West as cynical, self-sufficient, and uncommitted, as indeed in alliance with Balkan rampant masculinity and as uncommitted to a liberal project of gender equality? These are the destabilizing implications of the Balkan discourse's gendered constructions.

Table 9.1 summarizes the principal features of the three variants of the Genocide discourse.

Poststructuralism and David Campbell's *National Deconstruction*

Chapter 8 showed that the war in Bosnia was of key concern to neorealist scholars studying so-called ethnic or intra-state conflict. Turning to the IR

Table 9.1 Genocide discourse variations

Discourse	Rearticulated identities	Policy
European responsibility for Genocide	Splitting of the West into 'Europe' and 'America'	America should pressure Europeans to 'lift and strike'
Balkanizing Serbia	Serbia as the Balkan Other	Pro-Bosnian intervention
Gendering Genocide	Splitting of the Bosnian/Balkan subjects into men and women	Ambiguous: defense of women collides with masculinity of intervention

approach, usually held to be the furthest ontologically and epistemologically from neorealism, poststructuralism's take on Bosnia, and David Campbell's in particular, provided a thorough analysis of the war, the Western representations thereof, the policies pursued, and their ethical implications. Campbell's analysis was developed through a series of articles, book chapters, and conference papers, culminating in the publication of *National Deconstruction: Violence, Identity, and Justice in Bosnia* in 1998 (Campbell 1996a, 1996b, 1997, 1998a). Since *Security as Practice* is itself a poststructuralist work concerned with the discursive articulation of identity in foreign policy, it shares significant ontological and epistemological terrain with *National Deconstruction*. This raises the question how *National Deconstruction* should be positioned analytically, whether it should be read as any of the other texts engaged in the Western Bosnia debate or whether it should be read as an alternative, perhaps competing, discourse analysis. While *National Deconstruction* is *also* a text operating in the same analytical register as *Security as Practice*, there is nothing inherent in a deconstructivist text that prevents it from being read through the same discursive lens as the other texts discussed in chapters 7, 8, and 9. The meta-theoretical similarity between *National Deconstruction* and *Security as Practice* implies, however, that while the former can be read as any other text, it, and the reading of it, does raise a series of analytical, political, and methodological questions to discourse analysis. How should one draw the boundary between different discourses? How should one judge the judgment of the West? And, how should one arbitrate the methodological question of discursive evidence? The double status of *National Deconstruction* as being both a 'regular text' and a 'competitive meta-text' means that it will be read twice: first as a regular text (in this chapter), and then as a text which raises significant political, epistemological, and methodological questions for poststructuralist analysis of foreign policy (in the conclusion, chapter 10).[9]

Campbell's poststructuralist focus is, not surprisingly, on the representations of the war within Bosnia as well as the West. Focusing on his analysis of the latter, he argues that Western politicians, media, and academics converged around a reading of the war as 'ethnic cleansing,' as a 'civil war,' an 'ethnic war' of 'ancient' hatred or a 'humanitarian concern' on the one hand, or, on the other hand, as a 'genocide,' and as 'international aggression,' where 'vital interests' were at stake in protecting 'multicultural' and 'multireligious' Bosnia (Campbell 1998a: 33–55). The 'ethnic/civil' representation underpinned the policies of humanitarian intervention and mediation as well as the American withdrawals from 'lift and strike' and the 'international aggression/ genocide' representation called for a protection of 'Bosnia' and the multicultural and multinational Bosnian government. Contrasting this reading to the one developed here, Campbell's analysis defines discursive positions more broadly, particularly in the case of the 'ethnic/civil' representation. The ancient hatred of the Balkan discourse, the humanitarian responsibility of West European governments, and the neorealist advocacy of ambiguously modern/ intransient identities are all included within the 'ethnic/civil' discourse;

whereas the analyses in chapters 7 and 8 argued in favor of a more fine-grained reading of these discourses as both complimentary and diverging. Campbell's sharp juxtaposition of the two discourses and the inclusive status of the 'civil/ethnic' representation leads him to identify the latter as supported not only by Serbian and Western politicians but also by the majority of Western media and academe. This in turn implies 'The failure of the international community, the media, and the academy to heed the plurality of political positions and the nonnationalist voices that contested the identity politics of those prosecuting the war.' And that 'the dominant narratives of the media and the academy have operated in terms that have helped legitimize and sustain the geopolitical positions of extreme nationalists' (Campbell 1998a: 80–1).

What further characterizes Western discourse is its belief in 'the alignment between territory and identity, state and nation, all under the sign of "ethnicity," supported by a particular account of history' (Campbell 1998a: 80). This belief constitutes, in a term from Derrida, an ontopology: the 'ontological value of present-being to its *situation*, to the stable and presentable determination of a locality, the *topos* of territory, native soil, city, body in general' (quoted in Campbell 1998a: 80). The West's ontopological reading of Bosnia implies a desire for separate and coherent national identities, from neorealism's support for population transfers and a tripartite national division of Bosnia to the maps of ethnically distinct territories contained in various peace plans. Spatially, ontopology implies a fixing of identity within contiguous and mono-national, mono-cultural, and mono-religious territories; temporally, it situates identities within and across long unbroken centennial horizons, arguing that Serbian, Croatian, or Bosnian identities have particular cultural features which date back hundreds of years.

While there are enormous ontological and political differences between the representations of the Bosnian war as an ethnic/civil war and as a war of genocide/international aggression, there is also, argues Campbell, commonality insofar as many arguing in favor of the genocide representation have employed an ontopological logic. This discourse has argued in defense of a multicultural 'Bosnia,' whose identity stretches back for centuries and who has a 'very distinct history and culture'; an identity construction 'similar in form if not in content to those they are opposing' (Campbell 1998a: 49). A real multiculturalism, as defined by Campbell, moves beyond an understanding of multicultural tolerance as the protection of 'national minorities'—'largely a different mode of racism, albeit with a more humane face'—and into a 'commitment to heterogeneity' (Campbell 1998a: 48, 206). A genuine multiculturalism 'affirms cultural diversity without situating it,' which implies that 'Bosnian multiculturalism' should be a temporally and spatially open project, not one with particular and ancient roots or which is defined as the added participation of otherwise distinct national, ethnic, and religious groups (Campbell 1998a: 208). This understanding of multiculturalism is more demanding than normal definitions—perhaps it is even impossible for any collectivity to ever fully embody—but it has, argues Campbell, been enacted by the Bosnian government and Bosnian citizens on numerous occasions. With the support of the West, it would have flourished even further (Campbell 1998a: 209–43).

When read as a text engaged in the debate on Bosnia, *National Deconstruction* takes an analytical double position: on the one hand it identifies two opposing representations of the war and deconstructs the need for fixed identities at play in both. On the other hand, there is also a privilege bestowed upon a revised multicultural reading of Bosnia as a normative ideal as well as a description of what happened in Bosnia (Campbell 1998a: 218). While Campbell acknowledges that the genocide representation is competing (unsuccessfully) with the civil/ethnic/Balkan representation, it is also argued that the international community has avoided this representation due to the political and ethical demands which ensued, and that this opposition is made in the face of 'the evidence amassed to support the claim,' for instance by 'many nongovernmental sources' and 'a large body of international reportage,' which concluded that 'Bosnia has suffered genocide' (Campbell 1998a: 101–2).[10] This implies in sum that Campbell takes an analytical and political double position: he traces the discourses and their representations of identity and legitimation of foreign policy while also making a normative incision into the debate.[11]

Campbell's partial location within the Genocide discourse implies, not surprisingly, an assessment of the West as having failed. As shown by the statements above, Campbell makes a striking criticism of the international community's policies toward Bosnia, policies which were underpinned by an ontopological insistence on irreconcilable identities. Making a detailed analysis of the successive peace plans, Campbell argues that with the exception of the London Principles from August 1992, 'they all embodied to some extent the logic of partition' (Campbell 1998a: 155). The Vance–Owen Peace Plan (VOPP) was not the worst example of this logic: it expressed support for a multi-ethnic Bosnia, but its division of Bosnia into ten provinces was nevertheless followed by statements assigning ethnic identity, and homogeneity, onto each provincial territory. As the VOPP failed, 'The political assumption of homogeneity in otherwise heterogeneous areas that marked the VOPP had disastrous implications for communal relationships' (Campbell 1998a: 143). Turning to the Dayton Accord, its contiguous territories and fragile central structure 'institutionalized a form of "meta-racism" in which, in place of biological distinctions, "culture" is regarded as a naturalized property such that differences are inherently conflictual or threatening, and apartheid is legitimized as an "anti-racist" solution' (Campbell 1998a: 161–2). Those adopting the Genocide discourse would usually argue that Western interests were at stake in protecting the multiculturalism of Bosnia. Campbell, however, argues that the West failed to intervene not because Bosnia's multiculturalism was not recognized, but *because* of Western fear of multiculturalism, in Bosnia as well as within the Western Self. Defending multiculturalism in Bosnia would therefore 'require resolving in favor of plurality one of the most hotly contested cultural controversies in the United States and other Western nations' (Campbell 1998a: 170).[12] Another, more particular, Western fear was of an Islamic Bosnia generating local and regional problems and raising larger questions about European identity (Campbell 1998a: 52–3).

What policy then should the international community have pursued? Campbell chose to focus his analysis on the peace plans and hence to pay 'little attention to the military options and their assumptions.' This implies that there is limited explicit consideration of the discursive constitution of, or the ethical implications of, 'lift and strike' or the UN peacekeeping operation; neither is the policy difference between European troop contributors and America granted much discussion (Campbell 1998a: 125). In contrast to the American Genocide discourse, Campbell is noteworthy for *not* advocating 'lift and strike' as the Western response. Rather, he states, his argument is '*not* to suggest that large-scale military intervention should have been undertaken' (Campbell 1998a: 226). Indeed, in his view, the convergence of Western debate on the strategic feasibility of different policy proposals implied that questions of responsibility were avoided and that truly multicultural proposals were marginalized or unimaginable. Concluding *National Deconstruction* with a series of such proposals, Campbell advocates the support of independent media, local and NGO peace initiatives, and analysis and archives which contest the homogenized and homogenizing understanding of identity protected by the international community and nationalist political and military leaders (Campbell 1998a: 232–43).

Reading *National Deconstruction* as any other text engaged in the Western debate on the Bosnian war, it is situated within the Genocide discourse in that it takes the genocide representation to be factually, politically, and normatively superior to the competing ethnic, civil, or Balkan representations in play in the debate. Yet, its reading of multiculturalism challenges that part of the Genocide discourse which sees multiculturalism simply as the co-existence of otherwise coherent national, ethnic, or religious groups. And, the refusal to embrace 'lift and strike' in favor of a multitude of local and NGO activities challenges the Genocide discourse's call for Western military intervention, particularly in the American context, through the 'lift and strike' policy.

But *National Deconstruction* is not like any other text, in that it is also a poststructuralist reading of the Western Bosnia debate which complements or competes with the analysis advocated in this book. Therefore, comparing the two analyses raises a series of theoretical, methodological, and political questions: how should one identify opposing discursive positions? Should one distinguish between European and American approaches, as is done in chapter 7, or is a combined analysis, as conducted in *National Deconstruction*, sufficient to prove the diplomacy of the West? Is the discourse identified as humanitarian responsibility separate from the Balkan discourse or are the two, as claimed by Campbell, indeed alike? Was the West articulating a uniform ontopological position across diplomats, politicians, the media, and academe, or were there, as argued by *Security as Practice*, variations across the Atlantic, across different sites of discourse, and across different genres? What should be the methodological foundation for identifying a discourse and did the West abstain from a more proactive course because of its fear of multiculturalism and Islam? These are questions that arise from reading *National Deconstruction* through a poststructuralist lens, and because these are simultaneously questions that summarize the central analytical issues and the political issues at stake in understanding and developing poststructuralism as a perspective on international politics they are further discussed in chapter 10.

Memorializing negotiations

As illustrated by Campbell's analysis of international diplomacy, the Genocide discourse combined a construction of the West as an ethical failure with more concrete criticism of the peace plans put forward by negotiators and their teams. These negotiators, David Owen and Richard Holbrooke most prominently among them, became the embodiment of the Western attempts to halt the war and achieve a solution that would be seen as just as well as strategically enforceable and stable. Speaking of the VOPP, the first major attempt to end the war, *The Washington Post* called it 'an enforced compromise between war criminals and their victims' (*The Washington Post* 1993), and Patrick Glynn of the *USA Today* labeled it a 'Munich-like program' and a 'craven plan of surrender' (Glynn 1993). Perhaps most spectacularly, *The New York Times* ran an editorial, 'Lord Owen's Googly,' that targeted Owen's past and persona, arguing that he was 'as vain as he is smart,' 'not infallible in his political judgment,' and set on a European attempt to implicate Washington in the liquidation of Bosnia (*New York Times* 1993).[13] Richard Holbrooke, by comparison, faired better, even within skeptical media assessments, in that however imperfect the Dayton Accord was, it *did* end the war and was voluntarily agreed to by the parties (*The Washington Post* 1995b).[14] Yet, as the analysis of *National Deconstruction* showed, there were significant voices that read the Dayton Accord as a partitioning of Bosnia and hence the final testimony to the West's inability and unwillingness to support the multicultural identity of Bosnia.

Considering how prominently Owen and Holbrooke figured, both as 'peace plans' and as individuals, it was not surprising to see them publish extensive memoirs detailing their experiences. Both Owen's *Balkan Odyssey* and Holbrooke's *To End a War* employed central elements of the autobiographical genre's narrative techniques, including the use of retrospection and formative experiences, in legitimizing their efforts as negotiators (Owen 1995; Holbrooke 1998). But there were also important differences between the two books in that Owen prefaced his acceptance of the task of negotiator by a powerful narrative of conversion, whereas Holbrooke's *To End a War* adopted a more complex use of formative experiences and retrospection.

Balkan Odyssey: conversion and the Balkan sewer

Balkan Odyssey provides almost 400 pages of densely packed chronological accounts of the hardship that David Owen faced as he struggled through three years as the EC/EU's representative on the International Conference on the Former Yugoslavia. Reading *Balkan Odyssey*'s immense wealth of detail through the analytical framework of basic discourses, it employs elements of the Balkan discourse as well as the Genocide discourse, and it legitimizes the achievements and failures of David Owen through five narrative and strategic moves that incorporate significant elements of the genre of autobiography. First, through an introductory narrative account of the conversion that Owen underwent to become a negotiator and the structural constraints implied by this identity. Second, through the deployment of elements from the Balkan discourse in observations about the difficulty of being a negotiator in the environment of 'the Balkans.' Third, through a narration of personal encounters, particularly with Milosevic and Izetbegovic, which create an ambiguous combination of distance and familiarity between these two characters and Owen. Fourth, through a continuous insistence that the VOPP did, contrary to Campbell's claims, support and further a multi-ethnic and multicultural Bosnia. And fifth, through a harsh criticism of the Clinton administration for continuously undermining the work of Owen and his associates. David Campbell argues that 'clarity and consistency on the question of identity were not among Owen's strong points,' and *Balkan Odyssey is* ambiguous in its articulation of Bosnian/Balkan identities (Campbell 1998a: 138). Yet reading *Balkan Odyssey* as a foreign policy autobiography might bring further clarity on where and how this ambiguity is established, in particular of how a writing of the Self brings legitimacy to the VOPP and Owen's performance and persona.

Balkan Odyssey begins with Owen's account of his conversion in the summer of 1992, from Genocide discourse advocate to incorporating the Balkan discourse and the humanitarian responsibility discourse of the West European governments. This transformation was deeply tied to his acceptance of the structural requirements of the position of 'negotiator' and a linkage of negotiation and 'peace.' Owen describes how the disclosure of the Serbian run concentration camps in Bosnia in July 1992 lead him to send a letter to the *Evening Standard*, which was published on 30 July, 1992. This letter, addressed to the Prime Minister, John Major, argued that 'It is not an exaggeration to say that we are witnessing, 50 years on, scenes in Europe that mirror the early stages of the Nazi holocaust under the dreadful description of "ethnic cleansing." I urge you not to accept the conventional wisdom that nothing can be done militarily to stop the escalation of fighting and the continuation of such grotesque abuses of human rights' (Owen 1995: 14–15). Owen argues further that NATO should threaten to conduct air strikes, and that the larger cities under attack should be 'reinforced by air with troops acting under the authority of the UN, if necessarily parachuting men and materials in to secure air communications' (Owen 1995: 15). His prediction is that 'If no action is taken now there will be virtually nothing left of Bosnia for the Muslim population to negotiate about' (Owen 1995: 15). Owen proceeds to give a detailed description of the reception of his letter, which was a 'political hand grenade into the Whitehall/Westminster nexus' and the subject of conversation in a lunch between Owen and Stephen Wall, Major's private secretary, the day after. Wall described the war as 'essentially a civil war' and Owen 'admits' that he lacked good answers as to the consequences of applying air power if it proved insufficient to deter the Serbs or if the Serbs retaliated by taking hostages from international humanitarian organizations (Owen 1995: 16). Wall's questions brought Owen 'face to face with the harsh choices that accompany power and can be all too easily ignored by protest' (Owen 1995: 17). Wall, for his part, was 'clearly disappointed with my logic and thought I was being self-indulgent and not facing the real issues of government honestly' (Owen 1995: 17). This challenge, Owen recalls, 'was a good discipline for me, for he put me back in the Foreign Secretary's seat and did not allow me the luxury of playing to the gallery' (Owen 1995: 17).

Analyzing this episode as a prelude to Owen's acceptance of the role of negotiator, it constructs Owen as someone who knows the arguments of the Genocide discourse, precisely because he has argued them himself. His narrative of conversion not only constitutes Owen as reflective but also implicates the reader in Owen's transformation: the reader is suggested to identify with Owen's initial position, but through his revision to embrace a similar change. The transformative effect is further stabilized through the use of retrospection. 'It was a good discipline,' argues Owen, speaking from a temporal, spatial, and emotional distance to the episode itself. This insertion of a 'voice of the present' into the writing of the past facilitates the construction of the discursive and political positions available to Owen as either having the 'luxury of playing to the gallery' or facing the 'real issues of government honestly.' The articulation of the latter position is attributed to Wall, but Owen's construction of his own alternative position as 'luxury' and 'playing to the gallery,' rather than, for instance, 'making a sound argument,' is effectively one which shows Owen's embrace of Wall's options. As discussed in chapter 4, the constitution of foreign policymakers as having a particular moral responsibility for assuming leadership is brought forth in Owen's pointing to 'the harsh choices' that distinguish government from those who are unencumbered and can 'play to the gallery.' This not only grants legitimacy to the discourse of Wall and the Foreign Office, but foreshadows the similar constraints and responsibilities that Owen would be subjected to as he assumes the role of negotiator.

The rendition of meetings with Wall, John Major, and Cyrus Vance build up to Owen accepting the role as the EC's representative to the International Conference on the Former Yugoslavia. Reiterating the dichotomous choice between the responsible politician and the free-riding commentator, Owen argues that his decision was based on a consideration of 'whether to go on being a voice in the wilderness over Yugoslavia or join in the quest for peace' (Owen 1995: 23). 'The quest for peace' constructs the negotiator as embarking on a morally applauded endeavor, rather than, for instance, as a technocratic arbiter of opposing demands, and Owen further supports his choice through a revision of what were the 'facts of war': 'the facts were not all as I had first thought. While the terms "aggressor" and "victim" were being brandished as weapons in a propaganda war, the true situation was obviously far more complex than that dichotomy implied—and anyhow, they were terms better avoided publicly by a negotiator' (Owen 1995: 27). This passage underscores Owen's move away from the Genocide discourse, but the last sentence, the necessity to 'publicly avoid such terms,' destabilizes the 'factual revision' insofar as Owen's role is now determining discourse: being a 'negotiator' forces Owen not to 'take sides.' This final twist implies that the carefully narrated attempt to construct a story of conversion that legitimizes a more qualified support for the Genocide discourse—perhaps even a Balkan discourse—on factual grounds is marred by Owen's concluding message that when going into the negotiations he had to suspend attempts to question the construction of 'equal sides.'

This ambiguous invocation of factual and structural reasons for a turn toward a humanitarian responsibility discourse is supported by Owen's second narrative move, which consists of continuous references to the difficulties of operating in a 'Balkan environment.' The articulation of the war as Balkan comes in the book's very first sentence: 'Nothing is simple in the Balkans,' and Owen goes on to state that he had never before operated in 'such a climate of dishonour, propaganda and dissembling' where many of the people he dealt with were 'literally strangers to the truth' (Owen 1995: 1). Balkan history shows 'a readiness to solve disputes by the taking up of arms' and a 'culture of violence within a crossroad civilization' which has the marks of 'a dark and virulent nationalism' (Owen 1995: 3). Making an intertextual reference to *Black Lamb and Grey Falcon*, Owen sees a 'labyrinth of history, weaving a complexity of human relations that seemed to bedevil the whole region' (Owen 1995: 6). These initial deployments of the Balkan discourse are reiterated later in the book as Owen emphasizes the difficulties of negotiating; 'In the Balkans, intransigence is believed to be the only stance to pay off' (Owen 1995: 76), and as all parties were of the Balkans they proved themselves to be 'masters of disinformation, propaganda and deceit' (Owen 1995: 88, 200, 207, 334, 341). As in the humanitarian responsibility discourse, this construction of Balkan parties is combined with a differentiation between leaders who were 'impossibly negative' and ordinary 'decent people' who wanted to live in peace (Owen 1995: 123).

These articulations of Balkan identity allowed Owen to construct his task as immensely difficult, and in contrast to Balkan discourse texts, which constituted the Balkan Other from afar, Owen could refer to his personal encounters with the Balkans as giving him epistemological authority. This implied further that Owen could point to personal exasperation, asking how long he could 'ask my family to put up with my time and energy being spent swimming hard to keep my head up in this Balkan sewer' (Owen 1995: 242). A passage which not only constructs the Bosnian and the Balkan, but also constructs Owen's negotiating self as hard-working and sacrificing his own domesticity in the service of the larger good. Although *Balkan Odyssey* employs rather few explicit references to Owen's personal life, this juxtaposition of family and the Balkans effectively constitutes him as a family man and someone who is considerate of their needs.

Owen's initial generalized observations about the Balkans are supported by a series of personal experiences, but *Balkan Odyssey* also employs, in the book's third narrative move, personal encounters to construct central Bosnian and Yugoslavian characters. Although quite a few Serbs, most noticeably perhaps Karadzic, are constituted within the specter of Balkanness, it is striking that several of the main characters are written in ways which qualify the identity of the Balkan Other. Two of the most, if not indeed *the* most, significant characters in Owen's narrative are Milosevic and Izetbegovic, the former because Owen insists that he holds the key to settling the war, the latter because of the Genocide discourse's stress on the Western failure to protect Izetbegovic's multicultural Bosnia.

Zooming in on Milosevic, he shows 'ruthlessness and a pursuit of power,' but is also 'a considerate host' with 'plenty of time' who 'carries his nationalism lightly' and does not let it 'intrude in an offensive manner in conversation with foreigners' (Owen 1995: 127). Owen's privileged personal encounters, extensively described in *Balkan Odyssey*, make him declare that the 'private man is not a racist' (Owen 1995: 127). Generally, *Balkan Odyssey* adopts a steady chronological narrative pace, with few clearly designated formative moments; one striking exception is, however, of a day Owen and his wife, Debbie, spend with Milosevic and his wife, Mira Markovic, at one of Tito's old country residences, presumably now in the possession of Milosevic.[15] Using his personal conversation with the Yugoslavian couple as narrative evidence, Owen reiterates his earlier observations that he never believed Milosevic to be a nationalist, and the four of them had 'many hours that day of fascinating conversations' (Owen 1995: 272). The critical Genocide discourse reader's first response to this episode might be to question whether it was within the bounds of the ethically acceptable for a negotiator to stroll around the countryside on a double date with one of the key protagonists of the war, a reaction further spurred by Milosevic's later indictment and trial by the International Criminal Tribunal in The Hague. Owen, for his part, does not seem to consider that it might provide grist for the mill for those who constructed him as pro-Serb.

Leaving aside the potential unintended effects of this episode as far as Owen's potential pro-Serbianism is concerned, the constitution of 'the private Milosevic' involves an interesting negotiation of the boundaries between the public and the private, and the relevance of the latter for the former.[16] Broadly speaking, the boundary between the public and the private within liberal political theory, and Western political science built thereupon, is firmly demarcated, and the public is the unquestioned political realm. Put bluntly, how Milosevic reasoned, thought, and behaved as a private person would be irrelevant to an assessment of his public, political persona. Although Owen is careful to state that it will be for the tribunal in The Hague to decide on questions of guilt, the narration of the non-nationalist, hospitable Milosevic effectively dispenses with the tight regulation of the private by making this a relevant component of Owen's political analysis. Indeed, it is the deregulation of the public–private distinction which constitutes one of the important traits of the genre of political autobiography. The invocation of the private in the constitution of 'Milosevic' as a cunning, rational politician takes him out of 'the Balkans,' and this identity legitimizes the prominent role accorded to him within Owen's negotiations. Milosevic should be included, he argues continuously, and the West should acknowledge his importance, not only because of his power over the Bosnia Serbs but also because of his rational mind and genuine quest for compromise.

If the constitution of Milosevic is a case of normalization, the task at hand in writing Izetbegovic is to counter the Genocide discourse's charge that Owen, the peace plans he produced, and the process through which they were constructed, betrayed Izetbegovic and his multicultural Bosnia. As in the case of Milosevic, the narration of Izetbegovic breaks with the construction of a uniform Balkan identity, but where Milosevic is normalized as a reasoning and hospitable politician, it is through an employment of distance that Izetbegovic is described. Owen argues that he would 'go out of my way to talk informally to him [Izetbegovic] over a meal,' but that 'he kept to himself and was easiest to approach through his son or daughter.' Pondering the importance of Izetbegovic's imprisonment under communism, Owen decides that he has 'an inner toughness and a surrounding hard shell which is difficult to penetrate' (Owen 1995: 38). This implies that only few would know 'for certain' whether Izetbegovic was an Islamic fundamentalist, but Owen is emphatic that he 'always liked him and wanted to help him,' and that he disagrees with those who argue that Izetbegovic is 'manipulative and untrustworthy' and the worst to deal with of the former Yugoslavian leaders (Owen 1995: 38–9). This construction of Izetbegovic as the impenetrable Islamic Other has echoes of the traditional Orientalist articulation of the mysterious, indecipherable Eastern stranger; not necessarily the radical threatening Other, but nevertheless one whose identity sets it incomprehensibly apart from the rational West. Milosevic, by contrast, is constituted in terms more familiar to Owen's West. One should note further that while Owen declares himself in disagreement with the negative assessment of Izetbegovic, he does underline that this view is held by people 'who have also spent long hours negotiating with him' (Owen 1995: 38). Making this note of other, critical views of Izetbegovic introduces an element of instability, which gives Owen the possibility of presenting him as a difficult and indecisive part in later negotiations without incriminating his initial declaration of fondness and support for Izetbegovic.

Owen's articulation of himself as the protector of Izetbegovic becomes a move through which the charges against Owen for disregarding the Bosnians can be countered. 'The protector' is also a construction which situates Izetbegovic and his supporters as inexperienced in the game of diplomacy and which allows Owen a position of knowing the Bosnians'/Muslims' interests and deciding whether they act in accordance therewith. Owen's superior authority might in the final instance withstand Izetbegovic's and his government's potential opposition to his peace plans, yet Owen's political support for the Bosnians is also validated by Izetbegovic's approval; as when Owen points to Izetbegovic's 'crystal clear' desire for having Owen continue as the negotiator after the rejection of the VOPP (Owen 1995: 178, 194–5).

The construction of Owen as in the pursuit of Bosnian interests is further underscored by the fourth element of his defense against Genocide discourse criticism, an element which is particularly concerned with the charge that the VOPP was condoning ethnic cleansing and sanctioning partitioning. Owen insists in response that the VOPP both fostered and required a multi-ethnic Bosnia, and that he was in support of using air strikes to enforce it. Applying a retrospective evaluation of the negotiations and plans put forward, he argues that the implementation of the VOPP would have offered the Bosnian Muslims a better deal than did the Dayton Accord two and a half years later, and that its adoption would have spared numerous lives and hardships. The map suggested by the VOPP was 'just and equitable' and 'based on the fundamental premise that Bosnia-Herzegovina would remain a sovereign, independent, multi-ethnic state' (Owen 1995: 104). It 'did not accept the results of ethnic cleansing but was on the contrary designed to reverse them' (Owen 1995: 104). As Owen points out, the organization of entities within the VOPP did not create contiguous territories, something which constituted a major stumbling block with the Bosnian Serbs; for 'Vance–Owen Bosnia' to function politically, economically, and culturally, a high degree of cooperation within and between entities was therefore required. Comparing *Balkan Odyssey* with the understanding of multiculturalism advocated by Campbell, Owen's conception of multi-ethnicity does, however, appear limited. Owen's predominant categories are those of Muslim, Croat, and Serbian, and multi-ethnicity becomes as a consequence a matter of organizing co-existing but distinct identities that do not comprise the open and transversed multicultural Bosnian identity envisioned by Campbell.

The absence of contiguous territory made realists argue that the VOPP was unenforceable and unstable, but Owen insists that had it been supported by the Clinton administration it could have been implemented (Owen 1995: 38). However, and this constitutes *Balkan Odyssey*'s fifth defensive move, the Clinton administration failed spectacularly: it encouraged Izetbegovic to seek changes at impromptu times, it questioned the legitimacy of the VOPP, and it was unwilling to take any responsibility for its actions and inactions, yet it continued to scapegoat the Europeans. Perhaps worst of all, American policy was inconsistent to the point of indecipherability (Owen 1995: 162). Contrary to the claims of the American Genocide discourse, which held Europe and Vance–Owen responsible for the plight of the Bosnian government, it was, argues Owen, the Americans who 'totally let him [Izetbegovic] down' (Owen 1995: 173).

Summing up *Balkan Odyssey*, it is not surprising that Owen would use the genre of memoir to legitimize his past action. And, it is not surprising either to find a discourse which resonates with the humanitarian responsibility discourse discussed in chapter 7: Owen was the representative of the EC/EU and appointed through the channels of the British government. What is noteworthy, however, is that the genre of autobiography allows for the use of a powerful narrative of conversion and for the use of personal encounters as an epistemological foundation for reading the Balkans, the 'parties,' and the individual political and military leaders in ambiguous terms.

To End a War: formative experiences and Balkan bluff

Turning to Richard Holbrooke's *To End a War*, the mobilization of the narrative techniques of memoir is even more striking. Holbrooke is a self-conscious memoirist who points out in the preliminary 'Note to the reader' that 'A memoir sits at the dangerous intersection of policy, ambition, and history, where it is tempting to focus on instances of good judgment, and to blur or forget times when one made a mistake' (Holbrooke 1998: xvi–xvii). Holbrooke also invokes the epistemological authority of the personal encounter, arguing that 'Physical descriptions, anecdotes, and the personal background of participants are integral to the story; in diplomacy, as in architecture, details matter,' and these do indeed take up the majority of the book (Holbrooke 1998: xv). But Holbrooke is also aware of the authority of more conventional historiographical forms of knowledge as he prefaces his personal and cultural encounters by a long analysis of trans-Atlantic relations and American foreign policy after the Cold War. There are, he states, five factors which explain the tragedy of the war and the Western policy of inaction: 'first, a misreading of Balkan history; second, the end of the Cold War; third, the behavior of the Yugoslav leaders themselves; fourth, the inadequate American response to the crisis; and, finally, the mistaken belief of the Europeans that they could handle their first post-Cold War challenge on their own' (Holbrooke 1998: 21–2). Rather than ancient hatred, argues Holbrooke, the war was caused by 'bad, even criminal, political leaders who encouraged ethnic confrontation for personal, political, and financial gain' (Holbrooke 1998: 23). With Yugoslavia loosing its strategic Cold War importance, Bush tied down by the aftermath of Iraq, and an ineffective Europe, the outcome was 'the greatest collective security failure of the West since the 1930s'—a statement which begins chapter 2, but which stems from an article in *Foreign Affairs* from early 1995 (Holbrooke 1998: 21).[17] Holbrooke's support for a Genocide discourse is also articulate through his construction of the massacre at Srebrenica as 'a crime against humanity of the sort that we have rarely seen in Europe, and not since the days of Himmler and Stalin,' and his support for the bombings of Operation Deliberate Force (Holbrooke 1998: 90).

This introductory analysis constitutes Holbrooke as someone with historiographic and analytical authority and as critical of the Balkan discourse and 'Western inaction,' but the majority of the book articulates a more ambiguous construction of 'Bosnia,' its 'Balkan people,' and its leaders. This extensive narration of the Bosnian/Balkan Others is simultaneously intertwined with significant use of retrospection and formative experiences in writing Holbrooke's Self. Formative retrospection is employed first in the book's Prologue, which narrates the story of a 19-year-old Holbrooke hitchhiking through southeastern Europe in 1960, visiting the plaque commemorating the beginning of World War I as 'the first blow for Serb liberty' (Holbrooke 1998: xix). Holbrooke recalls being 'astonished' about the invocation of 'Serbian liberty,' and he 'never forgot that first brush with extreme nationalism, and it came back to me vividly when Yugoslavia fell apart' (Holbrooke 1998: xix). This anecdote situates Holbrooke as an adventurous and cultured young man and 'extreme nationalism' as a signifier of the Balkans. The Prologue continues with Holbrooke's return visit to Sarajevo in 1992, where he seeks out the old plaque. Asking John Burns, a correspondent for the *New York Times*, for directions, he laughs and replies that it 'had been destroyed by the Bosnian Muslims. But the spirit behind their inscription had been revived—murderously so' (Holbrooke 1998: xx). The Balkans is a space haunted by murderous and undifferentiated nationalisms.

The construction of Holbrooke's traveling Self continues in chapter 3, 'A Personal Prelude,' which chronicles how Holbrooke gets invited by the International Rescue Committee, a private refugee organization on whose board he serves, to go on a fact-finding mission to Bosnia in mid-August 1992. For this trip, he kept a diary, and in an explicit mobilization of retrospective analysis that creates another bond of continuity between past and present Selves, he argues that 'Rereading it for the first time four years later, I was struck by how this trip shaped my subsequent understanding of the situation' (Holbrooke 1998: 36). The reprinted journal states that 'It is the peculiar three-sided nature of the struggle here that makes it so difficult' (Holbrooke 1998: 36). Holbrooke witnesses the scene north of Banja Luka, 'terrible signs of war,' 'a systematic and methodical pogrom,' a 'horrorscape' and roadblocks commanded by 'awful-looking guards' (Holbrooke 1998: 37). 'The men in this country,' comments Holbrooke, 'act as if they would be impotent if they didn't carry guns' (Holbrooke 1998: 38). He continues, after the journal entries, that 'The trip had hooked me' (Holbrooke 1998: 39). Prompted by *Newsweek* he writes an article—reprinted in parts in *To End a War*—suggesting that the 'genocidal policies' of the Serbs should be countered by deploying international (probably UN) observers on the Bosnian border and in Kosovo and Macedonia, lifting the embargo, and bombing bridges between Serbia and Bosnia and Serb military facilities; policy suggestions that were repeated to Clinton's presidential campaign (Holbrooke

1998: 39–40). Bosnia had left so much of an impact that Holbrooke decided to spend New Year's Eve 1992 in Bosnia, ending up in Sarajevo, where the UN was becoming 'an unintentional accomplice to Serb policy' (Holbrooke 1998: 48–9). Returning to New York, Holbrooke writes another memo to the incoming Clinton staff reiterating the need for action and stating that the Vance–Owen plan should be given qualified public support, but that one should not become part of a war on the ground (Holbrooke 1998: 51–2).

These Bosnian travels constitute Holbrooke as familiar with Bosnia and with an established record of pro-Bosnian policies articulated within an American Genocide discourse. As in Owen's *Balkan Odyssey*, these formative experiences are not simply objective accounts of the past but a writing of the Self and its policies that previsions and preempts the criticism of the Dayton Accord and of Holbrooke himself for being insufficiently pro-Bosnian. Holbrooke's formative experiences are situated prior to his account of the negotiations, and one experience at the beginning of Holbrooke's work as a negotiator is so significant that it is placed as chapter 1, thereby breaking the chronological continuity of the book. This chapter, 'The Most Dangerous Road in Europe,' is devoted to Holbrooke's first trip as a negotiator in August 1995 and it functions as the springboard for the narration of his first encounters with the Bosnian leaders. Driving through Mount Igman in the attempt to get into Sarajevo, one of the vehicles—the one Holbrooke is not in—slips off the road, killing the core of Holbrooke's team: Robert C. Frasure, Joseph Kruzel, and S. Nelson Drew. Holbrooke gives a vivid description of the crash, and after making it into Sarajevo—the discussions with Izetbegovic and his government cancelled—he comments that 'The Bosnians, having lost so many people in the war, seemed relatively unmoved by three American dead. Finally, slightly annoyed with Izetbegovic, Menzies [an American diplomat about to become the Ambassador to Bosnia] pointedly said that, while we fully recognized how many Bosnians had died, these were the first Americans to lose their lives in Bosnia. This seemed to impress Izetbegovic, and he offered some words of condolences' (Holbrooke 1998: 15–16). Although Holbrooke acknowledges the losses of the Bosnians as a (partial) explanation for their detachment, he is nevertheless in agreement with Menzies's scolding of Izetbegovic, describing his comment as 'pointedly.' One might argue that in the heat of the moment, this might be an understandable reaction from Holbrooke and Menzies, however it is worth noticing that Holbrooke does not apply the possibility of the memoirist—otherwise mobilized throughout the book—to qualify retrospectively his demand on Izetbegovic's compassion.

The formative importance of the accident on Mount Igman is shown by Holbrooke's continuous articulation of its importance for him personally and for the administration as a whole. In the final chapter, he argues that the motives which pushed the United States to its involvement in 1995 were strategic as well as 'moral and humanitarian': 'After Srebrenica and Mount Igman the United States could no longer escape the terrible truth of what was happening in Bosnia ... Within the Administration, the loss of three friends

on Mount Igman carried a special weight; the war had, in effect, come home'
(Holbrooke 1998: 362). And Izetbegovic's response appears also to have had
a formative impact in that he is subsequently narrated in a manner that resonates with their first encounter. 'His eyes had a cold and distant gaze; after so
much suffering, they seemed dead to anyone else's pain.' Politically, 'although
he paid lip service to the principles of a multiethnic state, he was not the
democrat that some supporters in the West saw. He reminded me a bit of Mao
Zedong and other radical Chinese communist leaders—good at revolution,
poor at governance.' Although Holbrooke continues that 'without him Bosnia
would never have survived' (Holbrooke 1998: 97–8).

Turning to the Serbian characters, Karadzic 'had a sad face, with heavy
jowls, a soft chin, and surprisingly gentle eyes,' and Mladic came across as 'a
charismatic murderer' (Holbrooke 1998: 149). Milosevic, from their first
meeting, was 'smart, evasive, and tricky,' and his English was 'excellent'
(Holbrooke 1998: 4). He 'enjoyed late-night drama, perhaps in part because
his stamina and ability to hold liquor often gave him an additional edge over
others at that time,' and alcohol becomes a crucial demarcation of identity as
Holbrooke recounts numerous occasions where Milosevic urges him to drink
(Holbrooke 1998: 114, 181).[18] Milosevic shows, in contrast to Izetbegovic,
his sympathy with the deaths at Mount Igman, and in a manner that echoes
the Romantic construction of Balkan passion, 'He could range from charm to
brutality, from emotional outbursts to calm discussions of legal minutiae.
When he was angry, his face wrinkled up, but he could regain control of himself instantly' (Holbrooke 1998: 105, 114). Holbrooke's own personality is
presented through a juxtaposition to Warren Christopher: Holbrooke is 'intuitive
and impatient,' Christopher 'cautious and methodical' (Holbrooke 1998: 239).
But Holbrooke was not, he emphasizes, the 'bully' that the press's 'negotiating
folklore' had said him to be (Holbrooke 1998: 139).

As in *Balkan Odyssey*, these personal encounters are narrated to constitute a
difficult negotiation environment, hence making the reader acutely aware of
the immense challenges facing Holbrooke *and* the flexibility the reader must
assume in judging the process and outcome at Dayton. While the two memoirs differ on some accounts—Milosevic for instance is constituted as more
rational by Owen than by Holbrooke, who argues that the Western mistake
was to 'treat the Serbs as rational people' (Holbrooke 1998: 152)—they resonate in their construction of Izetbegovic as detached and introverted. None
of the leaders are constituted by Holbrooke in unambiguously positive terms,
and this ambiguity is reiterated in his articulation of 'the Balkans' as a 'savage' place and 'one of the most unstable regions of the world' (Holbrooke
1998: 9, 127). Lord Carrington warns Holbrooke that 'he had never met such
terrible liars in his life as the people of the Balkans,' and Holbrooke learns
that 'reneging on earlier offers was a basic style in the Balkans,' and that here
'nothing goes according to plan' (Holbrooke 1998: 30, 125, 138). Throughout
the negotiations, Holbrooke and his team confront 'Balkan bluff,' and the
articulation of 'the Balkans' as underdeveloped and unable to handle their

own problems comes through in the assessment that 'An aspect of the Balkan character was revealed anew: once enraged, these leaders needed outside supervision to stop themselves from self-destruction' (Holbrooke 1998: 165, 178). While Holbrooke early in *To End a War* disparages *Black Lamb and Grey Falcon* for its 'bad history,' he seems unaware of how the Balkanization discourse inserts itself into his own work (Holbrooke 1998: 22).

As the book moves into the account of the negotiation process, in particular at Dayton, the emphasis on personal encounters become even more predominant. In this, the narrative gaze lowers from abstract questions to concrete, daily statements on the parties' positions and stubbornness and their occasional decisions to compromise.[19] Moving from the level of foreign policy analysis and to the level of human interactions, Holbrooke finds the Bosnian Muslim delegation difficult to deal with and they have Holbrooke and his team on the verge of exasperation on several occasions: they are badly prepared and inexperienced; they are divided amongst themselves; they have a tendency to change their opinions, even when deals have been made; and, most importantly perhaps, they are not fully committed to stopping the war *and* to the preservation of Bosnia as a multi-ethnic country (Holbrooke 1998: 97, 224, 285, 288). One of his associates, Chris Hill, 'normally highly supportive of the Bosnians,' exclaimed that 'These people are impossible to help,' and Warren Christopher found the Bosnian position 'truly unbelievable' and 'irrational' (Holbrooke 1998: 302, 304).

The other delegations are difficult too, but from the point of countering the criticisms of the Genocide discourse, the narration of the shortcomings of the Bosnian one is the more significant. Holbrooke, in this light, becomes akin to the superior protector of Owen's discourse, who ensures the best possible deal for Bosnia as a whole. This construction is retrospectively validated by Holbrooke's return to Sarajevo five months after Dayton, where Izetbegovic 'seemed a changed man, cracking small jokes and smiling. He thanked me profusely for what I "had done for Bosnia," and noted that we had kept our promises to his government' (Holbrooke 1998: 341). This juxtaposition of a previously continuously dissatisfied Izetbegovic with a now happily transformed one not only bestows legitimacy on the Dayton Accord, it also constructs Holbrooke and his team—who fought till the end to get a very reluctant Bosnian Muslim delegation to sign—as capable of making better decisions than 'the Balkan leaders' themselves. This validation of the Dayton Accord rests, as in the American Genocide discourse discussed in chapter 7, on the prior construction of Izetbegovic and his associates as the legitimate representatives of 'the Bosnian people' and hence in a position of making decisions on their behalf. It is for Izetbegovic to confirm the legitimacy of the Dayton Accord, and the happiness of Izetbegovic diffuses the need for a closer scrutiny of the terms and justice of the accord, as for instance in the analysis by Campbell. Holbrooke does, however, acknowledge that criticism has been made, but transfers it onto the implementation. 'On paper, Dayton was a good agreement; it ended the war and established a single, multiethnic country' (Holbrooke 1998: 335). Many outside critics, argues Holbrooke, conflated the agreement with its implementation, although he concedes that the latter should have been better designed, and that he left the implementation process too early (Holbrooke 1998: 325, 363). Holbrooke, dutifully and correctly, notes on the final pages of his book that 'some criticized Dayton as a partition agreement, while others criticized it precisely because it was not one,' but he never explicitly addresses the former critique (Holbrooke 1998: 365).

Situating *To End a War* within the wider web of the Western Bosnia debate, the book seeks to legitimate the Dayton Accord through a mobilization of the American Genocide discourse in the preliminary historical chapters, but this discourse is later destabilized by articulations of the parties as Balkan and the Bosnian delegation as indecisive amateurs. Holbrooke, however, is written into a superior position, and his decisions are retrospectively validated by a grateful Izetbegovic. In the end, Dayton was the best outcome, and the burden of proof is put on the doorsteps of implementation.

Conclusions from Genocide: variations, policy, and genre

This chapter was devoted to an extensive analysis of the Genocide discourse: of its key text, Gutman's *A Witness to Genocide*; of its most theoretically interesting variations; of David Campbell's poststructuralist deconstruction and construction; and of the memoirs by the two negotiators most prominently embodying the international diplomacy of the West. Summarizing the studies above, it has been shown that the Genocide discourse's multiple subjects and demanding yet broadly delineated policy space allowed for a series of variations. Gutman argued within the American Genocide discourse (laid out in chapter 7), which constituted a policy of 'lift and strike' as militarily decisive and hence ethically responsive to the plight of Bosnia. Continuing within the American debate, the European responsibility discourse pushed the policy differences within the West to the level of a fundamental difference in identity. The Balkanization discourse unified the split Serbian subject while simultaneously destabilizing the articulation of a multicultural Bosnia and a liberal West, and the Gendering Genocide discourse shifted the constitution of subjects from a national-ethnic-cultural category to gender, where 'Balkan men' threatened vulnerable 'Balkan women.' Campbell's *National Deconstruction* offered an alternative discourse analysis of the representations of the West and made an argument in favor of a Genocide discourse that conceptualized multiculturalism as a constellation of heterogeneous and negotiable identities.

As the European responsibility for Genocide and the Balkanizing Serbia discourse were situated within the American debate, they were in concordance with the larger American Genocide discourse in criticizing UNPROFOR for being an inadequate response and in pointing to 'lift and strike' as a warranted, firmer support of the Bosnian government. Gendering Genocide was, by contrast, more ambiguous in that its radical feminist critique of militarism made it cautious of advocating Western military intervention, a caution echoed by Campbell, who argued in favor of Western support for alternative media, NGOs, and movements advocating truly multicultural projects.

The importance of genre for foreign policy discourses was also brought out: first, by Gutman's references to investigative journalism's authority as built on verifiable truths, and his subsequent self-reflection on why his discoveries failed to produce the active 'lift and strike' policy he thought immanent in his reports; and second by Owen and Holbrooke's memorializing legitimations of their negotiation efforts. Owen and Holbrooke both chronicled an initial support for the Genocide discourse that was later questioned by personal encounters and formative experiences narrated to produce an Othered 'Balkan' environment populated by ambiguous Bosnian characters.

10 Conclusion

The ambition of this book was to present a post-structuralist theory of identity and foreign policy, to develop an explicit discourse analytical methodology to go with it, and to bring both together in a detailed analysis of the Western debate on Bosnia. The previous nine chapters engaged the concept of identity, the theoretical and empirical intertextuality of official foreign policy, the mobilization of authority, knowledge, and responsibility in policy discourse, the importance of Romanticism and early twentieth century civilizational reasoning for contemporary debate, the usage of non-academic and literary genres in policymaking, and the ability of official discourse to withstand atrocities, ethnic cleansing, mass rape, and domestic criticism. This concluding chapter revisits the most important theoretical and methodological themes and links them to the analysis of chapters 6 to 9. The goal, however, is not only to summarize the points made, but to present a series of suggestions for a future post-structuralist research agenda. The loudest calls of the first chapter were for a more explicit intra-post-structuralist debate and for a heightened concern with methodological choices and their consequences. In response, this chapter ends by discussing the differences between the analyses of the Western debate on Bosnia argued by David Campbell in *National Deconstruction* and by chapters 6 to 9.

The politics of discourse

The ontological starting point for post-structuralist discourse analysis is a conceptualization of policy as always dependent upon the articulation of identity, while identity is simultaneously produced and reproduced through the formulation and legitimation of policy. To see foreign policies as both dependent on and constitutive of identity is to theorize the latter not as a property of states, individuals, or institutions but as a discursive and political practice. Those formulating foreign policy usually present identities as though they were objectively given, but these instantiations of objectivity are themselves necessary reproductive performances. Foreign policies are articulated to legitimize particular actions, thereby installing and constraining agency. Politicians, editors, and influential commentators construct a collective 'we' as the foundation for 'our' policy—and themselves as authoritative voices speaking on behalf thereof—and this 'we' has crucial political consequences for who is addressed and who can gain a voice and a presence.

Questions of representation are therefore not merely, or even predominantly, a matter of who are formally included in national or international institutions, but rather of the constitution of the subjectivity of the Other. Taking a historical view of Western discourses on the Balkans, chapter 6 showed that Romantic and civilizational discourses articulated a more positive view of the Other than the radical threatening Other of national security discourse or of the Balkan discourse, but that these Others were nevertheless disciplined by the West. The Romantic Other should not emulate the rational, urbanizing West, and the civilizational Other should plant trees and improve its personal hygiene. That the imposition of an Other onto the Balkans is not a thing of the past was brought out by the analysis of the humanitarian responsibility discourse in chapter 7. This discourse constituted a 'civilian victim' to whom humanitarian responsibility was extended, but this subject was only ethically privileged insofar as it maintained a separation from the realm of political and military agency. 'Innocence' in turn was depoliticized and dehistoricized.

As constraining as discursive structures might be, they do, however, dependent on human agency for their reproduction and humans (particularly those in political, media, and academic power), hold therefore a responsibility for their discursive choices. Discursive structures can be difficult to transform, but they do have the potential for destabilization and resistance. As the analysis of the Western discourses in chapters 6 to 9 showed, all discourses have a blank spot that they cannot address, be that the feasibility of 'lift and strike' or the history which produced 'innocent victims.' Uncovering it constitutes a critical component of post-structuralist discourse analysis that goes back to Foucault and Derrida. Another critical component used in this book is a critical historical analysis—in Foucault's terms a genealogy—which traces the formation of a concept, its evolution, and particular use in the present. The concept of the Balkans was identified as a dominant representation in the Western debate on Bosnia, and it drew upon a discourse that went back to the 1920s in constructing 'the Balkans' as violent, barbaric, and dangerously entrapping the West. Often, however, what is mobilized is not the history *of* the concept but the construction of history *within* the concept; the Balkan discourse of the 1990s drew extensively on a construction of the Balkan Other, not as born in the early twentieth century, but of 'ancient hatred' going back hundreds of years. Not only did the historical analysis of chapter 6 show the youth of the 'ancient' concept, it also brought out two marginalized discourses preceding the concept of Balkanization: a Romantic construction of the heroic and passionate Balkan, and a civilizational Enlightenment belief in the 'young clients of Balkan civilization.' The Romantic discourse was later shown to have influenced Robert D. Kaplan's *Balkan Ghosts*, although this influence has gone unnoticed in the de-Romanticized debate of the 1990s.

Post-structuralism's critical and political understanding of discourse implies, first, that as there is no place outside of language, there is no analytical place that does not make a political incision, and, second, that as there is no place outside of language, there is no analysis that can completely dispense with the vocabulary already in place. Hence, to return to the discussion of Campbell's analysis in chapter 9, he is perfectly post-structuralist in taking a political stance and in operating within as well as beyond the representation of the Bosnian war as genocide.

Identity and foreign policy debates

Moving from the ontology and politics of discourse to the development of an analytical framework, chapters 2 and 3 argued that identity should be conceptualized as relational and as analytically and empirically open. Identity, it was argued, is established not only through the radical delineation of difference, but through a multiplicity of Others, and even radical Others are usually stabilized through articulations of 'other Others' with less radical identities. The constitution of 'Balkan leaders' in the humanitarian responsibility discourse was, for instance, stabilized through the articulation of an 'innocent victim' which did not share the radical difference of 'its' leaders. That 'innocent victims' were also simultaneously depoliticized illustrates that the non-radical Other is not necessarily a place from which the Other can speak its history, agency and desires.

The analytically open Other should furthermore, chapter 3 suggested, be studied as articulated through spatial, temporal, and ethical identities, and these should be employed in a theory of foreign policy debates as structured around basic discourses.[1] Basic discourses are identified through striking representations—in chapter 6, 'the Balkans' and 'genocide'—and they articulate radically different constructions of identity. Basic discourses do not define one particular policy, but structure the policy space within which concrete decisions are being made. As chapter 6 showed, the Balkan discourse articulated a policy space where Western decisions were based on evaluations of Western interests and potential regional instabilities, not on assessments of the moral responsibilities and implications of the Bosnian war. The Genocide discourse, on the contrary, articulated a space where Western action was demanded on ethical grounds. Moving into the analyses in chapters 7 to 9, these basic discourses were modified and their policy spaces articulated to rather different effects: the humanitarian responsibility discourse modified the Balkan discourse in a legitimation of the deployment of UNPROFOR, but it also delimited Western intervention to a humanitarian mission; neorealists de-Balkanized the Balkans but retained a policy space unencumbered by ethical considerations in advocating 'lift and strike'; and the American Genocide discourse articulated 'lift and strike' as militarily feasible and ethically justified through a modification of the Genocide discourse that constituted 'Bosnian leaders' as a 'fighting party.'

This analysis shows that there is not a one-to-one relationship between identity and policy, that 'the Balkans' does not automatically lead to non-intervention, or 'genocide' to the deployment of ground troops. One cannot, as a consequence, deduce policy from representations, nor representations from policy—both need to be empirically uncovered and their exact linkages studied. The Western Bosnia debate also reveals that 'policy alliances' might occur between variations of opposing basic discourses. The analysis of the American debate identified a striking policy convergence on 'lift and strike,' a policy supported by the American Genocide discourse, Balkanizing Serbia, European responsibility for Genocide, and neorealists. Such policy convergence testifies to a political terrain where 'lift and strike' became the consensual oppositional policy. This 'lift and strike alliance' exerted pressure on the Clinton administration, but it also stabilized parts of his policy insofar as it reinforced the consensus on 'lift and strike' as the boundary of interventionism. 'No ground troops' was in turn the (negative) policy that was shared by oppositional and official foreign policy discourses. Does the policy alliance between modifications of different basic discourses weaken the analytical arguments of discourse analysis? Should one not expect that constructions of identity and policy line up more neatly than in the American case? Not necessarily, in that politics is a dynamic, not a schematic, process, where alliances do form and discourses develop and change. Moreover, while a policy alliance might at first appear as a homogeneous group, it is precisely their diverging discourses which indicates the (in)stability of their alliance and hence where policy splits might appear in the future.

Questions of discursive stability were brought to the fore in the Western Bosnia debate. Chapter 2 argued that discourse analysis is not adverse to the importance of 'facts' and 'events,' but that these should be theorized as discursively constituted phenomena. Once established as such, 'facts' and 'events' might be mobilized by critical discourses that challenge official representations. Decision-makers can respond by changing their discourse, articulate 'facts' and 'events' as accounted for within the discourse already in place, or by attempting to silence the challenge. The studies of governmental discourse in chapter 7 showed a remarkable resilience; particularly in the British case, where a construction of 'Balkan leaders' usurped a series of Bosnian Serbian atrocities. Clinton's presidency began with the articulation of an internally unstable combination of the Balkan discourse and the Genocide discourse, but having resolved instability in favor of the former this discourse was reproduced until the summer of 1995 and the massacre at Srebrenica. In short, 'facts', 'events,' and 'material factors' did not in and of themselves produce policy.

The relationship between materiality and discourse continues to resurface in the debate over post-structuralism and discourse analysis. Chapter 1 laid out how sympathetic skeptics argue that discourse analysis might make a contribution to the study of foreign policy, but that discourses' explanatory powers should be measured against material factors, national and strategic interests, and what is militarily feasible. Yet, to articulate a 'national interest' or a 'security threat' is not to speak from an extra-discursive, objective, or material foundation, but to mobilize an abstract discourse of 'state sovereignty,' the 'identity of Others' as well as objectivity and inevitability. The discursive, and hence contestable, nature of security discourse was brought out by chapter 7, which showed that foreign policy debate is precisely about the definition of what is 'objectively' at stake. Were Western vital interests at risk in the Bosnian war? Was there a threat of the conflict spreading to Kosovo, Macedonia, and beyond, thus creating a 'powder-keg' in a strategically important region of the world, drawing in NATO members Greece and Turkey? Were moral interests intertwined with strategic interests, in that the failure to protect the Bosnian Muslims would alienate the Middle East and turn it against America and Western Europe? Would undeterred ethnic cleansing have a cascading effect, where other governments or sub-state groups would employ similar destabilizing strategies? These claims were all repeatedly made by Western politicians, but the absence of any agreement pointed to the difficulty of moving from the abstract 'national interest' to its unequivocal manifestation on a particular issue (Weldes 1999).

Tied in with these discussions of Western and national 'interests' was the importance of military feasibility. Debates on Bosnia tried to define not only the identity of Bosnia and the Balkans but also what was militarily feasible and decisive. Articulating the 'feasible' within discourses that simultaneously constructed the identities of Self and Other, there were frequent references to the military identity of the Serbs, who had 'tied down German forces,' who could not be fought in the Bosnian mountains, and who were a heroic, warrior people. Furthermore, what the case of the Western debate brought out in a striking manner was that the realm of 'the feasible' was itself heavily contested. The discrepancy in the evaluation of military strategy between American and British discourses was a consistent finding of the study. Clinton, through parts of his presidency as well as large parts of Congress, argued that 'lift and strike' would change the balance of power to such an extent that the Bosnian government would be able to gain a larger territory and that it could be adopted without endangering UNPROFOR or its withdrawal, while the West Europeans blatantly rejected the validity of these claims.

The intertextuality of discourse

To speak with authority about foreign policy is not only to articulate identity but also to establish oneself as knowledgeable and, in the case of politicians, as responsible and forceful. Adopting the concept of intertextuality, chapter 4 argued that foreign policymakers articulate their policy through references to other texts and that they address other discourses within the public debate while seeking to establish their own discourse as hegemonic. Intertextual links within official foreign policy discourse point to genres not normally considered of relevance for foreign policy analysis, most strikingly travel writing and memoir; genres that mix narrative and subjective forms of knowledge with more conventional forms of historical, social, and political analysis. The intertextualization of foreign policy was systematized into three research models, which gradually broaden the scope of analysis from official foreign policy to the discourses of the political opposition, the media and corporate institutions, and to popular culture and marginal political discourses. These models provide different possibilities for investigating the hegemonic status of official discourse, how this status is produced and challenged through intertextual references, and the likelihood and form of future discursive changes.

The intertextuality of foreign policy discourse makes it vital that the particular construction of authority and knowledge within prominent genres are integrated into the analysis. This facilitates an understanding of genres' power and attraction—it would, for instance, be a mistake to try to explain the popularity of travel writing through its ability to provide factual knowledge—as well as an interrogation of the reading and political appropriation of texts. The Western Bosnia debate provides ample evidence of the linkability of foreign policy discourse and of the political mobilization of texts with an 'interpretative deficit': that is, historical texts, texts not explicitly concerned with policy, or texts from the genres of literary non-fiction. Clinton's policy on Bosnia had allegedly been changed by Robert D. Kaplan's *Balkan Ghosts*, and Rebecca West's *Black Lamb and Grey Falcon* was repeatedly quoted, although to various political effects. Analyzing these travelogues' reliance upon the narrative techniques of literary non-fiction as well as their articulation of a Romantic discourse, it was argued that the reading of Kaplan and West as examples of the Balkan discourse should be problematized. The discrepancy between the texts themselves and their intertextual mobilization shows that texts are being read through the discursive lenses of a particular time and place. Since the Balkan discourse was a prominent discourse in the 1990s, it is not surprising that older texts such as West's were read through this optic. Not only are texts read through the terms of the present debate, the debate itself generates a story of what the meaning of these texts are; of Kaplan as supporting ancient hatred and a passive policy; of West as pro-Serbian; and of the Carnegie Commission from 1914 as showing the repetitiousness of Balkan conflict. These stories then support the discursive construction through which they were read in the first place.

Those skeptical of intertextuality, in particular when it concerns the importance of literary non-fiction, might argue that the Western debate on Bosnia constituted an unusual case. In response, chapter 4 held that travel writing has played a prominent role for Western constructions of the world from the age of exploration onwards and hence has a deeper implication in the constitution of International Relations (Pratt 1992; Lisle 1999). Kaplan's prominent status within American foreign policy debate was another, more recent example of the porous boundary between travelogues and policy analysis. That said, it would be an interesting future research project to investigate more systematically whether, when, and how travel writing is mobilized by policymakers and journalists and to what discursive and political effects. Another task might be to study the hybridization of genres, as in politicians' use of autobiography and autobiographical speech, or the links between narrative forms of knowledge and journalism, for instance in reports from 'embedded' reporters 'on the road' with coalition forces in Iraq in 2003.

One crucial limitation of the discourse analysis of this book is the absence of an explicit discussion of visual forms of representation. How is identity articulated through images (photography, video, and drawings), how are pictures given verbal and political meaning, and is there a bigger or a smaller interpretive space between imagery and policy than between policy and words? Critical discourse analysts as well as post-structuralists have opened this research agenda, and it might be worthwhile to interrogate the terrain between these works and the framework and research design suggested in the first part of this book (Fairclough 1995; Chouliaraki 2005; Campbell 2002a, 2002b, 2003, 2004; Shapiro 1997, 1999; Der Derian 2001). The question of visual representation points further to the importance of new media, particularly the internet. Virtually all of the media texts used in this book could be found in digital archives, but the growth and development of the worldwide web since the end of 1995 constitutes an important difference between the Bosnian war and more recent foreign policy events. The web allows for real-time, interactive and global communications, which potentially reconfigures the public sphere and the way in which foreign policy debates evolve and resistance gets organized (Deibert 1997, 2000, 2003). Would there, for instance, have been an Abu Ghraib scandal without the ubiquity of digital cameras and email linking soldiers in Iraq with people 'back home'? (Sontag 2004).

A final intertextual expansion of the research agenda, and one which intersects with those of visual representation and new media, is to take more seriously the importance of popular culture (Der Derian and Shapiro 1989; Der Derian 1992; Shapiro 1999; Weber 2001; Weldes 2003). Popular culture was located within intertextual research model 3A, but its visual and interactive forms of representation—for instance in computer games (Totilo 2004)—reiterates the need for further theoretical and methodological research that incorporates its implications for foreign policy debate. A multitude of theoretical and empirical research projects could be imagined, and ones that build directly on the study of Bosnia would be to locate the war's representation in film and television within the framework of basic discourses (Iordanova 2001) or to make an analysis of the comics *Safe Area Gorazde* and *The Fixer: The Story of Sarajevo* by Joe Sacco and *Sarajevo Tango* by Hermann.[2]

The boundaries and methodology of discourse

This book began with a call for intra-post-structuralist debate and for explicit discussions of methodological choices and their consequences. An appropriate way to conclude it might therefore be to return to these questions and to compare David Campbell's analysis (described in chapter 9) with that of this book: not to determine who is right, but in an attempt to illuminate the relationship between analytical and methodological decisions and the analysis produced. The most significant points of divergence—and convergence—between the two readings concern the unity of the West, the boundary between the humanitarian responsibility discourse and the Balkan discourse, and whether the West abstained from a more forceful intervention out of a fear of multiculturalism and an Islamic Other.

Campbell argues, as noted in chapter 9, that the West took a political and discursive stance toward Bosnia that was informed by an ontopological fixing of uniform identities onto separate and continuous territories, hence there is no clear separation in Campbell's analysis between West European and American policies. This seems appropriate insofar as Campbell's analytical focus is on the response of the international community, primarily the peace plans put forward from 1992 onwards. In the terminology of this book, his study is an intertextual model 1 study with official discourse being that of the international community. But, even at the level of Western states, there were no major differences until the summer of 1995 insofar as Clinton refrained from a confrontation with West European governments. It is thus when the analytical scope is broadened to include wider domestic debate within intertextual model 2 that the differences between the two studies become apparent. There was, as shown in chapter 7, a powerful Genocide discourse within the US Senate, which pointed to the multicultural identity of Bosnia as a reason for intervention. Whether this discourse could be said to articulate the more demanding concept of multiculturalism as defined by Campbell could neither be confirmed nor disconfirmed from the debates in the Senate. It is, however, as argued in chapter 7, possible to problematize whether the constitution of the Bosnians as a 'party willing to fight' and of 'lift and strike' as a sufficient policy amounted to taking on an ethical responsibility for Bosnia.

Turning from the political unity of the West to Western media discourse, it should be noted that *National Deconstruction* takes a somewhat inconclusive stance; in places it argues that the dominant media representation has helped 'sustain the geopolitical positions of extreme nationalists' (Campbell 1998a: 80), and in other places it argues that 'a large body of international reportage' had supported the genocide representation (Campbell 1998a: 101–2). Media reports, editorials, and commentary were used in the analyses in chapters 7 and 9 mostly to identify criticism of governmental Balkan discourses. The analytical ambition was, however, modest in that the study was designed to show that Genocide discourse criticism *did* exist, *not* whether it was more dominant than the Balkan discourse. Both Campbell's study and the one conducted here illustrate that identifying dominant media discourse poses particular methodological problems for discourse analysis. It is not impossible to read all major parliamentary debates on a foreign policy issue, or even the total number of presidential statements within a shorter period, but media discourse is formed by a large number of outlets and an abundance of texts. It might therefore be worthwhile asking whether it would be desirable to couple discourse analysis with more specific quantifiable criteria for selecting media texts, thereby providing a firmer foundation from which to speak of discursive dominance and engage other forms of media analysis. Remembering that discursive dominance is constituted not simply through sheer number of text but through the intertextual power of key texts, how are studies of the two forms of influence to be brought more systematically together?

Another divergence between the two studies concerns the interpretation of the boundaries of the Balkan discourse, or the civil/ethnic representation in Campbell's optic. Campbell's analysis juxtaposes this representation against one of international aggression/genocide, but does not (unlike chapters 7 and 8) identify variations within the Balkan/ethnic discourse. Should one see the West European discourse on humanitarianism as a Balkan discourse or a variation? Again, there is no objective foundation from which to judge. The advantage of a more differentiated reading of humanitarian responsibility, as advocated in chapter 7, might be, however, that it shows explicitly how responsibility was circumscribed in being applied to a depoliticized and dehistoricized subject only. It also provides an understanding of how the deployment of almost 40,000 UN troops was legitimized, something which would have been very unlikely within an unmodified Balkan discourse.

Finally, Campbell suggests that the West failed to thoroughly engage Bosnia in part because of fear that the Bosnians might 'become an Islamic force in or near Europe' or because of problems with multiculturalism 'at home' (Campbell 1998a: 52, 170). Yet, of the material read for this book, the only articulation of 'the Muslim Other' as a reason not to intervene was made by Huntington, who also, although not in the same context, articulated the dangers of multiculturalism to American domestic identity (Huntington 1996, 2004; Hansen 2000b). It was not uncommon, however, to find that *critics* of Western inaction argued that if the West did not intervene this might have a negative impact on relations with the Islamic world, or that the West was not intervening because of the 'Muslim Other.' That the mobilization of 'the Muslim Other' was carried out predominantly by critics of Western inaction, and that this articulation was not similarly reflected in governmental discourse, raises an interesting theoretical and methodological question. Discourse analysis is, as laid out in chapter 2, focused on the legitimation of policies through the discursive construction of identities, which implies that discourse analysis cannot 'explain' foreign policies— in this case intervention in Bosnia—through recourse to non-discursive phenomena (Wæver 2002). The absence of 'Islam as Other' in Western Bosnia discourses does not preclude that decision-makers might have used it in secret; crucially, however, they abstained from employing this representation in public. Assuming, hypothetically, that it had been secretly used, a new research question appears: why would it be that governments refrain from legitimizing their policy through recourse to an 'Islamic Other,' particularly since even before September 11 this is a trope with a long history in Western thought? (Said 1978). Would it indicate a discursive shift within Western public discourse away from an accepted construction of Islam as Other and a split between leaders and public? However, rather than Western governments secretly deciding not to intervene in Bosnia because of the religion of (most of) the 'Bosnian' subjects but choosing not to use this representation because they feared alienating their publics and allies in the Middle East, it seems more likely that the 'Balkan Other' was 'Other enough.' That the construction of ancient hatred, entrapment, and a general uniform 'Balkan,' rather than a separate Bosnian Muslim identity, was the Other that stabilized the debate. That non-intervention was, in other words, more about 'the Balkans' than about the Bosnian 'Muslims.'

Notes

1 Introduction

1 A parallel move took place within the field of feminist research, with Keohane arguing in favor of a standpoint-rationalist research agenda (Keohane 1989, 1998; Tickner 1997, 1998; Weber 1994).

2 It should be noted, however, that Wendt referenced Ashley and Walker as influences on his work in 1992 (Wendt 1992: 394).

3 The work of Cox, Der Derian, Tickner, and Campbell is said to have made valuable contributions in the 1980s and early 1990s, but 'many of those at the vanguard of the Third Debate have seemed content to simply reiterate their long-standing epistemological and methodological critiques of the discipline' (Price and Reus-Smit 1998: 285).

4 As the presentation of post-structuralism is misleading, so too is the one of critical constructivism and the ostensible boundary between them. There are differences between post-structuralist discourse analysis that draws upon Derrida, Foucault, and Laclau and Mouffe (Campbell 1992, 1993, 1998; Neumann 1996a, 1999; Wæver 2002; Hansen and Wæver 2002) on the one hand and the Wittgenstein-inspired approach to language games as developed by Karin Fierke (1996, 1998, 1999) or the structural linguistic or narrative approaches adopted by authors such as Jennifer Milliken (2001) or Janice Bially Mattern (2001) on the other, but these are differences not well conveyed by rationalist or conventional constructivist accounts.

5 This is not to say that these practices and artifacts cannot be given political significance, as shown by the heated debate over the architectural design of the September 11 memorial in New York City.

6 This assessment requires a carefully selected pilot-study or an extensive body of secondary literature documenting the status of the official discourse's hegemonic status.

7 Studies of official discourse should, as discussed in chapters 3 and 4, ask how this discourse draws upon representations with a particular conceptual and political history. Post-structuralist analysis of official discourse, as in Campbell's *Writing Security*, often shows the articulation of official discourse along a multitude of areas not normally considered to be foreign policy, such as drug use and homosexuality (Campbell 1992).

8 The rationalist criticism of post-structuralism for being focused on texts seems to rest on the (implicit) argument that post-structuralists have devoted themselves

to studies of esoteric or strange material—spy novels, the link between sport and war, and film, for instance—which have no influence on 'real foreign policymaking' (see Der Derian and Shapiro 1989 and Ashley and Walker 1990 for early examples of intertextual studies). Chapter 4 responds to this critique by placing the study of popular culture inside a systematic consideration of this material's link with official foreign policy discourse.

9   Popular culture, film, television, computer games, and comics are also of potential relevance for foreign policy debates (Der Derian 1992; Shapiro 1997; Weber 2001; Weldes 2003). However, while my general theoretical framework allows for their inclusion, I do not attempt to build a full theory of the relationship between popular culture and official foreign policy, not least because this would require a thorough consideration of visual and interactive epistemologies.

10   Price and Reus-Smit modify this statement by adding that 'We are not suggesting that all work must attend to these issues,' but their faulting of the works of James Der Derian, David Campbell, and Bradley Klein for not assessing causality undermines this statement (Price and Reus-Smit 1998: 279).

11   It is not always clear, however, that causal theories comply with this definition. To take a prominent example, Wendt stresses that his constructivism in *Social Theory of International Politics* is positivist, but it is not apparent under which conditions his theory of three cultures of anarchy—Hobbesian, Lockian, and Kantian—and three degrees of internalization—coercion, self-interest, and legitimacy—could be falsified (Wendt 1999).

12   The focus on Western policy and debate implies that the study is 'told from the outside,' rather than from inside the Yugoslavian break-up. The applicability of discourse analysis to non-Western contexts will be addressed in the chapters on theory and methodology.

2   Discourse analysis, identity, and foreign policy

1   This account of the processes of linking and differentiation is inspired by Laclau and Mouffe's conception of the logics of equivalence and difference (Laclau and Mouffe 1985: 128–30). But Laclau and Mouffe collapse the question of linking and difference with the degree to which the Other is radicalized, while I prefer, for analytical, methodological, and pedagogical reasons, to separate the two (see chapter 3).

2   Andrew Moravcsik has argued, for instance, that the Copenhagen School of European integration assumes integration to be a 'battle between nationalist and European ideals' while disregarding the importance of national and financial interests (Moravcsik 1999b: 374; on the Copenhagen School see Wæver 1990, 2002; Holm 1993, 1997; Larsen 1997; and Hansen and Wæver 2002). For a discussion of the difference between the Copenhagen School of security studies and the Copenhagen School of European integration, as well as the difference between the latter approach and the work of Moravcsik, see Hansen 2002a.

3   For an example of the importance of spiritual forces in constructing identity in South Africa, see Ashforth 2000. Temporal and spatial identity constructions are further discussed in chapter 3.

4   It is possible that particular identities loose their saliency: the construction of monarchy as opposed to popular rule was central to the European concert of the nineteenth century but is not equally constitutive of contemporary European

political discourse (Kissinger 1957). It is therefore possible that 'democracy' could fade from its current status in an all-liberal world.

5 Wendt has more recently moved toward a relational understanding of identity by linking it with individual and collective recognition. He argues that 'it is through recognition by the Other that one is constituted as a Self in the first place' (Wendt 2003: 511). Yet his focus is on actors who arrive to the process of recognition with an identity already in place, whereas post-structuralism theorizes identity not as a meeting between two already constituted actors but as a process through which subjectivity is created.

6 Conventional constructivism adopts a thinner conception of discourse as ideational rather than as incorporating the discursive representation of materiality (Wendt 1999). A distinction between discourse and materiality is also adopted by Fairclough's critical discourse analysis (Chouliaraki and Fairclough 1999: 28).

7 Wallander's methodology also points to the difficulty of separating 'reality' and discourse: her analysis of NATO's post-Cold War transformation is built on NATO's primary sources and interviews with fifteen US officials from the Department of Defense, the Department of State, and the National Security Council involved in NATO's adaptation and one analyst 'deeply involved in policy on NATO' (Wallander 2000: 717). Her material is thus either NATO's own discourse or the discourse of those involved in constructing it, whereas a more methodologically rigorous analysis would have identified threats and instabilities from sources that were independent of NATO's own definitions.

8 For Risse-Kappen's analysis to become a theory of alliance stability it would need to be subjected to other cases, yet methodologically this would be difficult as NATO is the only military alliance which has been comprised by (largely) democratic members.

9 The post-Cold War emphasis on NATO's identity as a security community of culture and values was already argued by Secretary General Wörner in 1991: 'The Treaty of Washington of 1949 nowhere mentions the Soviet Union but stresses instead the need for a permanent community of Western democracies to make each other stronger through cooperation, and to work for more peaceful international relations' (Wörner 1991: 5). This construction was repeatedly articulated in NATO's legitimation of its 'intervention' in Kosovo in 1999.

10 It is thus misleading to say that the post-structuralist view of the relationship between identity and foreign policy implies that identity is easily changed or that history does not matter (Kaufmann 1996: 152–4). The post-structuralist focus on the reproduction of identities implies also that Buzan and Wæver's suggestion that constructivists and post-structuralists analyze the formative phases of identity and neo-realists the consequential phase does not fully take the reproduction of identity into account (Buzan and Wæver 1997).

11 This is not to say that making textual and deconstructivist analyses of official discourse is not important, but rather, as is discussed in more detail in chapters 4 and 5, that a more comprehensive discourse analysis situates official discourse within the context of a larger debate.

12 As Campbell notes, Hobbes is more concerned with a possible fall *back* into a state of nature than with the initial movement from the state of nature (Campbell 1992: 63–4).

13 Chapter 3 argues that while identity is necessary for the state, it might not necessarily be constructed through radical discourses of otherness.

3   Beyond the Other: analyzing the complexity of identity

1   Connolly's solution is to replace the logic of 'othering' with an agonism of difference, 'in which each opposes the other (and the other's presumptive beliefs) while respecting the adversary at another level as one whose contingent orientations also rest on a shaky epistemic grounds' (Connolly 1991: 178). David Campbell has later turned to Derrida and Levinas for an ethics toward the Other (Campbell 1998a).

2   As critics have pointed out, if *Writing Security* is read as a general theory of foreign policy discourse and identity rather than as study of a selected or selective part of one country's policy or discourse, the state's security politics takes on an almost monolithic character. The construction of countries and marginal groups as radical Others happens uncontested, and security politics seem to happen almost as a function—or cause—of state identity (Hansen 1994; Neumann 1996a).

3   This is not to say that the republican tradition is not of significance for contemporary American political identity; that the British royal family is not a fixture of extraordinary media coverage, or that monarchies cannot still be mobilized within Romantic nationalist discourse, as was the case in Danish debates on European integration in the 1990s (Hansen 2002b). The point is rather that it is no longer significant for the construction of international difference between Western states.

4   Laclau and Mouffe have coined the term 'nodal point' to identify the privileged sign within a discourse. I would argue that it is always possible to identify several nodal points depending on one's research question (Laclau and Mouffe 1985: 112–13).

5   Turning, for example, to Walker's *Inside/Outside: International Relations as Political Theory*, one finds subsections on 'historicity,' 'spatiality,' 'political community,' 'temporality,' 'ethics of exclusion,' and 'ethics of cooperation' (Walker 1993).

4   Intertextualizing foreign policy: genres, authority, and knowledge

1   To take one example, France's President Chirac turned down NATO participation in Iraq in June 2004, arguing that 'Any meddling by NATO in this region seems to us to carry great risks, including risks of clashes between the Christian West and the Muslim East' (Stevenson and Sanger, 2004).

2   The distinction between high and low culture is in fact more historically and sociologically bounded than substantial.

3   This is not to suggest that popular culture is always conspiring with official discourse, nor that it might always be easily decided whether popular culture reproduces or contests conventional representations, as illustrated by the 2003–4 American popularity of shows featuring gay men and lesbians: 'Queer Eye for the Straight Guy,' 'The L-Word,' 'Playing It Straight' and 'Will and Grace.'

4   The differences within these genres, for example between policy speeches and interviews, between newspaper editorials and field reporting, and between historians and quantitative social scientist, will be elaborated in chapter 5.

5   The standard distinction between autobiography and memoir is to define the former as more introspective and concerned with the impact of events and experiences on the self, and the latter as more focused on external events, more documentary, and oriented toward 'a historical field of reference' (Bjorklund 1998: 168; Eakin 1992: 142, 179). Since the political memoirs and autobiographies are of

particular concern in this book, and since these will lean more toward the inclusion of external events, memoir rather than autobiography is chosen to identify this form of writing. However, as Bjorklund adds, the distinction between autobiography and memoir is difficult to uphold in practice as memoirists 'often discuss their thoughts and feelings as well' (Bjorklund 1998: 212).

6 As a case in point see Cooper's review of *Balkan Ghosts* in *Slavic Review*, the best-established journal in Kaplan's field of writing (Cooper 1993). Cooper's review concludes: '*Balkan Ghosts* is deceptive, for it portrays itself as a lively account of the contemporary Balkans, based on history and first-hand experience. In fact it is a distasteful mix of tired clichés, undigested or incorrect historical fact, and personal bias. Let the reader beware' (Cooper 1993: 593). By 2002 *Balkan Ghosts* had sold over 300,000 copies! (Ringle 2002).

7 For the editors of *Bibliothèque Universelle des Romans*, who were writing at the same time, 'The taste for travels has always piqued the curiosity of readers ... we derive more pleasure indeed from the abbé Prévost and Captain Cook than from the most attractive book on morality' (quoted in Adams 1983: 75).

8 As Kenneth D. Barkin argues, the field of history has traditionally been reluctant to include autobiography because of its belief that 'consciously created documents, particularly autobiographies, are inherently suspect and are to be treated with bold scepticism' (quoted from Eakin 1992: 143).

9 The importance of formative experience for constructing the identity of the author as well as the identity of Others implies that one needs to read texts in full and carefully.

10 Moving into twentieth century autobiography, Bjorklund and Eakin point to the importance of psychoanalytic theory and a narrative that turns on the importance of cultural politics, often in ethnic minorities (Eakin 1992: 117–37).

11 The vast majority of academic discussions of memoir falls within the field of literary studies, which is not very concerned with questions of politics. Even Bjorklund, a sociologist, notes that she has not 'explored the political question, [however,] of how autobiography serves as ideology or a legitimation of the status quo' (Bjorklund 1998: 171).

12 See for example the use of four individual's stories, two of them refugees, in Bush's speech at the first national conference on faith-based and community initiatives: 'There is no better way to clarify for our fellow citizens the power of faith-based programs and [than?] to speak about examples, to hold up stories about lives who have been changed' (Bush 2004b).

5 Research designs: asking questions and choosing texts

1 It is possible to dispense with the linguistic requirement if the focus of analysis is on discursive encounters that play themselves out in an international arena where the 'translated' language of 'the Other' is English, French, Spanish, etc.

2 At the abstract level, all events and issues are of course related in that they concern the political discourse of the Self. For practical purposes, however, a separation into events or issues is useful.

3 Iver Neumann suggests using the term *pioneer texts* for historical key texts (Neumann 2001: 54).

4 Not that most political leaders write their own speeches, but they present them as if they were, and by being the speaking voice of the text, they make them 'their speeches,' erasing 'the actual writer.'

5 There is a difference between the practical research process and the way it is presented when written-up in its final form. The analysis begins with a presentation of the two basic discourses, but these could only be identified through readings of a wider body of literature, including key texts and general material.

6 The analysis does not, however, make a systematic comparison of the potential differences between the construction of identities and policy within reportage and editorials or of the stance of different newspapers.

7 Fiction and film did not appear to be equally influential. The most important instances were the heated discussions of Emir Kusturica's movie *Underground*, especially in France, and critical acclaim for *Before the Rain* by Manchevski (Iordanova 2001; Handke 1997). Later, more-mainstream movies *Welcome to Sarajevo* (a London journalist's experiences in Sarajevo and the rescue and adoption of a Sarajevan girl, featuring Woody Harrelson and Marisa Tomei in smaller parts) and *The Peacemaker* (a Bosnian Serb man whose family was killed in a mortar attack in Sarajevo seeking to blow up the UN in New York, chased by George Clooney and Nicole Kidman) got some attention but were not huge commercial or critical successes. The first season of Fox's '24' featured Bosnian Serbs as the villains.

6 The basic discourses in the Western debate over Bosnia

1 Todorova is a little unclear as to precisely when 'the Balkans' takes center stage. She argues that 'Until the Congress of Berlin in 1878, the most often used designations were derivative from the presence of the Ottoman Empire in the peninsula,' and later that 'In the second half of the nineteenth century "Balkan Peninsula" or simply "Balkans" was affirming itself in place of "European Turkey"' (Todorova 1997: 27).

2 For a discussion of empire as a political form of organization see Watson 1992, in particular 107–11 (on the Byzantine Empire), and 177–8 (on the Ottoman Empire).

3 While the area lacked a name, it was nevertheless, in Stoianovich's view, 'an area' and he could therefore, in the *Annales* tradition, write a study of 'the Balkans' which 'embraces eight or nine millennia' (Stoianovich 1967: viii).

4 This construction of 'the Balkans' as a bulwark against Islamic intrusion was also articulated by Serbs in the 1990s as they were seeking Western support against the 'Muslim' Bosnians.

5 Disraeli was reluctant to give Russia more power in the Balkans, as were subsequent generations of Western politicians.

6 Since neither Todorova nor Goldworthy addresses this discourses or the report by the Carnegie Commission, perhaps in part in the case of the latter because of her more literary focus, this section will take this report as an exemplar of a more general Western civilizational discourse and present a primary reading thereof.

7 Prior to the common use of 'civilization,' cultures had as far back as classical Greece thought about their relationship to others (Hartog 1988). The crucial point is thus not that the eighteenth century adoption of 'civilization' has no links to the past but that it constitutes a particular, and new, way of framing Self and Other.

8 However, it is worth noting that the concern with 'facts' was not necessarily coupled to 'observation' at least not in the early stages of the discovery of 'civilization.' Voltaire, who wrote about Russia never traveled further east than Berlin and Rousseau never visited Poland (Wolff 1994: 236).

9 Compared with the 1990s, there are remarkable few references to other 'outsiders' but Europe. There is one reference to 'the West' and two references to 'America' (Carnegie Endowment for International Peace 1914: 2, 3, 97).

10 Schoolteachers should encourage cleanliness in order to get rid of 'all obnoxious sights and smells' as well as 'tactfully suggest better plans for making the homes convenient and comfortable, by the use of proper floors, simple but useful furniture, better provisions for health and decency, and the planting of grass, shrubbery, and trees.' As a means of achieving this, a 'healthy rivalry' between villages should be encouraged (Carnegie Endowment for International Peace, 1914: 270–1). Interestingly, recommendations for adopting liberal democratic systems as a necessary means of becoming European were wholly absent.

11 Both discourses also converge on the construction of a 'Balkan subject' to which the 'real Balkans' have to conform. Thus while both discourses construct 'the Balkans' in progressing or attractive terms it is nevertheless a construction imposed by Western discourses onto a silent subject.

12 Paradoxically, this thematization of Balkan passion and brutality caused by the Ottoman influence appeared only clearly in Western discourse when the Ottoman Empire had lost its political hold on the Balkans (Todorova 1997: 122).

13 However, argued, Roucek, 'in reality the Balkan peoples have set amazing examples by heroic battles for the principles of freedom and independence' (Roucek 1948: 2).

14 The negative construction of the Balkans as a region of eternal conflict and instability within Western discourse has been countered, not surprisingly, by a number of 'Balkan strategies.' The first response is aimed at the meaning of the concept itself, to 'be Balkan' means not, within Greek discourse, to be a disruptive element, but to be abandoned by self-interested great powers who will let the Balkans fight on behalf of Europe only to treat it as an object (Stauersböll 2000). Another response is to argue that the border between Eastern Europe and Europe on the one hand and the Balkans on the other is located so that one's particular country falls within the European realm, but that one has the capacity to function as a bride or a mediator between 'Europe' and 'the Balkans' (Bakic-Hayden and Hayden 1992: 8–10; Hansen 1996). As Roucek pointed out in 1948: 'The Balkan intellectual resents being identified with what the term "Balkan" has come to connote' (Roucek 1948: 9).

15 That the Byzantine past is articulated in more positive terms in the region is perhaps not surprising. For Paparriogopoulos, the most influential modern Greek historian, Byzantium provided the link between the ancient world and the modern era (Stauersböll 2000: 56–7). In 1988, when most 'Eastern' countries were eager to establish themselves as 'Central European' rather than Eastern European or Balkan, the following saying is reported from Belgrade: 'The Balkans gave the world two great civilizations: the Greek and Byzantine. Central Europe gave the world two ideologies: communism and fascism' (Bakic-Hayden and Hayden 1992: 13).

16 Baker was Secretary of State under George H. Bush.

17 In addition, it was argued that 'Bosnia' was an international recognized state with a 'legal, multinational government' (Magas 1993: xi), formally recognized by the EC, the US, and the UN, and yet 'allowed to be destroyed' by its powerful recognizers as 'Yugoslavia' collaborated with the Bosnian Serbs (Rieff 1996: 23).

18 Daniel Kofman argued that the Israeli construction of the first three years of the war was of 'an "imagined affinity" with Serbia,' in no small part because of Serbia's contribution to the defeat of Nazi Germany and the Independent State of Croatia (Kofman 1996: 92). This position was in stark contrast to many diaspora Jews, who adopted the opposite position by identifying with 'Bosnia' (Kofman 1996: 110).

19 See for example the statements by Senators Cranston, DeConcini, and Specter in the US Senate debate on August 10 1992.

20 The discursive appropriations of 'genocide' had in fact clashed inside Yugoslavia prior to the outbreak of war (Boban 1990; Knezevic 1993; Hayden 1992, 1993; Djilas 1991: 103–27). One of the themes was how many people had died in Jasenovac, the concentration camp run by the Independent State of Croatia and the Ustasha movement, another was the discovery of burial sites in 1990 which held the remains of people killed or massacred by the Communists at the end of World War II. These people were predominantly Croatian Ustashas, but Slovenian home guards and Serbian Chetniks were also discovered (Denich 1994: 378). After World War II the Communist leadership had decided on a policy of silence on the issue of the Ustasha genocide as well as on the Communist massacres, to the extent that the issue was addressed it was constructed within the categories of 'victims of fascism' on the one side and 'foreign occupiers and domestic traitors' on the other (Denich 1994: 370). As the political environment in Yugoslavia became radicalized throughout the latter part of the 1980s, the genocide discussion was reopened and located within an increasingly nationalized context, and the genocide of World War II moved from being a historical memory to a contemporary political tool in the construction of national identities.

21 *The Independent* pointed to 'the flowering of multicultural ideas so valued in Britain' (*The Independent* 1993c) and David Rieff made a similar observation about America and Bosnia (Rieff 1996: 10).

22 While tracing the construction of 'Croatia' would be an interesting research question, it is of lesser importance in this context since Serbia and Bosnia were constituted as the two major players and identities. There are differences within the Genocide discourse as to how positively or negatively 'Croatia' is constructed: some construct it within the same symbolic community of meaning as Bosnia (Mestrovic 1994; Cushman and Mestrovic 1996; Letica 1996: 174), some leave Croatia in the neutral dark, and some are more inclined to see Croatia somewhere in-between 'Serbia' and 'Bosnia,' in particular as Tudjman and Milosevic were reported to discuss the partitioning of Bosnia and the Bosnian Muslims and Bosnian Croats fell into war (Djilas 1992: 26).

23 There was a discourse, to be discussed further in chapter 9, which coupled the construction of genocide with a Balkanization of 'Serbia,' but this should be seen as a variation over the Genocide discourse rather than its basic form, first because it was less frequently argued; second because it is closer to the Balkan discourse in that it shifts the 'Balkan identity' onto the 'Serbian subject' rather than rearticulating it in full.

7 Humanitarian responsibility versus 'lift and strike': tracing trans-Atlantic policy discourses

1 See, for example, Wilkinson (1995). Later reports by the UN and the Netherlands Institute for War Documentation, the latter commissioned by the Dutch Government,

sought to establish the political background for the massacre and evaluate the actions of the UN and Dutchbat (Secretary General of the UN 1999; Netherlands Institute for War Documentation 2002).

2 Germany had actively lobbied for the recognition of Slovenia and Croatia but adopted a low profile on Bosnia. Sending German peacekeepers to Bosnia was ruled out for constitutional and historical reasons and Germany found herself torn between the United States on the one side, and France and Britain on the other (Maull 1995–6: 109).

3 French Foreign Minister Juppé declared that 'One cannot indefinitely send hundreds of millions of francs, leave thousands of men on the ground, if the belligerents refuse all political solution' (quoted from Wood 1994: 148). France showed a more pro-Bosnian attitude than Britain on a number of occasions; it was, for example, the driving force behind the NATO ultimatum to the Bosnian Serbs following the mortar attack in Sarajevo in February 1994. But being the largest contributor to the peacekeeping force, France shared the other European countries' opposition to American calls for a more aggressive 'lift and strike' policy (Wood 1994: 148; Lepick 1996).

4 One of the noticeable critical voices from Labour was Clare Short (later a Minister).

5 Although a detailed study of the British media discourse is beyond the scope of this chapter, it is noteworthy that all editorials on Bosnia from the three newspapers mentioned above from the months of August 1992, April 1993, and July 1995, nine in total, are critical, some highly so, of the policies of the West and Britain.

6 One should note that the media did not contest all components of Western policy; there was, for instance, general support for upholding the arms embargo.

7 The articulation of 'multi-ethnic' Bosnia is found in early media coverage and it became increasingly voiced as academic analyses presented more complex, and historically accurate, pictures of Bosnia. For an early media example see Burns (1992); for early academic and historical analysis see Banac (1992), Magas (1993), and Malcolm (1994).

8 For an editorial that points in this direction see *The New York Times* (1992), which argues in a critique of the London Conference's proposals for humanitarian assistance, that 'America and Europe can still stop Serbia from redrawing the boundaries of Bosnia by naked force. And they have a moral and legal duty to prevent genocide. Britain ... is blatantly promoting the seductive sellout.'

9 Thomas L. Friedman argued that policymakers 'concede that they have begun to talk about Bosnia differently, to cast the problem there less as a moral tragedy—which would make American inaction immoral—and more as a tribal feud that no outsider could hope to settle.' The analysis here shows, however, that both elements were present in Clinton's discourse from the start of his Presidency (Friedman 1993).

10 One cannot, as argued in chapter 2, determine whether this was an intentional instability, whether Clinton was simply uncertain of how to understand Bosnia, or whether he was getting conflicting advice. (For a thorough account of the internal discussions inside the Clinton administration, see Daalder 2000).

11 One should note that most politicians still articulated the simpler version of the Genocide discourse, which did not bring up the 'multiethnic' Bosnia and the 'failure' of the West.

12 In Dole's words, he does not suggest risking 'one American life' (Dole S5622, 103rd Congress, May 12, 1994).

8 Writing the past, predicting the future: travelers, realism, and the politics of civilization

1 Later in the book Kaplan writes of drinking episodes in which he takes part, but these always depict him in the role as the reluctant foreigner complying with local habits.

2 The significance of alcohol in constituting 'the Balkans' as well as for forging links between drinking Westerners and Serbs is mentioned by UNPROFOR Director of Information in Zagreb, Michael Williams, who argued in an interview in 2000 that there was a much more congenial relationship between the British officers, including General Rose, and the Serbs than with the Bosnian Muslims. The Bosnian Serbs in Pale would 'make an entire evening of it, and quite lavish meals with quite a lot of alcohol would be provided' (quoted from Simms 2001: 178). Holbrooke's memoir, discussed in chapter 9, also makes prominent note of the Serbs' ability to drink.

3 It also calls forth a gendering of the Balkan discourse, which is further discussed in chapter 9. If Balkan men are particularly significant in constructing the 'barbaric Balkan' does this leave 'Balkan women' as the victims of 'Balkan masculinity'? If so, does the West not have a responsibility for offering them (masculine) protection?

4 The fame of Rebecca West was not only derived from her writings, but also from her ten-year long affair with H. G. Wells, and their illegitimate son Anthony West (Rollyson 1996). Even the biographical introduction in the Penguin classic edition of *Black Lamb and Grey Falcon* describes West's love life before her literary achievements and it is perhaps a cosmic irony that it took the violent sundering of her beloved Yugoslavia and the renewed popularity of *Black Lamb and Grey Falcon* in the 1990s to finally free Rebecca West from the H. G. Wells connection she sought to escape for the last sixty years of her life. It is beyond the scope of this chapter to discuss the relationship between *Black Lamb and Grey Falcon* and West's personal life, but it should be noted that her relationship with her son was strained at best, and that there is no mention of him, nor of the future grandchild, in *Black Lamb and Grey Falcon* and thus little support for the earthly granny that Kaplan romantically conjures (Rollyson 1996; Garis 1982).

5 On an anecdotal note, every Barnes and Noble I visited in New York City around Christmas 2003 had a copy in their history section. *Balkan Ghosts* was in the travel aisle.

6 By 2005, the book is still listed on NATO's website as suggested reading for understanding the history of Bosnia and was described as 'a chronicle' with 'insightful digressions into the history, politics and culture of the region' (NATO 2004).

7 Schweizer argues that 'the politics of *Black Lamb and Grey Falcon* is, for better or worse, impressionistic and philosophically informed. Rather than being capable of serving as a policy-maker's manual, this work belongs solidly to the realm of literature, history, and philosophy, setting out a tragic historical predicament within its wider cosmic context' (Schweizer 2002: 90). This takes too narrow a view of politics by equating it to 'policy-maker's manuals' and ignores the political and intertextual appropriations of West's book.

8 *Black Lamb and Grey Falcon* is perhaps as much a book about gender as it is a book about Yugoslavia, and there have been competing assessments of her potential as a feminist epistemological role model within the fields of literary criticism and women's studies (Stec 1997; Schweizer 2002).

9 Victoria Glendinning, West's first biographer, overlooks the references to the 1936 trip and argues, mistakenly, that the book 'was written as if based on a single extensive visit' (Glendinning 1987: 154).

10 The strongholds of resistance on the Dalmatian coast are thus privileged over Croatia proper (for example West 1941: 216).

11 The abolishment of popular representation also sits uneasily with West's insistence that both Serbs and Croats are 'intensely democratic people' (West 1941: 158, 554, 617).

12 West kept a brief diary of her trips, but it was impossible that she could have remembered word-for-word conversations that were five years old—and nowhere does she make a mention of having forgotten parts of a conversation. She also did not speak the local languages and hence relied upon interpreters.

13 It is frequently argued that Constantine was a vehicle for (Serbian) government propaganda (Rollyson 1996: 213). Yet, it is doubtful whether he was able to shake West's Romantic appropriation of the Yugoslav peoples.

14 West approves, however, of the Turks' architectural preference for light and uncluttered spaces, their love of nature, their 'tradition of tranquil sensuality,' and their appreciation of pleasure (West 1941: 288, 298, 389).

15 'Natural man, uncorrected by education, does not love beauty or pleasure or peace; he does not want to eat and drink and be merry; he is on the whole averse from wine, women, and song. He prefers to fast, to groan in melancholy, and to be sterile … natural man is mean' (West 1941: 172).

16 West is not entirely clear as to the applicability of the dynamics of sacrifice, which seems in some places to be ascribed to Christianity and in others to be located within human nature.

17 Kaplan, in a more recent article from 2002, points to Huntington as one of his main influences when he began as a traveling journalist in the 1980s (Ringle 2002).

18 The Sinic civilization was labeled Confucian and the Orthodox Slavic-Orthodox in 1993. When describing each of the civilizations, Huntington curiously leaves out the Orthodox civilization (Huntington 1996: 45–8).

19 Huntington predicted in 1993 that fault-line conflicts would become more frequent than intra-civilizational conflicts. By 1996 it was left open when this transformation would be completed. His 1996 statistical material is inconclusive as to which type is numerically dominant, however more important than sheer numbers is the fact that inter-civilizational conflicts are seen as posing the greatest danger to global stability (Huntington 1993: 48; Huntington 1996: 36 and 257).

20 Huntington's policy advice differed therefore from Robert D. Kaplan's civilizational reading in *The New Republic*, which argued for American support for the Bosnian government to prevent it from turning to the Middle East (Kaplan 1993b).

21 Neorealists have more recently argued in favor of a 'rationalist' reading of Bin Laden and Al Qaeda as well as Saddam Hussein (Mearsheimer and Walt 2003; Posen 2001).

9 The failure of the West? The evolution of the Genocide discourse and the ethics of inaction

1 Omarska was eventually closed down and opened to the International Red Cross and the media, but this did not put an end to ethnic cleansing or create an accountability for the disappearances that had occurred (Gutman 1993: xxxii).

2 This raises the question of whether some discourses provide for more discursive variations than others. While the number of subjects and the delineation of policy space are significant, they do not, however, determine how many variations are articulated empirically.

3 This, however, was a marginal discourse within the media. *The New York Times* was critical of Europe, but did not adopt the genocide representation after 1992, and it was more supportive of Clinton, arguing for instance on February 6, 1994, that 'Europe has failed miserably in its efforts to control the war in Bosnia,' while Clinton had 'responded well to a situation fraught with diplomatic duplicity' and that his 'firm stand is paying off' (*New York Times* 1994b, 1994a).

4 David Rieff was a notable exception to the American insistence that 'lift and strike' was sufficient. He argued that those who held that air strikes were 'enough' were 'wanting to deal with a great historical tragedy on the cheap,' and that those advocating the 'lifting' were being naive as to the capabilities of the Serbian side, 'Perhaps they thought that because the Bosnian Serb Army had committed great crimes, it was also stupid or incompetent. In fact it was neither, and NATO soldiers would have had to kill and die to get the weapons in. It should be said that, to their credit, at least most of those who opposed intervention seemed to understand its gravity in a way that many of those who backed it did not' (Rieff 1996: 13). Rieff is somewhat unfairly described by James Gow as an example of 'the impassioned and monodimensional assaults ... which betray little understanding of international relations' (Gow 1997: 5).

5 The construction of Western intervention as in the interest of the Serbian population was more frequently argued during NATO's intervention into Kosovo in 1999.

6 That this representation came under pressure during NATO's intervention in Kosovo in 1999, where Serbs positioned themselves on bridges thought to be bombing targets, shows that practical politics does not always conform with the categories neatly assigned to it. Whether this practice made bridges/Serbs legitimate targets is a long and complex discussion.

7 I have dealt specifically with the representation of mass rapes in Bosnia within the Balkan discourse, the Genocide discourse, and the radical feminist discourse in Hansen (2001). Bosnia also put the question of gendered warfare on the research agenda of IR more broadly (Jones 1994; Carpenter 2003).

8 Not all feminist analysis articulated a radical Gendering Genocide discourse.

9 It should be noted that the analysis below is focused on the articulation of identity and the evaluation of policy in *National Deconstruction*, and that the analysis does not go into a detailed discussion of David Campbell's reading of Derrida and Levinas, or his suggestions for post-structuralist ethics. There is, in other words, much more to *National Deconstruction* than I can do justice to in this context.

10 Campbell's claim that the Genocide Convention precludes the consideration of a Bosnian genocide because Bosnia's multinational and multireligious status would make the convention inapplicable appears less convincing, particularly in the light of the later proceedings at the International Criminal Tribunal in The Hague (Campbell 1998a: 108). One should note that this assessment of international reporting questions Campbell's earlier statement that Western media was in support of the assumptions of the ethnic/civil representation of the war.

11 Why that does not constitute a violation of post-structuralist principles is an issue addressed in chapter 10.

12 Comparing Campbell's analysis of multiculturalism to the European responsibility for Genocide discourse, the difference runs between the former's articulation of

multiculturalism as a problem within the West as a whole and the latter's claim that it is a sign of the Unites States and an absence within Europe.

13 The British media was slightly less hostile to Owen; for instance, *The Guardian* argued that although the VOPP would carve the Bosnian nation into bits, the two negotiators were nevertheless 'trying to stop the slaughter now' (*The Guardian* 1993a; *The Independent* 1993a).

14 Holbrooke was described as a 'tough costumer' by *The Washington Post*, which also took a swing at those who defined Holbrooke as 'swaggery or pushy or self-promoting' (*The Washington Post* 1995a).

15 The steady chronological pace implies also, in one reviewer's words, 'a weight of detail under which the reader at times feels close to suffocation' (Mortimer 1995).

16 Another striking employment of the public–private boundary is in Owen's account of the Bosnian Serbian commander Mladic, who is argued never to lower his guard. The only intimate moment with Owen is following Mladic's daughter's suicide, where Owen offers consolation, 'For a brief spell we were fathers first and foremost; but within minutes we were back to a wary confrontation and mock jocularity' (Owen 1995: 157). Here the narrative effect is slightly ambiguous: on the one hand, it creates an—however circumscribed—intimacy between Owen and the most notorious Bosnian Serb commander; on the other hand, it is the unwillingness of Mladic to transgress this boundary which sets him aside from Milosevic and relegates him to the Balkan Other.

17 At the time Holbrooke was Assistant Secretary of State for European and Canadian affairs; he continues in *To End a War* that the statement was 'intended to apply to events between 1990 and the end of 1992,' but adds somewhat defensively that 'there was concern that some people might also apply it to events as late as 1994, halfway into the Clinton Administration's first term' (Holbrooke 1998: 21).

18 Holbrooke disputes claims that Milosevic was intoxicated at Dayton and therefore made concessions that would have been unlikely under sober conditions (Holbrooke 1998: 285).

19 This part of the narrative draws extensively on the tradition of the strenuous travelogue: Holbrooke's team travels incessantly, works through weekends and holidays, gets little sleep, eats only sandwiches and cold pizzas, and has to stay in 'college dormitories' (Holbrooke 1998: 233).

10 Conclusion

1 Representations of foreign policy also imply constructions of gender, either through privileging the subject of 'women,' as in Gendering Genocide, or through the mobilization of gendered representations, as in Robert O. Kaplan's articulation of Rebecca West and drunken Balkan men. A future research project could couple the discourse analytical framework more fully to feminist approaches that trace the articulations of masculinity and femininity embedded in all foreign policy discourses (Elshtain 1987; Tickner 2001; Zalewski and Parpart 1998).

2 Sacco's work on Bosnia and Palestine has been prominently reviewed; David Rieff, for instance, called *Safe Area Gorazde* 'the best dramatic evocation of the Bosnian catastrophe,' and Sacco's work is often favorably compared to factual accounts of the Bosnian war (Rieff 2000; Giovanni 2004).

References

Adams, P. G. (1983) *Travel Literature and the Evolution of the Novel*, Lexington: The University Press of Kentucky.

Adler, E. (1997) 'Seizing the Middle Ground: Constructivism in World Politics,' *European Journal of International Relations*, 3 (3): 319–63.

Allcock, J. B. (1991) 'Constructing the Balkans,' in J. B. Allcock and A. Young (eds) *Black Lambs and Grey Falcons: Women Travellers in the Balkans*, Huddersfield: Bradford University Press.

Allen, B. (1996) *Rape Warfare: The Hidden Genocide in Bosnia-Herzegovina and Croatia*, Minneapolis: University of Minnesota Press.

Almond, M. (1994) *Europe's Backyard War: The War in the Balkans*, London: Mandarin.

Anderson, B. (1983) *Imagined Communities: Reflections on the Origin and Spread of Nationalism*, 2nd edn, London: Verso.

Anzulovic, B. (1999) *Heavenly Serbia: From Myth to Genocide*, New York: New York University Press.

Ashforth, A. (2000) *Madumo, A Man Bewitched*, Chicago: University of Chicago Press.

Ashley, R. K. (1981) 'Political Realism and Human Interests,' *International Studies Quarterly*, 25 (2): 204–36.

—— (1984) 'The Poverty of Neorealism,' *International Organization*, 38 (2): 225–86.

—— (1987) 'The Geopolitics of Geopolitical Space: Toward a Critical Social Theory of International Politics,' *Alternatives*, 12 (4): 403–34.

Ashley, R. K. and R. B. J. Walker (eds) (1990) 'Speaking the Language of Exile: Dissidence in International Studies,' *International Studies Quarterly*, 34 (3): 259–68.

Aspin, L. (1994) 'New Europe, New NATO,' *NATO Review* 42 (1): 12–14, www.nato.int/docu/review/1994/9401-3.htm

Baker III, J. A. (1995) 'Bosnia; Balkans Long History of Drifting Into Chaos,' *Los Angeles Times*, June 25, M2.

Bakic-Hayden, M. and Hayden, R. M. (1992) 'Orientalist Variations on the Theme "Balkans": Symbolic Geography in Recent Yugoslav Cultural Politics,' *Slavic Review*, 51 (1): 1–15.

Banac, I. (1984) *The National Question in Yugoslavia: Origins, History, Politics*, Ithaca: Cornell University Press.

—— (1992) 'The Fearful Asymmetry of War: The Causes and Consequences of Yugoslavia's Demise,' *DAEDALUS*, 121 (2): 141–74.

Bennett, C. (1995) *Yugoslavia's Bloody Collapse: Causes, Course and Consequences*, New York: New York University Press.

Berlin, I. (1990) 'Alleged Relativism in Eighteenth-Century European Thought,' in his *The Crooked Timber of Humanity: Chapters in the History of Ideas*, London: Fontana Press.

Bjorklund, D. (1998) *Interpreting the Self: Two Hundred Years of American Autobiography*, Chicago: University of Chicago Press.

Boban, L. (1990) 'Jasenovac and the Manipulation of History,' *East European Politics and Societies*, 4 (3): 580–92.

Booth, K. (1991) 'Strategy and emancipation,' *Review of International Studies*, 17 (4): 313–26.

Browning, C. S. (2002) 'Coming Home or Moving Home?: "Westernizing" Narratives in Finnish Foreign Policy and the Reinterpretation of Past Identities,' *Cooperation and Conflict*, 37 (1): 47–72.

Brownmiller, S. (1975) *Against Our Will: Men, Women and Rape*, New York: Fawcett Columbine.

—— (1994) 'Making Female Bodies the Battlefield,' in A. Stiglmayer (ed.) *Mass Rape: The War against Women in Bosnia-Herzegovina*, Lincoln and London: University of Nebraska Press. [First published in *Newsweek*, January 4, 1993: 37.]

Buk-Swienty, T. (1996) 'Vesten Mod Rester' ('The West Against the Rest'), interview with Samuel P. Huntington, *Weekendavisen*, December 19–26.

Burns, J. F. (1992) 'Bosnia's Nightmare,' *The New York Times*, May 24, section 4, p. 1.

Bush, G. H. W. (1992a) 'Remarks on the Situation in Bosnia and an Exchange With Reporters, in Colorado Springs,' August 6, *Public Papers of the Presidents of the United States*, vol. 2: 1315–18.

—— (1992b) 'The President's News Conference,' August 7, *Public Papers of the Presidents of the United States*, vol. 2: 1319–23.

Bush, G. W. (2003) 'President Discusses Operation Iraqi Freedom at Camp Lejeune,' Office of the Press Secretary, April 3, www.whitehouse.gov/news/releases/2003/04/20030403-3.html

—— (2004a) 'President Addresses the Nation in Prime Time Press Conference,' Office of the Press Secretary, April 13, www.whitehouse.gov/news/releases/2004/04/print/20040413-20.html

—— (2004b) 'America's Compassion in Action,' Bush's speech at the first national conference on faith-based and community initiatives. Office of the Press Secretary, June 1, www.whitehouse.gov/news/releases/2004/06/20040601-10.html

Butler, J. (1990) *Gender Trouble: Feminism and the Subversion of Identity*, London: Routledge.

Buzan, B. (1997) 'Civilisational *Realpolitik* as the New World Order?,' *Survival*, 39 (1): 180–3.

Buzan, B. and Diez, T. (1999) 'The European Union and Turkey,' *Survival*, 41 (1): 41–58.

Buzan, B. and Wæver, O. (1997) 'Slippery? Contradictory? Sociologically Untenable? The Copenhagen School Replies,' *Review of International Studies*, 23 (2): 241–50.

Buzan, B., Kelstrup, M., Lemaitre, P., Tromer, E., and Wæver, O. (1990) *The European Security Order Recast: Scenarios for the Post-Cold War Era*, London: Pinter.

Buzan, B., Wæver, O., and de Wilde, J. (1998) *Security: A New Framework for Analysis*, Boulder: Lynne Rienner.

Campbell, D. (1992) *Writing Security: United States Foreign Policy and the Politics of Identity*, Manchester: Manchester University Press.

Campbell, D. (1996a) 'Political Prosaics, Transversal Politics, and the Anarchical World,' in M. Shapiro and H. Alker (eds) *Challenging Boundaries: Global Flows, Territorial Identities*, Minneapolis: University of Minnesota Press.

———— (1996b) 'Violent Performances: Identity, Sovereignty, Responsibility,' in Y. Lapid and F. Kratochwil (eds) *The Return of Culture and Identity in IR Theory*, Boulder: Lynne Rienner.

———— (1997) '"Ethnic" Bosnia and Its Partitioning: The Political Anthropology of International Diplomacy,' paper presented at the ISA conference in Toronto, March, 1997.

———— (1998a) *National Deconstruction: Violence, Identity, and Justice in Bosnia*, Minneapolis: University of Minnesota Press.

———— (1998b) *Writing Security: United States Foreign Policy and Politics of Identity*, 2nd edn, Manchester: Manchester University Press.

———— (1999) 'Contra Wight: The Errors of Premature Writing,' *Review of International Studies*, 25 (2): 317–22.

———— (2002a) 'Atrocity, Memory, Photography: Imaging the Concentration Camps of Bosnia—The Case of ITN Versus *Living Marxism*, Part 1,' *Journal of Human Rights*, 1 (1): 1–33.

———— (2002b) 'Atrocity, Memory, Photography: Imaging the Concentration Camps of Bosnia—The Case of ITN Versus *Living Marxism*, Part 2,' *Journal of Human Rights*, 1 (2): 143–72.

———— (2003) 'Cultural Governance and Pictorial Resistance: Reflections on the Imagining of War,' *Review of International Studies*, 29 (Supplement 1): 57–73.

———— (2004) 'Horrific Blindness: Images of Death in Contemporary Media,' *Journal for Cultural Research*, 8 (1): 55–74.

Carnegie Endowment for International Peace (1914) *Report of the International Commission To Inquire into the Causes and Conduct of the Balkan Wars*, Washington, D.C.: The Carnegie Endowment.

———— (1993) *The Other Balkan Wars: A 1913 Carnegie Endowment Inquiry in Retrospect with a New Introduction and Reflections on the Present Conflict by George F. Kennan*, Washington, DC: Carnegie Endowment.

Carpenter, R. C. (2003) '"Women and Children First": Gender, Norms, and Humanitarian Evacuation in the Balkans 1991–1995,' *International Organization*, 57 (4): 661–94.

Carr, E. H. (1993[1939]) *The Twenty Years' Crisis 1919–1939: An Introduction to the Study of International Relations*, London: Papermac.

Chouliaraki, L. (2000) 'Refleksivitet og senmoderne identitet: et studie i Mediediskurs,' in T. B. Dyrberg, A. D. Hansen and J. Torfing (eds) *Diskursteorien på Arbejde*, Frederiksberg: Roskilde Universitetsforlag.

———— (2005) *Discourse and Culture*, London: Sage.

Chouliaraki, L. and Fairclough, N. (1999) *Discourse in Late Modernity: Rethinking Critical Discourse Analysis*, Edinburgh: Edinburgh University Press.

Clarke, R. A. (2004) *Against All Enemies: Inside America's War on Terror*, New York: Free Press.

Clines, F. X. (1995) 'Balkan History Lesson: Not With a 10-Foot Pole,' *New York Times*, November 29.

Clinton, W. J. (1993a) 'The President's News Conference With Prime Minister Brian Mulroney of Canada,' February 5, *Public Papers of the Presidents of the United States*, vol. 1: 53–6.

Clinton, W. J. (1993b) 'Remarks at a Town Meeting in Detroit,' February 10, *Public Papers of the Presidents of the United States*, vol. 1: 73–85.

———— (1993c) 'Interview With Dan Rather of CBS News,' March 24, *Public Papers of the Presidents of the United States*, vol. 1: 346–54.

———— (1993d) 'The President's News Conference With Prime Minister Kiichi Miyazawa of Japan,' April 16, *Public Papers of the Presidents of the United States*, vol. 1: 438–45

———— (1993e) 'The President's News Conference,' April 23, *Public Papers of the Presidents of the United States*, vol. 1: 484–93.

———— (1993f) 'Question-and-Answer Session With the Newspaper Association of America in Boston,' April 25, *Public Papers of the Presidents of the United States*, vol. 1: 505–10.

———— (1993g) 'Exchange With Reporters Prior to Discussions With European Community Leaders,' May 7, *Public Papers of the Presidents of the United States*, vol. 1: 591–6

———— (1993h) 'Interview With Don Imus of WFAN Radio, New York City,' May 12, *Public Papers of the Presidents of the United States*, vol. 1: 628–34.

———— (1993i) 'The President's News Conference,' May 14, *Public Papers of the Presidents of the United States*, vol. 1: 659–68.

———— (1993j) 'Exchange With Reporters on Bosnia,' May 21, *Public Papers of the Presidents of the United States*, vol. 1: 713–14.

———— (1994a) 'Remarks to the Greater Houston Partnership in Houston,' February 7, *Public Papers of the Presidents of the United States*, vol. 1: 192–9.

———— (1994b) 'Remarks to the World Jewish Congress,' February 9, *Public Papers of the Presidents of the United States*, vol. 1: 216–18.

———— (1995a) 'Remarks at the United States Air Force Academy Commencement Ceremony in Colorado Springs, Colorado,' May 31, *Public Papers of the Presidents of the United States*, vol. 1: 765–70.

———— (1995b) 'The President's Radio Address,' June 3, *Public Papers of the Presidents of the United States*, vol. 1: 804–5.

———— (1995c) 'Remarks on the Arrival in Honolulu, Hawaii,' August 31, *Public Papers of the Presidents of the United States*, vol. 2: 1273–5.

———— (1995d) 'Remarks to the Community at Abraham Lincoln Middle School in Selma,' September 5, *Public Papers of the Presidents of the United States*, vol. 2: 1305–8.

———— (1995e) 'The President's Radio Address,' September 23, *Public Papers of the Presidents of the United States*, vol. 2: 1464–5.

———— (1995f) 'Remarks on the Peace Process in Bosnia and an Exchange With Reporters,' September 26, *Public Papers of the Presidents of the United States*, vol. 2: 1493–4.

———— (1995g) 'Address to the Nation on Implementation of the Peace Agreement in Bosnia-Herzegovina,' November 27, *Public Papers of the Presidents of the United States*, vol. 2: 1784–7.

———— (2004) *My Life*, London: Hutchinson.

Clinton, H. R. (2003) *Writing History*, New York: Simon and Schuster.

Cohen, R. (1993) 'It's Not a Holocaust; Rhetoric and Reality in Bosnia,' *The Washington Post*, February 28, C1.

Cohen, R. (1994) 'Conflict in the Balkans: United Nations,' *The New York Times*, April 17, section 1, p. 12.

Connolly, W. E. (1991) *Identity\Difference: Democratic Negotiations of Political Paradox*, Ithaca: Cornell University Press.

Conversi, D. (1996) 'Moral Relativism and Equidistance in British Attitudes to the War in the Former Yugoslavia,' in T. Cushman and S. G. Mestrovic (eds) *This Time We Knew: Western Responses to Genocide in Bosnia*, New York: New York University Press.

Cooper, H. R. (1993) review of *Balkan Ghosts*, *Slavic Review*, 53 (3): 592–3.

Crawford, B. and Lipschutz, R. D. (1997) 'Discourses of War: Security and the Case of Yugoslavia,' in K. Krause and M. C. Williams (eds) *Critical Security Studies*, Minneapolis: University of Minnesota Press.

Cushman, T. and Mestrovic, S. G. (1996) 'Introduction,' in T. Cushman and S. G. Mestrovic (eds) *This Time We Knew: Western Responses to Genocide in Bosnia*, New York: New York University Press.

Daalder, I. O. (2000) *Getting to Dayton: The Making of America's Bosnia Policy*, Washington: Brookings Institute Press.

de Constant, d'Estournelles (1914) 'Introduction,' in Carnegie Endowment for International Peace *Report of the International Commission To Inquire into the Causes and Conduct of the Balkan Wars*, Washington, D.C.: The Carnegie Endowment.

Deibert, R. (1997) *Parchment, Printing, and Hypermedia: Communication in World Order Transformation*, New York: Columbia University Press.

———— (2000) 'International Plug n' Play? Citizen Activism, the Internet, and Global Public Policy,' *International Studies Perspectives*, 1 (3): 255–72.

———— (2003) 'Civil Society Activism on the World Wide Web: the Case of the Anti-MAI Lobby,' in D. R. Cameron and J. G. Stein (eds) *Street Protests and Fantasy Parks: Globalization, Culture and the State*, Toronto: UBC Press.

Denich, B. (1974) 'Sex and Power in the Balkans,' in M. Z. Rosaldo and L. Lamphere (eds) *Woman, Culture, and Society*, Stanford: Stanford University Press.

———— (1994) 'Dismembering Yugoslavia: Nationalist Ideologies and the Symbolic Revival of Genocide,' *American Ethnologist*, 21 (2): 367–90.

———— (1995) 'Of Arms, Men, and Ethnic War in (Former) Yugoslavia,' in C. R. Sutton (ed.) *Feminism, Nationalism and Militarism*, Arlington: Association for Feminist Anthropology/American Anthropological Association.

Denitch, B. (1994) 'Now, Bosnia Without Bosnians,' *The Washington Post*, February 13, C1.

Der Derian, J. (1987) *On Diplomacy: A Genealogy of Western Estrangement*, Oxford: Basil Blackwell.

———— (1992) *Antidiplomacy: Spies, Terror, Speed, and War*, Oxford: Basil Blackwell.

———— (2001) *Virtuous War: Mapping the Military-Industrial-Media-Entertainment Network*, Boulder: Westview Press.

Der Derian, J. and Shapiro, M. J. (eds) (1989) *International/Intertextual Relations: Postmodern Readings of World Politics*, Lexington: Lexington Books.

Derrida, J. (1976) *Of Grammatology*, Baltimore: The Johns Hopkins University Press.

———— (1978) *Writing and Difference*, London: Routledge and Kegan Paul.

Djilas, A. (1991) *The Contested Country: Yugoslav Unity and Communist Revolution 1919–1953*, Cambridge, Massachusetts: Harvard University Press.

———— (1992) 'The Nation That Wasn't,' *The New Republic*, 207 (13): 25–31.

Dobbs, M. (1995) 'Bosnia Crystallizes U.S. Post-Cold War Role,' *The Washington Post*, December 3, A1.

Doder, D. (1993) 'Yugoslavia: New War, Old Hatreds,' *Foreign Policy*, issue 91: 3–23.

Doty, R. L. (1996) *Imperial Encounters*, Minneapolis: University of Minnesota Press.

Drew, E. (1994) *On the Edge: The Clinton Presidency*, New York: Simon and Schuster.

Dyrberg, T. B., Hansen, A. D, and Torfing, J. (eds) (2000) *Diskursteorien på arbejde*, Frederiksberg: Roskilde Universitetsforlag.

Eakin, P. J. (1992) *Touching the World: Reference in Autobiography*, Princeton: Princeton University Press.

Edkins, J. (2003) *Trauma and the Memory of Politics*, Cambridge: Cambridge University Press.

Elshtain, J. B. (1981) *Public Man, Private Woman: Women in Social and Political Thought*, Princeton: Princeton University Press.

—— (1987) *Women and War*, Chicago: The University of Chicago Press

Fabian, J. (1983) *Time and the Other: How Antropology Makes Its Object*, New York: Columbia University Press.

Fairclough, N. (1995) *Media Discourse*, London: Edward Arnold.

—— (2001) 'Critical Discourse Analysis as a Method in Social Scientific Research,' in R. Wodak and M. Meyer (eds) *Methods of Critical Discourse Analysis*, London: Sage.

Febvre, L. (1930) '*Civilisation*: Evolution of a Word and a Group Of Ideas,' reprinted in Burke, P. (ed.) (1973) *A New Kind of History: From the Writings of Febvre*, London: Routledge and Kegan Paul.

Fierke, K. M. (1996) 'Multiple Identities, Interfacing Games: The Social Construction of Western Action in Bosnia,' *European Journal of International Relations*, 2 (4): 467–97.

—— (1998) *Changing Games, Changing Strategies: Critical Investigations in Security*, Manchester: Manchester University Press.

—— (1999) 'Dialogues of Manoeuvre and Entanglement: NATO, Russia and the CEECs,' *Millennium*, 28 (1): 27–52.

Foucault, Michel (1970) *The Order of Things: An Archaeology of the Human Sciences*, New York: Random House.

—— (1974[1969]) *The Archaeology of Knowledge*, London: Tavistock Publications.

—— (1977) *Discipline and Punish: The Birth of the Prison*, London: Penguin Books.

—— (1984) 'Nietzsche, Genealogy, History,' reprinted in P. Rabinow (ed.) *The Foucault Reader*, London: Penguin, first published in *Language, Counter-Memory, Practice: Selected Essays and Interviews*, Oxford: Basil Blackwell, 1997.

Friedman, T. L. (1993) 'Bosnia Reconsidered: Where Candidate Clinton Saw a Challenge The President Sees an Insoluble Quagmire,' *New York Times*, April 8, A1 and A6.

Garis, L. (1982) 'Rebecca West,' *The New York Times*, April 4, section 6, p. 30.

Gati, C. (1992) 'From Sarajevo to Sarajevo,' *Foreign Affairs*, 71 (4): 64–78.

George, J. (1994) *Discourses of Global Politics: A Critical (Re) Introduction to International Relations*, Boulder: Lynne Rienner.

Giovanni, J. di (2004) 'In the Belly of the Balkans,' *The Times*, July 31.

Gladstone, W. E. (1876) *Bulgarian Horrors and the Question of the East*, London: John Murray.

Glendinning, V. (1987) *Rebecca West: A Life*, London: Weidenfeld and Nicolson.

Glenny, M. (1996[1992]) *The Fall of Yugoslavia: The Third Balkan War*, 3rd edn, London: Penguin.

Glynn, P. (1993) 'Beware of Bosnia Sellout,' *USA Today*, February 5, p. 10A.

Goldstein, J. and Keohane, R. O. (eds) (1993) *Ideas and Foreign Policy: Beliefs, Institutions and Political Change*, Ithaca: Cornell University Press.

Goldsworthy, V. (1998) *Inventing Ruritania: The Imperialism of the Imagination*, New Haven: Yale University Press.

Gow, J. (1997) *Triumph of the Lack of Will: International Diplomacy and the Yugoslav War*, London: Hurst.

Grau, L. W. (no date), review of Kaplan's *Eastward to Tartary: Travels in the Balkans, the Middle East and the Caucasus*. Foreign Military Studies Office, fmso.leavenworth.army.mil/bookrevu/tartary.htm

The Guardian (1992) 'Berets for Bosnia,' leading article, May 5, 1992, p. 18.

―――― (1993a) 'In the Long Haul,' leading article, February 12, p. 18.

―――― (1993b) 'The Dismal Failure to Save Bosnia,' leading article, April 6, p. 19.

Gutman, R. (1993) *A Witness to Genocide: The First Inside Account of the Horrors of 'Ethnic Cleansing' in Bosnia*, Massachusetts: Elements.

Hall, B. (1996) 'Life and Letters: Rebecca West's War,' *The New Yorker*, April 15.

Handke, P. (1997) *A Journey to the Rivers: Justice for Serbia*, New York: Viking.

Hansen, L. (1994) *The Poststructuralist Conceptualization of Security*, MA Thesis, Department of Political Science, University of Copenhagen.

―――― (1996) 'Slovenian Identity: State Building on the Balkan Border,' *Alternatives*, 21 (4): 473–95.

―――― (1997) 'A Case for Seduction? Evaluating the Poststructuralist Conceptualization of Security,' *Cooperation and Conflict*, 32 (4): 369–97.

―――― (1999) 'NATO's Balkan Engagement: Institutional Reconstruction and the Representation of Bosnia and Kosovo,' paper presented at BISA's annual conference in Manchester.

―――― (2000a) 'The Little Mermaid's Silent Security Dilemma and the Absence of Gender in the Copenhagen School,' *Millennium*, 29 (2): 285–306.

―――― (2000b) 'Past as Preface: Civilizational Politics and the "Third" Balkan War,' *Journal of Peace Research*, 37 (3): 345–62.

―――― (2001a) 'Gender, Nation, Rape: Bosnia and the Construction of Security,' *International Feminist Journal of Politics*, 3 (1): 55–75.

―――― (2001b) 'Feminism in the Fascist Utopia: Gender, Citizenship and World Order in *Starship Troopers*,' *International Feminist Journal of Politics*, 3 (2): 275–83.

―――― (2002a) 'Introduction,' in L. Hansen and O. Wæver (eds) *European Integration and National Identity: The Challenge of the Nordic States*, London: Routledge.

―――― (2002b) 'Sustaining Sovereignty: The Danish Approach to the EU,' in L. Hansen and O. Wæver (eds) *European Integration and National Identity: The Challenge of the Nordic States*, London: Routledge.

―――― (2005) 'The Politics of Digital Autobiography: Understanding www.johnkerry.com,' in K. B. Jensen (ed.) *Interface://Culture: The World Wide Web as Political Resource and Aesthetic Form*, Copenhagen: Samfundslitteratur.

Hansen, L. and Wæver, O. (eds) (2002) *European Integration and National Identity: The Challenge of the Nordic States*, London: Routledge.

Harper, J. L. (1994) *American Visions of Europe: Franklin D. Roosevelt, George F. Kennan, and Dean G. Acheson*, Cambridge: Cambridge University Press.

Hartog, F. (1988) *The Mirror of Herodotus: The Representation of the Other in the Writing of History*, Berkeley: University of California Press.

Hayden, R. M. (1992) 'Balancing Discussion of Jasenovac and the Manipulation of History,' *East European Politics and Societies*, 6 (2): 207–12.

——— (1993) 'On Unbalanced Criticism,' *East European Politics and Societies*, 7 (3): 577–82.

Herr, M. (1977) *Dispatches*, London: Picador.

Herzfeld, M. (1987) *Anthropology Through the Looking-glass: Critical Ethnography in the Margins of Europe*, Cambridge: Cambridge University Press.

Higate, P. and Henry, M. (2004) 'Engendering (In)security in Peace Support Operations,' *Security Dialogue*, 35 (4): 481–98.

Hjort, K. (ed.) (1997) *Diskurs: Analyser af tekst og kontekst*, Frederiksberg: Samfundslitteratur.

Holbrooke, R. (1998) *To End a War*, New York: Random House.

Holland, P. and Huggan, G. (1998) *Tourists with Typewriters: Critical Reflections on Contemporary Travel Writing*, Ann Arbor: University of Michigan Press.

Holm, U. (1993) *Det franske Europa*, Aarhus: Aarhus University Press.

——— (1997) 'The French Garden is No Longer What it Used To Be,' in K. E. Jørgensen (ed.) *Reflective Approaches to European Governance*, London: Macmillan.

Huntington, S. P. (1993) 'The Clash of Civilizations?,' *Foreign Affairs*, 72 (3): 22–49.

——— (1996) *The Clash of Civilizations and the Remaking of World Order*, New York: Simon and Schuster.

——— (1997) '"The Clash of Civilizations" – A Response,' *Millennium*, 26 (1): 141–2.

——— (2004) *Who are We?*, New York: Simon and Schuster.

Huysmans, J. (2002) 'Shape-shifting NATO: Humanitarian Action and the Kosovo Refugee Crisis,' *Review of International Studies*, 28 (3): 599–618.

The Independent (1992) 'The key decision on Bosnia,' leading article, August 5, p. 12.

——— (1993a) 'Bosnia May Still be Saved,' leading article, January 6, p. 16.

——— (1993b) 'Bold Thoughts on Bosnia,' leading article, April 15, p. 23.

——— (1993c) 'Fears for Muslims as Bosnia Burns,' leading article, June 19, p. 16.

——— (1995) 'Cold Comfort in Bosnia's Peace,' leading article, November 22, p. 22.

Iordanova, D. (2001) *Cinema of Flames: Balkan Film, Culture and the Media*, London: British Film Institute Publishing.

Jachtenfuchs, M., Diez, T., and Jung, S. (1998) 'Which Europe? Conflicting Models of a Legitimate European Political Order,' *European Journal of International Relations*, 4 (4): 409–45.

Jepperson, R. L., Wendt, A., and Katzenstein, P. J. (1996) 'Norms, Identity, and Culture in National Security,' in P. J. Katzenstein (ed.) *The Culture of National Security: Norms and Identity in World Politics*, New York: Columbia University Press.

Joenniemi, P. (1990) 'Europe Changes—The Nordic System Remains,' *Bulletin of Peace Proposals*, 21 (2): 205–17.

Jones, A. (1994) 'Gender and Ethnic Conflict in ex-Yugoslavia,' *Ethnic and Racial Studies*, 17 (1): 115–34.

Jørgensen, M. W. and Phillips, L. (1999) *Diskursanalyse som teori og metode*, Frederiksberg: Samfundslitteratur and Roskilde Universitetsforlag.

Kaplan, R. D. (1993a) *Balkan Ghosts: A Journey Through History*, New York: Vintage.

——— (1993b) 'Ground Zero: Macedonia: The Real Battle Ground,' *The New Republic*, 209 (5): 15–16.

Katzenstein, P. J. (ed.) (1996) *The Culture of National Security: Norms and Identity in World Politics*, New York: Columbia University Press.

Katzenstein, P. J., Keohane, R. O., and Krasner, S. (1998) 'International Organization and the Study of World Politics,' *International Organization*, 52 (4): 645–85.

Kaufmann, C. (1996) 'Possible and Impossible Solutions to Ethnic Civil Wars,' *International Security*, 20 (4): 136–75.

Kennan, G. (1947) ('X') 'The Sources of Soviet Conduct,' *Foreign Affairs*, 25 (4): 566–82.

––––––– (1972) *Memoirs 1950–1963*, Boston: Little, Brown and Company.

––––––– (1993) 'Introduction—The Balkan Crises: 1913 and 1993,' in Carnegie Endowment for International Peace, *The Other Balkan Wars: A 1913 Carnegie Endowment Inquiry in Retrospect with a New Introduction and Reflections on the Present Conflict by George F. Kennan*, Washington, DC: Carnegie Endowment.

Keohane, R. O. (1988) 'International Institutions: Two Approaches,' *International Studies Quarterly*, 32 (4): 379–96.

––––––– (1989) 'International-Relations Theory—Contributions of a Feminist Standpoint,' *Millennium*, 18 (2): 245–53.

––––––– (1998) 'Beyond Dichotomy: Conversations Between International Relations and Feminist Theory,' *International Studies Quarterly*, 42 (1): 193–7.

King, G., Keohane, R. O., and Verba, S. (1994) *Designing Social Inquiry: Scientific Inference in Qualitative Research*, Princeton: Princeton University Press.

Kirkpatrick, D. D. (2004) 'In 12th Book of Best-Selling Series, Jesus Returns,' *The New York Times*, March 29, A1.

Kissinger, H. (1957) *A World Restored: Metternich, Castlereagh and the Problems of Peace 1812–1822*, Boston: Houghton Mifflin Company.

Klein, B. S. (1994) *Strategic Studies and World Order: The Global Politics of Deterrence*, Cambridge: Cambridge University Press.

Knezevic, A. (1993) 'Some Questions about a "Balanced" Discussion,' *East European Politics and Societies*, 7 (1): 155–66.

Kofman, D. (1996) 'Israel and the War in Bosnia,' in T. Cushman and S. G. Mestrovic (eds) *This Time We Knew: Western Responses to Genocide in Bosnia*, New York: New York University Press.

Kratochwil, F. (1989) *Rules, Norms and Decisions: On the Conditions of practical and legal reasoning in international relations and domestic affairs*, Cambridge: Cambridge University Press.

Kratochwil, F. and Ruggie, J. (1986) 'International Organization: A State of the Art on an Art of the State,' *International Organization*, 40 (4): 753–75.

Krause, K. and Williams, M. C. (1996) 'Broadening the Agenda of Security Studies? Politics and Method,' *Mershon International Studies Review*, 40 (2): 229–54.

Kristeva, J. (1980) *Desire in Language: A Semiotic Approach to Literature and Art*, New York: Columbia University Press.

Kupchan, C. A. (1995) 'Reclaiming the Moral High Ground; In Bosnia; What Does the West Stand for If It Does Nothing?,' *Los Angeles Times*, July 23, M1.

Kurki, M. (forthcoming) 'Causes of a Divided Discipline: Rethinking the Concept of Cause in International Relations Theory,' *Review of International Studies*.

Laclau, E. and Mouffe, C. (1985) *Hegemony and Socialist Strategy: Towards a Radical Democratic Politics*, London: Verso.

Laffey, M. and Weldes, J. (1997) 'Beyond Belief: Ideas and Symbolic Technologies in the Study of International Relations,' *European Journal of International Relations*, 3 (2): 193–238.

Lapid, Y. and Kratochwil, F. (1996) 'Revisiting the "National": Toward an Identity Agenda in Neorealism?,' in Y. Lapid and F. Kratochwil (eds) *The Return of Culture and Identity in IR Theory*, Boulder: Lynne Rienner.

Larsen, H. (1997) *Foreign Policy and Discourse Analysis: Britain, France and Europe*, London: Routledge.

Lepick, O. (1996) 'French Perspectives,' in A. Danchev and T. Halverson (eds) *International Perspectives on the Yugoslav Conflict*, London: Macmillan.

Letica, S. (1996) 'The *West Side Story* of the Collapse of Yugoslavia and the Wars in Slovenia, Croatia, and Bosnia-Herzegovina,' in T. Cushman and S. G. Mestrovic (eds) *This Time We Knew: Western Responses to Genocide in Bosnia*, New York: New York University Press.

Lewis, A. (1995) 'Abroad at Home; Leadership and Duty,' *New York Times*, Editorial desk, Section A, p. 17.

Lisle, D. (1999) 'Gender at a Distance: Identity, Performance and Contemporary Travel Writing,' *International Feminist Journal of Politics*, 1 (1): 66–88.

Los Angeles Times (1992) 'A Rottenness at Europe's Core; Will No One Act to Save Bosnia's Muslims,' October 10, Editorial Writers Desk, Part B, p. 7.

Lytle, P. F. (1992) 'U.S. Policy Toward the Demise of Yugoslavia: The "Virus of Nationalism",' *East European Politics and Societies*, 6 (3): 303–18.

MacKinnon, C. A. (1994) 'Rape, Genocide, and Women's Human Rights,' in A. Stiglmayer (ed.) *Mass Rape: The War against Women in Bosnia-Herzegovina*, Lincoln and London: University of Nebraska Press.

MacMillan, J. (2003) 'Beyond the Separate Democratic Peace,' *Journal of Peace Research*, 40 (2): 233–43.

Magas, B. (1993) *The Destruction of Yugoslavia: Tracking the Break-up 1980–92*, London: Verso.

Malcolm, N. (1994) *Bosnia: A Short Story*, New York: New York University Press.

Marcussen, M., Risse, T., Engelmann-Martin, D., Knopf, H. J., and Roscher, K. (1999) 'Constructing Europe? The Evolution of French, British and German Nation State Identities,' *Journal of European Public Policy*, 6 (4): 614–33.

Mattern, J. B. (2001) 'The Power Politics of Identity,' *European Journal of International Relations*, 7 (3): 349–97.

Maull, H. W. (1995–96) 'Germany in the Yugoslav Crisis,' *Survival*, 37 (4): 99–130.

Mearsheimer, J. J. and Pape, R. A. (1993) 'The answer: A partition plan for Bosnia,' *The New Republic*, 208 (24): 22–8.

Mearsheimer, J. J. and Van Evera, S. (1995) 'When Peace Means War: The Partition that Dare Not Speak its Name,' *The New Republic*, 213 (25): 16–21.

Mearsheimer, J. J. and Walt, S. M. (2003) 'An Unnecessary War,' *Foreign Policy*, issue 134: 50–60.

Mestrovic, S. G. (1994) *The Balkanization of the West: The Confluence of Postmodernism and Postcommunism*, London: Routledge.

—— (ed.) (1996) *Genocide After Emotion: The Postemotional Balkan War*, London: Routledge.

Miles, J. (1994) 'Don't Ask Gorazde to Surrender,' *Los Angeles Times*, April 26, B7.

Milliken, J. (2001) *The Social Construction of the Korean War: Conflict and its Possibilities*, Manchester: Manchester University Press.

Moravcsik, A. (1999a) '"Is Something Rotten in the State of Denmark?" Constructivism and European Integration,' *Journal of European Public Policy*, 6 (4): 669–81.

—— (1999b) 'The Future of European Integration Studies: Social Science or Social Theory?,' *Millennium*, 28 (2): 371–91.

Morokvasic, M. (1998) 'The Logics of Exclusion: Nationalism, Sexism and the Yugoslav War,' in N. Charles and H. Hintjens (eds) *Gender, Ethnicity and Political Ideologies*, London: Routledge.

Mortimer, E. (1995) 'Painstaking Progress of a Peacemaker,' *Financial Times*, November 9, p. 24.

Mousavizadeh, N. (ed.) (1996a) *The Black Book of Bosnia: The Consequences of Appeasement, by the Writers and Editors of The New Republic*, New York: Basic Books.

—— (1996b) 'Preface,' in N. Mousavizadeh (ed.) *The Black Book of Bosnia: The Consequences of Appeasement, by the Writers and Editors of The New Republic*, New York: Basic Books.

NATO (2002) *AFSOUTH Fact Sheets: Operation Deliberate Force*, updated December 16, 2002, www.afsouth.nato.int/factsheets/DeliberateForceFactSheet.htm.

NATO (2004) *SFOR—History of Bosnia and Herzegovina From the Origins to 1992*, www.nato.int/sfor/indexinf/bihistory.htm, updated December 3, 2004.

Netherlands Institute for War Documentation (2002) *Srebrenica—A 'Safe' Area*, http://213.222.3.6/srebrenica/.

Neumann, I. B. (1996a) *Russia and the Idea of Europe: A Study in Identity and International Relations*, London: Routledge.

—— (1996b) 'Collective Identity Formation: Self and Other in International Relations,' *European Journal of International Relations*, 2 (2): 139–74.

—— (1999) *Uses of the Other: 'The East' in European Identity Formation*, Minneapolis: University of Minnesota Press.

—— (2001) *Mening, materialitet, makt: En innføring i diskursanalyse*, Bergen: Fagbokforlaget.

Neumann, I. B. and Welsh, J. M. (1991) 'The Other in European Self-Definition: An Addendum to the Literature on International Society,' *Review of International Studies*, 17 (4): 327–46.

The New York Times (1992) 'Peace in Our Time, Bosnia-Style?,' August 23, Editorial desk, section 4, p. 14.

—— (1993) 'Lord Owen's Googly,' February 4, Editorial desk, Section A, p. 22.

—— (1994a) 'NATO's Bosnia Sideshow,' January 13, Editorial desk, Section A, p. 20.

—— (1994b) 'Lift the Embargo Now,' February 6, Editorial desk, section 4, p. 16.

—— (1994c) 'Bosnia: Keep Diplomacy Honorable,' February 13, section 4, p. 14.

—— (1995) 'Bosnia: Not America's War,' June 3, Editorial desk, p. 18.

Nikolic-Ristanovic, V. (1996) 'War Against Woman,' in J. Turpin and L. A. Lorentzen (eds) *The Gendered New World Order: Militarism, Development, and the Environment*, London: Routledge.

Oguzlu, H. T. (2003) 'An Analysis of Turkey's Prospective Membership in the European Union from a "Security" Perspective,' *Security Dialogue*, 34 (3): 285–99.

Onuf, N. G. (1989) *World of Our Making: Rules and Rule in Social Theory and International Relations*, Columbia, SC: University of South Carolina Press.

Orel, H. (1986) *The Literary Achievement of Rebecca West*, London: Macmillan.

Oren, I. (1995) 'The Subjectivity of the "Democratic Peace": Changing U.S. Perceptions of Imperial Germany,' *International Security*, 20 (2): 147–84.

OSCE (1996) *Lisbon Document*, available at www.osce.org/documents/mcs/1996/12/4049_en.pdf.

Ó Tuathail, G. (1996a) *Critical Geopolitics: The Politics of Writing Global Space*, Minneapolis: University of Minnesota Press.

—— (1996b) 'An Anti-geopolitical Eye: Maggie O'Kane in Bosnia, 1992–94,' *Gender, Place and Culture*, 3 (2): 171–85.

Owen, D. (1995) *Balkan Odyssey*, New York: Harcourt Brace & Company.

Paris, R. (2001) 'Human Security,' *International Security*, 26 (2): 87–103.

Pateman, C. (1983) 'Feminist Critiques of the Public/Private Dichotomy,' in S. Benn and G. Gaus (eds) *Public and Private in Social Life*, London: Croom Helm.

Posen, B. (1993a) 'The Security Dilemma and Ethnic Conflict,' *Survival*, 35 (1): 27–47.

—— (1993b) 'Nationalism, the Mass Army, and Military Power,' *International Security*, 18 (2): 80–124.

—— (2001) 'The Struggle Against Terrorism: Grand Strategy, Strategy, and Tactics,' *International Security*, 26 (3): 39–55.

Pratt, M. L. (1992) *Imperial Eyes: Travel Writing and Transculturation*, London: Routledge.

Price, R. and Reus-Smit, C. (1998) 'Dangerous Liaisons?: Critical International Theory and Constructivism,' *European Journal of International Relations*, 4 (3): 259–94.

Ramet, S. P. (1994) 'The Yugoslav Crisis and the West: Avoiding "Vietnam" and Blundering into "Abyssinia",' *East European Politics and Societies*, 8 (1): 189–219.

—— (1996) *Balkan Babel: The Disintegration of Yugoslavia from the Death of Tito to Ethnic War*, 2nd edn, Boulder: Westview.

Republic of Turkey, Ministry of Foreign Affairs (2004) 'Turkish Foreign Policy: A Synopsis. Last Updated: 21 July 2004,' at www.mfa.gov.tr/grupg/gb/default.htm, accessed June 21, 2004. [Notice that the day of updating is a month into the future of the day accessed.]

Rieff, D. (1996) *Slaughterhouse: Bosnia and the Failure of the West*, New York: Touchstone. [First Touchstone edition with a new afterword by the author.]

—— (2000) 'Bosnia Beyond Words,' *The New York Times*, December 24, section 7, p. 5.

Ringle, K. (2002) 'Oracle of a New World Disorder; Robert Kaplan's Global Journeys Took Him Into the Culture of War,' *The Washington Post*, February 21, p. C01.

Risse-Kappen, T. (1996) 'Collective Identity in a Democratic Community: The Case of NATO,' in P. J. Katzenstein (ed.) *The Culture of National Security: Norms and Identity in World Politics*, New York: Columbia University Press.

Roberts, A. (1995) 'Communal Conflict as a Challenge to International Organization: The Case of Former Yugoslavia,' *Review of International Studies*, 21 (4): 389–410.

Rodgers, J. (1998) 'Bosnia, Gender and the Ethics of Intervention in Civil Wars,' *Civil Wars*, 1 (1): 103–16.

Rogel, C. (1994) 'In the Beginning: The Slovenes from the Seventh Century to 1945, in J. Benderly and E. Kraft (eds) *Independent Slovenia: Origins, Movements, Prospects*, London: Macmillan.

Rollyson, C. (1996) *Rebecca West: A Life*, New York: Scribner.

Rosenbaum, D. E. (2004) 'In the Fulbright Mold, Without the Power,' *The New York Times*, May 3, A21.

Roucek, J. S. (1948) *Balkan Politics: International Relations in No Man's Land*, Stanford: Stanford University Press.

Ruggie, J. G. (1992) 'Multilateralism: The Anatomy of an Institution,' *International Organization*, 46 (3): 561–98.

Rutenberg, J. (2004) 'TV Shows Take on Bush, and Pull Few Punches,' *The New York Times*, April 2, A1 and A16.

Rutenberg, J. and Kirkpatrick, D. D. (2004) 'Timing of Clinton Memoir Is Everything, for Kerry,' *The New York Times*, April 13, A1 and A23.

Rumelili, B. (2004) 'Constructing Identity and Relating to Difference: Understanding the EU's Mode of Differentiation,' *Review of International Studies*, 30 (1): 27–47.

Sadkovich, J. J. (1996) 'The Former Yugoslavia, the End of the Nuremberg Era, and the New Barbarism,' in T. Cushman and S. G. Mestrovic (eds) *This Time We Knew: Western Responses to Genocide in Bosnia*, New York: New York University Press.

Said, E. W. (1978) *Orientalism*, New York: Pantheon Books.

Schweizer, B. (2002) *Rebecca West: Heroism, Rebellion, and the Female Epic*, Westport, Connecticut: Greenwood Press.

Secretary General of the UN (1999) *Report of the Secretary-General pursuant to General Assembly resolution 53/35: The fall of Srebrenica*, www.un.org/peace/srebrenica.pdf.

Shapiro, M. J. (1981) *Language and Political Understanding: The Politics of Discursive Practices*, New Haven: Yale University Press.

—— (1988) *The Politics of Representation: Writing Practices in Biography, Photography, and Policy Analysis*, Madison, Wisconsin: The University of Wisconsin Press.

—— (1990) 'Strategic Discourse/Discursive Strategy: The Representation of "Security Policy" in the Video Age,' *International Studies Quarterly*, 34 (3): 327–39.

—— (1997) *Violent Cartographies: Mapping Cultures of War*, Minneapolis: University of Minnesota Press.

—— (1999) *Cinematic Political Thought: Narratives of Race, Nation, and Gender*, New York: New York University Press.

Silber, L. and Little, A. (1997) *Yugoslavia: Death of a Nation*, London: Penguin [revised and updated edition].

Simms, B. (2001) *Unfinest Hour: Britain and the Destruction of Bosnia*, London: Penguin Books.

Sontag, S. (2004) 'Regarding The Torture Of Others,' *The New York Times*, May 23, Section 6, p. 25.

Stanley, P. (1999) 'Reporting of Mass Rape in the Balkans: *Plus Ca Change, Plus C'est Même Chose?* From Bosnia to Kosovo,' *Civil Wars*, 2 (2): 74–110.

Stauersböll, H. (2000) *Between Byzantium and Hellas: Understanding the Greek Policy Towards Macedonia in the 1990's*, MA thesis, Department of Political Science, University of Copenhagen.

Stec, L. (1997) 'Female Sacrifice: Gender and Nostalgic Nationalism in Rebecca West's *Black Lamb and Grey Falcon*,' in J. Pickering and S. Kehde (eds) *Narratives of Nostalgia, Gender and Nationalism*, London: Macmillan Press.

Steel, R. (1992) 'Let them sink: The perils of Bosnian intervention,' *The New Republic*, 207 (19): 15–16.

Stevenson, R. W. and Sanger, D. E. (2004) 'Bush Doesn't See NATO Sending In Troops for Iraq,' *The New York Times*, June 11, A1 and A12.

Stiglmayer, A. (ed.) (1994a) *Mass Rape: The War against Women in Bosnia-Herzegovina*, Lincoln and London: University of Nebraska Press.

—— (1994b) 'The Rapes in Bosnia-Herzegovina,' in A. Stiglmayer (ed.) *Mass Rape: The War Against Women in Bosnia-Herzegovina*, Lincoln and London: University of Nebraska Press.

Stoianovich, T. (1967) *A Study in Balkan Civilization*, New York: Alfred A. Knopf.

Swales, J. M. (1990) *Genre Analysis*, Cambridge: Cambridge University Press.

Swofford, A. (2003) *Jarhead: A Marine's Chronicle of the Gulf War and Other Battles*, New York: Scribner.

Tickner, J. A. (1997) 'You Just Don't Understand: Troubled Engagements Between Feminists and IR Theorists,' *International Studies Quarterly*, 41 (4): 611–32.

Tickner, J. A. (1998) 'Continuing the Conversation…,' *International Studies Quarterly*, 42 (1): 205–10.

Tickner, J. A. (2001) *Gendering World Politics: Issues and Approaches in the Post-Cold War Era*, New York: Columbia University Press.

The Times (1993) 'Taking Bosnia seriously,' April 15.

———— (1995a) 'Endgame in Bosnia,' July 21.

———— (1995b) 'Bosnia, Ohio,' November 24.

Titscher, S., Meyer, M., Wodak, R. and Vetter, E. (2000) *Methods of Text and Discourse Analysis*, London: Sage.

Todorov, T. (1992) *The Conquest of America: The Question of the Other*, New York: HarperPerennial.

———— (1995) *The Morals of History*, Minneapolis: University of Minnesota Press.

Todorova, M. (1994) 'The Balkans: From Discovery to Invention,' *Slavic Review*, 53 (2): 453–82.

———— (1997) *Imagining the Balkans*, Oxford: Oxford University Press.

Torfing, J. (1999) *New Theories of Discourse: Laclau, Mouffe and Zizek*, Oxford: Blackwell.

Totilo, S. (2004) 'A Belated Invasion: Vietnam, the Game,' *The New York Times*, April 1, Section G, p. 1.

Turnipseed, J. (2003) *Baghdad Express: A Gulf War Memoir*, New York: Penguin.

United Nations Security Council (1995) *3564th Meeting, August 10, S/PV.3564, Agenda: The situation in the republic of Bosnia and Herzegovina*, http://daccessdds.un.org/doc/UNDOC/PRO/N95/858/26/PDF/N9585826.pdf?OpenElement.

Van Evera, S. (1994) 'Hypotheses on Nationalism and War,' *International Security*, 18(4): 5–39.

Väyrynen, R. (1989) 'Common Security and the State System,' in R. Nakarada and J. Øberg (eds) *Surviving Together: The Olof Palme Lectures on Common Security 1988*, Hampshire: Dartmouth Publishing Company.

Wæver, O. (1990) *With Herder and Habermas: Europeanization in the Light of German Concepts of State and Nation*, Working Paper no. 16/1990, Copenhagen: Centre for Peace and Conflict Research.

———— (1995) 'Securitization and Desecuritization,' in Ronnie D. Lipschutz (ed.) *On Security*, New York: Columbia University Press.

———— (1996) 'European security identities,' *Journal of Common Market Studies*, 34 (1): 103–32.

———— (1997) 'The Baltic Sea: A Region after Post-Modernity?,' in Pertti Joenniemi (ed.) *Neo-Nationalism or Regionality: The Restructuring of Political Space Around the Baltic Rim*, Stockholm: NordREFO.

———— (1998) 'The Sociology of a Not so International Discipline: American and European Developments in International Relations,' *International Organization*, 52 (4): 687–727.

———— (2002) 'Identity, Communities and Foreign Policy: Discourse Analysis as Foreign Policy Theory,' in L. Hansen and O. Wæver (eds) *European Integration and National Identity: The Challenge of the Nordic States*, London: Routledge.

Walker, M. (1997a) 'China Preys on American Minds,' *Guardian Weekly*, April 6.

———— (1997b) 'Arms, Aid and a Reordered Europe,' *Guardian Weekly*, March 30.

———— (1997c) 'Martin Walker's American: Bill's Dream Offer Hides a Nuclear Nightmare,' *The Observer*, March 23, p. 12.

Walker, R. B. J. (1987) 'Realism, Change and International Political Theory,' *International Studies Quarterly*, 31 (1): 65–86.

Walker, R. B. J. (1990) 'Security, Sovereignty, and the Challenge of World Politics,' *Alternatives*, 15 (1): 3–27.

Walker, R. B. J. (1993) *Inside/Outside: International Relations as Political Theory*, Cambridge: Cambridge University Press.

Wallander, C. (2000) 'Institutional Assets and Adaptability: NATO after the Cold War,' *International Organisation*, 54 (4): 705–36.

Walt, S. M. (1991) 'The Renaissance of Security Studies,' *International Studies Quarterly*, 35 (2): 211–39.

—— (1997) 'Building Up New Bogeymen,' *Foreign Policy*, issue 106: 177–89.

Waltz, K. N. (1979) *Theory of International Politics*, New York: McGraw-Hill.

The Washington Post (1993) 'What Kind of Peace in Bosnia?,' January 17, opinion editorial, p. C6.

—— (1995a) 'A Word About Richard Holbrooke,' October 7, editorial, p. A28.

—— (1995b) 'A Peace of the Weary,' November 22, editorial, p. A16.

Watson, A. (1992) *The Evolution of International Society: A Comparative Historical Analysis*, London: Routledge.

Weber, C. (1994) 'Good Girls, Little Girls and Bad Girls: Male Paranoia in Robert Keohane's Critique of Feminist International Relations,' *Millennium*, 23 (2): 337–49.

—— (1995) *Simulating Sovereignty: Intervention, the State, and Symbolic Exchange*, Cambridge: Cambridge University Press.

—— (1998) 'Performative States,' *Millennium*, 27 (1): 77–95.

—— (2001) *International Relations Theory: A Critical Introduction*, London: Routledge.

Weldes, J. (1999) *Constructing National Interests: The United States and the Cuban Missile Crisis*, Minneapolis: University of Minnesota Press.

—— (2003) (ed.) *To Seek Out New Worlds: Science Fiction and World Politics*, Basingstoke: Palgrave Macmillan.

Wendt, A. (1987) 'The Agent-Structure Problem in International Relations Theory,' *International Organization*, 41 (3): 335–70.

—— (1992) 'Anarchy is What States Make of It: The Social Construction of Power Politics,' *International Organization*, 46 (2): 383–92.

—— (1999) *Social Theory of International Relations*, Cambridge: Cambridge University Press.

—— (2003) 'Why a World State is Inevitable,' *European Journal of International Relations*, 9 (4): 491–542.

West, R. (1941) *Black Lamb and Grey Falcon: A Journey through Yugoslavia*, New York: Viking Press.

Wetherell, M., Taylor, S., and Yates, S. J. (2001) *Discourses as Data: A Guide for Analysis*, Milton Keynes and London: Open University and Sage.

Wieseltier, L. (1993) 'Curses,' *The New Republic*, 209 (17): 46.

Wight, C. (1999) 'Meta Campbell: the Epistemological Problems of Perspectivism,' *Review of International Studies*, 25 (2): 311–16.

Wilkinson, T. (1995) 'Refugees tell of Serb Atrocities in Fall of "Safe Area",' *Los Angeles Times*, July 14, A1.

Williams, M. C. (1998) 'Identity and the Politics of Security,' *European Journal of International Relations*, 4 (2): 204–25.

—— (2001) 'The Discipline of the Democratic Peace: Kant, Liberalism and the Social Construction of Security Communities,' *European Journal of International Relations*, 7 (4): 525–54.

Williams, M. C. and Neumann, I. B. (2000) 'From Alliance to Security Community: NATO, Russia, and the Power of Identity,' *Millennium*, 29 (2): 357–88.

Wodak, R. and Meyer, M. (eds) (2001) *Methods of Critical Discourse Analysis*, London: Sage.

Wolfe, P. (1971) *Rebecca West: Artist and Thinker*, Carbondale: Southern Illinois University Press.

Wolff, L. (1994) *Inventing Eastern Europe: The Map of Civilization on the Mind of the Enlightenment*, Stanford: Stanford University Press.

Wood, P. C. (1994) 'France and the Post Cold War Order: The Case of Yugoslavia,' *European Security*, 3 (1): 129–52.

Woodward, S. L. (1995) *Balkan Tragedy: Chaos and Dissolution After the Cold War*, Washington, D.C.: The Brookings Institution.

Wörner, M. (1991) 'NATO transformed: the significance of the Rome Summit,' *NATO Review*, 39 (6): 3–8.

Yuval-Davis, N. (1997) *Gender and Nation*, London: Sage.

Zalewski, M. (1995) 'Well, What is the Feminist Perspective on Bosnia?,' *International Affairs*, 71 (2): 339–56.

Zalewski, M. and Parpart, J. (eds) (1998) *The 'Man' Question in International Relations*, Boulder: Westview.

Zarkov, D. (1995) 'Gender, Orientalism and the History of Ethnic Hatred in the Former Yugoslavia' in H. Lutz, A. Phoenix, and N. Yuval-Davis (eds) *Crossfires: Nationalism, Racism and Gender in Europe*, London: Pluto Press.

Zehfuss, M. (2001) 'Constructivism and Identity: A Dangerous Liaison,' *European Journal of International Relations*, 7 (3): 315–48.

Zimmermann, W. (1996) *Origins of a Catastrophe: Yugoslavia and Its Destroyers — America's Last Ambassador Tells What Happened and Why*, New York: Times Books.

UK parliamentary debates

Located from www.publications.parliament.uk/pa/cm/cmhansard.htm
Dates on debates cited in this book:

- September 25, 1992

- April 29, 1993

- May 5, 1995

- May 9, 1995

- July 19, 1995

- November 22, 1995

- December 12, 1995

US Senate debates

Located from http://thomas.loc.gov/
Titles and dates on debates cited in this book:

- 'Authorization of Multilateral Action in Bosnia-Hercegovina,' August 10, 1992.

- 'Sarajevo on the Abyss: The Fatal Moment before Bosnia's Tragedy and the West's Shame are Complete,' August 03, 1993.

- 'Foreign Relations Authorization Act,' January 27, 1994.

- 'Lifting the Arms Embargo on Bosnia and Herzegovina,' May 10, 1994.

- 'Lifting the Arms Embargo on Bosnia and Herzegovina,' May 12, 1994.

- 'Deployment of United States Armed Forces in Bosnia and Herzegovina,' December 13, 1995.

Index

Note: Page numbers in **bold** refer to figures and tables

eBooks – at www.eBookstore.tandf.co.uk

A library at your fingertips!

eBooks are electronic versions of printed books. You can store them on your PC/laptop or browse them online.

They have advantages for anyone needing rapid access to a wide variety of published, copyright information.

eBooks can help your research by enabling you to bookmark chapters, annotate text and use instant searches to find specific words or phrases. Several eBook files would fit on even a small laptop or PDA.

NEW: Save money by eSubscribing: cheap, online access to any eBook for as long as you need it.

Annual subscription packages

We now offer special low-cost bulk subscriptions to packages of eBooks in certain subject areas. These are available to libraries or to individuals.

For more information please contact webmaster.ebooks@tandf.co.uk

We're continually developing the eBook concept, so keep up to date by visiting the website.

www.eBookstore.tandf.co.uk